FRAMINGHAM STATE COLLEGE

3 3014 00328 8976

D1222222

Fundamentals of
Earthquake Prediction

Fundamentals of Earthquake Prediction

Cinna Lomnitz
Institute of Geophysics
Universidad Nacional Autónoma de México
Mexico City, Mexico

John Wiley & Sons, Inc.

NEW YORK / CHICHESTER / BRISBANE / TORONTO / SINGAPORE

Framingham State College
Framingham, Massachusetts

This text is printed on acid-free paper.

Copyright © 1994 by John Wiley & Sons, Inc.

All rights reserved. Published simultaneously in Canada.

Reproduction or translation of any part of this work beyond
that permitted by Section 107 or 108 of the 1976 United
States Copyright Act without the permission of the copyright
owner is unlawful. Requests for permission or further
information should be addressed to the Permissions Department,
John Wiley & Sons, Inc., 605 Third Avenue, New York, NY
10158-0012.

This publication is designed to provide accurate and
authoritative information in regard to the subject
matter covered. It is sold with the understanding that
the publisher is not engaged in rendering legal, accounting,
or other professional services. If legal advice or other
expert assistance is required, the services of a competent
professional person should be sought.

Library of Congress Cataloging in Publication Data:
Lomnitz, Cinna.
  Fundamentals of earthquake prediction / Cinna Lomnitz.
    p. cm.
  Includes index.
  ISBN 0-471-57419-8
  1. Earthquake prediction. I. Title.
QE538.8.L66 1994
  551.2'2—dc20   93-40909

Printed in the United States of America

10 9 8 7 6 5 4 3 2

QE
538.8
L66
1994

Contents

Preface

Seismology has been defined as "the science based on data called seismograms" (Aki and Richards, 1980). The definition misses the urgency of human suffering caused by the complex phenomena called earthquakes. It also tends to restrict membership of our club to people who know their way around seismograms, rather than to those who make use of other kinds of input such as theoretical physics, fault displacements, or time series of seismic events. Actually seismograms tell us far less about earthquakes than we need to know. They are like unreliable couriers sent abroad with a long complicated message: By the time they get to their destination they tell us all about the incidents along the way but the original message has been forgotten.

Seismic signals are severely modified as they travel through the earth: High frequencies are damped out and wave fronts are reflected, bent, and scattered at myriad obstacles and discontinuities. It is hard to recover the original waveform unless the intervening structure is exceptionally well known. Besides, the instrumental information is frustratingly incomplete: For example, we miss out on the amount of rotational ground motion that can be felt during a large earthquake on soft ground. We need accessory data even for interpreting the seismogram itself. Basic insights in the field of seismology have been contributed by geologists and engineers, whose distinctive approaches represent much-needed complements and correctives to our own. As for the immediacy of a description provided by some keen witness of earthquake phenomena, such as Charles Darwin, it is often worth a dozen seismograms.

We shall be talking about large earthquakes. They differ from small earthquakes as a python does from a garden snake—they belong to different species. Truly large earthquakes are rare events in terms of the human life span. Because of their rarity they are not always studied with the depth and care they deserve. Well-documented phenomena such as earthquake lights and visible ground waves, which are observed only in large earthquakes, are apt to be dismissed as optical illusions merely because relatively few people have witnessed them. In recent years, general descriptions of destructive earthquakes have been virtually banned from the scientific literature. The *Bulletin of the Seismological Society of America* turns down such papers as a matter of policy.

Thus, in addition to the few parameters that may be derived from seismograms, we are often obliged to rely on published accounts in the press. Journalists reporting on large foreign earthquakes are not specialists; they are apt to miss significant aspects of the story. Their situation is awkward: Stranded on distant shores at exceptional times, without an adequate grip of the unfamiliar scene, they are under pressure to provide instant appraisals of what is clearly a freak situation. Just how much is due to the earthquake and how much is the everyday disaster of a strange way of life? Journalists are apt to have trouble obtaining reliable information in time for meeting their deadlines.

In the 1985 Mexico earthquake, hundreds of small children were trapped alone in the dark under the steel-and-concrete rubble of what used to be their "earthquake-proof" homes. Some were lucky to die quickly; others could be heard crying for days. Few were rescued alive. This may have been the most significant aspect of the Mexico story, but few correspondents picked it up in the news media. It was the same again in the 1992 Cairo earthquake. Efforts to prevent the recurrence of such calamities can only be described as noble and worthwhile; but they won't succeed unless we face the facts squarely. And the facts are mostly missing.

Getting hold of the facts in order to prevent the recurrence of earthquake disasters is what earthquake prediction is about—or ought to be. It is the very soul of seismology. But is it feasible? We are like scared children huddled together in some brightly lit room, daring each other to explore the dark outside. From time to time one of us darts out and rushes back breathlessly grasping a leaf or a twig torn off the unknown. From such shreds of evidence we piece together the tall tales we proudly call *scientific models*.

In his inaugural speech at the 1992 International Geological Congress, Charles F. Drake reminded his colleagues that model building, not truth, was what earth science is all about. One model is as good as another if it represents reality tolerably well. Galileo, however, chose to quarrel with a perfectly serviceable model due to Claudius Ptolemy, which predicted the known motions of the planets as well as the Copernican model did. The idea that the earth moved through space was "entirely ridiculous," said Ptolemy; it had already been held by Pythagoras in the 6th century B.C. and was now utterly discredited. Ptolemy's model managed to explain the available observations in those modern times without offending the equivalent of today's religious right. In short, it seemed infinitely preferable to the weird ideas of the Copernicans. There was only one thing wrong with it—it was barren. It couldn't lead to new discoveries. The ideas of Galileo could and did—until Einstein's model came around.

Today it would take a Galileo to find his way in the earth sciences. Scientific meetings have come to resemble automobile shows: so many models! Shopping around is half the fun, but everyone buys at his own risk in the end. This book is not a shopping guide for models of earthquake prediction. It does not attempt to cover the field or to be fair to all authors. There are wiser and more comprehensive books about earthquake prediction, notably the ones by T. Rikitake (1976) and by K. Mogi (1985). There are also excellent interdisciplinary reviews of recent seismological research such as the book by Christopher H. Scholz (1990). But earthquake prediction is not just any field of modern science; it is also a public issue. It impinges on a number of raw nerve endings in our society that have to do with the role of science and the obligations of science to society.

What is a disaster?—and is science successfully dealing with the complex and subtle problems involved in earthquake prediction? These questions deserve to be raised in a book, at a level that is accessible to scientists in other disciplines as well as to the scientifically literate public.

FEASIBILITY OF EARTHQUAKE PREDICTION

Earthquake prediction is feasible: it is commonly practiced today. The prediction of amplitudes and spectra of ground motion is a flourishing scientific subject. Seismicity gaps are used to pinpoint hazardous areas at plate boundaries. Statistical procedures can predict earthquake risk to within 5%, saving money for shareholders of insurance companies if not always to policyholders. Much more can and should be done.

The new field of earthquake prediction is scientifically challenging, and we shall be talking about some of its successes in this book. But there is one important sense in which earthquake prediction is not feasible today. This is *calendric* prediction—the forecasting of earthquakes in terms of dates and places of occurrence. Here our success has been less than impressive. Perhaps our expectations were unrealistic: Earthquakes, we should recall, are chaotic phenomena. In a sense God alone could have predicted the destruction of Sodom and Gomorrah. Yet a study of the tectonics of the Dead Sea Rift can do wonders in predicting and preventing future Sodom-Gomorrah-type disasters. There have been definite advances in the earth sciences. There is no turning back —see what happened to Lot's wife!

On the other hand, even if we could predict earthquakes to the nearest split second, we might not necessarily save more lives or more dollars. We cannot pick up our homes and businesses, snail fashion, and move them to less hazardous spots. Besides, earthquakes are not disasters in themselves; structures make them so. Technology advances, but the poor designs will always be with us. Our main problem is to know not *when* the next earthquake will strike, but what kind of structure it takes to survive the earthshock when it comes—at this very spot and not half a block away.

Those are good reasons for earthquake prediction being foremost in the minds of government agencies. But there is another. Earthquake prediction is invariably the first subject that occurs to anyone on meeting a seismologist. Hardly another question is capable of fascinating lay people and scientists alike to such a degree. The question is, do people really *want* earthquake prediction? I think they do. We hate uncertainty even worse than death or damage. This is why countries such as China and the United States have laws requiring government agencies to predict earthquakes.

We may argue forever whether prediction is a dead end or a worthwhile field of scientific endeavor. Anyone can knock earthquake prediction by pointing out that no operational forecasting method has yet worked. We must not dodge this issue, and we shall certainly consider the argument that earthquakes might be essentially unpredictable. Does the earthquake process reflect a process of self-organized criticality? Are there strange attractors? Is there a meaning to the major regularities (such as aftershock sequences) that are the constant companions of the "earthquake cycle"? On the other hand, it would be very strange if earthquake precursors didn't exist. Those who reject the feasibility of earthquake prediction out of hand may be compared to Arjuna on the plain of Kurukshetra. Arjuna challenged his heavenly mentor to reveal himself in his real form, but when Krishna obliged, Arjuna couldn't stand it. He entreated him to resume his former familiar shape.

Some of the failures of earthquake prediction may well have been treated with too much leniency in the past. There have been scientifically dubious prediction ventures in several countries. Scientists, like any human beings, can make mistakes under political pressure. Students should be able to learn from our failures, provided that we can bring ourselves to admit them.

Uncritical manipulation of the data, public announcements of predictions for self-promotional purposes, and other features of pathological science or pseudoscience have long plagued the field. Earthquake prediction was totally discredited for decades. It was revived in the 1960s—sometimes for political purposes. Thirty years later, as the International Decade of Natural Disaster Reduction 1990–2000 gets under way, the situation has not changed a great deal. If anything, the world disaster situation is more critical than it was in 1960. Yet we may be close to achieving an effective control of earthquake hazard. This possibility should not be overlooked: It may depend on the continuity of earthquake prediction programs. It would be the wrong time to give up.

EARTHQUAKE PREDICTION AND ETHICS

Minerva, the goddess of wisdom and science, sprang fully armed from the recesses of Jupiter's brain. Similarly, earthquake prediction was born of the deep pockets of government science in the 1960s and 1970s. The bounty has dried up but the birthmark remains.

There is some cause for concern, since false alarms may cost lives and research costs money. In the early 1980s attempts were made by seismologists to restrain each other by devising special codes of ethics. Commissions of earthquake prediction evaluation were appointed as watchdogs, but instead of cracking down on the offenders, they were soon hawking predictions of their own.

Does science have an ethics? What could it be based on? If model building is our sole business, truth is no longer of immediate concern. Our publications are reviewed by peers, not by Olympian gods. Genuine thought is not always easy to identify in a scientific paper. It may be a hindrance in getting work past the reviewer. All this leaves little solid ground on which to base a code of conduct.

Yet some protection against misconduct in earthquake prediction is desirable. Safeguards are needed, of the kind that protect the public against unscrupulous medicine peddlers. The Federal Drug Administration of the United States, which is far from perfect, requires double-blind tests to be performed before a new drug can be released. In this book I suggest similar tests that might be applicable to earthquake prediction.

Every preface is an appointment with a particular kind of reader. Thoreau hoped to be read by poor students. There are worse audiences, aside from the fact that my own students have largely belonged to that reluctant category. They were majors in geophysics, in geology, in physics, in statistics, in engineering, in disaster prevention—or in just plain puzzlesolving. It didn't matter in the end. Earthquake prediction is a highly eclectic, nonlinear challenge, and we should welcome people from all fields. We must be prepared to tolerate each other's data, methods, or quirks. A certain open-minded inquisitiveness is the only prerequisite. Scientists are an independent lot who prefer making up their own minds, which is as it should be.

Many colleagues have contributed ideas and results to this work, and I have tried to acknowledge their contributions at the appropriate passages. I owe thanks to Hans Berckhemer, who first suggested this book, and to my wife, Betty, who made it possible and who contributed especially to Chapter 8. I am indebted to my editors, Philip Manor and Diana Cisek, and to Susan Middleton who copyedited the manuscript as if someone were actually going to read the book. In a special sense I also owe thanks to my colleagues from China and Japan, for their gallant forays in the dark.

CINNA LOMNITZ

January 1994
Mexico City, Mexico

Fundamentals of
Earthquake Prediction

Part I

The Spiral of Practice

1

Introduction

Nature has much to say but won't talk.
—Zhuang Zhou (300 B.C.)

INTRODUCTION

The grim human experience of living through disaster provides a distinctly different outlook on science and on life in general. Subtle shifts of perspective can affect even purely technical matters. I survived the 1960 Chile earthquake, the 1967 Caracas earthquake, and the 1985 Mexico earthquake, not to mention on-the-spot investigations in the aftermath of a score of other seismic disasters.

Earthquake prediction (in the sense of forecasting the date, location and magnitude of an earthquake) is not feasible today. A practical method or system for predicting earthquakes is possibly five to 25 years in the future.

In his 1965 report on earthquake prediction, Frank Press noted that "even today, without spending a lot of money, much can be done to mitigate the hazard due to large earthquakes." This was an honest statement, but it may have cost the first American proposal for earthquake prediction its passage by Congress. The latter decided to let the seismologists try to mitigate the hazard without spending a lot of money. To make sure, they gave seismologists nothing.

We know better now than to tell politicians that the earthquake problem will just go away. Of course, the original statement of the Press Committee remains substantially true. Today, as in 1965, much could be done to mitigate earthquake hazard. But how? And what is the best way to achieve this objective? This chapter is an initial attempt to get both questions in focus.

THE CHANGING NATURE OF EARTHQUAKE DISASTERS

Casualties and damage from seismic disasters are everywhere on the increase (Boullé, 1990). The fact can be blamed largely, but not exclusively, on population growth and shifts in land use. Urban population has increased greatly and will continue to increase all over the world (Table 1.1).

Notice from Table 1.1 that with the exception of New York, the 20 largest cities in the 21st century will be non-Western or will belong to the developing world. Some of them, like Seoul and Lagos, were not even on the list of the 50 largest cities in 1950. In 2000 they will exceed the population of Los Angeles.

The word *developing* (as in "developing nation") has become a misnomer or a sarcasm. Developing into what? Some of our ancient nations may barely make it into the Information Age; others will sink back into barbarism. In terms of environmental threats there are some objective differences. None of the developed Western nations (northern and central Europe, the United States, Australia, and Canada) fronts on a subduction zone, yet 85% of the energy released in earthquakes occurs at subduction zones. Plate-boundary earthquakes account for over 95% of all seismic energy release. However, with the exception of Los Angeles and San Francisco, none of the Western cities in Table 1.1 is threatened by proximity to an active plate boundary.

The annual number of deaths from earthquakes has averaged about 17,000 since 1900. There was a steadily decreasing trend after 1935 which reflected advances in earthquake engineering and the worldwide adoption of reinforced concrete-frame construction for housing. But the trend was suddenly and dramatically reversed around 1955 (Fig. 1.1). This reversal cannot be wholly explained by fluctuations in seismicity; the global population began to increase very rapidly or to "explode" at about that time.

Traditional masonry construction had been the cause of most seismic disasters in the past. However, since the 1950s and particularly after the 1967 Caracas and 1968 Tokachi-Oki earthquakes, the collapse of reinforced concrete-frame structures on soft ground began to account for a rising share of earthquake casualties. Recent examples include the 1985 Mexico earthquake, the 1988 Armenia earthquake, the 1989 Loma Prieta earthquake, and others. The death rate from earthquakes is still rising. Modern reinforced-concrete buildings, however, are Western imports. If they are becoming the favorite target of Mexican earthquakes, as appears to be the case, blaming the Mexicans won't do. The same observation applies to Venezuela, Puerto Rico, Egypt, Indonesia, China, Armenia, the Philippines, India, Ecuador, Turkmenia, and many others. The list grows longer day by day.

Partly as a result of the rising rate of urbanization the instances of poor performance of engineered urban structures on soft ground have reached such alarming proportions that some engineers are beginning to suspect a *knowledge gap* in the general area between the disciplines of soil mechanics, seismology, and earthquake engineering (Suh, 1985). Such gaps are like blank

TABLE 1.1   Projected Population of the World's 50 Largest Cities in the Year 2000[a]

Rank	Metropolis	Country	Population in Millions
1	Mexico City	Mexico	24.44
2	São Paulo	Brazil	23.60
3	Tokyo/Yokohama	Japan	21.32
4	New York	U.S.A.	16.10
5	Calcutta	India	15.94
6	Bombay	India	15.43
7	Shanghai	China	14.69
8	Teheran	Iran	13.73
9	Jakarta	Indonesia	13.23
10	Buenos Aires	Argentina	13.05
11	Rio de Janeiro	Brazil	13.00
12	Seoul	Korea	12.97
13	Delhi	India	12.77
14	Lagos	Nigeria	12.45
15	Cairo	Egypt	11.77
16	Karachi	Pakistan	11.57
17	Manila	Philippines	11.48
18	Beijing	China	11.47
19	Dacca	Bangladesh	11.26
20	Osaka	Japan	11.18
21	Los Angeles	U.S.A.	10.91
22	London	U.K.	10.79
23	Bangkok	Thailand	10.26
24	Moscow	Russia	10.11
25	Tianjin	China	9.96
26	Lima	Peru	8.78
27	Paris	France	8.76
28	Milan	Italy	8.74
29	Madras	India	7.85
30	Bangalore	India	7.67
31	Baghdad	Iraq	7.66
32	Chicago	U.S.A.	6.98
33	Bogotá	Colombia	6.94
34	Hong Kong	China	6.09
35	Lahore	Pakistan	5.93
36	St. Petersburg	Russia	5.84
37	Pusan	Korea	5.82
38	Santiago	Chile	5.58
39	Shenyang	China	5.50
40	Madrid	Spain	5.42
41	Medan	Indonesia	5.36
42	Ankara	Turkey	5.19
43	Alger	Algeria	5.16
44	Ahmedabad	India	5.09
45	Belo Horizonte	Brazil	5.01
46	Hyderabad	India	4.94
47	Caracas	Venezuela	4.79
48	Casablanca	Morocco	4.63
49	Guangzhou	China	4.49
50	Wuhan	China	4.47
	TOTAL		496.17

[a] After R. Bilham, 1988. Earthquakes and Urban Growth, *Nature, 336,* 625–626.

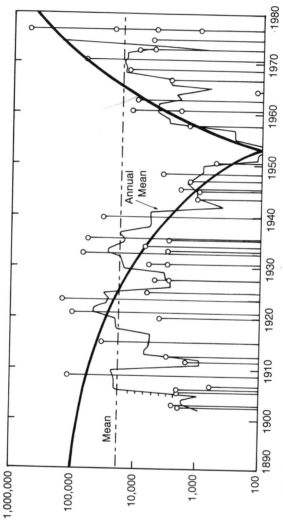

Fig. 1.1 Worldwide casualties from earthquakes (after Mogi, 1992, published by II Cigno-Galileo Galilei, Rome).

spots on the map of science. They raise important scientific and social questions. They are capable of generating the kind of new emerging syntheses called scientific (and social) revolutions.

The term *knowledge gap* may seem puzzling. After all, the relevant facts have been known for years. Strain, not acceleration, has long been suspected to be the major factor of damage on soft ground: "the cyclic shear strains, not the cyclic shear stresses, control the cyclic pore pressures . . . and govern the associated reduction of soil stiffness during earthquakes" (Vucetic and Thilakaratne, 1989). Practicing engineers have long recognized that the wavelengths of surface waves can shorten during an earthquake and that torsion and rocking are very often as critical in terms of damage causation as the peak horizontal accelerations (see, e.g., Trifunac, 1982). Nevertheless, these insights are not always being translated into actual engineering practice.

A gap between theory and practice is typical of fields in which the state of knowledge is in flux. There are many examples. In this case structures on soft ground are designed against uncorrelated random seismic accelerations, as if the shaking were of infinite wavelength, when actually the damage is done by surface waves of short wavelength. Torsion and rocking are neglected in formal design, as if they were the exceptional cause of damage rather than the normal one. Strong-motion instruments are incapable of recording the rotational components of ground motion; and since the rocking of the ground is not recorded it is easy to forget about it.

The correlation between local geology (particularly wedges in the topsoil formation) and damage is often striking. Surface geology is a major factor of damage in earthquakes. Nevertheless, damage continues to occur because of this unrecognized missing link between theory and practice. The soil is hidden under city pavements. In the 1989 earthquake that struck San Francisco Bay, the damage to the Marina and to the Nimitz Freeway could have been predicted on the basis of local geology. This would have been earthquake prediction at its best.

ARE EQUINOXES EARTHQUAKE PRECURSORS?

Yet the idea that earthquake prediction is hopeless or plain wrong is subscribed to by many geophysicists. My teacher Charles F. Richter definitely thought so. He once surprised us with the announcement that he had discovered a reliable way to predict earthquakes: "All major earthquakes occur within three months of an equinox." "Richter's Law" (as it came to be called) is infallible. Everything occurs within three months of an equinox, and so do earthquakes. But Richter's joke had some interesting serious implications. How relevant is it to know exactly when the next earthquake will occur? To what accuracy do we really need to predict? Also, it is not at all obvious that equinoxes fail to qualify as earthquake precursors.

Two main criteria for earthquake precursors have been proposed: (a) "precursors . . . always precede the target earthquake"; (b) "individual precursors almost always give false alarms".[1] Equinoxes qualify on both counts. They regularly precede the target earthquake by at most six months. Used by themselves, they nearly always yield a false alarm.

Let us pursue this idea a bit further. Equinoxes occur regularly twice a year. Their occurrence is rare enough to generate a large probability gain. But this is precisely what one is looking for in a promising earthquake precursor!

Thomas Bayes, an English churchman, became interested in the theory of probability (or *doctrine of chances*, as it was then called). A few months before his death in 1761 he proved one of the pivotal theorems in statistics, which has since given his name to a scientific school or faction, the Bayesians. Bayes' Theorem enables one to compute the probability that some hypothesis is true provided that one knows the probable truth of all supporting arguments. These arguments have often been evaluated subjectively and not in terms of hard data, but this was hardly Bayes' fault. Anyway, Bayesian statistics tend to be controversial.

Suppose that we wish to compute the probability gain from "Precursor X"—in this case, an equinox. Precursor X unfailingly turns up twice a year, earthquake or no earthquake. Thus we may write $\Pr(X) = 1/(6 \text{ months}) = .0055/\text{day}$. This is the probability of having an equinox fall on any given day of the year. Now Bayes' Theorem states that

$$\Pr(M|A,B,C, \ldots) = \frac{\Pr(A,B,C, \ldots |M)\,\Pr(M)}{\Pr(A,B,C, \ldots |M)\,\Pr(M) + \Pr(A,B,C \ldots |\tilde{M})\,\Pr(\tilde{M})}$$
(1.1)

In words, the probability of occurrence of an earthquake of magnitude M given the previous occurrence of some precursory set of phenomena A, B, C, . . . equals the probability of occurrence *of the phenomena given that the earthquake actually does occur*, times the probability of occurrence of an earthquake of magnitude M, over the sum of all possible products of the same type. But there are only two possibilities: either the earthquake occurs (M) or it doesn't $(\tilde{M})$. Therefore the denominator can have only the two terms shown in Eq (1.1).

Now if it is true that "the precursors always precede the target earthquake", the probability of the syndrome formed by the precursors [A, B, C, . . .] must be unity. Thus the numerator is reduced to $\Pr(M)$. Then Bayes' formula boils down to

---

[1] The quotes, as well as other quotes and derivations in the rest of this section, are from Aki (1984), Utsu (1979), and some Chinese sources.

$$\Pr(M|A,B,C, \ldots) = \frac{\Pr(M)}{\Pr(M) + [\Pr(A)\,\Pr(B)\,\Pr(C)\cdots]} . \qquad (1.2)$$

Here it has been assumed that the precursors occur independently of each other so that, if the earthquake does not occur, we may write

$$\Pr(A,B,C, \ldots |\tilde{M}) = \Pr(A)\,\Pr(B)\,\Pr(C)\cdots, \qquad (1.3)$$

following Aki (1981) and Utsu (1979). Notice how strongly Eq (1.2) depends on the value of the product $\Pr(A)\,\Pr(B)\,\Pr(C)\cdots$ in the denominator. When this product is underestimated one automatically overestimates $\Pr(M|A,B,C, \ldots)$. But who guarantees that the phenomena A, B, C, $\ldots$ are actually precursors? The question is crucial: it is fundamental for applying Bayes' theorem to this problem. Most researchers simply assume that the phenomena must be precursors since there is a probability gain associated with their use as precursors. But the probability gain is a consequence of the assumption that the phenomena A, B, C, $\ldots$ "always precede the target earthquake." It begs the question of their being precursors at all.

The probabilities $\Pr(A)$, Pr (B), $\ldots$ are very small numbers. For every precursor one adds to the list, the probability of a future earthquake may be made to increase. Sometimes this increase can be quite dramatic. Take the 1978 Izu-Oshima, Japan, earthquake —an earthquake that was almost predicted, though not on Bayesian probabilistic considerations. An equinox occurred less than a month before the earthquake. Since the probability rate $\Pr(M)$ for the occurrence of an earthquake of magnitude $M = 6.5$ in Izu-Oshima had been estimated by Utsu at $P_0 = 10^{-4}$/day, we may write:

$$\text{Probability gain due to equinox} = \Pr(X)/P_0$$
$$= 0.0055/10^{-4} = 55.$$

A superb probability gain! Compare it with the *combined* probability gain from radon anomalies, changes in water level, and volumetric strain changes used in the Izu-Oshima prediction, which only amounted to 33 (Utsu, 1979). There is no trick: We played by the rules. The earthquake did occur; hence the use of the equinox as a precursor was justified. We can even ascertain that equinoxes are indeed statistically independent of the other precursors, as Eq (1.3) requires. This happens to be true because equinoxes are semiannual, periodic phenomena while any periodic components in other precursors have been previously removed by filtering.

Whoever wishes to pursue the matter further will find that equinoxes do better in terms of probability gains than any of the long- and medium-term precursors reported for the Chinese earthquake predictions of Haicheng, Longling, or Tangshan.

A precursor is held to be useful to the extent that it produces a large probability gain. "A tremendous gain is possible if a particular short-term precursor is expected with a high degree of certainty," says Aki. Here no precursor can beat equinoxes: they are expected with *total* certainty.

In conclusion, Richter's tongue-in-cheek proposal of equinoxes as earthquake precursors cannot be lightly dismissed. We ought not laugh it off, just because we think we know what equinoxes are and what an earthquake precursor is. The less we know the more openminded we ought to be. A connection between earthquakes and astronomical phenomena has in fact been suggested from ancient times to the present, and not just by astrologers. Recently such a connection was again proposed by Ogata and Abe (1991).

CREDIBILITY OF EARTHQUAKE PREDICTION

The official Japanese earthquake prediction program, begun in 1964, is now in its sixth five-year plan. It will face renewal in March 1994. The forecast of a large earthquake in the Tokai region, which might affect the Tokyo Metropolitan Area, has spawned an unparalleled array of precautionary measures. Japan is today the best-protected nation against disasters in spite of the high incidence of major earthquakes.

And yet there is a great deal of uneasiness. Because no actual method of prediction has yet been produced, some of the younger Japanese seismologists have voiced doubts about the wisdom and effectiveness of the program, and even about the soundness of the preventive measures. Many interest groups have emerged around the earthquake problem. Politicians are beginning to point out that 30 years of research have yet to produce a viable system of earthquake prediction.

Similar comments are being voiced in China, in Russia, and in the United States. Those are, with Japan, the four countries where significant resources have been channeled into official earthquake prediction programs. Such programs will be continued into the near future, if only to comply with commitments made under the 1990–2000 International Decade of Natural Disaster Reduction subscribed by the United Nations. But probing questions are increasingly likely to be asked by engineers, geologists, geophysicists, and the public at large.

The pigeons have come home to roost. Scientists of the 1970s had been optimistic about earthquake prediction being just around the corner. Their naive statements are now apt to be remembered by critics, as new generations of scientists are turning their back or thumbing their nose at the prediction problem.

IS EARTHQUAKE PREDICTION POSSIBLE?

One factor affecting the credibility of earthquake prediction programs is a general trend toward science promotion evident in some countries. Popularization of science is not always to the good. "Very often the expected benefits of any given scientific advance are puffed up to many times their real value," complains Leo Kadanoff in *Physics Today* (1992). "We are fast approaching a situation in which nobody will believe anything we say in any matter that touches upon our self-interest."

There is a strong temptation to claim that someone is engaged in earthquake prediction when actually he or she is merely recording some sort of signal produced by the earth. Yet the systematic instrumentation of the earth over large regions is undeniably a necessity if we want to produce the data that will make earthquake prediction possible.

On the other hand, there are many promising approaches to earthquake prediction that have hardly been tried. The comparison with weather prediction has often been mentioned—only to be dismissed—but has never been taken seriously. The interior of the earth is much less accessible to observation than the atmosphere, and there are other important differences as well. But there are also similarities. It is possible to find practical methods of imaging the accumulation of strains or moments in the earth, and we should seriously aim for this as an important step toward understanding the earthquake process.

In a two-page commentary in *Nature,* Robert J. Geller (1991) has rendered a significant service to geophysics by raising the question as to whether earthquakes can be predicted. If the dynamics of large earthquakes are chaotic, the earth itself does not "know" when and where the next event will occur. Any two arbitrarily close neighboring states may lead to divergent histories of the system even if we knew the initial state, the history, and the dynamics.

Thus nonlinear complex dynamic systems such as the atmosphere, the earth's interior or the world economy are chaotic. But this does not mean that prediction is a fraud. Short-term economic forecasts exist; so do weather forecasts. Both are feasible. Earthquake prediction does not yet exist. That is the main difference.

Strictly speaking, none of these phenomena can be predicted. No two earthquake ruptures are ever the same. But their general pattern is predictable. Through careful observation we can discern precursory changes that may indicate whether a major disturbance is approaching. Suppose a cyclonic pattern is forming over the Gulf of Mexico. If detected in time, such a pattern may be extrapolated and used as a warning for ships and aircraft to avoid the area, even when we are not sure whether a cyclone will actually develop, which path it will travel or how strong it will be. In a similar way, certain unstable economic trends, if heeded, may help governments avert a major crisis. Finally, millions of citizens all over the world watch the weather report and dress accordingly, or carry an umbrella. They would hardly keep doing this day after day if weather prediction didn't work.

Geller (1991) argues that every prediction ought to specify the region, the time, the magnitude and the probability of occurrence "within narrow limits''. But such strictures are unreasonable and unnecessary. Large earthquakes ''predictably'' occur at plate boundaries within limits that may not be as narrow as we once thought, but for practical purposes this will do. What matters is our ability to anticipate them and to take appropriate measures against the hazards they entail. I submit that this definition of predictability is more relevant.

Suppose a large earthquake could be predicted years in advance to the nearest year or month; what would be gained? Would people move away? They do not seem to be leaving Tokyo, even though such a prediction (or a closely equivalent one) was made in 1978. The city did not stop growing. People have roots and are attracted to jobs and to places. Employment and buildings cannot be moved at short notice. As a matter of fact, economic activity in Tokyo has greatly increased since 1978, and so has the construction of high-rise buildings.

On the other hand, a short-term prediction involving the detection of precursors might be useful in taking precautionary measures. This is one type of prediction we have in mind. After the 1985 Mexico earthquake two friends and I designed an earthquake warning system for Mexico City. The system detects the earthquake at the epicenter and transmits a signal to Mexico City, more than 230 miles away. Owing to the lag of seismic over electromagnetic waves, a one-minute warning time is available for people to take cover or to look after the safety of their family. The system was awarded a patent: it proved feasible in the earthquake of May 14, 1993 which triggered an alarm in Mexico City about 50 second in advance of the strong motion. Systems based on a similar principle exist in Japan and the United States.

I submit that this is a simple application of earthquake prediction of the kind that supposedly doesn't exist. ''There might arguably have been reasons for supposing, in 1962, that such precursors existed, but there is no longer room for such a belief'', writes Geller (1991). He would probably argue that a P wave at the epicenter does not constitute a true precursor of an earthquake in Mexico City. But the average citizen of Mexico City disagrees.

We can carry this one step further. Was the sequence of giant ($M > 7$) earthquakes that preceded the great 1960 Chile earthquake by 33 hours the result of a coincidence that had nothing to do with this earthquake? A sequence of small shocks began the day before the 1975 Haicheng earthquake; more earthquakes were felt that day than had been felt in all of Liaoning Province since 294 A.D. The main shock was certainly the largest ever felt in the province. But let us assume, for the sake of argument, that foreshocks don't exist. The changes in groundwater levels recorded in Tangshan before the 1976 earthquake were the largest since 1923: the Tangshan Steel Mill, the New Tangshan Manufacturing Corp., the Xinjuntu Fertilizer Plant, and the No. 422 Cement Plant had to close down because their water supply wells dried out. After the earthquake the groundwater level rose immediately by several meters and some wells flowed over. To summarize: we may develop an analogy between earthquakes and other events such as cyclones or economic crises, which occur in nonlinear systems exhibiting chaotic behavior and self-organization. These systems exhibit certain regularities (called *attractors*) that may be asymptotically stable and reproducible. In such systems a limited form of prediction is possible, in the sense that the onset of the phenomenon can often be detected before it "hits" (Mexico City, the coast or the economy). Whether or not this limited form of forecasting deserves to be called "prediction" is beside the point. Its possibility is what matters.

The purpose of seismology is, first to understand earthquakes and next to teach people how to build safer homes, safer schools, safer bridges and a safer environment. First and foremost, we need to predict how earthquakes will affect specific structures in specific locations. Today earthquake prediction is the best reason for becoming a seismologist.

2

The Earthquake Hut

I would fain say something, not so much concerning the Chinese and Sandwich Islanders as you who read these pages, who are said to live in New England.
—*H.D. Thoreau*

EARTHQUAKE PREDICTION IN CHINA

The successes of Chinese earthquake prediction are better known, by and large, than its attendant struggles and failures. Both deserve to be carefully studied. If we wish to understand and applaud the true extent of Chinese achievements we need to gain some perspective of the situation of Chinese geophysics in the mid-1960s.

On March 22, 1966, an earthquake of magnitude 7.2 occurred at a focal depth of 9 km at 115.0°E, 37.3°N near the town of Xingtai, about 300 km SSW of Beijing. Some 8,000 people died in this densely populated area of Hebei Province. Premier Zhou En-lai, while talking to survivors, was impressed by stories concerning various precursory phenomena such as foreshocks, ground water level fluctuations and changes in the behavior of domestic and wild animals. Highly critical of the performance of seismologists (who, he suspected, had been shutting themselves up in an ivory tower), he challenged scientists to "go find out on the spot, and get hold of the Xingtai earthquake for research." Severe penalties were in store for the small and hardy scientific community of China unless it came up with an answer to earthquake prediction. As a matter of fact, the government didn't wait for an answer from the scientists. It went ahead and established numerous "People's Stations" for ordinary citizens to predict earthquakes by observing fluctuations in wells and changes in the behavior of animals.

The scientists mobilized as best they could but were overtaken by events. Several further destructive earthquakes occurred; one in 1967 in Cangzhou, uncomfortably close to the capital; another beneath the Gulf of Bo, near

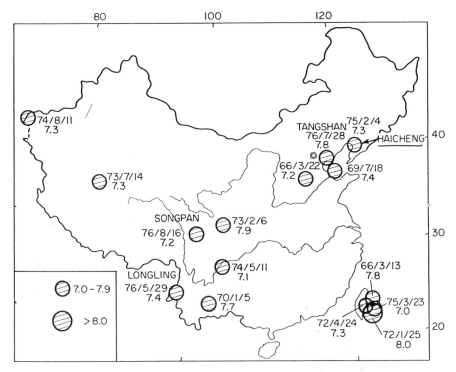

Fig. 2.1 *Major recent earthquakes in north China (up to 1976). Reprinted by permission from* Earthquake Prediction *by Ma Zongjin et al. (1990), Springer-Verlag, New York.*

Tianjin, in 1969; another in early 1970 near Tonghai in southern Yunnan (this one had a magnitude of 7.7 and caused considerable damage). Fifty days later, the Dayi earthquake occurred in Sichuan Province, and in December 1970 the Xiji earthquake killed over 100 people (Fig. 2.1). At the time, the relations between Chairman Mao and the intellectuals were strained. Mao Zedong, with a personality as big as China, was influentiable and had a mean pedantic streak. Party circles close to the Leader had become increasingly hostile to the scientific community. In 1970 the central government decided to create a separate government agency, the State Seismological Bureau, in order to carry out the earthquake prediction work independently of the Academy of Sciences and the universities. The new agency got to work on a set of scientific and administrative guidelines, which were eventually approved at the 1972 National Seismological Conference of China.

These guidelines were to become decisive in shaping the Chinese prediction effort. They took the form of a five-point directive:

(1) Priority to be given to prevention over basic research;
(2) Scientists to cooperate with amateurs on an equal footing;

(3) Chinese and Western scientific approaches to be merged;

(4) "Rely on the Masses"; and

(5) Everybody to join forces in waging battle under the leadership of the Party.

These instructions carried the weight of an executive order. The authority of the Communist Party stood behind them. Scientists were left in no doubt about the fate of skeptics. They would be "reeducated" at concentration camps. Academic degrees and the positions of directors of institutes were useless: they had been abolished in the Cultural Revolution. All scientific institutes in China were controlled by political activists. Twice-weekly training sessions in Mao-Thought and self-criticism were mandatory. Scientists had to spend a compulsory "sabbatical year" on a collective farm for every three years spent at an institute.

Conditions such as they were in 1966–1976 may be difficult to visualize now. Furthermore, the development of seismology in China had been rather weak. Most crippling was the comparative lack of exposure of seismologists to modern advances in physics and geophysics. The structure of science in China was in need of cross-fertilization: it had remained isolated since before the war years. Professional gatherings to discuss earthquake prediction were rarely attended by scientists from related fields.

The Chinese colleagues did their best under the circumstances. In the absence of a rational strategy for earthquake prediction they searched Mao's writings for guidance. They came up with an ingenious solution. The key to earthquake prediction, they suggested, was to be found in the following quote from Mao's text *On Practice* (1937):

To catch the tiger's cubs
you must enter the tiger's lair.

Conveniently cryptic, like a message in a fortune cookie, this ancient folk saying was meant by Mao to convey the need for rolling up one's sleeves and getting to work on the problems at hand. But the seismologists had another interpretation ready.

The *tiger*, they argued, is the earthquake. The *tiger's cubs* are the precursors. The *tiger's lair* is the epicentral region. Thus what the Leader was trying to say was something like this:

To detect the precursors
You must enter the epicentral region!

But where was the epicentral region? Here was precisely the vital element of the prediction to be achieved. But the Helmsman had foreseen this difficulty: Didn't he wisely order to blanket the country with stations? Thus the epicenter would automatically be covered. But there were not enough professional seismologists in the world to run so many stations! Hence the key to a Maoist strategy for earthquake prediction was precisely to be found in point (4) of the new directive: "Rely on the masses."

After 1972 nearly 5,000 People's Stations were created and staffed by local volunteers equipped with homemade instruments, such as magnetometers made of a piece of string with a small magnet dangling from it, bouncing a light beam off a piece of mirror stuck on the magnet. I saw such an instrument and others like it in Yunnan in 1977—just before the People's Stations were gradually phased out. At its peak the program may have enlisted more than 100,000 volunteers. In Yunnan alone there were 750 People's Stations served by 4,000 amateurs, in addition to 25 professional stations. During 1970–1976 more than 20 local predictions were issued in Yunnan.

The system of People's Stations conveniently fitted the Zhou Directive, since (a) station heads had to be Party members, and participation as volunteers was counted as a credit towards Party membership; (b) one important aim of the volunteers was to propagandize the countryside against "superstitions," including Buddhism; (c) the volunteers were coached by scientists working for the Seismological Bureau of each province; (d) Western methods taught by the scientists were combined with indigenous methods invented by the volunteers; and (e) the predictions that eventually ensued were the result of a joint effort between the scientists, the volunteers and the People.

PRECURSORS

Mao's epistemology was a powerful blend of Marxism (filtered through Engels-Lenin-Stalin pragmatism) and traditional Chinese aphoristic philosophy. The model of knowledge outlined in his 1937 lectures at the Yenan Red Army military academy combined the idea of progress with that of the eternal return. Knowledge (said Mao) advances yet always seems to come back to its starting point. The Wisdom of the People stems from its traditions; yet Leaders are wise to the extent that they are able to reject these traditions and be revolutionary. This dialectical model was represented as a spiral moving between theory and praxis. Knowledge moves upward in cycles: a half-cycle of theory, a half-cycle of praxis, another half-cycle of theory, and so on. Each half-cycle builds on the preceding. It is foolish and counterrevolutionary to theorize before the corresponding praxis is solidly in place.

Such epistemological concepts originated well before Marxism; one thinks of Hegel, for instance, but also of mystical doctrines such as the Tree of Life of the Cabalists, and of course the *yin-yang* paradigm. It is tempting to replace Mao's model of knowledge by a double helix: the Spiral of Theory and the Spiral of Praxis, two intertwining structures fertilizing each other.

Chinese earthquake prediction was nonetheless based on some theoretical ideas. The main one was the idea that there exists a certain class of phenomena called *precursors*, each of which enhances the probability that an earthquake will occur. This model was rooted in Chinese traditional scientific thought: Precursors played a role analogous to *symptoms* in Chinese medicine. A symptom (in this tradition) may seem to be wholly unrelated to the illness; it may appear at some remote spot of the body, connected to the diseased organ by invisible channels or *meridians* (*jing luo*); a fluid, usually called *energy*, circulates in these channels. A pattern of symptoms, or *syndrome*, precedes every ailment, but we cannot know in advance which syndrome will be present in a particular patient. All illnesses were attributed to an imbalance between positive and negative forms of energy (the *yin-yang* paradigm), caused by the blocking of certain meridians.

A given collection of earthquake precursors was likened to a syndrome, related to the unknown disturbance that caused the earthquake. Such precursors could hardly be independent: according to Bayes' Theorem they should fail to enhance each other's effect as predictors. In order to circumvent this difficulty, it was proposed that precursors occurred in four groups according to their lead time (long-term, medium-term, short-term, and imminent.) These stages were assumed to be widely separated in time, and it was proposed that precursors belonging to different stages should be practically independent from each other.

Precursors were normally selected from among a wide assortment of possible "signatures." The following effects were listed as relevant "medium-term precursors" preceding earthquakes by one to a few years (Zhang et al., 1984):

- Anomalous patterns of seismicity, etc.
- Changes in the velocity, source mechanism and spectral features (of seismic waves), etc.
- Crustal deformation in large area and motion of tectonic belt, etc.
- Anomalous changes in crustal strain and stress
- Changes in the gravity, geomagnetic field, earth current and resistivity, etc.
- Anomalous changes in behavior of underground water and contents of Rn, F, CO_2, NO_3 in the water, etc.
- Anomalies of rainfall, air pressure, temperature and ground temperature, etc.

One or the other of these fluctuations cannot fail to be present in every geophysical record of "one to a few years'" length anywhere on earth. Earthquake or no earthquake, even in active seismic regions there are always more precursors than there are seismic events: thus there are many precursors to choose from. Even in the unlikely event that there should be more earthquakes than there are precursors, every precursor could be positively assigned to at least one earthquake. In either case a prediction may be truthfully claimed to be successful. The hitch is that the assignment of precursors to earthquakes is done *a posteriori*.

If done in this way, the identification of one or more precursors preceding any earthquake (actually any date selected at random) seems a virtual certainty. The probability Pr(X) to be assigned to a precursor X is estimated from its long-term frequency as if it had been selected independently of the search—when in reality it was picked out from a myriad of possible precursors.

THE PREDICTION OF AN EARTHQUAKE

Thus the Chinese seismological community gradually became receptive to conceptual models of the earthquake process that were fundamentally alien to Western scientific tradition. Another one of these models was the concept of *earthquake preparation*. This is to be understood as analogous to the *incubation* of an illness. The earthquake was thought to be present in a state of latency, and the precursors were interpreted in terms of this latency and not necessarily of the earthquake itself.

During the period of "preparation" it is not yet clear if, when and where an earthquake will *break out*. Hence the precursors are scattered over a large region, the *preparation area*. As the earthquake approaches, the precursors tend to concentrate in space and draw closer to the eventual epicenter.

Up to this point the analogies were mostly drawn from Chinese medicine. But a new and intriguing aspect of Chinese earthquake prediction intervened at this point. Its origins go back to the roots of Chinese civilization. I am referring to *military science*. The earthquake was likened to an enemy who must be tracked down and surrounded. Mao's watchword "Prepare for war and disaster" was interpreted to mean that disaster prevention is a kind of warfare. Brigades of *earthquake fighters* were organized. Some concepts such as *stepwise earthquake prediction* cannot be fully appreciated without studying *The Art of War* by Sun Tse, a manual of the fifth century B.C. acknowledged by Mao as the main source of his military tactics.

Sun Tse defined warfare as an art based on deception. What matters is not so much attacking the enemy as the enemy's strategy. This means outguessing the enemy and acting in an unpredictable way. A general, to be consistently successful, must be wily as well as truthful and incorruptible. Sun Tse's strategy involved complicated energy calculations based on the *yin-yang* paradigm. The best of generals, he maintained, can merely make himself invincible but cannot cause the enemy to be vulnerable. He cannot be defeated, but he can only win if the enemy cooperates. Victory is made possible by enemy weaknesses shrewdly perceived and boldly exploited.

Earthquake disasters were seen as caused by deficiencies in human knowledge or social organization, which the earthquake enemy could successfully exploit in the form of surprise attacks. The initial failures of the Chinese earthquake prediction program were attributed to momentary setbacks or local defeats in a long-term campaign against a cunning foe. It was not going to be easy to win since the earthquake fought with *deception*, as Sun Tse said it should. The only effective way to fight back was by getting to understand the *earthquake's strategy*; but this turned out to be extremely difficult. In the meantime, it was necessary to render society invulnerable. Frequent unreliable predictions and false alarms had to be taken in stride.

The idea of stepwise prediction arose originally out of a strategic need, namely to divide the prediction campaign into four stages: long-term, medium-term, short-term, and imminent. Originally these were meant as a sort of strategy of encirclement of the earthquake enemy. Gradually it came to be believed that they were part of the enemy's strategy as well. *Rhythmical fluctuations* of short, medium, and long periods were assumed to exist and it was claimed that one might find out objectively in which stage of the process any given region happened to find itself at any particular moment.

The Bohai earthquake struck on July 18, 1969, under the Gulf of Bo in northern China, halfway between Haicheng and Tangshan. It had a magnitude of 7.4. After the 1966 Xingtai earthquake the epicenters of strong earthquakes had seemed to migrate across northern China in a northeast direction. The day before the Bohai earthquake, 20 different species of animals in the Tianjin Zoo acted strangely or seemed upset. This was reported by the keepers two hours before the earthquake. Here was the stuff of a short-term prediction, yet no prediction was issued. The migration trend of the epicenters had been recognized three years before the earthquake: it was interpreted *ex post facto* as a medium-term precursor. But no foreshocks had been felt.

In successive yearly National Situation Meetings (established after 1972) it was occasionally suggested that earthquakes might continue to migrate across the Gulf of Bo in the general direction of the Korean border, but nothing much seems to have been done about it. Strong earthquakes occurred in 1970–1974 in other parts of the country. The sensitive area around Beijing and northern China continued to attract the attention of seismologists, however; a failure to predict a damaging earthquake near the capital was the scenario they feared the most.

On May 11, 1974, an earthquake of magnitude 7.1 occurred near Zhaotong and Yongshan on the Jinsha River, astride the Yunnan-Sichuan state line. Rarely mentioned in the literature, this event claimed about 20,000 lives, mostly among members of the Yi minority. This was a severe blow to earthquake prediction in China, and the leadership became extremely concerned lest another such event should hit the vulnerable area of North China in the same manner. In June 1974, less than eight months before the Haicheng earthquake, a special consultation on the three northern provinces was convened. The meeting ended in dissent. Most seismologists felt that the hazard in northern China (including Liaoning Province, where Haicheng is located)

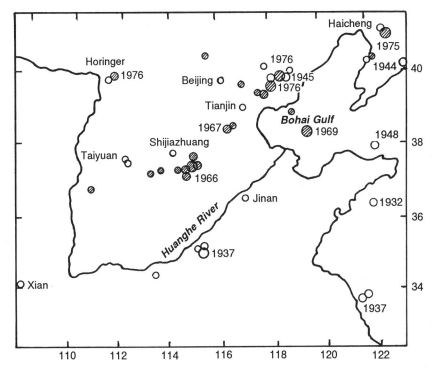

Fig. 2.2 *Distribution of damaging earthquakes in north China (up to 1976). Reprinted by permission from* Earthquake Prediction *by Ma Zongjin et al. (1990), Springer-Verlag, New York.*

was low as large historical shocks were rare. Since A.D. 294 only two shocks greater than magnitude 6 and none greater than magnitude 7 had occurred in Liaoning Province. This amounted to less than 0.3% of the total seismicity of China. Other scientists argued that earthquakes came in waves and that such a wave was now in progress in northern China, as suggested by the unusual number of damaging earthquakes since 1966 (Fig. 2.2). The meeting finally recommended that more stations of every kind be installed throughout North China, particularly in the sensitive area around the large cities of Beijing and Tianjin. This was done in October 1974. It was later claimed that the resolution amounted to a medium-term prediction for the Yingkou-Dalian-Haicheng area, particularly since the possibility of an earthquake in this general area had actually been discussed.

However, no new seismic station was installed in this area. At the time of the 1975 earthquake a single station capable of recording the foreshock sequence existed, namely Shipengyu station established in 1970 between Yingkou and Haicheng. An alleged radon anomaly at Lui-Hotang Hot Springs (72 km northeast of the epicenter) began three hours before the earthquake but was discovered *a posteriori*; it is doubtful and cannot be found in some later reports. No water-level recorders existed in wells in the area; though peasants had reportedly observed a falling water table since 1969 "there were no observations collected for earthquake purposes around the epicenter," according to Wang Chengmin (1990). The nearest quantitative groundwater observations were made once a day in Liaoyang, at some considerable distance from the epicentral region.

THE EARTHQUAKE

Haicheng is a small town and railroad station on the old Russian-built line from Lüda (the former Port Arthur) to Shenyang (also known as Mukden) and eventually to Harbin. The town is almost 50 km inland from Yingkou, main port on the Gulf of Liaodong (Fig. 2.3). A regional tilt about a hinge in the Yingkou region had been detected between the 1958 and 1971 geodetic

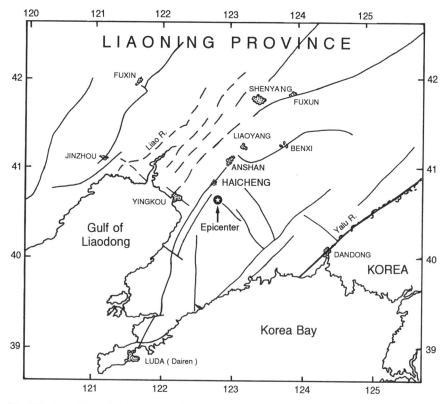

Fig. 2.3 Location of Haicheng and of major faults in Liaoning Province. Reprinted by permission from Earthquake Prediction by Ma Zongjin et al. (1990), Springer-Verlag, New York.

surveys. There seemed to be a relative uplift of Korea Bay with respect to Yingkou at the rate of about 6 cm in 13 years over a distance of 100 km. This tilting, however, appeared to be unrelated to earthquakes; it was already detected in the 1937–1958 period, and the possibility of a cumulative surveying error could not be ruled out (Gao, 1991). Perhaps the most significant precursor reported up to 1974 seemed to be a weak increase in background seismicity since about 1972, but even this observation was hard to confirm since the few seismic stations in the province had just barely been installed.

In the second half of 1974 some scattered observations in southern Liaoning Province (Liaodong Bandao Peninsula) suggested an increased precursor activity. Vertical fault creep measurements based on the elevation differences of three benchmarks (two on the east side and one on the west side of the fault) had been conducted across the right-lateral Jinzhou fault near Jinxian. The instrument used was a spirit level. The maximum range of observed displacements was 4 mm over a baseline of 560 m. Daily measurements had been carried out since late 1971. The difference in elevation between the benchmarks remained constant during the first 20 months; then it rose slowly after mid-1973 and reversed direction about October 1974. Similar observations were said to have been made near Yingkou. Measurements at intermediate benchmarks in Jinxian suggested that these displacements were not actually related to fault creep but to regional tilting of the surface of the ground. Since the reversal was opposed to the regional tilt determined geodetically in 1971, this anomaly became a crucial element in the story of the prediction of the Haicheng earthquake, which occurred four months later.

Yet the Haicheng earthquake did not alter the direction or the rate of tilting at Jinxian. It continued in the "reversed" direction into 1976 when the measurements were finally stopped. The tilt, if real, was unrelated to the earthquake. But this conclusion was reached after the earthquake. The Haicheng earthquake eventually occurred about 185 km away from Jinxian, on a fault trending normally to the Jinzhou fault.

In October 1974, as a result of the recommendations of the June meeting, a public information campaign was carried out throughout North China and "thousands" of temporary People's Stations were set up. I cannot find any mention of such stations having been established in the immediate Haicheng area. Shipengyu, about 20 km from the epicenter of February 4, 1975, may have been thought to be adequate. It remained the only professional station within a radius of 130 km from Haicheng. The nearest stations beyond that distance were Shenyang and Dandong.

In December 1974 a seismological brigade was detailed to Dandong, 160 km to the southeast of Haicheng. On December 20, 1974, the brigade issued a "synthetic short-term prediction" for a smallish earthquake somewhere in the general region. Such predictions were part of the routine and could be issued anytime by any brigade; since they were not made public, they didn't have to be cleared with the central authorities. They were often made just in case an earthquake should occur. It did, in this case. Two days after the prediction an earthquake swarm (maximum magnitude 4.8) broke out under Qinwo Reservoir, 150 km northwest of Dandong and 90 km northeast of Haicheng. The question facing the seismological brigade was, should they claim this as the event they had predicted? It was well beyond their area of activity, but the magnitude of the largest shock was in the anticipated range. The swarm was finally recognized as reservoir-induced, as it correlated with the location and water levels of Qinwo Reservoir.

The 1975 yearly National Situation Meeting went by and no specific or short-term prediction for Liaoning Province was issued. The whole of Liaodong Peninsula from the Gulf of Liaodong to the North Korean border (Fig. 2.3) continued to be mentioned in the final report as a "large-scale seismic area with no concrete place pinpointed," for an earthquake of magnitude up to 6 with no specific time or place mentioned. This was two weeks before the earthquake.

On February 1 a tiny shock (magnitude 0.5) was detected at Shipengyu seismic station. It was neither locatable nor felt. It must have been right under the station. The nearest other station was 100 km away, in the provincial capital of Shenyang. On February 2 and early on February 3 seven or eight more such tiny events were recorded at Shipengyu.

A recognizable foreshock sequence developed on February 3 after 6 P.M.,when earthquakes began to be felt in the Haicheng area at the rate of up to 20 shocks per hour. This was 24 hours before the earthquake. The Shipengyu seismic station recorded around 500 foreshocks, which they located very roughly by distance (about 20 km) and direction of first motion. It was later claimed that the epicenters of these foreshocks were densely concentrated, but this hardly amounted to more than a good guess. No instrumental locations were available.

Shipengyu station felt most of the foreshocks and issued "a very important prediction submitted to higher authority" about midnight or early dawn of February 4 (Tang, 1988). Earthquakes continued to be felt in Haicheng and Shipengyu through the night. The largest foreshock (M = 4.7) occurred at 7:50 A.M. on February 4. It was preceded by a surge of seismic activity beginning after midnight. More than 100 felt shocks followed within the hour. The population of Haicheng, kept awake by the foreshock sequence, went into a panic. Foreshocks could be heard like artillery fire in the immediate epicentral region. The large foreshock at 7:50 A.M. was recorded as far as Changchun station in northern Liaoning, but it is not clear whether many more foreshocks were also recorded there. The felt activity was going strong around 10 A.M. when an official earthquake alert was finally issued by the provincial government. Toward noon the seismic activity dropped to two to five felt shocks per hour, and the foreshock activity continued at this rate until 7:36 P.M. local time when the main shock (M = 7.4) occurred. A total of 1,328 people were killed, and a large but unknown number of people were hospitalized. Damage figures were not reported. Shipengyu station itself was severely damaged, thus preventing it from recording the aftershocks.

In conclusion, the earthquake has been successfully predicted. Chinese sources give the following account of the prediction. An emergency meeting was called by the Liaoning Revolutionary Committee (the government of the province) around 10 A.M. on the day of the earthquake:

> Having got this idea [i.e., that a strong earthquake was coming], the provincial government made emergent [*sic*] phone call at once to the entire province, and held an urgent meeting in Haicheng county; it was arranged to organize the masses to build temporary living huts, to move out the patients from hospitals, concentrate transportation facilities and important objects, organize medical teams, move the old and weak people to safe places . . . (Zhang et al., 1984)

It has widely been claimed that Haicheng was "evacuated" before the earthquake, though no such claim can actually be found in Chinese sources. It may be due to a misinterpretation of the facts by Western analysts, none of whom was present during the earthquake or able to visit the epicentral area until more than a year later. The earliest on-the-spot report is probably that of J.C. Savage, on an official U.S. Geological Survey mission in June, 1976.

Sources in the Liaoning Seismological Bureau suggest that they made an "imminent" prediction on February 4, 1975 at 10 A.M. (i.e., about 9 hours before the earthquake), and that the official warning went out around 10:30 A.M. to southern Liaoning Province (not specifically to Haicheng). The rate of foreshocks felt in Haicheng was then nearing its peak, after the large event in the morning. No details on the relative roles of the seismologists and the administrative authorities were given; the fact that the imminent prediction of the seismologists was simultaneous with the official warning is suggestive. No particular town or county was pinpointed.

An *earthquake hut* is a temporary shelter made of branches, wooden planks, and other light materials. It is built in front of the home according to age-old Chinese custom, whenever foreshocks are felt. The family moves out of the home and into the earthquake hut. I saw many of these freestanding emergency structures on the Beijing sidewalks as late as 10 months after the 1976 Tangshan earthquake. They had been erected because of the aftershock activity, spontaneously and not under government supervision. Any casual visitor couldn't help noticing them. The earthquake hut is not exclusively a Chinese invention: Similar temporary shelters were in use, as late as 1915, in southern Italy and parts of Latin America (Montessus de Ballore, 1915). In Calabria the earthquake shelter was among the facilities routinely specified in residential lease contracts.

When the foreshock sequence started in Haicheng, people did not wait to be told what to do. They built earthquake huts on the sidewalks in front of their homes. This would have taken a couple of hours at most. People moved in after the main foreshock struck in the morning, taking advantage of the unseasonably mild weather (up to 15°C). Even without access to an earthquake shelter many people would have had the good sense to stay outdoors. The earthquake occurred about 26 hours after the felt foreshock activity began. The local government had *arranged to organize the masses to build temporary living huts*, which implied an official blessing on what the population was doing. In view of the panic and the short time, there was hardly an opportunity to do much more, but it was appropriate and effective.

Evacuation means the physical removal of a population from an endangered town or geographical area. In this sense, no evacuation took place. The earthquake huts were the evacuation. Could the citizenry have been spurred to action by the predictions issued by the Liaoning Provincial Seismological Bureau? But no such predictions had been publicly issued. A smallish earthquake, at most of magnitude 6, was expected by the seismologists at some unspecified date and place within Liaoning Province. This conclusion had not been released to the public.

The alert ordered by the authorities was an appropriate precautionary response. It was issued at a time when the population was at a high pitch of excitement because of the continuing foreshocks. With the aid of hindsight it was later argued that the foreshocks, though credited with being *the key for the final imminent-term prediction* (cf. Zhu et al., 1984), were not exclusively relied upon, as many other precursors had played a part in the prediction. The fact is, however, that the alarm was issued on the strength of the foreshocks. The Qinwo Reservoir swarm had occurred less than two months before, and there was the arguable reversal of tilt measurements at Jinxian. Yet releasing such information to the public was unthinkable. Moreover, the "prediction" of a magnitude 6 earthquake somewhere in Liaoning had been "tentative," that is, not requiring any administrative action.

Liaoning Province had never experienced the like of the Haicheng foreshock sequence before, as far as anyone could remember. There was no stopping people from building earthquake huts; fortunately, no one tried to. This is to the everlasting credit of the good sense of the Liaoning Provincial Government. Under the rules established by the State Seismological Bureau in Beijing, a local or provincial seismological brigade or even a single seismological station such as Shipengyu could make discretionary predictions without checking back with headquarters. Long-distance phone calls were not an easy matter; anyhow, a prediction could only be relayed to authorities, and it was up to the latter to take action. Under no circumstances could a seismologist decide to release information on earthquake prediction directly to the public. The authorities (local, county, provincial or national) were alone empowered to issue alerts. In practice this meant that control of all matters concerning the population were in the hands of the Party, a tightly knit network of 3 million people spanning the entire Chinese territory.

Did the authorities at least require an expert opinion from scientists in order to issue the earthquake alert of February 4, 1975? They did not. The occurrence of foreshocks was reason aplenty for alerting the population, common sense being the best seismologist when the ground is shaking under one's feet. "Trust the People," the watchword of the Chinese Revolution, was the secret behind the success of the Haicheng prediction.

All sources agree that the Haicheng alarm was issued under the sole responsibility of the Revolutionary Committee of Liaoning Province. Some agricultural communes around Haicheng had in fact jumped the gun by alerting the locals as early as the previous evening. The Revolutionary Committees of these communes had no privileged information that improved on that of the Provincial Government, except that they were right on top of the epicenter and could feel foreshocks as well as the next person.

Were the members of the Provincial Revolutionary Committee at least aware of the prediction efforts made by the seismologists headquartered in Yingkou City? Some of them probably were, but no definite information exists on this crucial point. Perhaps it didn't make much difference whether they did or not. Antiearthquake propaganda campaigns were routinely carried out all over China, and it can be argued that this helped reduce the casualty rate in the earthquake. As for the Yingkou seismological brigade, it got to Haicheng on the day of the earthquake and because of the foreshock emergency. No local seismological station or brigade had been detailed to Haicheng. The drive to Haicheng from Yingkou was circuitous and took a couple of hours. By the time the seismologists arrived, it was shortly before 10 A.M. and they couldn't have done much local research before the alert was issued at 10:30 A.M. Interestingly, another large earthquake occurred near Haicheng on May 18, 1978 ($M = 6.0$), but there were no foreshocks and no prediction was claimed.

To issue a public warning is no problem. Public address systems are ubiquitous in China, even in small villages. Loudspeakers are available to local Party authorities and/or to the Revolutionary Committees of towns or communes, and the population is often saturated with messages of all kinds, starting with calisthenics at 6 A.M. It is not clear how the earthquake warning was actually broadcast in Haicheng or what its wording may have been, but messages to the population concerning the earthquake situation must have been issued repeatedly on February 4. The contact between the leadership and the masses is much more fluid in China than it is in the West. The literature on the Haicheng prediction merely mentions a phone call relayed to all cities and counties of southern Liaoning Province; but it seems fair to assume that after 10 A.M. no information was kept from anyone within earshot of a loudspeaker. A specific warning was perhaps superfluous as the population was sufficiently alarmed by the foreshocks. The large number of victims must be attributed to the fact that many people went back to their homes at nightfall to have a hot meal. They were fooled by the decrease in the number of foreshocks.

Then where did the persistent information about the evacuation of Haicheng come from? While Chinese seismologists never actually claimed to have evacuated Haicheng, neither did they deny it. They were eager to take credit for the relatively low number of casualties in the Haicheng earthquake. They had been under pressure for years. Mao was still alive in 1975.

According to an official Chinese source, Shipengyu seismic station in Yingkou issued a "very important prediction" early on February 4, 1975. So did the People's Station at nearby Panshan High School, manned by students. We don't know exactly to whom, what was said, or what evidence these predictions were based on. We know that the seismic coverage of Shipengyu station was inadequate for locating the foreshocks, except by distance and general azimuth. Dandong and Shenyang stations were too far away to record any but the larger aftershocks. Their readings became available after the earthquake. The nearest quantitative monitoring of groundwater levels was near Liaoyang City, but it may have been unnecessary as some wells near Haicheng were said to have become artesian around 8 A.M. on the day of the earthquake. The monitoring of other precursors was not extensive or detailed by Chinese standards. At the annual prediction meeting, less than a month before the earthquake, only a vague forecast had been routinely issued. Yet the 1976 technical report by J.C. Savage contained reservations about nearly all precursors except about the prediction itself. In 1990 a panel of the International Association of Seismology and Physics of the Earth's Interior officially endorsed the claim that the Haicheng earthquake had been successfully predicted (Wyss, 1991).

Consider now the alternatives before the State Seismological Bureau. The Bureau is a professional agency, like the U.S. Geological Survey, but it is much more than that. It is a *cadre organization*, a militant political organ reporting directly to the Council of State. It commands incomparably more power than scientific bodies like the Academia Sinica or university research institutes. As a foreign academic scientist I was not allowed to visit its headquarters in 1977. Should such an agency have issued a disclaimer, belittling its own role in preventing casualties in the Haicheng earthquake? A statement of this kind would most certainly have been misunderstood. It would have been unfair to the Bureau's own staff, who performed creditably in trying to predict the quake and in mitigating the hazard. Note that none of the available facts on the Haicheng earthquake can be construed as detracting from the merits of Chinese seismologists. They had been trained to trust the people and they did. This was just as well. They might have attempted to deter people from building earthquake huts. Chinese seismologists deserve all the credit because their expectations on the subject of earthquake prediction were modest and realistic. Earthquake prediction is still in the future, and they knew it. Under the circumstances they performed as well as they had been expected to.

Western observers have attempted to interpret some aspects of the official Haicheng story at various times with indifferent success. Consider the following comment in a discussion on snakes coming out of hibernation before the earthquake:

. . . the reported mean temperatures in Liaoning in January 1975 were a few degrees above their usual -10 to $-15°C$. . . . Experts on animal behavior in China do not think that such a slight increase in temperature would drive snakes out of their holes, even if it awakened them (Deng, Jiang, Jones and Molnar, 1981).

Compare this with the following description:

Haicheng: particularly hot in Jan., frozen surface melted, ice melted; grass grown on the shady mountain; temperature increased steeply and night temperature fluctuated. (Meteorological investigation:) getting warm nationwide in January and the monthly maximum temperature appeared first in Shenyang area [where the snakes were first found—C.L.] since 1960. On Feb. 3, 1975, the strong warm low pressure moved to the epicenter, surface temperatures as high as $14.8°C$. (Causal analysis:) weather effects (urban hot island effect), but the output of underground heat could not be ruled out (Liu Defu, 1990).

The discrepancy between the two versions is striking, despite the fact that it concerns an effect as easy to verify as the temperature. The Western observers subscribe to the theory that the weather was below freezing while the Chinese reference insists temperatures were in fact in the 40s and 50s Fahrenheit. The most likely explanation is as follows. The first quote, giving the impression that the temperature remained much below freezing, was based on reports concerning the behavior of snakes. All comments on this supposed animal precursor tended to dismiss the influence of the weather. The second quote was taken from a discussion of *thermal precursors*, that is, alleged weather changes before Chinese earthquakes: quite naturally such reports tended to emphasize the occurrence of abnormally high winter temperatures. The final comment that "the output of underground heat could not be ruled out" was added as an afterthought, in order not to offend the advocates of snake precursors. Such examples could be multiplied. In later Chinese accounts, the reports concerning abnormal animal behavior (including snakes) are usually downplayed or dismissed. At the same time, anomalies in animal behavior continue to be cited as a major basis for the "short-term prediction" supposedly made in mid-January, though the actual evidence is increasingly hard to find in modern references.

CONCLUSIONS

(a) The Haicheng earthquake was predicted by the Chinese seismologists.

(b) Imminent predictions were issued 9 to 24 hours before the earthquake occurred. As for short- and medium-term predictions, the effective time-space-magnitude window was not clearly defined. There was a medium-term prediction for an earthquake of magnitude about 6 that might be stretched to fit the description of the Haicheng earthquake. But a sizable part of the territory of China was covered by similar predictions at the time.

(c) The prediction of the Haicheng earthquake may be regarded as an unqualified success, as it still is in China and elsewhere. But this success should be weighted against the low expectations produced by earlier and later failures.

(d) Despite initial claims, the number of victims of the Haicheng earthquake (1,328 dead) was inadmissibly large. For comparison, 200 people were killed in the 1985 Chile earthquake, which was also preceded by foreshocks but was much larger ($M = 7.9$), though no alert was issued. It seems likely that many inhabitants of Haicheng were allowed to regain their homes at nightfall. Alternatively, the lead time of the warning may have been too short for evacuation or other orderly measures of preparedness to be carried out.

Yet the alert was successful, together with the foreshocks and the fine weather, in getting people out of doors and in encouraging the building of earthquake huts on the sidewalks of Haicheng, thus arguably preventing a much larger number of casualties.

A similar successful prediction was made for the Songpan earthquake (Sichuan Province, August 16, 1976, $M = 7.2$). The warning was issued four days in advance, but the area of the prediction included a number of cities and counties in the general border area between Sichuan, Qinghai, and Gansu provinces. Since the Songpan earthquake, no further major shock has occurred and many seismologists assume that the "high tide" of earthquake activity in north-central China is now over.

(e) The various versions of the Haicheng prediction have changed noticeably over time. Six years after the earthquake, Zhang and Fu (1981) still cited a dozen anomalies including ground tilt at Jinxian ($\Delta = 140$ km), electrical potential at Yingkou, magnetic and self-potential anomalies, resistivity anomalies, animal behavior and groundwater anomalies at Dandong, and radon fluctuations at Liuhetang. Illustrations of such precursors are still widely reproduced. However, in the authoritative book by Ma et al. (1990), which discusses many precursors in separate chapters, all but the foreshocks were downplayed with comments such as "very few convincing anomalies were registered, mostly due to poor observation conditions and to instrumental instability" (re. ground tilt). It appears that many precursors used in the prediction turned out to be unreliable or doubtful. Most importantly, none of the precursors had been recorded with enough lead time to permit an evaluation of background fluctuations.

(f) It seems possible that the antiearthquake propaganda carried out by seismological brigades was effective in alerting the population of Haicheng to the danger of earthquakes, thereby preventing many casualties. This has been interpreted as a positive effect of the prediction. But in this case, the absence of active measures for increasing the detection capabilities for precursors in the Haicheng area seems puzzling and may require some explanation.

Thus, only 33 of the 500 foreshocks recorded at Shipengyu were of magnitude 1.5 or greater, and not many of those could be reliably read at Shenyang station. Besides, these readings only became available after the earthquake. Hence no extensive location of foreshocks could have been done prior to the earthquake. Yet, especially among Japanese scientists, the gradual concentration of foreshocks to within 5 km of the epicenter is cited as a precursor that contributed to the successful prediction of the Haicheng earthquake. But no temporary seismic station was established as a result of such a prediction, though it was known that there were not nearly enough stations for locating foreshocks anywhere in the province. Similar comments could be made with respect to other observations: water level in wells, radon, and geodetic or geoelectric measurements.

The story of Haicheng has played a role in buttressing bids for government support to earthquake prediction programs in other parts of the world. The claim of the successful Haicheng evacuation has been endorsed by government agencies and has been conceded even by skeptics such as Professor Donald L. Turcotte (1991, p. 268):

> Certainly no precursory phenomena have provided reliable predictions of earthquakes. However, it should be noted that a successful earthquake prediction was made by the Chinese and resulted in the evacuation of the city of Haicheng.

Western analysts might have had more reservations if it hadn't been so expedient to believe in the evacuation of Haicheng. As mentioned above, no claim of an evacuation can be found in Chinese sources. Neither can pictures of earthquake huts, though this was the factor credited with preventing larger casualties. The considerable logistic effort involved in the evacuation of a medium-sized town might normally have given pause to the analysts. Providing food and emergency shelter for a hundred thousand people can take elaborate groundwork and may cost millions of dollars. The spontaneous construction of earthquake huts is a vastly simpler affair, requiring no organization to speak of and costing next to nothing. It was in line with the official philosophy of the Chinese government in the mid-1970s, which promoted self-reliance schemes such as the "barefoot doctors," widely publicized at the time as a convenient way of supplementing scarce professional health care.

As long as the mechanism of earthquakes is still imperfectly understood, the Chinese approach to earthquake prediction may well represent one of the most effective tools for controlling earthquake hazards in seismically active regions. It is often a first step toward prevention. Earthquakes were predicted in practically all hazardous areas of China; and when an earthquake actually occurred the activities of the predictors were demonstrably useful in mitigating the hazard.

It doesn't always work. Four hundred kilometers southwest of Haicheng and 18 months later, the disastrous Tangshan earthquake struck. The number of casualties was in the hundreds of thousands. There had been no foreshocks . . .

3

A Blundering Oracle

INTRODUCTION

In 1957 the Russians launched *Sputnik,* the first earth-orbiting satellite. The brilliant success of Sputnik represented a powerful challenge to the Americans, who immediately responded by embarking upon a scientific and technological effort without precedent in world history. This was made possible by a system of education and research that had been totally overhauled since the war. The success of the Manhattan Project group and of other war research teams, such as the Group for Undersea Warfare, had made a deep impression on Washington. The three main prongs of the American Cold War scientific effort were aerospace, electronics, and computing, but in fact all fields of research and development were swept along by the momentum of what was to become the most amazing adventure of discovery in human history.

Around 1959 the Pentagon decided that a nuclear test-ban treaty with the Russians was not in the best interest of the United States. America was ahead in the technology race. Besides, there were too many loopholes. The test sites of both countries had purposely been located in seismically active regions: Nevada and Kazakhstan. There was no good way of telling an explosion from an earthquake, except for being on the spot. But here the Americans had spotted a fundamental Russian weakness. For political reasons Russia could not afford American inspection teams to visit their territory. Thus the Americans were able to manipulate the Russian response at will, merely by insisting or not insisting on *in situ* inspection.

But if there was to be no test-ban treaty, there would be a definite technological advantage for the United States being able to tell an explosion from an earthquake at a distance. As a result, a special research program was created under the code name *VELA-Uniform* for the purpose of solving the problem of monitoring nuclear tests at large distances. The first worldwide network of seismic stations was set up under this program, which was secret at the top but unclassified at the bottom. Generous grants as well as exemptions from security clearance were provided for academic scientists who participated in VELA-Uniform.

Wolfgang K.H. Panofsky, American physicist and an acute observer of his country's science policies, has pointed out that "confidence that science can perform on command is unwarranted." Yet the relevant fundamental knowledge was available in this case, and the problem was solved in record time. Earthquakes had a quadrantal distribution of first motions: They originated from shear displacements on deeply buried faults. Explosions were pulses from shallow, homogeneous, compressional sources. Technical procedures were quickly developed for distinguishing one from the other. By 1965 VELA-Uniform had attained its primary objective. It was phased out, and the academic scientists were left high and dry.

Frank Press, an American seismologist then based at Caltech, set out to find an alternate source of funding for seismological research. In those years a Russian group around Nersesov had reported some intriguing successes in earthquake prediction. The Japanese scientists had successfully persuaded their government to invest in a long-term earthquake prediction program. In 1964 the first of a succession of well-funded Japanese five-year plans on prediction research got underway.

Frank Press called for a similar program in the United States. His working group prepared a proposal to Congress tentatively calling for $242 million to be spent over a 10-year period on earthquake prediction and mitigation of earthquake hazard (Press, 1965). The proposal was a brilliant plea for support of the earth sciences but it had a weak spot. An annex entitled "Alternatives", which was appended to the proposal, began innocently:

> Using existing knowledge, without a major research program much could be done to reduce the potential loss of life and property from future earthquakes.

This sounded like a second line of defense. It created the suspicion in Washington that the asking price of $242 million was too high. It was not, and yet the statement in the annex rang true. If so much could be done so cheaply to reduce earthquake risk, why not just do it? In short, the proposal was turned down and nothing was done about earthquake hazard for 10 years. It took that long for American seismology to live down this defeat.

By 1976 the "Alternatives" to the earlier proposal had been dropped and the tune had become more sanguine about earthquake prediction. The alleged Chinese success in evacuating Haicheng had come to the rescue; it was brandished as proof that earthquakes could be successfully predicted. The new project was approved by Congress and the 1977 National Earthquake Hazards Reduction (NEHR) Act was born.

The new law put four federal agencies in charge of different aspects of the NEHR program. The U.S. Geological Survey (USGS) was made "responsible for earthquake prediction research and technological implementation. The USGS has adopted a goal that is stated quite simply: predict the time, place and magnitude of damaging earthquakes," according to *Earthquakes & Volcanoes,* an official USGS publication.[1]

This was easier said than done. Research groups were organized and some important scientific results were achieved; but the problem of predicting earthquakes turned out to be tougher and more complex than just telling an earthquake from an explosion. As far as Washington was concerned, not enough was happening. In the spring of 1982 the NEHR Act came up for reauthorization by Congress. At that time, the review of past performance led to "concern that the USGS was not moving agressively toward an operational earthquake prediction system". Senator Harrison Schmitt, a former astronaut and Chairman of the Senate Subcommittee on Science, Technology and Space at the time, bluntly suggested that a more "appropriate lead agency for earthquake hazards prediction and mitigation" might be found unless something happened soon. He casually mentioned the National Oceanic and Atmospheric Administration (NOAA) as a likely candidate to replace the USGS, citing NOAA's experience in weather prediction.

NOAA is under the Department of Commerce while the USGS is under the Department of Interior. Obviously, they are rival organizations. Science has little to do with turf warfare; just in case his point was missed, Senator Schmitt wrote to the Director of the USGS: "I feel strongly that some type of prototype earthquake prediction system needs to be in place in the U.S. within four to five years."

The USGS obliged: "in 1983, in response to Sen. Schmitt's concern, James Dieterich, the USGS Program Manager for earthquake prediction at the time, published a report entitled 'Assessment of a Prototype Earthquake Prediction Network for Southern California' ". This was to become known as the *Parkfield Project.*

The announcement satisfied politicians on Capitol Hill. The USGS was reconfirmed as the lead agency for earthquake prediction in the United States.

NEPEC

Now all eyes were on Parkfield, California (population 34), where an earthquake of magnitude 5.5–6 was now predicted to occur in 1988 ± 5 years,

---

[1] All quotes in this section are from *Earthquakes & Volcanoes—mainly from Filson (1988).*

that is to say, before December 31, 1992, at midnight. Political pressure was to be applied to the earth's crust in southern California.

Instruments were hurriedly emplaced around Parkfield for fear that the announced earthquake would be missed. Nothing happened. As the deadline for the prediction drew near, Menlo Park (where the USGS West Coast headquarters are located) became noticeably fidgety. The prediction had been announced with a confidence of 95%. Scientists went on the air with dire forecasts. No earthquake has ever been more anxiously awaited.

A candle or two might have been lit to St. Jude, the celestial patron of desperate causes. The Parkfield prediction had not just been made public by USGS; it had been endorsed by the National Earthquake Prediction Evaluation Council (NEPEC), a panel of 12 scientists created in 1980 for the purpose of evaluating proposed earthquake forecasts. The NEPEC panel consists of up to six USGS scientists, the rest being mostly university professors appointed by the director of the USGS.

NEPEC had barely been formed when an awkward initial case came before it. Brian T. Brady and William Spence, two American geophysicists who worked for government agencies, had predicted a series of three major earthquakes to occur off the coast of Peru in June–September 1981. The prediction was based on work carried out by the authors since 1976 and published (some of it) in reputable scientific journals. In view of the amount of research involved in the prediction, the two-day hearing held by NEPEC in January 1981 was widely perceived as inadequate. But the panic generated by the prediction in Peru and particularly in the capital city of Lima admitted no further delay.

The Council discussed and formally refused to endorse the Brady-Spence prediction, thus complying with a specific request of the president of Peru. But it did so rather lamely (Olson, 1989). Even though Spence and Brady had recanted, NEPEC failed to repudiate or disqualify their prediction explicitly; instead, the chairman of NEPEC offered to go to Peru on the critical dates as a token of his personal conviction that no earthquake would occur.

Lingering misgivings about the case were reflected in the comments by Professor Clarence N. Allen, chairman of NEPEC at the time:

> It clearly represented a very delicate situation, involving freedom of scientific expression and the willingness of the scientific "establishment" seriously to consider seemingly aberrant points of view, but also involving the economic and social well-being of literally millions of people. Was the public (in this case, the citizenry of Peru) well served by the scientific community? Should the National Evaluation Council have acted sooner and more positively to renounce the prediction? Should the Peruvian scientific community have acted more positively, or perhaps have sought outside advice sooner, in repudiating the prediction? Were the predictors given adequate and fair opportunities to defend the scientific basis of their predictions? Was an open hearing, with the television cameras rolling, the fairest and most effective form for the scientific evaluation of the prediction? In our efforts to be professionally fair to the

predictors, were we being equally fair to the people of Peru? Should the National Evaluation Council have refused to evaluate the prediction until it was published, or at least until it was written in some sort of formal scientific statement? Should the employers of the predictors—in this case, agencies of the U.S. government—have been more active in "controlling" the announcements of their employees? What role should the professional societies play in such a circumstance, and, in particular, should they be more vigorous in formulating a prediction "code of ethics"? Did the U.S. State Department, in its somewhat overzealous effort to help the Peruvians prepare for the possible earthquakes, add undue credence to the prediction? (Allen, 1983).

Stripping the statement of its sackcloth and ashes, it boils down to a veiled criticism of the Peruvian scientists for dumping their problem into NEPEC's lap instead of making mincemeat of Brady and Spence, as they might well have done. But the Peruvians had been paralyzed by the circumstance that they had made the initial move of inviting Dr. Brady to Peru. Thus they had unwittingly provided the launching pad for his unfortunate public declarations. A belated attempt at invalidating or dismissing their guest's predictions would have made them look even worse. In any case, their credibility was close to zero.

I was a frequent visitor to Peru at the time. In May 1981 (after the NEPEC ruling) the panic caused by the Brady-Spence prediction continued unabated. NEPEC had made little if any dent in public opinion. There was a run on outbound air travel tickets, and the flights to Miami were booked solid through September. The government made halfhearted attempts to counter the effects of the panic, but these efforts were ridiculed by the opposition press. The U.S. embassy kept a dignified silence. Brady and Spence were allowed to keep their government jobs.

I bought a newspaper on arrival in Lima. It reported on a witches' convention being held in town. A gentleman who claimed to be president of the Sorcerers' and Witches' Association of Peru had offered to perform a special sabbath—in order to find out "the truth about the earthquake!" The performance was luridly described in the centerfold of the paper. Graphic artists had showered the page with sketches of black cats and other esoteric paraphernalia. The ceremony culminated in a spell for summoning "Brady's ghost" (his body being unavailable for comment), and requesting a definite answer as to whether or not there was going to be an earthquake in Lima. According to the paper the "ghost" did in fact show up. When the fateful question was put to him, he replied like NEPEC: "Hoy día sí, mañana no" (yes today, no tomorrow).

"FORECASTED BUT NOT PREDICTED"

Just as the USGS was getting ready for the Parkfield earthquake, the Loma Prieta earthquake of October 17, 1989 occurred. It caused $6 billion of damage in the San Francisco Bay area and killed 68 people, most of them in the collapse of an elevated interstate freeway in Oakland. The USGS promptly claimed to have predicted it—a claim that caused some squirming among USGS scientists. San Francisco was not exactly the same as Parkfield. It was not even in southern California. Actually some scientists of the USGS had published a "speculation" (not a formal prediction) that an earthquake might occur soon near Calaveras Reservoir east of Stanford with potential damage to San Francisco. This was a few months before the Loma Prieta earthquake. A Loma Prieta foreshock was ironically found afterwards on the map containing the flawed prediction (Fig. 3.1).

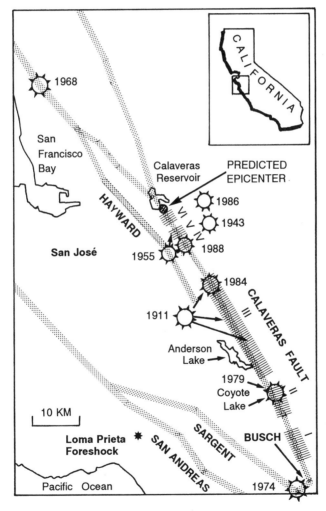

Fig. 3.1 *Prediction of an earthquake near Calaveras Reservoir, California in 1988. After R.A. Kerr, 1988. From* Earthquakes & Volcanoes, 21, *U.S. Geological Survey, p. 117.*

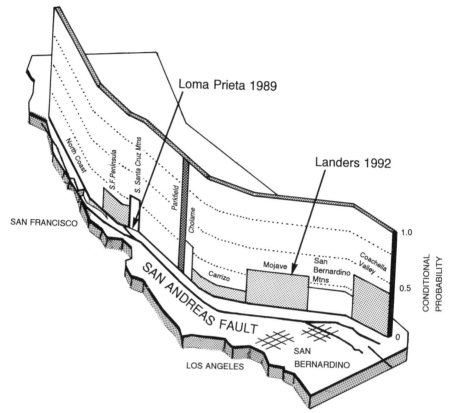

Fig. 3.2 *Forecasted probabilities of occurrence of California earthquakes, as issued by the Working Group on California Earthquake Prediction and endorsed by NEPEC in 1988. From* Earthquakes and Volcanoes, 20, *U.S. Geological Survey, p. 59.*

A paper published in June 1991 by James C. Savage, a respected seismologist of the USGS, was interpreted as a signal of unrest among the rank and file. Savage took the NEPEC to task for having endorsed the set of forecasts of California earthquakes (shown in Fig. 3.2), issued in 1988 by the Working Group on California Earthquake Prediction (WGCEP). These forecasts included the Parkfield prediction and were based on the hypothesis that the times of recurrence between characteristic earthquakes in California are lognormally distributed with unit (or normalized) variance $\sigma = 0.21$. Savage tested this hypothesis and found it wanting. It didn't seem to fit the data terribly well. As a matter of fact, the recurrence intervals of the four best-documented data sequences were only marginally consistent with the proposed lognormal fit.

Savage (1991) argued that the uncertainties in the estimation of the mean recurrence times were so large as to make most of the 1988 predictions "virtually meaningless." The forecast, he wrote, should have taken the scatter of the estimates into account. At the very least, it should have assigned somewhat lower conditional probabilities of occurrence to Parkfield (assigned a 95% probability to rupture before 1993), as well as the Southern Santa Cruz Mountains (assigned a 30% probability to rupture before 2018). Now for the unkindest cut of all: Savage reminded NEPEC that the Loma Prieta earthquake did occur in 1989, though the likelihood of this happening had been estimated at less than 5% just a year before, using the very forecasting method approved by NEPEC. In the meantime, the Parkfield earthquake was still unaccountably delayed.

The Loma Prieta earthquake ruptured the trace of the San Andreas fault along the Santa Cruz segment, previously broken in the great San Francisco earthquake of 1906. Nothing had happened there for 80 years. Then in June 1988 and again a year later, in July 1989, two moderate earthquakes occurred in the Loma Prieta area. They were correctly identified as possible foreshocks, but the major earthquake was expected in Parkfield.

In 1988 a working group on California earthquake prediction proposed a division of the San Andreas fault into 11 segments, one of which was the Santa Cruz segment. Forecasts for each segment were issued; they involved an estimation of probabilities of rupture within the next 30 years for each segment of the fault (Fig. 3.2). All bases were covered. Records of the discussions in NEPEC show that a number of different scenarios were considered and that a rupture on the Calaveras or other East Bay faults was assigned a higher probability than a rupture on the Loma Prieta segment. After the 1988 foreshock and again after the July 1989 event, the California Office of Emergency Services issued public warnings that a large earthquake might occur within 5 days; nothing happened.

These forecasts and attempted predictions were made on the broad basis of the *hypothesis of characteristic earthquakes,* which assumes that earthquakes on the San Andreas fault recur essentially on the same segments and in much the same manner. But the 1989 rupture did not occur *exactly* on the same fault plane that ruptured in 1906. Even the mechanisms were different. The 1906 earthquake had taken place on a vertical fault which broke the surface for many miles. The Loma Prieta earthquake did not break the surface—and the fault plane now had a significant dip. The displacement involved about equal amounts of reverse and strike-slip motion, while the 1906 earthquake had been purely strike-slip.

Now, after a year of more careful study [wrote Tom Heaton of the USGS in 1991], many researchers are questioning whether the Loma Prieta earthquake was the earthquake forecast in the 1988 report. In particular, there is growing evidence that the 1906 and 1989 earthquakes may have been on separate subparallel faults, and that the repeat time for earthquakes similar to the 1989 earthquake may be larger than several hundred years. Ironically, while the Loma Prieta earthquake seemingly fulfilled the forecast of a characteristic earthquake, it provided evidence that earthquakes may not be characteristic and that forecasting their occurrence may be even more difficult than previously believed.

NEPEC might have countered by pointing out that the arguments of Heaton and Savage about the 1989 Loma Prieta earthquake owed a great deal to hindsight. They had not spoken up in 1988, when the forecast was made. But no reply of NEPEC came forth. No one apparently wished to probe further.

In the following chapters we will cautiously develop Heaton's view "that earthquakes may not be characteristic." In a certain sense, the question about the "repeat times" of earthquakes along specific faults might be meaningless. No fault breaks twice along an identical rupture. The closer we look at a fault "segment" the less we can speak of repetitions. By analogy, in the case of a watershed, the drainage pattern is evolving and shifting with every successive flood. According to Heraclitus, we cannot step twice into the same river. Similarly, in the case of a plate boundary, no constant configuration exists: Strain will find its channels.

Yet there is such a thing as a characteristic length of rupture for a given region. In the Amazon Basin, primary affluents have a characteristic length (which is smaller than the length of the Amazon), and so have secondary, tertiary affluents, and so on. The paradox is resolved through randomness and self-organization. The major predictable feature of seismicity is the pattern of regional strain release, not the specific break on which the next event will occur.

The attempted prediction (or the "successful forecast," as some insisted on calling it) of the 1989 Loma Prieta earthquake was complicated by a series of extraneous events. The first of these contingencies was a 1987 letter to NEPEC by Dallas L. Peck, director of the USGS, following up on a recommendation of his Subcommittee on Earthquake Research. The relevant paragraph stated:

> Finally I have a specific charge for the Council regarding the evaluation of the earthquake threat to southern California. Considerable work has been done during the past few years in this region, and it is appropriate that earlier estimates of the earthquake potential in the region be revised and refined in the light of this work. Specifically, I would appreciate your assessment by the end of the year on the likelihood of a great earthquake in southern California during the next few decades.

This charge exceeded the formal authority of NEPEC (which is supposed to pass judgment on predictions but not to formulate any of its own). Therefore a special Working Group on California Earthquake Prediction (WGCEP) was set up. As the membership of both councils more or less overlapped, the result was that NEPEC gradually slipped into the role of issuing predictions. The main difference was that WGCEP's action was confined to California while NEPEC's was nationwide.

The other event was the prediction made by V.I. Keilis-Borok of the Soviet Union, for an earthquake with a magnitude in excess of 7.5 to occur in California or Nevada before December 31, 1988. As a result of this prediction, Keilis-Borok was invited to expound his methodology before NEPEC, which he did in Los Angeles on June 6, 1988. At that time he also announced that he was extending his prediction window to the end of 1991. The record of the discussion that took place in the meeting reveals that Keilis-Borok failed to convince NEPEC. In some critical aspects, including the prediction probabilities for the announced earthquake, members of NEPEC failed to nail down the foxy visitor, who remained amusingly elusive and noncommittal. At the end of the day the Keilis-Borok prediction was summarized by NEPEC as follows (cf. Updike, 1989):

- In a diameter of 900 km centered in north-central California with a 100 km extension north and south (which included most of California and western Nevada), an earthquake greater than magnitude 7.5 would occur up to the end of 1991.
- In northern California, an earthquake greater than 6.4 was expected up to February 1989.

None of these predictions came true. The Loma Prieta earthquake did occur in 1989, but it only had a magnitude of 7.1. Keilis-Borok later claimed that his prediction window for the *second* ($M > 6.4$) event had actually extended beyond February 1989—which would have included Loma Prieta. Anyway, partly because of the prestige of the author of the prediction, several members of NEPEC felt that earthquake patterns over very large areas (exceeding the size of the segments for characteristic earthquakes) should be looked into for predictive purposes.

The algorithm used by Keilis-Borok was independently tested by J.B. Minster (University of California, San Diego) and by J.H. Healy (USGS). They found that the algorithm was far from robust: It depended critically on the occurrence or nonoccurrence of small distant events and on the choice of parameter settings. Healy thought that most major earthquakes in 1985–1991 may have been successfully predicted by the algorithm; Minster disagreed. On the other hand, the 1992 Landers earthquake had been predicted according to Minster but not according to Healy.

As a touch of savage irony, the Northridge, California earthquake (January 17, 1994, $M = 6.6$) was a replay of the 1971 San Fernando earthquake—except that the area had become more vulnerable. No one seems to have had an inkling that such an event could occur at this particular spot. The quake originated off the San Andreas fault, on an unknown blind thrust fault running somewhere under the San Fernando Valley. More than 55 people died, and the cost exceeded all previous world records for earthquakes. If, as the Chinese believe, earthquakes are actually cunning enemies of humankind, this one could not have planned a more stunning or a more unexpected strike. The American earthquake prediction program was utterly shattered. All that remained now was picking up the pieces.

1992 LANDERS EARTHQUAKE

Earthquake prediction was complicated, among other things, by the fact that the problem was not well posed. Seismologists didn't agree about what we should be looking for. Throwing money at the problem was no substitute for hard thinking.

On October 20, 1992 an earthquake of magnitude 4.7 near Parkfield triggered the California emergency system. An alert was broadcast over five counties in California. Was the Parkfield earthquake—magnitude 6–7—finally going to occur within the following 72 hours? Again, nothing happened. The alert caused anxiety as far away as Mexico City, where a part of the public believes for some reason that the San Andreas fault goes through the city.

No alert was issued before the largest earthquake to strike California in 40 years: the Landers quake. On June 28, 1992, a shock of magnitude 7.6 ruptured a length of 70 km across the Mojave fault block in San Bernardino County (Fig. 3.3). The earthquake caused one death and about $100 million of damage. Three hours later another earthquake occurred near Big Bear Lake ($M = 6.5$). The area had been carefully mapped, but despite the explicit charge of the director of the USGS, no activity had been predicted in that particular location. Ten years earlier, the Landers fault could not have been found on a map purporting to show the pattern of major faulting in southern California. After consulting a dozen recent papers I am still unsure that anyone had an inkling that such a large event might occur at this location. The right-lateral slip along the fault was the largest ever measured in California: up to 6.2 m. But the rupture was not continuous; individual segments were offset. Contrary to the characteristic-earthquake hypothesis, the faulting had hurdled the offsets with ease.

Once again the earthquake was "forecasted but not predicted". The USGS had unsuspectingly scheduled a major review meeting (on the Parkfield prediction) to take place 12 hours after the Landers earthquake! Fig. 3.2 suggests that an earthquake may have been expected to occur on the Mojave segment of the San Andreas fault. Because of the length of the segment the magnitude was expected to reach 7.5: This segment had previously been described as quiescent (Fig. 3.4). It still is. How long the quiescence will last is anybody's guess, but the Landers quake did not occur on the trace of the San Andreas fault. No one believes that it has taken the load off the fault; on the contrary, many seismologists suspect that a larger earthquake is more likely than ever.

A large foreshock of Landers occurred on April 22, 1992 ($M = 6.1$). Called the "Joshua Tree earthquake," it was not recognized as a foreshock. Mogi (1992) had stated shortly before that "I would not expect to find strong foreshocks before an earthquake in central California in the United States, where the geological structure is very simple." Simple or not, large-scale deformations of the earth's crust over an area of 200×200 km were detected after the shock. The deformation pattern was reconstructed by radar interferometry and fitted the predicted strain from the observed faulting. It is practically certain that important precursory deformations occurred as well. An extension of the 1959–1974 Palmdale "bulge" had its maximum uplift in the

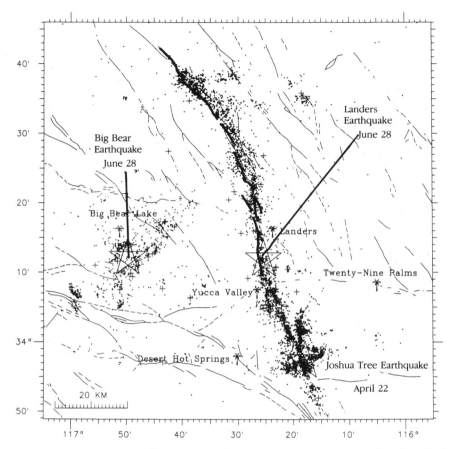

Fig. 3.3 The 1992 Landers, California, earthquakes, including the Joshua Tree foreshock and the Big Bear earthquake (probably triggered by the main shock). Surface ruptures (thick lines) were produced by the main shock. From j. Mori, K. Hudnut, L. Jones, E. Hauksson, and K. Hutton, compilers, 1992. Rapid seismic response to Landers quakes, EOS, 73, 417–418. Published by the American Geophysical Union.

1992 epicentral region. At this date (1994), many California seismologists tend to believe that strong foreshocks do occur regularly before California earthquakes.

SWALLOWING CAMELS

Actually NEPEC had painted itself into a corner. It had ruled that the lognormal distribution of intervals with unit variance 0.21 was recommended for predicting the likelihood of future characteristic earthquakes in the state of California.

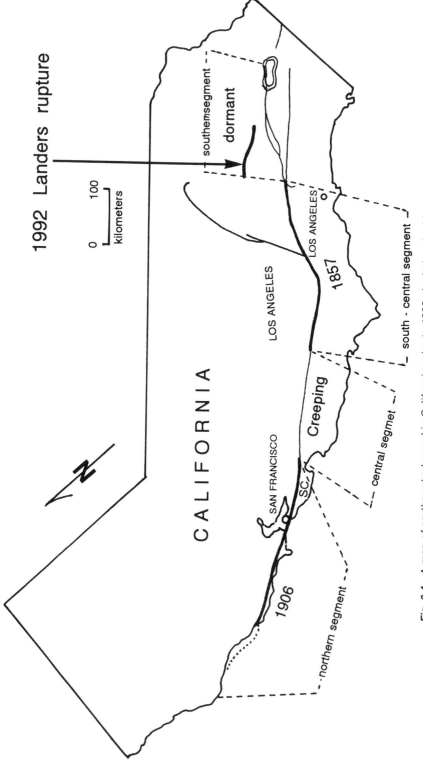

Fig. 3.4 A map of earthquake hazard in California prior to 1992, depicting the Mojave segment of the San Andreas fault as "dormant".

A characteristic earthquake is a seismic event that ruptures one and the same fault segment time and again and by so doing, defines the segment independently of adjacent segments. The circularity of the definition is inevitable: There seems to be no other way of subdividing a continuous plate boundary into discrete regions. But this makes the recognition of an earthquake as characteristic strongly dependent on the interpretation of earlier events in the same region. The NEPEC predictions had been based on observations of 48 intervals between characteristic earthquakes in 14 segments of plate boundaries around the world. This is not a large sample: It makes an average sample size of only 3.43 observations per segment. A typical segment produced the following data set (Nishenko and Buland, 1987).

Region	Events	Interval T	Mean
San Marcos	1907–1845	62	
	1957–1907	50	56.0

This defines a segment called "San Marcos" in southern Mexico in terms of three characteristic earthquakes that took place in 1845, 1907, and 1957, with intervals of 62 and 50 years. The mean recurrence interval was 56 years. But another paper printed in the same issue of the *Bulletin of the Seismological Society of America* contained the following statement on this region (Nishenko and Singh, 1987):

> . . . both the 1937 to 1950 and 1957 shocks each represent a partial rerupturing of the 1907 zone. . . . Accordingly, the observed recurrence intervals for the Acapulco–Ometepec region during this century range from 30 + to 50 years (i.e., 1937 to 1907 and 1957 to 1907).

The Acapulco-Ometepec region includes the San Marcos region. The two interpretations seem incompatible in terms of the characteristic-earthquake hypothesis. The 1907 earthquake could not be characteristic for both segments at once. If it had been, the events in the two adjacent segments could not be independent and hence were not characteristic. Moreover, the case of the 1907 earthquake was not unique. All through the list one could find similar instances of overlaps, partial ruptures, and precession.

Two segments on the San Andreas fault, Parkfield and Pallett Creek, were defined in terms of characteristic earthquakes with average intervals of 21.8 and 194.3 years. The disparity between recurrence times is larger than between any other pair of segments in the worldwide sample, yet these are nearby segments on the same fault. Could this be because Parkfield earthquakes have been clocked to the nearest hour while Pallett Creek earthquakes have been dated by radiocarbon methods to the nearest decade or so? Clearly the two data sets cannot refer to the same kind of events: One average interval on Pallett Creek would exceed the total historical record on the San Andreas fault. The list is not homogeneous.

The statistical procedure consisted in normalizing the intervals T by dividing them by the mean interval for each segment. Then the "normalized" intervals were merged and fitted to a single lognormal distribution. It was then claimed that "the distribution of recurrence intervals for each fault segment is also lognormal and $\ln(T)$ is normally distributed" (Nishenko and Buland, 1987). But this claim is invalid as lognormality is not conserved under superposition.

One and the same unit variance was proposed to apply to all segments; in other words, the logarithmic variance for each segment was proposed to equal 0.21 scaled by the sample mean. This was inconsistent with the data. Finally, the Parkfield prediction, which NEPEC had previously espoused, was based on a totally different and probably incompatible statistical model. It too was based on the idea of characteristic earthquakes but it used a different variance. These inconsistencies turned out to be beneficial as they eventually helped discredit the concept of characteristic earthquakes.

THE PARKFIELD PREDICTION

But what was the Parkfield prediction? A paper by Bakun and Lindh (1985) (hereafter referred to as PARKFIELD) had proposed to model the process of characteristic earthquakes on the Parkfield segment of the San Andreas fault. PARKFIELD suggested a constant repeat time of 21.8 ± 5 years between earthquakes in this area. In other words, Parkfield earthquakes were assumed to be largely deterministic (i.e., the opposite of random).

This idea was not proposed as a general result to be applied to all earthquakes, or even to all segments of the San Andreas fault. On the contrary: PARKFIELD suggested that the Parkfield sequence was unusual and possibly unique. Four of its six known events were almost evenly spaced, with a mean interval of 21.8 years. Scholz (1990) has provided a careful and detailed discussion of the geophysical arguments. In spite of some reservations he too concluded that "by any reckoning the next earthquake in the series is imminent."

This confidence was based on the erroneous assumption that the cycle of tectonic loading and relaxation at a given segment of a plate boundary can be analyzed and understood more or less independently of what happens elsewhere along the same boundary. The complete Parkfield sequence was as follows:

1857, 1881, 1901, 1922, 1934, 1966.

The corresponding intervals T were (in years):

24, 20, 21, 12, 32.

This sequence was described as "shocks of approximately magnitude 6 occurring every 21 to 22 years and having the same epicenter and rupture area" (Bakun, 1988). The implication was that the next earthquake would occur approximately in 1988. But how valid was such an extrapolation? The first three intervals were about the same, but not the last two. The 1934 event was ten years closer to 1922 than it was to 1966.

Suppose, however, that we just eliminate this one data point on the grounds that it doesn't belong. Then the sample of intervals (after tampering with 20% of the data) would look as follows:

$$24, \ 20, \ 21, \ 44.$$

But this makes the case for equal intervals even worse. On the other hand, if the 1934 earthquake is *not* eliminated, the sample mean is 21.8 years as claimed, but the *range* of intervals is 12–32 years: a scatter of about ± 10 years, nearly half the sample mean. Such a scatter would be expected for a Poisson process. It would make the prediction of the next earthquake quite uncertain. The easy way out was pretending that the 1934 event had actually occurred in 1944. This was ludicrous, but it was the course of action PARK-FIELD eventually adopted. It assumed that the 1934 event had been prematurely triggered by a foreshock of magnitude 5.0 which occurred two days before.

Let us make a blindfold test. Suppose that, instead of moving the date of the 1934 event, we just eliminate the last observation (1966). In other words, suppose that the 1966 earthquake has not yet occurred. Could we have predicted this event? The sample mean would then have been $T_{ave} = 19.25$ years with a standard deviation of 4.42 years. If we extrapolated this sequence in the manner of PARKFIELD we should have predicted the next event to occur in 1934.45 + 19.25 ± 4.42 = 1953.7 ± 4.42. The true date (1966) would have been missed by more than a decade.

On a different tack, let us assume that the 1934 event was on schedule and that the 1966 event was delayed. Then discarding 1966 and taking 1934 as our benchmark we may extrapolate twice the mean interval of 21.8 years. Then we get a totally different prediction target for the next earthquake, namely 1978 ± 4 years instead of 1988 ± 5 years. This makes 10 years of difference with the prediction adopted by NEPEC. The prediction would have lapsed in 1982.

This example shows how sensitive a prediction can be to the logic behind it, especially if it is based on few data points. The NEPEC prediction had agreed to dismissing the true date of the 1934 earthquake as irrelevant, yet the dates of the other earthquakes were retained. An error of ten years was accepted for the 1934 event while the 1966 event was assumed to be known with zero error. This was a major inconsistency. Since there was no objective reason for assuming delays or premature occurrences in one event rather than in another, the same error bars should have been assigned to all data points. But if all six data points had error bars of ± 10 years, the Parkfield prediction would make no sense.

Let us now attempt a nonstationary prediction. The optimal prediction for a nonstationary random walk is obtained by repeating the last observation, that is, by extrapolating the last interval into the future. The last interval was 32 years. Thus we obtain a mean prediction for the next Parkfield earthquake of 1966 + 32 = 1998.

So far we have not questioned the basic premise that the six Parkfield events were in fact characteristic earthquakes that could be singled out unequivocally from among other events on this particular segment of the San Andreas fault. But Bakun (1988) was careful to point out that "the quantity and quality of the information decrease dramatically for the earlier shocks." In other words, the earlier events should have been given smaller weights (or assigned larger error margins) than the observations made after 1901. But the two most recent intervals are 12 and 32 years. The recent observations are precisely the ones that deviate the most from the hypothesis of a constant deterministic increment of 21.8 years. The more reliable the observations, the less they support the hypothesis of the prediction.

How unusual is in fact the occurrence of a run of six equally spaced events in a region? If the answer is "extremely unusual," this should have cautioned NEPEC into considering randomness as a null hypothesis. If the answer is "moderately unusual but not terribly surprising," the PARKFIELD hypothesis loses credibility. In either case we need to examine the following question: What is the probability of obtaining a run of five equal intervals in a random point process—assuming that the Parkfield events were actually evenly spaced?

Let us make some quick computer experiments using the type of forward stochastic modeling known as the *Monte Carlo method* among seismologists. Assuming a pure Poisson process with a mean interval of $T_{ave} = \lambda^{-1} = 21.8$ years the intervals T may be generated by

$$T = -\lambda^{-1} \ln (1 - R) \tag{3.1}$$

where R is a uniformly distributed random number in the range [0,1]. Eq (3.1) was obtained by solving for x in the exponential interval distribution

$$F_T(x) = 1 - e^{-\lambda x}, x > 0 \tag{3.2}$$

and replacing the distribution function F by a random number. Every value of R corresponds to a different value of T. In this way one can quickly and efficiently generate long Poisson time series for different values of the parameter λ.

I counted the number of runs of five consecutive intervals T in a Poisson process of mean interval $\lambda^{-1} = 21.8$ years, such that no single interval would deviate more than 10 years from the sample mean. This happened about 45 times in a thousand trials. In other words, the Parkfield sequence appears to be compatible with the Poisson hypothesis at the 4.5% level. This is certainly too high for rejecting the Poisson hypothesis on the basis of a single trial. I raised the question with some gamblers, who are familiar with odds. I asked them to consider the likelihood of rolling two aces ("snake-eyes") twice in a row with a new pair of dice. None of the gamblers would conclude that this was enough reason for rejecting the dice as unfair. Yet the probability of twice rolling snake-eyes with an honest pair of dice is $6^{-4} = 0.0008$ or almost *57 times less* than 4.5%.

The above test assumes that the mean of the process is 21.8 years, but of course the true mean was unknown. For a Poisson process (and, in fact, for every reasonable point process we care to assume), the sample mean is smaller than the mean of the process. For a Poisson process with $\lambda^{-1} = 21.8$ years, the average sample mean was 9.5 years. If we assume $\lambda^{-1} = 50$ years, for example, runs of 5 intervals with a sample mean of 21 years still occur 0.02% of the time—which comes near the probability of rolling snake-eyes twice in a row. Actually, as λ^{-1} is unknown, the likelihood of the Parkfield run having been generated by a Poisson process is significantly higher.

On the other hand, the Poisson process is but one of a family of likely earthquake processes: the renewal processes (see Chapter 7). Consider, for example, the Benioff-Shimazaki distribution

$$F_T(x) = 1 - e^{-\xi x^2} \tag{3.3}$$

to be discussed later. Solving for $x = T$ and replacing F by R we obtain the Monte Carlo algorithm

$$T = [-\xi^{-1} \ln (1-R)]^{1/2}. \tag{3.4}$$

Carrying out the same experiment as before with $\lambda^{-1} = 21$ years we find that five sequential near-equal intervals now occur 10% of the time. Since neither the type of process nor the mean sample interval were known *a priori*, we get extremely high odds that the sequence was actually generated by a number of possible processes, each of which is at least as likely as the one proposed in PARKFIELD.

In fact, what is the likelihood that alone the Parkfield segment produces earthquakes by means of a quasi-deterministic process, while all other segments on the San Andreas fault and elsewhere generate events by a renewal process, as NEPEC suggested? On the strength of only six Parkfield earthquakes as against hundreds if not thousands of "normal" events, one can hardly assign a very high probability to such an hypothesis. Probability theory is constructed on the basis of simple axioms, for example: "the probability of an event is the frequency of occurrence of the event over a sufficiently long series of tests" (Kolmogorov, 1956). It is based on simple logic. But the human mind often experiences trouble following all but the simplest logical steps. PARKFIELD proposed a process with a single spectral line at a period of 21.8 years, on the strength of a five-point data run. What would have been the return period if 10, 50, or 1,000 Parkfield earthquakes were available? Does it seem believable that it would still be 21.8 years?

A more correct procedure would have been to model the proposed process with an *unknown* interval and then to carry out an analysis of variance. The various possible mean intervals (19, 20, 21 years, and so on) should have been assigned equal probabilities, and the probability of a run with a sample mean of 21.8 should have been estimated for each hypothesis. The probability for the next earthquake occurring in 1988 ± 5 years would have been different in each case. Finally, the fact that the computation was carried out at a time when more than 20 years had gone by since the last earthquake should have been taken into account. This changes the probabilities very considerably since the occurrence of an interval of less than 20 years was automatically nil. In conclusion, there existed no reasonable way of obtaining a probability as high as 90% that the next Parkfield earthquake should fall within a prediction window as narrow as ±5 years.

Let Pr[dat|"Bak"] be the probability that the Parkfield data ("dat" = [1857. . . 1966]) were in fact generated by a process such as proposed in PARKFIELD. Similarly, let *Pr*[dat|"Ben"] be the probability that the same data were generated, say, by a Benioff-Shimazaki process. Then the posterior probability that the PARKFIELD hypothesis was correct may be expressed by

Pr["Bak"|dat]

$$
= \frac{\text{Pr[dat|"Bak"] Pr["Bak"]}}{\text{Pr[dat|"Bak"] Pr["Bak"]} + \text{Pr[dat|"Ben"] Pr["Ben"]} + \ldots} \cdot
$$

from Bayes' Theorem. The prior probabilities of type Pr[dat|"Bak"] or Pr[dat|"Ben"] can be calculated by Monte Carlo simulations as shown in the examples above.

But the probabilities of type Pr["Bak"] are subjective: They denote the likelihood that the corresponding hypothesis is correct. This likelihood cannot be estimated objectively, because in this case it would have to be obtained independently of the data input ("dat"); and there is no way of doing this except by guessing. In other words, the result depends on how firmly one believes, say, that characteristic earthquakes do exist and that Parkfield is a very special place where earthquakes, unlike elsewhere on earth, are perfectly predictable by extrapolation of six observation points. The Bayesian approach affords a possibility of doing this or at least hedging our bets and making a minimum of enemies. It suffices to assign the same probability to all models. But this way we learn nothing.

Consider now a worst-case scenario such as a more skeptical NEPEC might have used. Suppose the process underlying the Parkfield sequence

TABLE 3.1 The Parkfield Sequence

Events	1857		1881		1901		1922		1934		1966
Intervals T		24		20		21		12		32	
$T - 21.8$		2.2		-1.8		-0.8		-9.8		10.2	
Rank		3		-2		-1		-4		5.	

was actually a Poisson process. The standard deviation would equal the square root of λ^{-1} or $\sqrt{21.8} = 4.67$ years, which fits the data. But then the probability of occurrence of an earthquake within five years of the target date of 1988 could not have been 95% as originally claimed. It should have been much less than 50%, because (a) the true mean recurrence time is unknown, and (b) the target of 1988 had almost been reached when the prediction was formulated. The fact that no earthquake had occurred up to that time was not fed into the prediction. But the Poisson process was only one of many possible processes.

In other words, using standard logic the PARKFIELD prediction had a much less than even chance of coming true. NEPEC could have decided to back it anyway, if it stood to gain a lot in case that it worked and lose very little if it didn't. But the reverse was true. NEPEC stood to gain a five-year breathing space against high odds of losing its credibility for future earthquake prediction programs.

Finally, let us attempt a nonparametric test, that is, a test that does not assume any particular distribution *a priori*. As an example, consider again the PARKFIELD hypothesis that the sequence of earthquakes was generated by a deterministic renewal process. In other words, assume that the intervals were symmetrically distributed about $T_{ave} = 21.8$ years (Table 3.1). We apply the Wilcoxon one-sample test, a nonparametric test that consists in ranking the absolute differences between the sample values and the null hypothesis. The ranks are given the signs of the corresponding observations. As seen in Table 3.1, the sum of the positive ranks is 8 and of the negative ranks -7. The Wilcoxon criterion is the probability P of getting a rank sum equal to or more extreme than these observed values.

The total number of possible rank combinations is $2^5 = 32$ since any rank is equally likely to be positive or negative. For such a small sample it is just as quick to enumerate all possible ways in which the negative rank sum can be equal or larger than -7:

$$1, \quad 2, \quad 3, \quad 4, 5 \qquad\qquad\qquad\qquad\qquad\qquad\qquad\qquad (1)$$
$$-1, \quad 2, \quad 3, \quad 4, 5 \qquad 1, -2, \quad 3, \quad 4, 5 \qquad 1, \quad 2, -3, \quad 4, \quad 5 \; \ldots \; (5)$$
$$-1, -2, \quad 3, \quad 4, 5 \qquad -1, \quad 2, -3, \quad 4, 5 \qquad -1, \quad 2, \quad 3, -4, \quad 5 \; \ldots \; (4)$$
$$1, -2, -3, \quad 4, 5 \qquad -1, -2, \quad 3, -4, 5 \qquad 1, -2, \quad 3, \quad 4, -5 \qquad (3)$$
$$1, \quad 2, -3, -4, 5 \qquad\qquad\qquad\qquad\qquad\qquad\qquad\qquad\qquad (1)$$
$$-1, -2, -3, \quad 4, 5 \qquad -1, -2, \quad 3, -4, 5 \qquad\qquad\qquad\qquad\qquad (2)$$

Framingham State College
Framingham, Massachusetts

thus yielding a total of $1 + 5 + 4 + 3 + 1 + 2 = 16$ combinations. In conclusion, the value of P is $16/32 = 0.5$ which means that the null hypothesis is just as likely to be accepted as to be rejected.

This result was predictable. It was due to the small sample size. Definitely, nothing could be said about the PARKFIELD hypothesis except that it was doubtful. "So much for a blind obedience to a blundering oracle" (Thoreau).

BRUNE'S DILEMMA AND OTHER CURIOSITIES

In conclusion, the Parkfield earthquake was "successfully predicted" in terms of the state of the art. It will certainly occur sooner or later. The questions it raises are of another order.

Seismologist James N. Brune wrote a brief discussion on the subject of the predictability of earthquakes (Brune, 1979). Suppose, Brune argued, that large earthquakes are always triggered by small earthquakes. Then we must either be able to tell the small shocks that trigger a large earthquake from the enormously more numerous small shocks that don't, or else predict every small earthquake that occurs on every plate boundary. This dilemma seems to rule out earthquake prediction for the foreseeable future. For the same reasoning would be applicable to radon anomalies, groundwater fluctuations, animal behavior, or any other precursors.

Brune's dilemma has a kind of solution: Small shocks and large earthquakes are not the same kinds of events. They are different classes of phenomena. Precursors differ from small random fluctuations. The confusion may lie in the idea of *triggering*. Large earthquakes are not triggered by precursors, or by anything: they are embedded in a larger transient that starts ahead of the earthquake and lasts beyond its occurrence. This transient is the cause of precursors, such as foreshocks.

Consider a plate boundary such as the San Andreas fault, compounded by a large number of subfaults. A large earthquake is a complex event consisting of a sequential rupture of N subfaults, such as to minimize the entropy production

$$\Delta S = kN [\log \Pi_{\text{after}} - \log \Pi_{\text{before}}] - E/T, \tag{3.5}$$

where E is the seismic energy release, T is the temperature, and k is Boltzmann's constant. Each product Π is of the form

$$\Pi = \sum_i e_1^i \sum_i e_2^i \cdots \sum_i e_N^i, \tag{3.6}$$

where e_j^i is the energy of the j-th subfault for the i-th state of the subfault.

Thus each Π is a product of N terms, each of which is a summation over all possible states of the subfault.

Now, if $\bar{e}$ is the mean energy release on a subfault, the total seismic energy release may be written

$$E = N\bar{e} \ . \tag{3.7}$$

Since the products Π are functionals of N, Eq (3.5) may be written

$$\Delta S = N \, f(N). \tag{3.8}$$

No matter how many variables are involved in the rupture process, we may assume that they are independent of N. Then the condition of minimum entropy production can be written

$$\partial(\Delta S) = f(N) \, \partial N + N \, \partial f(N) = 0, \tag{3.9}$$

which is a differential equation in N. Let $[N^*]$ be a set of solutions for some set of initial conditions of the system. Then each solution represents a characteristic earthquake—not in the old and doubtful sense of "an earthquake which repeatedly ruptures the same fault segment and whose source dimensions define that fault segment" (Nishenko and Buland, 1987): There is no such thing as an exact repetition anywhere in the universe—but in the physically more meaningful sense of an earthquake having a critical size for a given geological environment.

Thus it appears that the approach followed at Parkfield might have been correct but naive. The strategy of NEPEC never included the possibility that the forecast might fail. As we have seen above, failure had a considerable likelihood attached to it. Savage (1993) has argued that the "fallacy" of NEPEC consisted in neglecting some "less-contrived" explanations of the Parkfield earthquake sequence, such as "that the intervals between earthquakes are randomly drawn from a normal distribution with mean 21.9 years and standard deviation 7.2 years." But this hypothesis is as contrived as NEPEC's. Why should a fault work like a pendulum clock? And why should the mean be equal to the sample mean of a particular set of five intervals?

I believe that the Parkfield caper cannot be shrugged off as some "fallacy" in scientific reasoning, or a miscalculation caused by a lack of awareness of the principles of statistics. There may have been all of this, but it adds up to a serious blunder with major policy implications. If there was a "fallacy" it did not consist in selecting a particularly "contrived" statistical model over less contrived ones. The basic error of NEPEC was failing to consult a professional statistician. An arbitrary subset of six events was treated as if it represented the entire event space. Thousands of earthquakes had occurred near and far; and the available evidence suggested that the interval distribution of earthquakes could not be represented as resulting from a clockwork mechanism. This evidence was reckoned as naught.

The original proposal by Frank Press (1975) had included a plan for instrumenting the entire San Andreas fault at reasonable intervals. This seemed to guarantee that most major earthquakes in California would fall within the prediction network. The USGS might have been able to nail down the precursors and other near-field phenomena for the Loma Prieta, Petrolia, Landers, and Northridge earthquakes. Instead, 28 different observational networks were installed around Parkfield and more are being put in, in the hope of catching the precursors of a moderate earthquake at best. Thus even if the Parkfield earthquake had occurred on schedule, the prediction experiment should have been judged to have failed as those much larger events in California were not predicted. Thus a basic mistake of the Parkfield experiment was confining the prediction to an area so small as to make the occurrence of an earthquake within the period of the forecast unlikely.

Reasenberg and Jones (1989) and Agnew and Jones (1991) have argued that foreshocks might be the most reliable way to predict earthquakes in California. Since there is no way of telling an isolated foreshock from an ordinary smallish earthquake, this seems to imply that we must be content with a success rate of 10–20%. It is unlikely that an earthquake prediction system with such a high rate of false alarms would be socially acceptable. The strategies of *Vela-Uniform* and of the manned mission to the Moon were unqualified successes. This was possible in the Sixties, because the basic scientific problems had already been solved. Those were immensely complex yet basically straightforward technological enterprises. Nuclear test discrimination did not require any new science to be developed. Neither did Apollo. The same approach, however, worked poorly on the uncharted territory of earthquake prediction.

Plate boundaries are partitioned into finite, characteristic zones of rupture, but these zones are not stationary. They shift with each occurrence. The events precess along the boundary. Every rupture modifies the boundary irreversibly. The fault trace shifts every time. Instabilities in a boundary may develop over days or months, but also over years or decades. They evolve in time as a result of the occurrence of other events, large and small, seismic as well as aseismic. Shifting patterns of energy release may eventually pinpoint the area where the next large event is due to occur, but we have not yet learned how to recognize these patterns.

If, according to the famous Chinese simile, *earthquake* is equated with *tiger*, the precursors are not the *tiger's cubs*. They are the footprints of the tiger, the whiskers of the tiger, the stripes of the tiger. They may be the tiger breathing down our neck. But they don't tell us when the tiger is going to jump.

4

Trial by Water

Rabbi Eliezer, to make a point, caused a stream to flow uphill. His opponent,
Rabbi Joshua, said, "What does this water mean to prove by flowing backwards?
It's got no business meddling in our argument."
—Ernst Jünger

WATER IS EVERYWHERE

The KTB Drilling Project is one of the most exciting research projects ever planned. It expects to reach a record depth of 10,000 m under Central Germany by means of what might easily become the most expensive hole ever drilled. The technical difficulties are gigantic. Because of high temperatures there is considerable doubt that the target depth could be reached by 1994 if at all. Once it has been successfully attained, there still remain 99.85% of the earth's radius to get to the center of the earth.

These figures are meant to give an idea of the tiny amount of hard information available about the earth's interior. Recovery of 4,000 m of sample cores from a pilot KTB drill hole was a major achievement and represented an immeasurable contribution to the knowledge of the earth. It proved, among other things, that there are open water-filled cracks in rocks at all depths. A sudden increase in water flow was found at a depth of 3,900 m, where a strong reflecting layer had been reported from surface seismic surveys: Yet no major geologic interface turned up. The cause of the reflection is still unknown.

Most tectonic earthquakes originate well below 3,900 m; it seems unlikely that typical focal depths of earthquakes will soon be reached by drilling. If our civilization should take a sudden turn for the worse, the human race might never again get a chance to explore the earth at depths in which earthquakes occur. The physical properties of materials at those depths would remain a mystery forever.

From what little we know we may, nevertheless, piece together some sort of a coherent story. The ubiquity of water in deep crustal rocks is a major discovery. The German scientists succeeded in recovering large amounts of it directly from the KTB hole. This water was not chemically bound: it actually flowed. At a depth of 3,900 m it was a heavy brine twice as salty as seawater. It had a temperature of 118°C (244.4°F). It contained 80% by volume of gases in solution, mainly nitrogen (70%) and methane (29%). In conclusion, we must expect flows of water to take place in the earth's crust in response to pressure transients caused by earthquakes.

There is an ocean under our feet. Its dynamics are of prime relevance to the possibility of earthquake prediction. We may safely suppose that this ocean has tides, currents, and waves like other oceans, though little is known on the subject. We shall be particularly interested in transient flows caused by pressure differentials.

THE KERN COUNTY GROUNDWATER ANOMALY

The Kern County earthquake of July 21, 1952 ($M = 7.7$) was the largest California earthquake since 1906—not excepting the 1992 Landers earthquake ($M = 7.6$). It was also the largest in California history ever to occur off the San Andreas fault. Unfortunately, little groundwater monitoring existed in the state at that time. No very detailed studies are available on the dramatic flow changes observed in dozens of wells and natural springs over the epicentral region.

There was practically no rainfall in the region for two months after the earthquake; this made it possible to infer the changes in the net discharge of wells and streams due to the earthquake, as climatic effects could be discarded. It was estimated that the Kern County earthquake generated an excess outflow of more than 10^7 m^3 (several billion gallons) of groundwater over a two-month period, within a monitored area of 1,000 km^2. It is important to note that this flow was juvenile: It originated from deep within the earth and not from surface sources. It consisted entirely of increased water production from hard-rock springs in the Sierra Nevada Batholith and not, for instance, from consolidation of saturated sediments by seismic vibrations.

The increase in discharge was *coseismic*; that is to say, it was simultaneous with the earthquake itself. Precursory changes in flow were likely, but none were reported. The coseismic increase was observed right after the earthquake, or at most within a few hours. It was attributed by Sibson (1981) to the hypothetical formation of cracks or fractures in the rock. However, the instantaneous response of the groundwater system to the earthquake strongly suggests that the cause must have been a regional pressure transient in the ocean of groundwater at our feet and not a change in permeability at depth. The latter would not have generated an instantaneous change of discharge simultaneously at many distant surface points in the mountains, nor would it necessarily have increased the flow of surface springs. Casing pressures in oil wells in the valley also peaked immediately after the earthquake and recovered slowly during the aftershock sequence (Johnston, 1955).

The excess surface discharge was everywhere strongly correlated with aftershock activity, both in time and in space. Over half the transient flow originated in the area around the northern end of the fault break, where C.F. Richter had located most of the aftershock activity. The flow decayed in time at the same rate as the number of aftershocks. Incidentally, there were a few isolated instances of coseismic drops in discharge, but in every such case the decrease could be traced to the appearance of new springs surging nearby. Thus the instances of decreased flow were merely instances of diversion of the flow into new channels.

In conclusion, the groundwater anomaly recorded after the 1952 Kern County earthquake must be attributed to a regional pressure transient. This transient was probably generated by the stress drop caused by the earthquake. If precursory stress transients occurred before the earthquake, they should also have been detectable as groundwater fluctuations, but no continuous monitoring of water levels in wells was practiced at the time.

The correlation of the discharge anomaly with the aftershock activity is very interesting. It suggests that aftershocks may also be caused by pressure transients, the same that produce changes in fluid flow. It appears that both aftershocks and changes in groundwater flow are recovery phenomena, in the sense that the seismic stress drop generates a negative pressure gradient, which causes water to flow into the region. The resulting stress recovery triggers the aftershocks. This idea will be developed more fully below.

MONITORING GROUNDWATER IN WELLS AND SPRINGS

Coseismic fluctuations in the water table are widely observed in practically all large earthquakes. Most of the published observations refer to changes of water level in wells; the crucial information about wells that failed to exhibit any change is often omitted. Most reports also fail to provide the needed background information on the amplitudes of seasonal changes of the water table, which determine the sensitivity of the well. Finally, well records tend to be so short that the signal cannot reliably be separated from the background fluctuations. For all these reasons the mistrust of groundwater anomalies reported after large earthquakes may often be justified.

Another reason for this distrust is the lack of good models capable of providing explanations of the observations. Geophysicists mostly assume that changes in water flow are generated by volume changes in the focal region. Actually pressure changes are a more likely mechanism than changes in volume. Seismic processes involve large stress drops preceded by lengthy

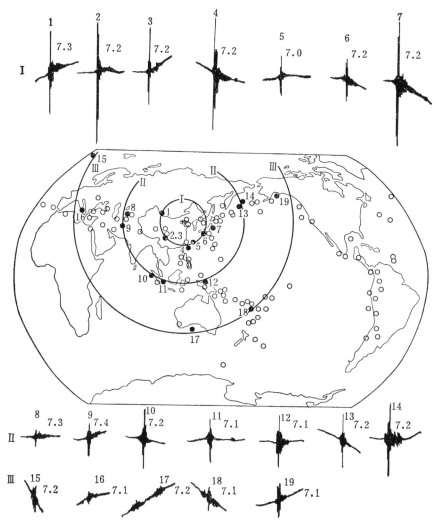

Fig. 4.1 *Teleseisms detected at epicentral distances of up to 100° by water-level recorders in deep wells (China). From Wang Chengmin et al., 1984, p. 507.*

periods of stress accumulation. It would be strange indeed if no regional pressure changes were associated with earthquakes.

Some wells appear to be more "sensitive" than others. Deep wells in China are capable of recording tiny pressure transients due to seismic waves originating from earthquakes halfway around the world (Fig. 4.1). They function as pressure meters. The sensitivity of these wells may be due to their being relatively protected from surface noise caused by rainfall and other seasonal factors. The behavior of each well depends on the aquifers that it taps. Often, however, reliable hydrogeologic information is unavailable.

Wells used exclusively for earthquake prediction research are rare. Most monitored wells are simultaneously used for purposes of water supply or irrigation. Pumping, especially when it is intermittent, disturbs the record. Artesian wells are sometimes preferred for research purposes; in this case, however, there may be no reliable record of pressure at the head of the well.

The water-level record must be corrected for effects of the earth tides and of changes in atmospheric pressure. Earth tides can have a very important effect on wells (Fig. 4.2). This effect is often attributed to volume changes in fractured aquifers produced by tidal strains, but the change in the acceleration of gravity may be sufficient to account for the observed amplitudes. The maximum amplitude equals the difference between the oceanic tide and the solid-earth tide. Wells are sometimes calibrated against the earth-tide signal, on the misleading assumption that the tidal component is entirely due to strain in the rock.

For commercial reasons, medicinal springs in health resorts are frequently monitored in real time for both flow and temperature. Often the chemical composition is also monitored. Such valuable records provide essential long-term information on regional groundwater fluctuations. Hot springs feed on fluids circulating in a network of channels in the hard rock. Reports of dramatic earthquake-related changes in discharge, temperature and turbidity of hot springs can be found in almost any seismic region. Unfortunately, no careful systematic investigation of these reports seems to be available.

The monitored variables, such as water discharge, radon concentration, and temperature, are causally interrelated in ways that are not fully under-

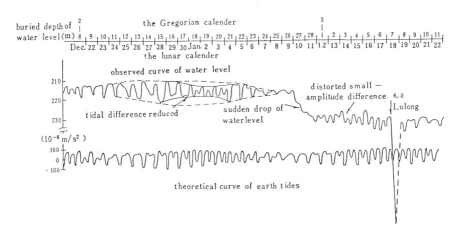

Fig. 4.2 *Effect of earth tides on water level recordings before a* M=6.0 *earthquake in China. Reprinted by permission from* Earthquake Prediction *by Ma Zongjin et al. (1990), Springer-Verlag, New York.*

stood. All records must first be filtered and detrended. Because of the world-wide increase in water consumption, the water table tends to fall in most parts of the world. This effect can easily be confused with a long-term earthquake precursor. Climate change may also be a factor.

Irrigation is a major seasonal disturbance in some regions. It may tend to raise the water table, and it is obviously out of phase with the hydrologic cycle. Thus, correcting for rainfall on well records can be a tricky business.

Reported precursory fluctuations attributed to earthquakes are often of the order of the background noise or smaller; hence the importance of having several years' recording in order to subtract the trend and the seasonal fluctuations with any confidence. Outside China and Japan, few wells have long and accurate monitoring data. Even in these countries, wells drilled for prediction purposes are often only a few hundred meters deep and a few years old.

RADON MONITORING IN WELLS

Radon (^{222}Rn) concentrations in groundwater are often monitored for purposes of earthquake prediction. Radon anomalies were accidentally discovered by monitoring the water supply of the city of Tashkent, Uzbekistan, before the destructive earthquake of April 26, 1966 ($M = 5.5$). The radon concentration in Tashkent increased steadily over a period of several years before the earthquake; then it began to decrease shortly before the earthquake occurred.

Radon is a decay product of radium (^{226}Ra); it is a gas that belongs to the helium-argon-neon series. It is preferred as a geochemical tracer because it is chemically inert and relatively easy to monitor using α-scintillation counters. However, its half-life is only 3.8 days, which means that it would normally be capable of seeping only a few hundred yards away from its point of release before decaying. Yet the detection of radon both in groundwater and in soil is widespread. Equipment for continuous on-stream monitoring includes the widely used Chinese FD-128 automatic radon meter and similar instruments.

In China practically all professional observation wells are equipped with radon measuring equipment. These wells are mostly located in north-central China, that is to say, in the agricultural and industrial heartland north of the Yangtze River. Their number is much larger than anywhere else on earth. At least 105 wells have been drilled to depths of more than 1000 m for purposes of earthquake prediction. Continuous monitoring of water levels to an accuracy of 0.5 cm and of water temperature to the nearest 0.01° are standard features. The radon concentration measurements seem to vary considerably in accuracy from well to well; but anomalies of the order of 10^{-10} Ci/l are often reported. Sources of external pollution, particularly from atmospheric nuclear testing (in China) must be carefully excluded.

So-called amateur wells are much more numerous than the professional wells—around 4,000 in China alone—and their geographical distribution is also broader. Here equipment is either rudimentary or absent. The groundwater research program in China began right after the 1966 Xingtai earthquake; more than 430 reports of precursory fluctuations of water level in wells were reported for this event, mostly by farming collectives after the earthquake.

In Japan altogether 93 wells (some originally intended for water supply or for controlling ground subsidence) are monitored for earthquakes. Most of them are located in south-central Honshu (in the Kanto and Chubu regions, especially). In other countries, including the United States, it is customary to monitor a few mineral springs and, rarely, irrigation wells.

Altogether the scientific effort invested in monitoring and interpreting groundwater fluctuations may be described as insignificant, especially if one considers that ground water fluctuations probably represent the most promising earthquake precursor today.

THE TANGSHAN GROUNDWATER ANOMALIES

The tragedy of the Tangshan earthquake (Hebei Province, July 28, 1976, at 3:42 A.M. local time, $M = 7.8$) was that no one foresaw it. The region was thought to be relatively nonseismic, so earthquake ordinances were not considered necessary in local construction even though all buildings were relatively recent. The number of casualties was depressingly large.

In 1977 I was invited to a special one-week seminar on Tangshan held in Beijing. I was the only outside participant. Many precursors of the Tangshan earthquake were described by dozens of researchers, one after another. I finally asked why the earthquake had not been predicted, but no immediate reply was given. In the evening two young members of the Hebei Seismological Brigade, a man and a woman, visited me in my hotel room and explained carefully that none of the alleged precursors had been detected before the event.

Long-term and medium-term predictions were nevertheless claimed to have been issued; for example: "At the National Consultative Meeting on the Earthquake Situation in early 1976, it was estimated that an earthquake with magnitude 5 or 6 might occur in the Tangshan-Liaoxi region, and intensification of work in this region was recommended" (Ma, 1990, p.7). To my knowledge no recent Chinese earthquake has yet failed to be "predicted" in this way. Statements like the above were scattered far and wide at all successive National Consultative Meetings. Hardly any likely area was omitted. On the other hand, Chinese seismologists have freely admitted that the basic seismological situation in Tangshan was not correctly assessed. For example, some precursors were mistaken for aftershocks of two smaller events—one in Inner Mongolia and the other near Tianjin. The truth is that most seismologists thought that the 1975 Haicheng earthquake had relieved the accumulated stress in North China for centuries to come.

Tangshan, an industrial city of about 1 million population founded in the late 19th century, is a major rail center and the largest coal mining town in the country. It is located about 90 km from Tianjin and 150 km from Beijing, in the heart of China's most sensitive industrial region. As Professor Ma Zongjin (1990) points out, "for issuing an earthquake prediction in the Beijing-Tianjin region, it was unavoidable to take the extremely serious social impact into consideration." A false alarm in this heavily populated region would not have been taken lightly by the central government. The disruption to communications, industry, and mining might have been very costly.

To make matters worse, 1976–1977 was a time of production drives in China. The central economy was faltering. "Learn from Daqing" (a record-breaking oil field) was the slogan at the time of my visit. Local leaders were leery of allowing their production quotas to slip. Unfortunately Tangshan was terribly vulnerable. Housing consisted largely of rows of aging unreinforced brick tenements. Even major concrete structures were not visibly designed against lateral forces. The earthquake occurred in the middle of the night, without foreshocks. It claimed 240,000 lives according to the official count, though much larger estimates (up to 655,000 victims) have been unofficially published abroad. The shaking was extremely violent, especially on soft ground. Casualties occurred as far away as Beijing and Tianjin. It was the worst earthquake disaster anywhere in the world since the great 1556 Guanzhong earthquake in Shaanxi Province, China.

Large disasters have political implications. The official infatuation with earthquake prediction in China was certainly motivated (at least in part) by a desire to counteract the popular belief in earthquakes as harbingers of political upheaval. The origin of this belief is unknown, but it certainly goes back to well before the unification of China in 221 B.C. Chang Heng (78–139), the inventor of the first seismograph, notified the Emperor of the occurrence of a large distant earthquake three days before the news reached the Court, thus enabling the sovereign to claim foreknowledge. It might otherwise have cost him his throne. Understandably, the "struggle against superstition" carried out by earthquake brigades between 1966 and 1976 was largely directed against such a dangerous belief. All their effort was wasted: A month after the Tangshan earthquake Chairman Mao died, thus striking a posthumous blow for ancestral wisdom. After that, superstitions were left alone.

The right-lateral Tangshan fault runs right across town. It was accurately mapped as an Oligocene fault, but it was not recognized as active. The Chinese geologists are hardly to blame for this miscalculation: It is the rule rather than the exception for intraplate earthquakes. Even in seismically active California the seismic potential of the Landers fault was not recognized prior to the 1992 earthquake. In the case of Tangshan some trenching carried out afterwards suggested that an earlier, large seismic event might have occurred 7,500 years ago. No earthquake activity was attributable to this fault in historical times. Thus it must be concluded that the available historical record of observations (about 3,000 years!) had not been long enough to assess the seismicity in Tangshan.

The subsurface geology of the area was rather well known because of the mining activity. Yet most water-level anomalies were found in retrospect, perhaps because wells in the Tangshan area were very noisy due to intense domestic and industrial water use. The data set on Tangshan groundwater anomalies is the largest ever collected anywhere. Three to four years before the earthquake a slow decline of the water table set in, with total amplitudes of up to several meters in some cases. Three or four months before the main shock, several wells in the Tangshan- Ninghe-Fengnan triangle reached their lowest levels ever, and a few dried up altogether. This forced a number of industrial or agricultural concerns to shut down.

Hours before the earthquake, the groundwater level started to pick up again (Fig. 4.3). Ma (1990) points out that some wells "even became artesian from 4 min to 3 h before the main shock." An upward anomaly of 8 cm was recorded as far away as the Biaokou well (Δ = 125 km). At the precise time of the earthquake the rise of the groundwater table accelerated and eventually reached several meters; in many instances the wells flowed over.

Consider now the fluctuations in the pumping record at the Tangshan coal mine (Fig. 4.4). The pumping rate reflects the mean rate of water seeping into an extensive underground network of deep mining shafts or tunnels. Records have been kept since 1923, and the pumping rate has been exceptionally stable. It shows hardly any ripples due to seasonal variations.

Note the sudden increase at the time of the 1976 Tangshan earthquake: the main shaft was less than 10 km away from the epicenter. The pumping rate appears to have increased from 25 m³/min to more than 75 m³/min immediately before the earthquake; this amounts to an increment of 200%. An

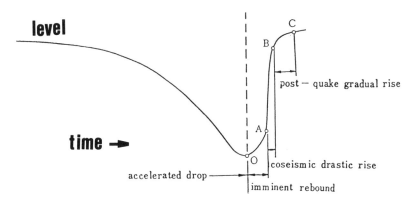

Fig. 4.3 *Pattern of groundwater anomalies according to Chinese researchers. Note the precursory reversal ("imminent rebound"). Reprinted by permission from* Earthquake Prediction *by Ma Zongjin et al. (1990), Springer-Verlag, New York.*

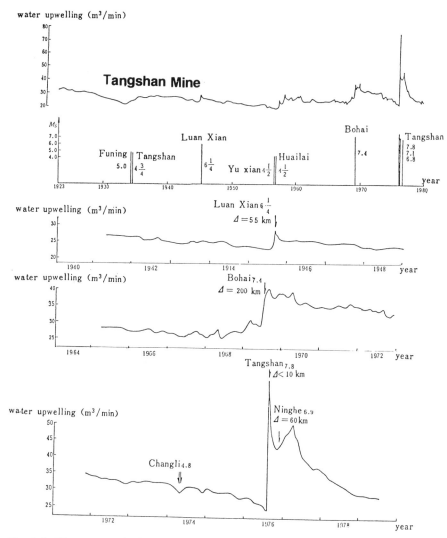

Fig. 4.4 *57-year record of pumping rates from the Tangshan coal mines (top), with a record of major regional earthquakes. Magnified sections of the same record are shown below for the Luan Xian, Bohai and Tangshan earthquakes. Reprinted by permission from* Earthquake Prediction *by Ma Zongjin et al. (1990), Springer-Verlag, New York.*

exponential decay in the pumping rate seems to have followed after the main shock; it was interrupted by a secondary perturbation caused apparently by two large aftershocks at distances of up to 60 km from the mine.

Local seismologists insist that the increase in flow started *before* the main shock. This is consistent with the well records though difficult to confirm because of the small scale of the available graphs. The Tangshan Mine has many miles of underground tunnels at different depth levels, and seepage must have varied widely from place to place. We are looking at an integrated record of the seepage. There was a generalized power failure at the time of the earthquake: A widely publicized rescue of miners trapped in the flooding mine was described as having been carried out without operational pumps or electric light or elevators. City power was out for at least one week after the earthquake. The continuity of the pumping record in Fig. 4.4 may seem puzzling; evidently pumping resumed shortly after the earthquake by means of emergency or mobile power plants.

Minor but clearly noticeable coseismic disturbances can be observed at the time of other regional earthquakes that occurred in this region since 1923. The largest of these anomalies coincides with the 1969 Bohai earthquake, which was 200 km away and had a magnitude of 7.4. The record is somewhat noisy between 1967 and 1970. A cleaner though smaller anomaly occurred at the time of the Luan Xian earthquake of 1945, which had a magnitude of 4.3 but was merely 55 km away.

Should the slow downgoing trend before each of these earthquakes be interpreted as a long-term precursor? Wang Chengmin and other Chinese colleagues think so. A general downward trend can be noticed over the entire record, however. In other words, the regional water table was dropping consistently for 53 years, which is hardly unusual given the increase in water use. On the other hand, each coseismic anomaly seems to have retarded this trend. Coseismic anomalies were all compressional, suggesting a coseismic pressure recovery, just as in the Kern County earthquake. A rising water level is considered normal among Chinese investigators ("Rapid rises of water level after almost all earthquakes are usually considered as coseismic effect"—Wang et al., 1984).

The rapid precursory rise of groundwater level called *imminent rebound* in the Chinese literature began up to three hours before the Tangshan earthquake—for example, at the Biaokou well. Taken by itself this rise at Biaokou was not recognized as significant. On the other hand, some precursory effects were said to have amounted to pressure changes of over 1 bar (or 10 m of water column), which could hardly have been overlooked.

The general pattern of groundwater anomalies reported in Tangshan, and generally in China, is as follows: a steady decreasing trend for months or years before the earthquake, followed by an accelerating decrease, and then a rapid rise of groundwater level a few hours (or at most two or three days) before the quake. This is the imminent rebound and is assumed to have an important diagnostic value (Fig. 4.3).

Finally there is the large coseismic rise. A similar history of variations in the groundwater level was recorded before the 1966 Xingtai, 1969 Bohai, 1975 Haicheng, 1976 Longling, 1976 Tangshan, 1976 Songpan, and other Chinese earthquakes. The anomalous pattern is not recorded everywhere: A carefully monitored deep-water supply well ("Running Water Factory") in downtown Tangshan showed no anomalies at all. Precursory rises occurred in a few wells, but no consistent pattern emerged: It seems that down-

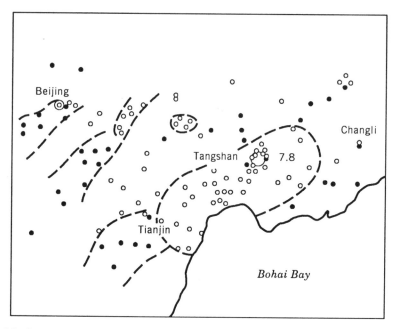

Fig. 4.5   *Geographical distribution of water-level precursors for the 1976 Tangshan earthquakes.* Open circles, *down. Reprinted by permission from* Earthquake Prediction *by Ma Zongjin et al. (1990), Springer-Verlag, New York.*

draw was more statistically significant, as suggested by Fig. 4.5. Some authors feel that the long-term anomalies were more consistently recorded over the available set of well data, while the imminent rebound and the coseismic surge were more spotty and less consistent in character.

In conclusion, large anomalies in groundwater level preceded the Tangshan earthquake. For various reasons these anomalies were not recognized or used for predicting the earthquake, though they were more significant than anything recorded before the 1975 Haicheng earthquake. They could certainly have helped predict this important seismic event, if a theory of groundwater precursors had been available at the time.

THE COALINGA EARTHQUAKE

On July 22, 1983 a large aftershock ($M = 6.4$) of the Coalinga earthquake (May 2, 1983, $M = 6.7$) occurred about 10 km northwest of the town of Coalinga, California. The Husky Oil Company was running a pressure survey in well KCDC 41–8 LS located in the Tulare Lake oil field, Kings County, about 60 km southeast of the epicenter. Some 20 hours before the large aftershock the bottom-hole pressure recorder detected a series of erratic pressure drops that were seen as deviations from the previous smooth pressure buildup. These pressure anomalies continued through the earthquake and stopped about 23 hours after the shock, when the normal increasing pressure trend was reestablished.

At first, because of the distance between the epicenter and the oil well, no particular importance was attached to this observation. However, eventually A.S. Bakr, a senior staff engineer of the oil company, contacted Drs. Paul Segall and Art McGarr of USGS, to whom I owe this information. The well was producing from a Miocene sandstone formation that happens to be the main producing horizon in the Coalinga oil field. Transmission of groundwater anomalies over distances of 60 km are quite common in other parts of the world. In the Coalinga area, the producing formation occurs at a depth of only about 600 m because of the presence of the Coalinga Anticline; in the Tulare Lake field it is 4,000 m deep. But since the formation is continuous, there is a definite likelihood of pressure transients being transmitted from the epicenter toward the Tulare Lake field.

The fault mechanism of the earthquake suggested east-west compression; this is approximately consistent with the tectonics of the anticline. The focal depth was about 10 km. If the observed fluctuations were a precursor, they would suggest a dilatational transient, which is consistent with the fact that the well was located in the dilatational quadrant. Unfortunately no distinct coseismic anomaly was positively identified.

This observation is interesting because downhole pressure is not continuously monitored in oil wells. Pressure surveys are carried out occasionally. No similar observations are available for the main shock or for other oil fields near the epicenter. The erratic fluctuations suggest that slow strain transients were occurring before and after the large aftershock. Aftershocks still represent the single major regularity of the earthquake process. If we could understand the cause of aftershocks, we would be close to an understanding of the earthquake process as a whole.

TILT PRECURSOR OF THE 1985 CHILE EARTHQUAKE

The central Chile earthquake of March 3, 1985 ($M = 7.9$) was an important subduction event with a fault slip of 1–2 m. Leveling carried out after the earthquake disclosed important postseismic geodetic changes including approximately 48 cm of coastal uplift and up to 12 cm of inland subsidence (Fig. 4.6). The same pattern of inverted-S flexure had been observed in other Chilean earthquakes, notably in the great 1960 earthquake where both the offshore uplift and the near-coastal depression attained several meters. Darwin (1860) investigated some effects of coastal uplift from the 1835 Concepción earthquake and suggested that the uplifted terraces along the coast indicated some of the uplift was permanent. Rapel Reservoir is located about 34°S, in the Coastal Range and at the edge of the aftershock region. Water

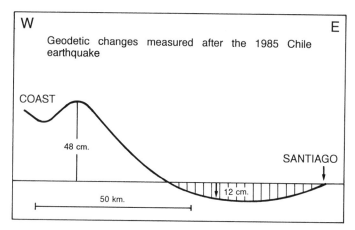

Fig. 4.6 *Geodetic deformations observed along a precise leveling profile from Santiago to the coast after the 1985 earthquake. After S. Barrientos and E. Kausel (1990), Pre- and postseismic time-dependent signals associated with large subduction earthquakes, EOS, 71, 1451. Published by the American Geophysical Union.*

levels in the reservoir were monitored continuously since five years before the 1985 earthquake and are still monitored now. The reservoir was elongated toward the epicentral region. The difference of levels between the near and far sides of the reservoir thus provided an accurate measure of regional ground tilt, as the spacing between the two extreme points was 20 km (Barrientos and Kausel, 1990).

A 10-year graph of daily average level differentials (Fig. 4.7) shows a significant tilt anomaly beginning about eight months before the earthquake and increasing up to nine months beyond the date of the shock. The maximum tilt reached 13 cm over a 20 km baseline, or 6×10^{-6} rad. Since 1986 the tilt has been slowly decaying, but the deformation was not totally recovered. The earthquake occurred as the tilt had reached about 2×10^{-6}, or one-third of the final amplitude. No significant tilt perturbation is visible at the time of the earthquake. The earthquake did not generate a very large wave in the reservoir.

Since the earthquake occurred well after the beginning of the tilt anomaly, it is inferred that the earthquake transient was embedded in a much larger strain process of regional extent. The magnitude of the tilt agrees with the observed leveling anomalies (Fig. 4.6). Thus the tilt anomaly was not a local phenomenon. It extended over much of central Chile. The time history of the Rapel anomaly is instructive. It begins eight months ahead of the main shock and six months before the foreshock sequence.

By taking the elevation differences between two points located at opposite ends of the reservoir, Barrientos and Kausel were able to get rid of noise due to climate, rainfall, runoff, and water consumption for power generation. The observed noise was due to tidal fluctuations, wind waves, or long-period eigenvibrations (seiches) of the reservoir. Similar geodetic observations reported before large earthquakes elsewhere use smaller baselines or contain large leveling errors. Leveling lines are repeated at large intervals, and the continuous shape of the anomaly can rarely be documented as it was in this case.

Rapel Reservoir is located above and beyond the edge of the seismic rupture, as inferred by the spatial extent of the aftershock activity. For this reason no tilt offset corresponding to the earthquake was recorded. We have no tilt data inside the ruptured region, but we may infer that the coseismic or instantaneous deformation was equal to the accumulated deformation since the beginning of the anomaly (Fig. 4.8).

I suggest that the precursors are due to the difference between the actual strain and the strain that would have been measured if the fault had not been locked (shaded area, Fig. 4.8). For example, the landward tilt of the Rapel region should have produced a withdrawal of groundwater from the epicentral region and a corresponding increase of groundwater levels beyond the epicentral region. The coseismic anomaly should have been in the opposite direction (Fig. 4.9). If this interpretation is correct, the imminent rebound recorded in China would suggest that there is some precursory yielding on the fault just before an earthquake. Such yielding has indeed been found in short leveling lines in Japan (Fig. 4.10).

The shape of the geodetic anomaly is very simple. It can be interpreted in terms of a relatively simple slip dislocation on a dipping plane (Barrientos

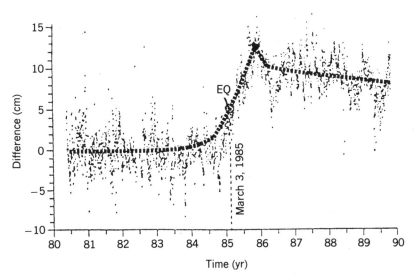

Fig. 4.7 Tilt of Rapel Reservoir, Chile, before and after the 1985 earthquake, computed from the difference in water levels between two gauges 20 km apart. Note that the anomaly begins in mid-1984. After Barrientos and Kausel (1990). EOS, 71, 1451. Published by the American Geophysical Union.

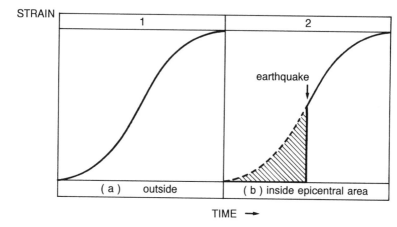

Fig. 4.8 *Inferred coseismic deformation in the 1985 Chile earthquake* (shaded).

and Ward, 1990). Rapel Reservoir was located at an epicentral distance of 100 km and just outside the foreshock area. Thus no coseismic effects were detected. No long-term precursor was detectable either. I suggest that no significant long-term strain precursors should be detectable in magnitude 8 subduction earthquakes. Long-term prediction of large earthquakes must rely entirely on the world pattern of moment release.

In conclusion, an earthquake is a mechanical transient embedded in a slip

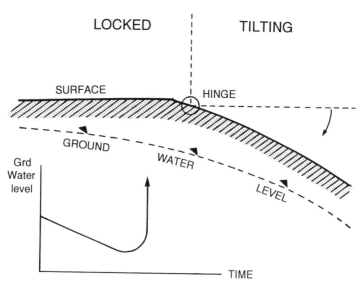

Fig. 4.9 *Inferred precursors of ground water level in the 1985 Chile earthquake. In the epicentral region the level first went down, then up* (below).

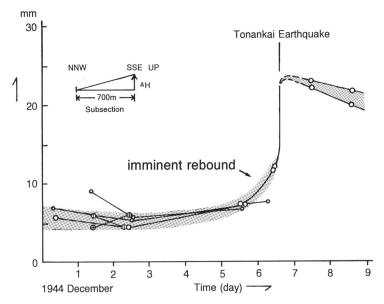

Fig. 4.10 *Geodetic precursor of the 1944 Tonankai, Japan, earthquake showing the imminent-rebound effect. From Mogi (1992), published by Il Cigno-Galileo Galilei, Rome.*

instability that propagates mainly aseismically over a large region (Fig. 4.10). It may or may not generate a violent rupture. The true slip area may be somewhat larger than the area of the rupture. For a subduction earthquake of magnitude 8 the duration of the slip transient is of the order of 12–24 months. The rupture could presumably occur at any time during this window. This means that the lead time of the precursors varies between 0 and 24 months.

THE 1978 IZU-OSHIMA (JAPAN) EARTHQUAKE

The Izu-Oshima earthquake of January 14, 1978 ($M = 7.0$), is well documented. The earthquake was not predicted, though many Japanese seismologists feel that it would be predicted if it occurred today. At the time, the seismologists responsible for earthquake prediction were surprised at the severity of the shock. None had expected such a large earthquake. As in Haicheng, there was a high rate of foreshock activity beginning on the day before the earthquake, but a number of other significant precursors had also been detected.

   The east coast of the Izu Peninsula is a popular resort area dotted with small picturesque beaches and hot springs. By tradition it had been favored by people in the Tokyo Metropolitan Area as a holiday destination. Less than 10 miles offshore lies the active volcanic island of Oshima ("Big Island''), where a major eruption took place nine years after the 1978 earth-quake (Fig. 4.11). Other smaller earthquakes occurred during the 1970–1991 period. The 1974 Izu-hanto-oki earthquake ($M = 6.9$) appears to have desta-bilized the area, which continues to be abnormally active at present. As-sorted precursors included a geodetic uplift over part of Izu Peninsula: It was monitored before the 1978 earthquake. We are thus talking about a complex sequence of seismic and volcanic events, and it is hard to tell which events were precursors of which.

Some water wells in the area showed precursory activity before the 1978 earthquake, while others failed to record either precursory or coseismic anomalies—presumably because of excessive background noise. Fig. 4.12 shows the anomaly recorded at well SKE-1, drilled by the University of Tokyo in 1975 into the floor of a quiet, narrow valley a couple of miles from the village of Nankaizu, at an elevation of 270 m above sea level. The epicen-ter of the earthquake was 25 km away. The well was 350 m deep: it reached below sea level. A pressure pulse could presumably propagate unimpeded between the focus and the well. The anomaly in the radon concentration stands out clearly. Since the well was artesian, no water-table level was recorded; however, a nearby well (I-6) registered precursory as well as co-seismic changes in water level as well as water temperature (Fig. 4.12c). The precursory or ''imminent'' drop in the water level began about a month before the earthquake. The signatures of these two wells (located within 5 km of each other) were strikingly similar.

Equally striking was the fact that another nearby well (RHB-1, also be-longing to the University of Tokyo) recorded nothing. This well was located at an elevation of 440 m and was only 150 m deep. The site overlooks the quiet little valley where SKE-1 was recording. But RHB-1 was very different from SKE-1. Aside from not reaching below sea level, it was not artesian. It was used to supply water to a sanatorium. The record was extremely noisy due to intensive intermittent pumping. It seems questionable whether any anomaly, if present, could have been detected.

Two other wells in the Nankaizu area also reported precursors. Both were artesian hot-water wells (this being an area of abundant hot springs) and had depths of 500 m and 700 m. Both reached below sea level. They showed a drop or erratic changes in water temperature beginning seven to 35 days before the earthquake. Wakita (1981) believes that the change in temperature was related to a decrease in the water flow, but the actual discharge was not monitored. There was a sudden coseismic rise in temperature of up to 12°C (from 38° to 50°C), followed by a very gradual decrease (Fig. 4.12b).

At Funabara, inland from Nankaizu and on the prolongation of the main fault trace, a deep well (600 m) registered a coseismic drop of 7 m in the water level (Fig. 4.12e). A precursory (''imminent'') drop in water level amounting to about 1 m began a month before the earthquake. The well was located about 35 km from the epicenter.

At Omaezaki, on the far side of Suruga Bay and beyond the epicentral

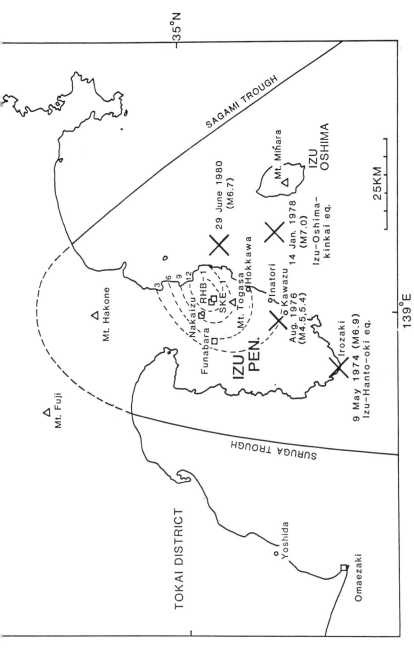

Fig. 4.11 Map of the 1978 Izu-Oshima-kinkai earthquake and related events. Squares, precursory observations in wells; dashed contours, geodetic uplift; large crosses, major seismic events. The boundary of the Philippine Plate is indicated. From H. Wakita (1981), in Earthquake Prediction, D.W. Simpson and P.G. Richards, Eds., Maurice Ewing Series, vol 4. Published by the American Geophysical Union.

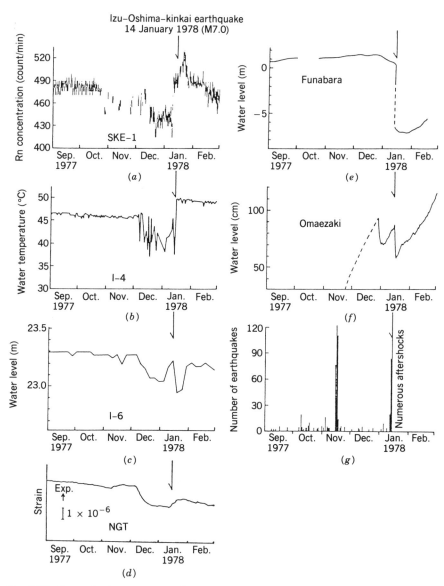

Fig. 4.12 Groundwater precursors in the Izu Peninsula and in Omaezaki (across Suruga Bay) for the 1978 earthquake. A strain record (d) is also shown. The seismic activity (g) shows a swarm in November 1977 and the January 1978 foreshock sequence. From H. Wakita (1981), in Earthquake Prediction, D.W. Simpson and P.G. Richards, Eds., Maurice Ewing Series, vol 4. Published by the American Geophysical Union.

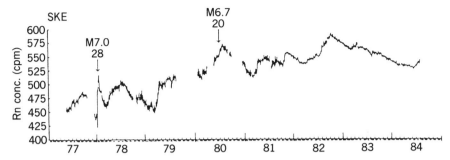

Fig. 4.13 *Eight-year radon record from the artesian well SKE near Nankaizu, Izu Penin-sula. Compare with the precursor in Fig. 4.12. No radon precursor occurred before the 1980 earthquake. From Wakita (1981), in* Earthquake Prediction, D.W. Simpson and P.G. Richards, Eds., Maurice Ewing Series, vol 4. Published by the American Geophysical Union.

region, a coseismic drop of the order of 30 cm in the water level was reported (Fig. 4.12). The well had been recently drilled and had not yet reached stability: Hence this particular observation should arguably be discarded, though I feel that it is significant.

All the experimental wells reporting anomalies (five out of nine) were located in the dilatational quadrant of the main shock; from the compressional quadrant no anomalies were reported. However, a volunteer group did observe anomalous changes in water level and water temperature in about 30 shallow wells scattered all over the coseismic area and beyond, up to an epicentral distance of 150 km.

Fig 4.13 shows the radon record of the SKE-1 artesian well for the period May 1977-August 1984. Except for occasional interruptions due to malfunction, the background is reasonably quiet. The precursory anomaly features an abrupt rise in radon concentration five days before the Izu-Oshima earthquake. The coseismic anomaly is smaller but recognizable (Fig. 4.12a). A "medium-term" anomaly is claimed to have begun in October 1977, three months before the earthquake; but it is only marginally steeper than other ramps found in the record and I suspect that it would not have been identifiable as anomalous.

Radon is an unstable gas with a half-life of only 91.8 hours. It is a product of the breakdown of uranium and thorium in crustal rocks. By the time it has diffused to the surface of the earth, there should be little radon left to detect; yet radon anomalies are detected before some large earthquakes. Since normal diffusion would be too slow, the detection of radon anomalies at the surface seems to require an active flow of groundwater.

Two years later, on June 29, 1980, a shock of magnitude 6.7 occurred nearby (Fig. 4.11). This was interpreted as an independent shock unrelated to the Izu-Oshima earthquake: Its focal mechanism was different (though tectonically consistent with the 1978 event). No precursory or coseismic anomalies are seen in Fig. 4.13, nor are any observed at the other stations mentioned above. The wells of the Nankaizu area (which had been in the dilatational quadrant of the 1978 event) were now close to a nodal line, which may be the reason why nothing was recorded (Fig. 4.11).

At Usami Hot Springs, northwest of the epicenter, a major temperature anomaly was observed. The temperature of the spring rose by nearly 2°C beginning four days before the 1980 earthquake; the anomaly was quite clear. The coseismic change was even more dramatic: The spring dried out. It resumed flowing four or five days later but at a lower temperature. Usami is a seashore resort to the northeast of Nankaizu and well within the dilatational quadrant of the 1980 earthquake.

TECTONIC INTERPRETATION OF THE IZU-ASHIGARA REGION

I visited the area three times (in 1985 and twice in 1992). This is a key area for understanding the tectonics of the Tokai earthquake, predicted by Professor K. Ishibashi in 1977. The Tokai area is behind Suruga Bay, just

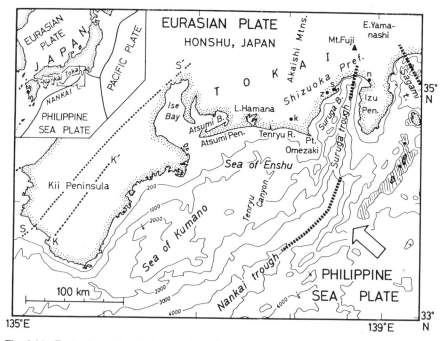

Fig. 4.14   Tectonics of the Philippine-Eurasian Plate boundary. The Nankai Trough bends northward into Suruga Bay. Subduction of the Eurasian Plate by the Philippine Plate is supposed to take place obliquely along the Suruga Trough. From Mogi (1992), published by Il Cigno–Galileo–Galilei, Rome.

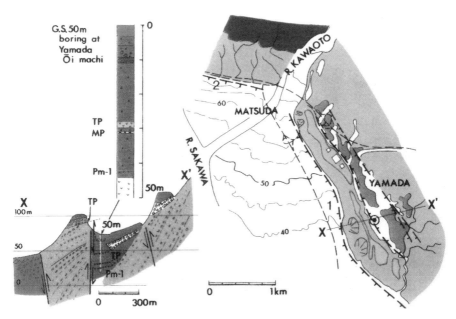

Fig. 4.15 *Tectonics of Ashigara Plain. 1, eastern plate boundary (Kozu-Matsuda fault) indicated as a doubtful inverse or thrust fault. Note the Yamada graben just behind it.*

off the west coast of the Izu Peninsula. Since about 1980 the government of the Tokyo Metropolitan Area has been actively preparing for this earthquake and a large number of instrumental observation points have been installed by various organizations in order to catch the eventual precursors.

The prediction was largely based on the fact that no large earthquake had occurred in the Tokai region for about 120 years. The area features some of the most unusual tectonics to be found anywhere in the world (Fig. 4.14). The Philippine Plate forms a wedge that drives into the Japanese island arc. The Izu Peninsula is on the Philippine Plate, and its base is a collision boundary; right on this boundary sits the active Hakone Volcano (with Mt. Fuji just 20 miles inland). Since the crust of the Izu Peninsula is continental, we have a continent-continent collision. For comparison, think of India which is also in collision with the Eurasian Plate (like the Izu Peninsula): There are no active volcanoes in the Himalayas—and there is no major collision-type mountain range to be found north of the Izu Peninsula. Instead the peninsula is bordered on the east by a flat sedimentary valley, the Ashigara Plain, which has been subsiding since the mid-Pleistocene (Fig. 4.15). Here the plate boundary is the Kozu-Matsuda fault, which runs along the edge of the low Oiso Hills; its main trace has not been identified. It is supposed to be a steep reverse fault, but the evidence is thin. The Oiso Hills contain clear tensional features (small grabens only 300 m from the boundary and parallel to it), as can be seen on the same figure.

A field trip to the collision area north of Hakone Volcano was arranged on September 29, 1992, under the guidance of Professor Tanio Ito, a Japanese structural geologist with considerable field experience in the area whose scientific contribution is gratefully acknowledged. The supposed main thrust boundary north of the Izu Peninsula was examined. This boundary is segmented and offset by a sequence of lateral faults. As an active continent-continent convergence zone it seems less than impressive: It certainly cannot be compared to the Alps or the Himalayas. There is a 40-km-long fault running along the spine of the Izu Peninsula that seems to split the Philippine Plate wedge symmetrically in two halves, but which does not quite reach the thrust zone: the Tanna-Hirayama fault (Fig. 4.16). The peninsula is bulging actively along this spine. The old somma of Hakone Volcano happens to sit precisely astride the fault, which has an undefined character: It changes from reverse to normal and back to reverse without rhyme or reason.

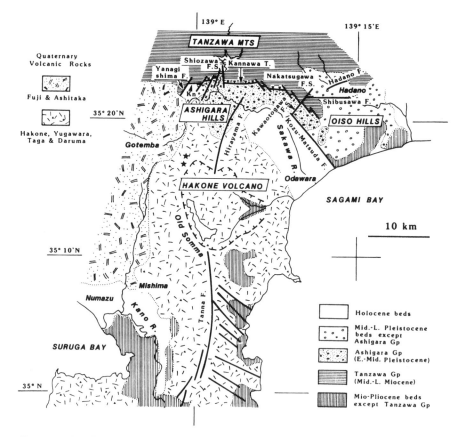

Fig. 4.16 *The Tanna-Hirayama fault runs along the spine of the Izu Peninsula but vanishes as it approaches the plate boundary. From Ito et al. (1989), Tectonic evolution along the northernmost border of the Philippine Sea plate since about 1 Ma, Tectonophysics, 160, 305–326. By permission of Elsevier Science Publishers, Amsterdam.*

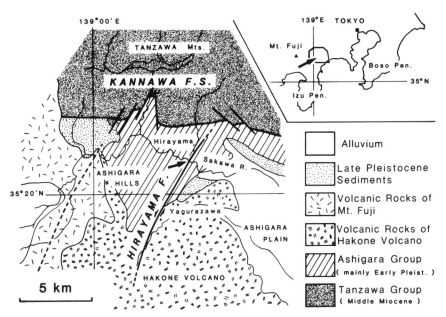

Fig. 4.17 *Detail of the Hirayama fault. Type locality (arrow) is on the right bank of the Sakawa. This river originates in the Eurasian Plate (Tanzawa Mountains, a granitic intrusion); then it traverses the presumed collision boundary (crossing what should be the continental divide) into the Philippine Plate. It drains the Ashigara Plain and eventually flows into Sagami Bay. From Ito et al. (1989), Tectonic evolution along the northernmost border of the Philippine Sea plate since about 1 Ma, Tectonophysics, 160, 305–326. By permission of Elsevier Science Publishers, Amsterdam.*

We examined the type locality of the Hirayama fault at the bottom of a hanging cliff on the south bank of the pretty Sake River, or Sakawa (Fig. 4.17). This must have been an idyllic spot in old Japan a few years ago. The name of the river comes from the reputedly intoxicating quality of the water. The site may be reached by means of a knotted rope. Here the fault plane is beautifully exposed; it is a steep-angle thrust with about equal amounts of inverse and left-lateral motion. Miocene mudstones are underthrust along the bedding planes by Ashigara gravels (Fig. 4.18). The velocity of fault motion must have been highly variable along the section. The fault gouge is about 1 m thick. The Gotemba mudflow (unit Yvs-II), a regional marker that can be dated to a Fuji eruption of around 400 B.C., was not cut by the Hirayama fault (Ito et al., 1989).

Thus the fault is not active. How long has it been inactive? A 21,000-year-old layer of Ashigara gravel is clearly displaced by the Hirayama fault. The lack of recent activity also applies to other faults in the area—and it agrees with the generally low seismicity found at present.

The granitic core of the Tanzawa Mountains, just north of the collision

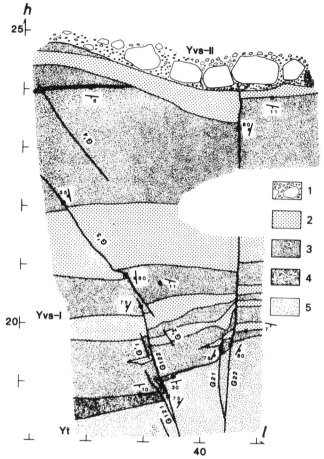

Fig. 4.18 *Stratigraphy of the Hirayama fault exposed at the right bank of the Sakawa. Note that the fault does not displace the Gotemba mud flow (Unit Yvs-II). From Ito et al. (1989), Tectonic evolution along the northernmost border of the Philippine Sea plate since about 1 Ma, Tectonophysics, 160, 305–326. By permission of Elsevier Science Publishers, Amsterdam.*

zone, was intruded 4 to 5 million years ago. It may correspond to the final stage of buoyant subduction. At present, seismic activity is minor but volcanic activity is high. I asked about the offshore continuation of the plate boundary into the Sagami and Suruga troughs and was told that shallow seismic activity occurs mostly along the midplate lineament, which comprises the east coast of Izu Peninsula, Oshima Volcano, and the Izu-Bonin Ridge leading into the back-arc spreading zone behind the Marianas Arc (Fig. 4.19). This ridge may be in an early stage of becoming a spreading center (Klaus et al., 1992). A recent joint Japanese-French expedition has

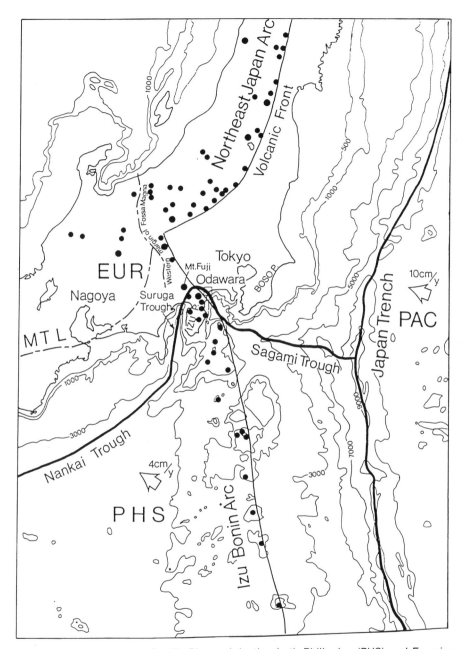

Fig. 4.19 Position of the Pacific Plate subducting both Philippine (PHS) and Eurasian (EUR) plates at a rate of 10 cm/year. Note the trend of the volcanic front and the young spreading ridge of Izu-Bonin (black dots, major volcanoes). From Mogi (1992), published by Il Cigno–Galileo Galilei, Rome.

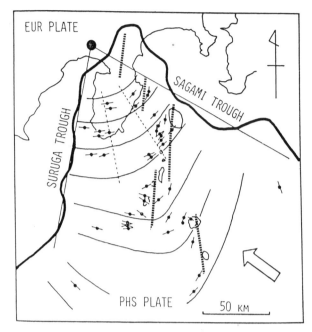

Fig. 4.20 *Focal mechanisms suggesting a possible spreading of the Izu-Bonin Ridge. Trends of the spreading centers are suggested.* Heavy line, Eurasian Plate boundary. The epicenters are shown as dots, with the trend of strike-slip faulting as indicated. From Mogi (1992), published by Il Cigno–Galileo Galilei, Rome.

discovered a new ocean trench that is being formed south of Izu Peninsula. Thus the present "collision" plate boundary is in the process of being shunted out.

All this is exciting and intriguing. The region is in rapid evolution. Japanese geologists believe that there may have been several successive episodes of collision between the Philippine and the Eurasian plates in the past. Separated by what? Geologists still claim that the volcanic activity can be attributed solely to subduction of the Pacific Plate (Fig. 4.19). I believe that this concept must be revised, since there is continuity between the Japanese Volcanic Front and the back-arc spreading center behind the Marianas, where a microplate (the Mariana Plate) has been suggested. Where does subduction volcanism grade into a spreading oceanic ridge? At Mt. Oshima? At Mt. Fuji? There certainly must be a transition somewhere.

All this seems to be suggestive of the importance of tensional tectonics in the region. The focal mechanisms of earthquakes are consistent with the idea that the Izu-Bonin Ridge is spreading (Fig. 4.20). If the Philippine-Eurasian collision has now come to a virtual standstill, present features of volcanic and seismic activity can be explained by active east-west spreading along the Oshima-Bonin axis. In conclusion, I suggest that the complexity of present tectonics in the Izu region cannot be due to frontal collision only. The Philippine Plate may be splitting along its center line, and the two halves may be drifting apart along the Izu-Bonin Ridge. The Izu Peninsula itself may be tearing or breaking apart lengthwise.

How does this affect the prediction of a major earthquake in the Tokai region? A major question is whether the 1944 and 1946 earthquakes on the Nankai Trough increased the pressure on its northern extension or whether, on the contrary, the pressure on the Suruga Trough was relieved. The latter interpretation seems to be consistent with modern research on the tectonic evolution of southwest Japan (see, e.g., Sugiyama, 1990, 1992). After all, informations on large earthquakes in the Tokai area rely on historical data, and the present evidence for activity of the Tokai segment is marginal.

SEISMIC EVIDENCE FOR TENSIONAL TECTONICS

Roeloffs (1988) proposed that upward and downward coseismic water-level anomalies "are consistent with regions of contraction and extension, respectively." This may be a key to understanding the tectonics of regions such as the Izu Peninsula. The downward direction of water-level anomalies observed in the Izu-Oshima earthquake of 1978 contrasts with the upward direction of anomalies observed in China. But China is in compression between the hammer of the Indian Plate and the anvil of the Eurasian Plate. On the other hand, the North Palm Springs, California, earthquake (July 8, 1986, $M = 5.9$) featured a clear coseismic *drop* in water level (Fig. 4.21). This is

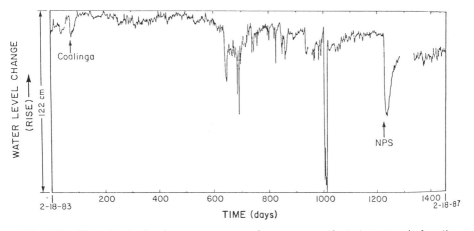

Fig. 4.21 *Alleged water level precursors occurring seven months to two years before the 1986 North Palm Springs, California earthquake (NPS). Note the coseismic drop, suggesting tensional tectonics. From Ben-Zion et al. (1990). Permission granted by the Seismological Society of America.*

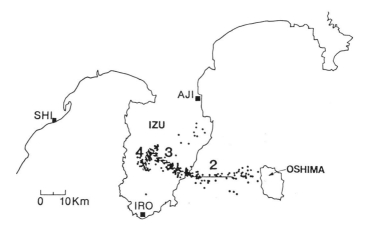

Fig. 4.22 *Sequence of rupture in the 1978 Izu-Oshima earthquake. Foreshocks near Oshima Island, then (2) main shock, (3) slow earthquake followed by aftershocks inland, and (4) slow earthquake on a cross-fault, also followed by aftershocks. The three volumetric strain stations are indicated by square symbols. From I.S. Sacks et al. (1981). A slow earthquake sequence following the Izu-Oshima earthquake of 1978, in* Earthquake Prediction, *D. Simpson and P. Richards, Eds., Maurice Ewing Series vol. 4, pp. 617–628. Published by the American Geophysical Union.*

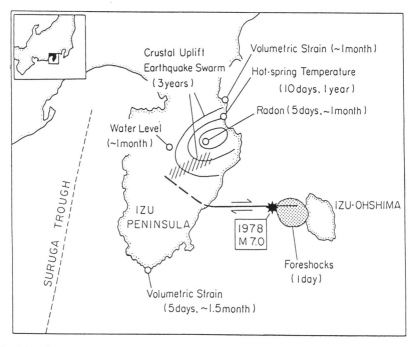

Fig. 4.23 *Summary map of Izu-Oshima precursors (precursor times in parentheses). From Mogi (1992), published by Il Cigno–Galileo Galilei, Rome*

in contrast with the rise in water level observed during the 1952 Kern County earthquake. The Palm Springs area may be an area of predominantly extensional tectonics.

The Izu-Oshima earthquake ($M = 7.0$) occurred on January 14, 1978, at 12:24 P.M. local time (Fig. 4.22). It was a right-lateral event on a submarine fault that extended from Oshima Volcano to the east coast of the Izu Peninsula. It had been preceded by numerous foreshocks that began the day before (Fig. 4.23). A group of seismologists from the Carnegie Institution of Washington, in cooperation with the Japan Meteorological Agency, had set up three Sacks-Everton strainmeter stations, one on the east coast south of Odawara (AJI), another at the tip of the Izu Peninsula (IRO), and the third (SHI) on the far side of Suruga Bay (Sacks et al., 1981). All three stations were within 80 km of the epicenter (Fig. 4.22).

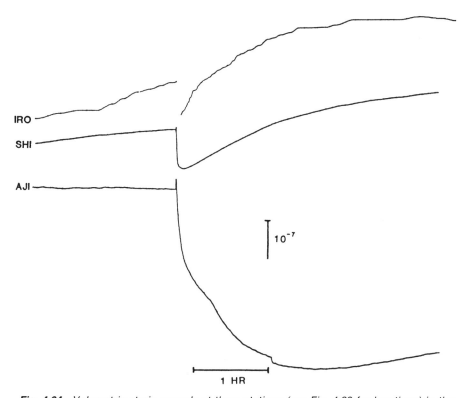

Fig. 4.24 *Volumetric strain records at three stations (see Fig. 4.23 for locations) in the 1978 Izu-Oshima earthquake. Dilatation is up. Note the dilatational pulse caused by passage of the seismic signal at AJI, followed by a compressional offset. Recovery is dilatational at all three stations. From I.S. Sacks et al. (1981), A slow earthquake sequence following the Izu-Oshima earthquake of 1978, in* Earthquake Prediction, *D. Simpson and P. Richards, Eds., Maurice Ewing Series vol. 4, pp. 617–628. Published by the American Geophysical Union.*

The Irozaki (IRO) station at the southern tip of the Izu Peninsula was in the compressional quadrant of the main shock, and the Ajiro (AJI) station was near a nodal plane; both showed coseismic dilatation (up) followed by rapid recovery and a large compressional overshoot. The initial dilatation was caused by the passage of the radiated seismic pulse, since both AJI and SHI were located in the dilatational quadrant of the main shock (Fig. 4.24).

The compressional overshoot was interpreted by Sacks et al. (1981) as a sequence of strain events ("slow earthquakes"). These slowquakes occurred along the prolongation of the fault break and also at right angles to it (Fig. 4.22). The coseismic change at AJI was 2.4×10^{-7} and the additional strain attributed to the slow earthquakes was about on the same order. The slowquakes had the same focal mechanism as the main shock, but due to their location their effect on the strain meters at IRO and AJI was in opposite directions.

The respective seismic moments were as follows: 11×10^{25} dyne-cm for the main shock and 4.45×10^{25} dyne-cm (or 40% of the main shock moment) for all slow earthquakes combined. A highly active aftershock sequence began immediately after the slowquakes.

As the Izu-Oshima earthquake occurred in a tensional environment, the coseismic strain release may have been compressional. Indeed the main strain step was seen as a compression at all stations. Regardless of quadrantal

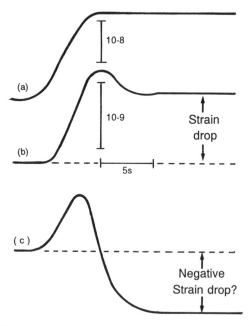

Fig. 4.25 Strain steps as a result of an earthquake: (a) pure compression, (b) compression with the passage of a seismic wave front, (c) tension.

distribution, there was a large compressional transient immediately after the passage of the seismic wavefront (Fig. 4.25).

If the coseismic strain drop was compressional, the flow of water after the earthquake must have been outbound, not inbound as in regions of convergent tectonics. As a matter of fact, the water level went *down* nearly everywhere during the main shock. It recovered to a large extent within about 10 days. The water temperature went up, which is consistent. The radon concentration increased before the earthquake, in agreement with a precursory flow increase toward the epicentral region. The slow strain effects do show a clear quadrantal distribution, suggesting that the slowquakes represented a delayed seismic deformation.

In conclusion, there appears to be a difference in polarity of precursors depending on whether the tectonics is tensional or compressional. The unusual precursors recorded in the 1978 Izu-Oshima earthquake suggest that the region is under tension, in agreement with the idea that the collision between the Philippine and Eurasian plates has been replaced by spreading along the Izu-Bonin axis. There is abundant evidence that the tectonic pattern in this region is rapidly changing.

As Ito et al. (1987, 1989) have pointed out, fault motion obtained from geologic evidence should not be extrapolated for purposes of earthquake prediction in rapidly changing island arc environments. The Hirayama fault has featured frequent changes or pulses of activity and is now largely inactive. It is important to consider the general activity of a fault over the last 2 or 3 million years, but recent trends, which may modify very markedly the assessment of seismic hazard in a region, should not be neglected.

5

Scars and Healing: the Power of Seismic Gaps

INTRODUCTION

There are two main reasons why earthquake prediction is such a difficult proposition: (a) Plate tectonics is incomplete, and (b) there is no practical way of imaging tectonic processes.

Recall from Chapter 3 the discussion that took place in NEPEC after Volodya Keilis-Borok had presented his prediction of a large California earthquake. Professor H. Kanamori of Caltech chimed in with a subtle remark no one picked up at the time. He pointed out that, while Keilis-Borok claimed to use pattern recognition in order to predict earthquakes, he "actually used a standard seismicity approach." Thus he suggested that "someone in the United States" ought to have a look at the same approach, provided that "there must be a complete catalog of seismicity for southern California, and the global seismic catalog must be cleaned up" (Updike, 1989).

At the time, no one may have understood what Kanamori meant by a "standard seismicity approach". The model he had in mind was a model no one was explicitly using. No general theory of seismicity existed. In a sense it was necessary to build one from scratch. Keilis-Borok had begun his 1988 presentation before NEPEC by stating that, "because an adequate theoretical model for the earthquake process does not exist," he would propose to fit the data to a set of discrete models, or *algorithms*, and then extrapolate these algorithms to obtain predictions. The idea turns out to have doubtful merit because there is no objective way of choosing the best model among a million possible algorithms that may fit the data equally well.

Plate tectonics does provide an excellent kinematic model for the earthquake process. But it is not matched by a model of the dynamics. Early proponents of plate tectonics, such as Xavier Le Pichon, tried to make this into a virtue. However, a mechanical theory that consists of a kinematics without a dynamics stands on one leg. It is incomplete.

A THUMBNAIL INTRODUCTION TO PLATE TECTONICS

The earth is roughly 4.6 billion years old. Plate tectonics began 2.5 billion years ago, just as the earth was recovering from an attack of severe bombardment by asteroids. The period prior to plate tectonics, known as the Precambrian, contains early imprints of small, soft life forms, though actual animal skeletons have only been found after the Precambrian. Higher life forms are conditioned by plate tectonics.

In the human sense, plate tectonics gave its name to a revolution in our thinking about the earth. It began in 1967 (McKenzie and Parker, 1967; Morgan, 1968; Isacks, Oliver and Sykes, 1967). The period prior to the introduction of plate tectonics was a time when earth scientists would attribute most tectonic deformations either to gravity or to shrinking of the earth as a whole. The interior of the earth was pictured as relatively quiescent.

Plate tectonics is pictured as a global process of large plates moving against or past or away from each other over the earth's surface (Fig. 5.1). Frictional motion of one plate against the other occurs either as continuous sliding or in discrete jumps. Jumps, or *earthquakes,* may also occur in the interior of a plate; but these intra-plate earthquakes are insignificant in terms of their energy contribution as compared to plate-boundary activity. By far, most actual motion occurs along the plate boundaries, though intraplate earthquakes may represent a serious hazard to humans.

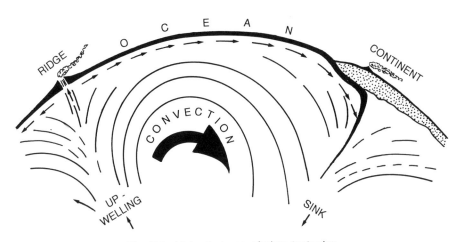

Fig. 5.1 *Major features of plate tectonics.*

Convection is the driving mechanism of plate tectonics. The early continents (remains of which may be found in Africa, Australia, Antarctica, Brazil, Canada, India, Scandinavia, and Siberia) were lighter than the underlying mantle of the earth. They may have been segregated from the mantle by buoyancy. No oceans existed at the time. Convection continually brought fresh, deep-seated materials to the surface. The viscosity in the upwelling regions is quite large (about 10^{18} Pa-s), but still about 1,000 times smaller than under the continents. It is small enough to allow small convection rolls or eddies to form near the oceanic ridges, in the boundary layer.

Plate tectonics makes things both easier and more complicated for earthquake prediction. It explains the origin of surface features, but it does so by appealing to deep-seated processes that we know very little about. There are few data on the earth's interior, and what we know fits poorly together.

Oceanic plates are generated continuously by upwelling of heavy mantle material, which leaks through long tension cracks, the mid-ocean ridges (Fig. 5.1). The oceanic crust is strained at a rate of about 3×10^{-16} rad/s; it inches toward the coasts of the continents at a final rate of the order of 5 cm (2 inches) per year. At the continental margins it is swallowed up and recycled (Fig. 5.2): This process is called *subduction*. The total seismic energy generated by plate motion is around 10^{18} Joules/year. Some oceanic materials stick to the underside of the continental plate and build it up by accretion: this

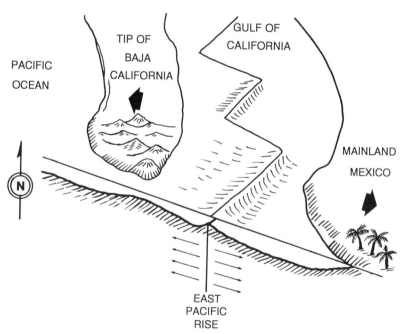

Fig. 5.2 *Mechanics of displacements at plate boundaries: the opening of the Gulf of California.*

is called *underplating*. As the oceanic crust descends further beneath the continent, some of its upper layer begins to melt and to rise percolating into the crust; eventually this alien material may ooze out as lava or be expelled as volcanic fumes or ash. Molten material also rises spottily under the plates: these so-called mantle plumes or *hot spots* (e.g., Hawaii) remain stationary while the plates move over them.

In short, plate tectonics is the main agent of geologic transformation of the earth. At subduction boundaries it creates mountains, fault systems, volcanoes, and earthquakes. Volcanoes emit steam, which condenses and forms oceans. Life originated in the shallow coastal waters of subduction zones. Vegetation generated the free oxygen found in the atmosphere. Carbon dioxide from the volcanoes ends up as limestone via the tiny skeletons of animals that live in shallow seas. Everything is in a turmoil of creation. Only the *cratons*, or cores of the old continents, have remained relatively quiet and stable. Earthquakes are, so to speak, the background music of plate tectonics. The faster the plates move against or past each other, the higher is the seismic activity. Around 90% of all earthquakes occur at plate boundaries, most of them in subduction zones.

The average rate of plate motion has slowed down substantially since the end of the Cretaceous, some 70 million years ago. But it also fluctuates periodically with the extinctions and the earth's encounters with external bodies, every 26 or 27 million years (Rampino and Caldeira, 1993). The motion of plates can be irregular or jerky even over shorter time spans. A segment of plate boundary may get stuck for decades or centuries; suddenly the plate will jump forward by several meters in a major earthquake. Small earthquakes, of course, occur all the time. Every 15 min, somewhere on earth, an earthquake strong enough to be felt occurs: a boon to earthquake forecasters. Anytime is a good day for predicting an earthquake.

CHARACTERISTIC EARTHQUAKES

The dynamics of plate tectonics is being explored from various angles. An early deterministic model was suggested by Reid (1910), who assumed that the fault was a plane and that the adjacent blocks moved in opposite directions at a constant rate. This model is still widely used (e.g., Shimazaki and Nakata, 1980). Later, as it developed that faults are merely components of larger structures called plate boundaries, the question arose as to what were the basic modules or building blocks of such boundaries. If the plate moves as a whole, the process can hardly be deterministic or independent of location, and the question of how the motion is partitioned over discrete segments of the boundary also arises.

In our hydrologic analogy, which we shall be using throughout the book, the strain accumulation corresponds to rainfall, the faults to watersheds, and the plates to the oceans. The building blocks of the hydrologic system are the primary watersheds, such as the Mississippi or the Amazon, to name but the world's largest, that drain directly into an ocean. Thus large floods are characteristic. On the other hand, neighboring watersheds are coupled through rainfall, so that flood conditions can "propagate" to several adjacent watersheds.

The statistical dynamics of faults were explored by Lomnitz-Adler (1985, 1989), who followed the general approach of Knopoff (1971). The dynamical equation was obtained by Knopoff, and the time-dependent properties were derived by Lomnitz-Adler. The basic assumption is that each fault is *characteristic* or well defined in spatial extent. For example, the component faults of the San Andreas system are segments of about 30 km length that are often separated by small lateral offsets. Each fault may be described by a probability density $f(\sigma,t)$, which describes the likelihood that the fault will be in a state σ at a time t. The state σ is usually defined in terms of a loading stress.

Each fault is made up of an array of elementary subfaults of small dimensions, which can fail either singly or all together. In the latter case a characteristic earthquake is generated. The propagation of a rupture over the fault surface is studied by means of a percolation model, assuming that the dimension of the system equals 2 (the fault is a plane). It is found that the fault has a critical state: No matter where the rupture starts the earthquake always breaks the entire fault. On the other hand, below the critical state the ruptures are partial, so that smaller earthquakes occur (Fig. 5.3). When the calculations are carried out for actual examples, it is found that there is a modal repeat time for characteristic earthquakes, which is time-dependent (Fig. 5.3). After each critical event there is a dead time, during which the probability of occurrence of another characteristic earthquake is essentially zero. In the case of the coast of Oaxaca, Mexico, it is found that the most probable repeat time is 37 years and the dead time is 17 years, in good agreement with available earthquake statistics for this region (Lomnitz-Adler, 1989).

In conclusion, the more closely earthquakes conform to the characteristic hypothesis (i.e., the more each segment works as a well-defined independent unit), the more they are predictable by statistics. Note that the peaks in Fig. 5.3 are quite sharp. For medium-sized events (Fig. 5.3, middle), the most probable interval is about two years shorter than that of characteristic events; thus the occurrence of medium-sized events could be used as an earthquake precursor. Finally, if there is coupling between two adjacent characteristic segments, some ruptures will propagate over two or more segments, thus generating extremely large earthquakes. In this case, however, the "noise" in the component systems will dominate the dynamics, so these supercharacteristic earthquakes will tend to have a stationary or time-independent distribution of intervals (Lomnitz-Adler, oral communication).

SEISMICITY GAPS

Since about 1980 it is widely believed that most large earthquakes around the Pacific Ocean have occurred in certain segments of plate boundary that

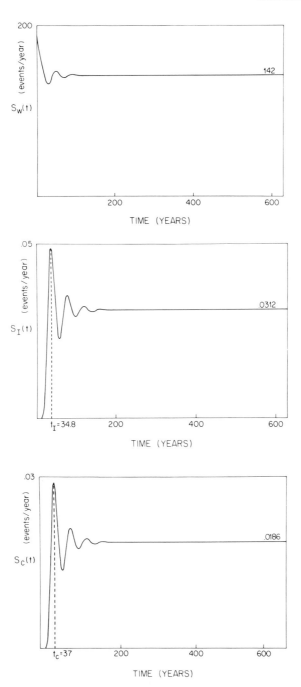

Fig. 5.3 *Theoretical seismicity as a function of time after the previous earthquake.* Top, *low-magnitude shocks;* middle, *medium-magnitude events;* bottom, *characteristic events. From J. Lomnitz-Adler (1989). Statistical dynamics calculations of time-dependent seismicity,* Tectonophysics, 169, *207–213. Permission granted by Elsevier Science Publishers, Amsterdam.*

had been previously designated as seismicity gaps. Gaps are thought to be the most effective long- to medium-term precursors of earthquakes. An explicit seismicity gap hypothesis was first enunciated by Lynn Sykes (1968) on the basis of earlier ideas by Imamura, Fedotov, and Mogi. Sergei Fedotov (1965) had observed that the segments of a seismic belt where no events had occurred in a long time tended to be the first to rupture. He mapped 13 gaps in the Kurile-Kamchatka active belt where earthquakes of magnitude greater than $7\frac{3}{4}$ were likely to happen. The following subsequent large events verified this prediction: the 1968, 1969, 1971, 1973, and 1978 earthquakes fell in the previously designated gaps.

Sykes proposed to predict the probable location of future large earthquakes on the basis of a deficiency of strain release in some segment of a plate boundary. The gap hypothesis was redefined as follows: "If a section of a long seismic belt has not ruptured recently . . . and adjacent sections have had large earthquakes, the probability of a large earthquake in the 'gap' is proportionally increased" (Brune, 1991).

But how recent is "recently"? How large is "large"? How to define a "section"? "Proportionally increased" in terms of what? Consider a plate boundary of length $\mathscr{L}$ (Fig. 5.4), and suppose that characteristic ruptures of mean length ℓ occur at random on the boundary once a year on the average. Then two ruptures will overlap on the average every $\mathscr{L}/\ell$ years. The quantity $\mathscr{L}/\ell$ is called the *mean repeat time.*

Now suppose that the process is not independent but that there is a tendency for *gaps* to be formed, that is, the probability of a future rupture increases with the preceding interval T. How can we tell this from the case of perfectly random ruptures?

Seismologists were initially divided on this question. Some felt that the oftener earthquakes occurred in a region the higher was the hazard, while others argued that, on the contrary, the hazard was highest whenever the seismic activity was *lowest* in a known active region. The middle ground was occupied by skeptics who thought that it didn't make much difference since earthquakes occurred pretty much at random.

In more relaxed days—before plate tectonics, when research scientists

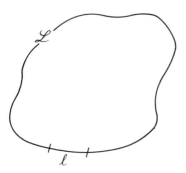

Fig. 5.4   *Random gaps ℓ along a plate boundary $\mathscr{L}$.*

were a mere handful who knew each other personally worldwide—seismologists used to gather over coffee or a hand of bridge (Richter loved bridge) in order to invent private jokes about earthquake prediction. Perry Byerly took the prize with "The longer it's been since the last one, the sooner it'll be till the next one." This was solemnly christened Byerly's Law. It had soothing properties, because it produced instant agreement among members of the warring factions—no doubt because it was a truism.

THE PATROL OFFICERS' DILEMMA

Consider the following thought experiment. Cars are traveling on a one-lane highway. Three patrol officers are asked to predict the times of passage of vehicles past a checkpoint. The first officer clocks each car as it passes; he finds that, as time elapses from the passage time of any car, less time remains for the passage of the next car. This is Byerly's Law.

The other officers scoff: "Your discovery is merely an effect of the forward direction of time." The second officer decides to measure the number of vehicles per unit time instead. He notices that whenever traffic is heaviest,

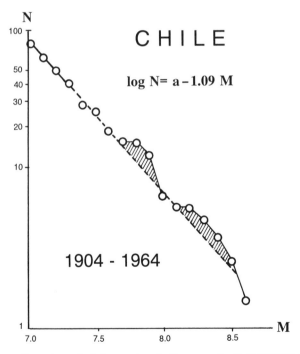

Fig. 5.5 *"Bumps" or characteristic maxima in the magnitude-frequency distribution of earthquakes along the Chile plate boundary. One maximum is at* M = *7.75 and the other about* M = *8.3. From C. Lomnitz (1985), Tectonic feedback and the earthquake cycle, Pageoph, 123, 667–682. Reprinted with permission of Birkhäuser Verlag, Basel.*

the probability of the passage of a car also increases. Conversely, the lighter the traffic the longer is the gap between cars. This is another interpretation of Byerly's Law. A knowledge of the distribution of intervals, while essential, is not necessarily promising in terms of predicting the actual passage times of cars.

The third officer notices an interesting anomaly. Sometimes the traffic is heavy yet temporarily cars stop passing altogether. Usually when this happens, a large truck is slowing down traffic just ahead of the checkpoint. This officer has hit upon a way of predicting the passage of large trucks with some confidence: They are preceded by a substantial gap in the traffic.

This thought experiment suggests that the usefulness of gap observations hinges on the dependence between events, and especially on the presence of two different types of events with different statistical properties. Each type of event has a different mode, which appears as a distinct peak in the frequency distribution of earthquake magnitudes (Fig. 5.5). The mode in the high-magnitude range (corresponding to the trucks in the example) is caused by characteristic earthquakes.

HOW TO PROVE (OR DISPROVE) A HYPOTHESIS BY STATISTICS

Around 1971 the plate boundaries around the Pacific Ocean were divided in segments of different seismic potential on the basis of the gap hypothesis. Gaps were tentatively defined as areas where no major earthquake had occurred in 30 years or more. This seemed to work: Subsequent earthquakes always appeared to occur in segments previously designated as gaps. But Kagan and Jackson (1991) disagreed. They found that "Places of recent earthquake activity have larger than usual seismic hazard, whereas the segments of the circum-Pacific belt which did not experience large earthquakes in recent decades have remained relatively quiet."

This finding was interpreted as contradicting the hypothesis of seismic gaps. Actually it may have meant something entirely different. Large earthquakes do occur in gaps; but this may be due to the fact that gaps are so common. An earthquake could hardly miss one. In other words, too many areas have been designated as gaps. On the other hand, few earthquakes occur in the *oldest* gaps, though they have been designated as "sites of highest seismic potential" (Fig. 5.6). The reason is that few areas have been so designated.

Clustering—a common feature of point processes—means that small intervals are more frequent (i.e., more likely) than large ones. The result of Kagan and Jackson could be interpreted as a trivial consequence of clustering.

Consider now Fig. 5.6, showing a well-known published map of seismicity gaps. Well over half the length of the plate boundary is rated as having higher than average potential for generating large earthquakes. Even if earthquakes

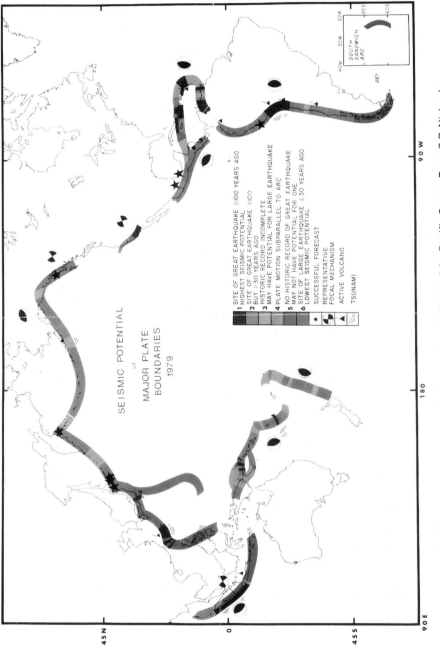

Fig. 5.6 Map of seismic potential for gaps located around the Pacific Ocean. From S.P. Nishenko and W.R. McCann (1981), Seismic potential for the world's major plate boundaries, in Earthquake Prediction, D. Simpson and P. Richards, Eds., Maurice Ewing Series, vol. 4, pp. 617–628. Pub-

occurred at random, most large earthquakes would have to occur in gaps. This is not a fair test of the gap hypothesis. Suppose that the plate boundary were made up entirely of gaps; then the hitting average of the gap hypothesis would be 100%.

This discussion suggests the need for quantifying the gap concept. The situation is similar, in some ways, to that of medicine before X-rays. Physicians knew the general position of the bones and organs, but they could not adequately treat fractures or internal disorders because there was no way of *imaging* the situation except by getting inside the patient. Advances in medical imaging have made possible the recent advances in diagnostic medicine. Something similar happened in weather prediction as a result of the introduction of satellite imaging.

It is tricky to try showing that some effect is not there. Kagan and Jackson may have merely shown that highly seismic regions are more seismic than regions of low seismicity—which we knew before. Much of our research is like that: tautological. We may demonstrate that everything is random and conclude that no purposeful action exists in the universe. But in this case, who created statistics? There is no substitute for hard thinking.

SOME GAP PREDICTIONS

Central Chile has been defined as a seismicity gap since about 1971. It was one of the gaps everyone agreed on. The last major earthquake in this area had been in 1906. Nishenko (1985) successfully predicted the 1985 Chile earthquake, using an argument based on the deficiency of slip release along the Chile plate boundary. His paper was about to be published in the *Journal of Geophysical Research* when the earthquake occurred. It turned out that Nishenko had anticipated a much larger area of rupture than the one that actually developed. Seismologists were so elated about the success of the prediction that they thought the earthquake had made a mistake. Nishenko must have been right and the rupture would soon extend southward into the segment of the 1928 earthquake (Fig. 5.7). But no further earthquake occurred.

In 1989 Nishenko predicted another earthquake to occur in the Nicoya gap, Costa Rica, with a 93% probability before 2009, again on the basis of gaps and slip rates. An earthquake of magnitude 7.0 did actually occur in the Gulf of Nicoya on March 25, 1990; This was a major earthquake, nearly as damaging as the Chile earthquake. Foreshocks began 16 hours before the main shock. But Protti and McNally argued that it didn't fit Nishenko's prediction: The rupture didn't fall squarely inside the gap.

Kisslinger et al. (1986) successfully predicted the earthquake of May 7, 1986 ($M = 7.7$) in the Andreanof Islands (Aleutians), largely on the basis of gap considerations. Unfortunately the earthquake occurred several months past the time limit specified by the authors, and the location of the rupture

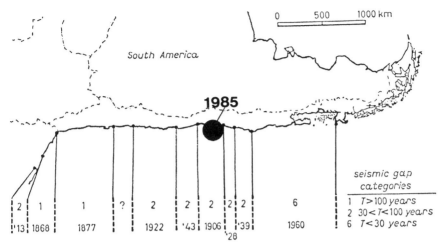

Fig. 5.7 *Map of suggested seismic gaps along the coast of Chile. After S.P. Nishenko, 1985. Published by the American Geophysical Union.*

failed to match the exact specifications of the forecast. As a result, Kisslinger (1988) conceded that the prediction had failed. Others might have been less particular.

Quiescence is defined as an abnormal decrease in low-level seismicity within a gap, interpreted as an earthquake precursor. It has been claimed that 17 reliable cases of seismic quiescence were reported and that three earthquakes were successfully predicted on the basis of such observations (Wyss and Habermann, 1987). Yosihiko Ogata (1991) examined the statistics of seismicity in Japan and claimed that a period of quiescence could be objectively detected before every large earthquake. However, Ogata's tests were parametric in the sense that *a priori* distributions of aftershocks and of background seismicity had been assumed. Thus the quiescence might have been introduced by way of the test itself.

The "successful" 1978 Oaxaca prediction was made on the basis of seismic quiescence. This case history is worth relating in some detail and will be given further below.

IMAGING THE EARTHQUAKE PROCESS

Earthquakes may be modelled as a four-dimensional point process in (a) latitude Φ; (b) longitude λ; (c) focal depth h; (d) origin time t_0. In addition, if the process is *marked*, it may carry one or more tags denoting magnitude, intensity, or some other descriptor. The *imaging problem* refers to the problem of how to represent this multidimensional process in some visually accessible way for diagnostic purposes. In practice this means projecting the process into two dimensions.

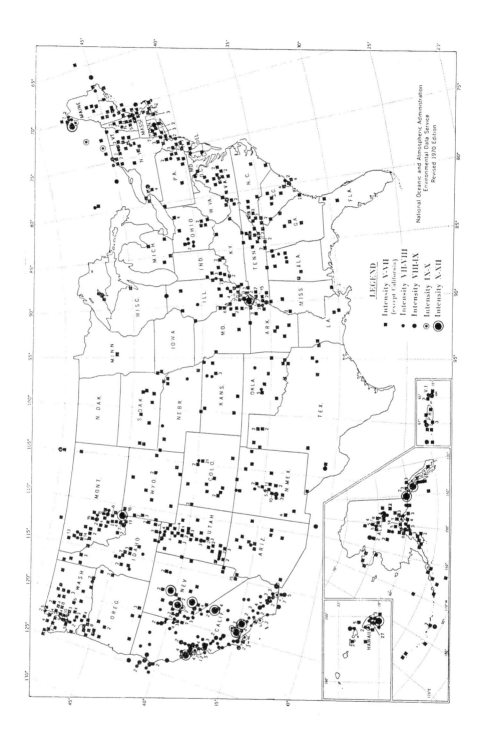

National Oceanic and Atmospheric Administration
Environmental Data Service
Revised 1970 Edition

LEGEND

Intensity V-VII
(except California)

■ Intensity VII-VIII

● Intensity VIII-IX

◉ Intensity IX-X

⬤ Intensity X-XII

Seismicity is a generic term used for describing the process of occurrence of earthquakes in space and time. Its assessment involves plotting the four dimensions of the hypocenter plus at least one mark, such as magnitude or seismic moment. The main problem seems to be the discovery of appropriate plotting variables. Russian investigators have devoted much thought to this issue. They tried to plot various energy functions, called variously *seismic weather, seismic climate,* or *seismic power* (see, e.g., Fedotov and Riznichenko, 1984). Nothing came of these investigations because the imaging problem of earthquake risk in terms of relevant energy functions could not be solved.

The main properties of a good plotting variable seem to be *stability, resolution,* and *contrast.* More importantly, we require finding a function of the data that is not subject to rapid fluctuations and which affords a well-defined image of the seismic source process as it evolves along a plate boundary. The image should clearly set off high-risk regions from adjacent lower-risk regions. It should provide a diagnostic tool for evaluating the changing patterns of earthquake hazard along the boundary. Some of the early options tried for seismicity imaging are described in the following.

(a) Seismicity Maps

These are maps of earthquakes represented as dots on a geographical grid (Fig. 5.8). Such maps were first produced by Montessus de Ballore (1907), who used dots of different sizes to denote the relative amount of severity or damage for each event. Nowadays the dots are proportional to the Richter magnitude. Seismicity maps are still issued by government agencies as a form of describing or dramatizing the earthquake hazard. Their usefulness in terms of risk analysis and hazard prevention is doubtful. Their main disadvantage is that they omit the time variable. (Sometimes the dates are written in small print next to the major events.)

(b) Energy Release

The earth releases about 10^{18} J/year of energy in earthquakes. However, a single large event, such as the 1960 Chile earthquake, can exceed this amount many times. Fig. 5.9 shows an example of logarithmic contouring of cumulative energy release. Here energy was used as a convenient mark of the process, rather than magnitude, which is not additive and has no direct physical interpretation.

Fig. 5.8 *Example of a seismicity map (United States). Each dot represents an earthquake felt with an intensity of at least V on the Modified Mercalli Scale. The small numbers refer to frequency of reported occurrences. The density of dots is not necessarily related to the hazard. From the National Oceanic and Atmospheric Administration.*

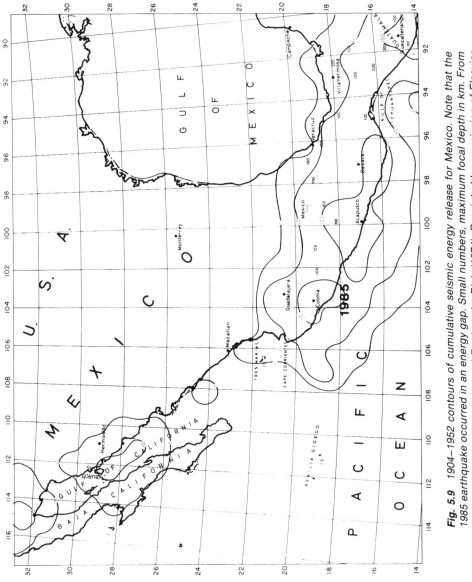

Fig. 5.9 *1904–1952 contours of cumulative seismic energy release for Mexico. Note that the 1985 earthquake occurred in an energy gap. Small numbers, maximum focal depth in km. From C. Lomnitz, Global Tectonics and Earthquake Risk (1974). Reprinted by permission of Elsevier Scientific Publishers, Amsterdam.*

Besides the fact that time is again omitted, the main drawback seems to be that energy is difficult to measure from earthquake records. It is usually evaluated indirectly from the magnitude M by the old empirical equation

$$\log_{10} E = 1.5\,M + 4.4 \,. \tag{5.1}$$

where E is the energy in joules and M is the Richter magnitude of the earthquake. Note that a magnitude error of ± 0.1 (magnitudes are determined to the nearest decimal) translates as an error of -29% to $+41\%$ in the energy.

In any large earthquake, the energy release is spread over an area of hundreds to thousands of square kilometers, called the *area of rupture*, while the location is given in earthquake catalogs as a geographical point $P(x, y, z)$. This is the *focus*, defined as the point where the rupture started. Its projection on the surface of the earth is the *epicenter*.

Since earthquake catalogs don't give the outline of the area of rupture, the energies were computed from Eq (5.1) and then smoothed by spreading the energy of each earthquake over a bell-shaped volume in proportion to its magnitude. Then all the energies were added and contoured. The contours must be logarithmic in energy; otherwise only the largest events will show up in the map. Since the Richter scale is also logarithmic in the energy, each contour may be loosely associated with a magnitude level. Energy goes up as magnitude to the power 1.5; thus one contour interval in log(energy) is equivalent to 1.5 magnitude steps.

(c) Contour Maps of Seismic Moment

The seismic moment M_0 is routinely calculated for all larger earthquakes. It is the force times the area of rupture. Seismic moment, unlike energy, can be obtained directly from individual seismograms; unlike magnitude, it has a clear physical interpretation. Thus it represents a better measure of earthquake size than either. If desired, the seismic moment may also be computed empirically from the magnitude:

$$\log_{10} M_0 = M + 12.9 \tag{5.2}$$

where M is the Richter magnitude and M_0 is the seismic moment in newton-meters (N-m). Using Eq (5.2) is necessary for evaluating the smaller shocks for which moment determinations are not routinely available. It is all right to use hybrid data sets that include direct evaluations of seismic moment for the larger earthquakes and estimates from approximation (5.2) for the smaller events. The contribution of the latter is small as compared with that of the larger shocks, and the error is within the error margin of moment determinations for large earthquakes.

SERENDIPITOUS REDISCOVERY OF SEISMIC GAPS

I was a skeptic on the subject of seismicity gaps until quite recently. I shared the views of Kagan and Jackson (1991) concerning the statistical soundness of the gap concept. However, my interest in seismic imaging led me to rediscover gaps by accident.

Back in 1965 I attempted to find a better way of imaging the probabilities of occurrence of maximum ground accelerations in earthquakes. I contoured the annual probability of accelerations exceeding 0.1 g on a base map of California (Fig. 5.10), assuming that earthquakes occurred at random according to a simple Poisson process. My input was a list of all earthquakes of magnitude greater than 4 that had occurred in California between 1932–1964.

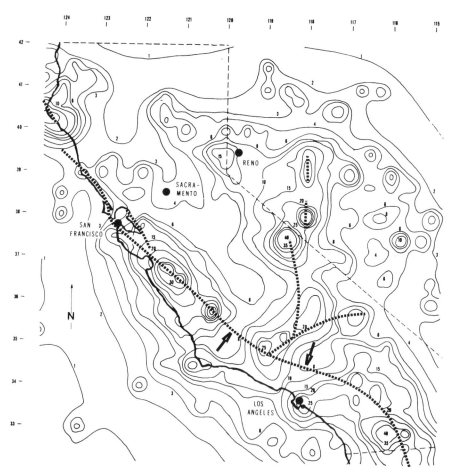

Fig. 5.10 *1932–1964 contours of seismic hazard for California. Note that the 1966 and 1971 earthquakes* (arrows) *occurred in seismicity gaps on the San Andreas fault* (dashed). *From C. Lomnitz,* Global Tectonics and Earthquake Risk *(1974). Reprinted by permission of Elsevier Scientific Publishers, Amsterdam.*

The result was intended to be used by engineers as a guide to predicting the earthquake hazard at different localities in the state.

Luckily the map was never published. It showed two saddlepoints on the San Andreas fault: one near Parkfield and the other near San Fernando. These should have been the least hazardous places on the San Andreas fault; instead they were the locations for the next two damaging California earthquakes. Parkfield occurred in 1966 and San Fernando in 1971. In both events the ground acceleration exceeded 0.1 g. According to my initial reasoning the probability for any such event should have been less than 6% in 30 years. Yet both earthquakes occurred within six years of the date of the map, and no earthquakes occurred in the areas designated as having maximum probability.

There were to be more serendipitous discoveries. The saddlepoints shown in Table 5.1 were discovered 15 years after publication of my maps of smoothed contours of cumulative earthquake energies of the world for the period 1904–1952 (Figs. 5.9, 5.11–5.14).

Some further successful gaps might have been identified in these maps with the aid of hindsight, but these examples seemed the most convincing. The case of the 1985 Mexico earthquake is interesting because there was an ongoing discussion at the time about whether the lack of large historical earthquakes in this particular segment of plate boundary indicated a seismicity gap or rather an absence of seismic hazard. The isolated gap in the energy contours might have helped in inferring that there was indeed a large seismic hazard in this region.

TABLE 5.1 Serendipitous Seismicity Saddles (1904–1952)

Location of Saddle Point According to Lomnitz (1974)	Subsequent Earthquake (after 1952)[a]
176°E	1965 Rat Islands earthquake, $M_w = 8.7$
178°W 174°W 167°W	1957 Fox Islands earthquake, $M_w = 9.1$ 1986 Andreanof Islands earthquake, $M = 8.0$
163°W 150°W	1964 Alaska earthquake, $M_w = 9.2$
18°N	1985 Mexico earthquake, $M_w = 8.1$
8°S	1970 Peru earthquake, $M_w = 7.9$
11°S	1974 Peru earthquake, $M_w = 8.1$
50°N	1963 Kurile earthquake, $M_w = 8.5$
49°N	1969 Kurile earthquake, $M_w = 8.2$
37°N	1964 Sea of Japan earthquake, $M = 7.5$
25°N	1990 Philippine earthquake, $M = 7.8$
150°E	1989 Macquarie Is. earthquake, $M = 8.2$

[a] M_w is the moment magnitude (as far as available) computed from the seismic moment M_0, while M is the Richter surface-wave magnitude.

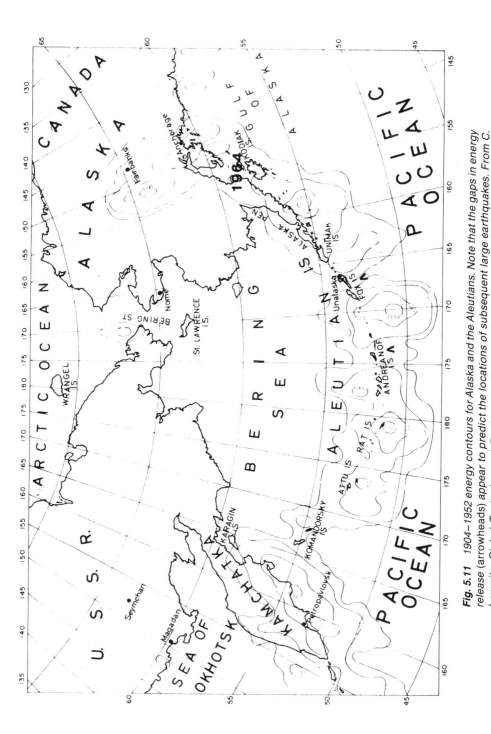

Fig. 5.11 1904–1952 energy contours for Alaska and the Aleutians. Note that the gaps in energy release (arrowheads) appear to predict the locations of subsequent large earthquakes. From C. Lomnitz, Global Tectonics and Earthquake Risk (1974). Reprinted by permission of Elsevier

Scientific Publishers

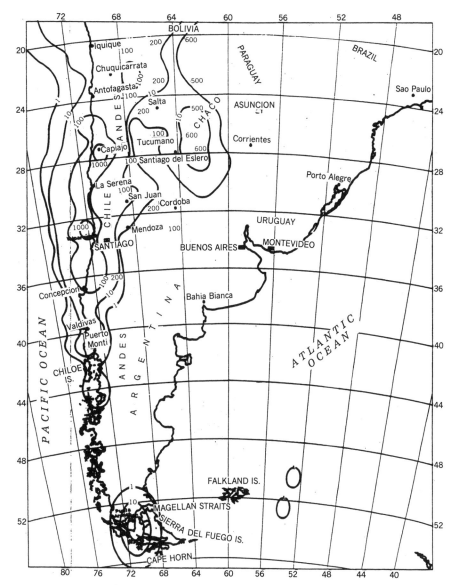

Fig. 5.12 *1904–1952 energy contours for southern South America. No energy gaps are visible, because the contours of the 1906 central Chile event still dominate the pattern 46 years later. From C. Lomnitz,* Global Tectonics and Earthquake Risk *(1974). Reprinted by permission of Elsevier Scientific Publishers, Amsterdam.*

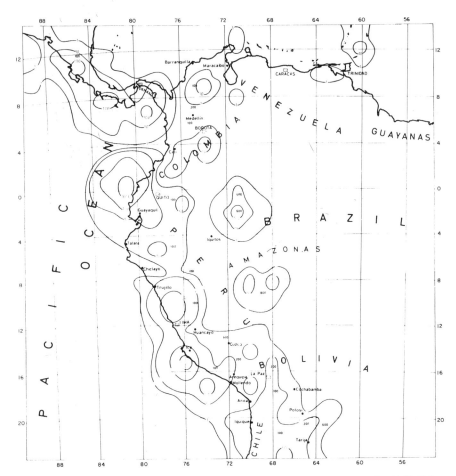

Fig. 5.13 *1904–1952 energy contours for Peru. The gap corresponding to the 1970 Chimbote earthquake is visible. From C. Lomnitz,* Global Tectonics and Earthquake Risk *(1974). Reprinted by permission of Elsevier Scientific Publishers, Amsterdam.*

Some question remains as to whether these gaps could have been found *a priori.* Energy mapping is rather unstable: it is strongly affected by the occurrence of every large earthquake. On the other hand, the destructive 1990 Philippines earthquake was associated with a saddle in the energy contours since well before 1952. This earthquake occurred on the Luzon fault, one of the major strike-slip features of the world, which had been recognized as active by C.R. Allen and other geologists—but apparently no major historic earthquakes had occurred on this fault (Fig. 5.14).

THE HEALING HYPOTHESIS

Let us now introduce the concept of healing.

On Fig. 5.12 it may be noticed that the central Chile gap is not visible in

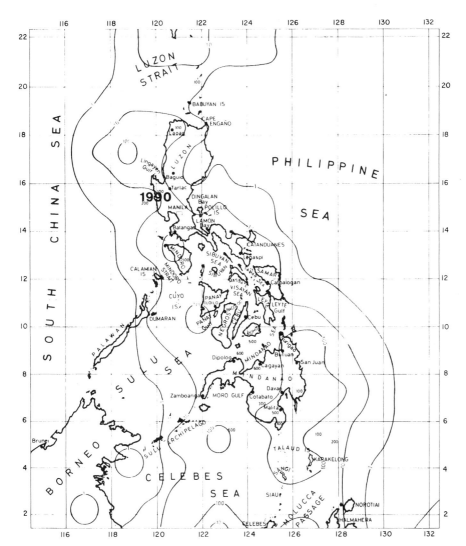

Fig. 5.14 *1904–1952 energy contours for the Philippines. Note the gap corresponding to the 1990 earthquake in central Luzon. From C. Lomnitz,* Global Tectonics and Earthquake Risk *(1974). Reprinted by permission of Elsevier Scientific Publishers, Amsterdam.*

the energy contours. The reason is the persistence of the energy from the previous large earthquake, which occurred in 1906. The 1906 energy release is still sitting squarely on the gap and won't budge to make room for the next earthquake. Yet an important strain deficiency was detected here in 1971. Stuart Nishenko used it successfully to predict the 1985 earthquake.

In a steady-state system, after a perturbation in any state variable there is *recovery*. The best-known (though not necessarily the simplest) example of such a recovery process is the healing of a wound. When the skin is broken, the organism starts rebuilding it, beginning from the ragged edge of the wound and gradually working toward the center. Since the rate of healing is a function of the length of the perimeter, the rate of healing decays with time. Such processes are common in nature and called *rate processes*. They typically generate an exponentially decreasing rate of recovery.

In seismology it has been customary instead to assume that the stress and/or the strain *accumulates* at the boundary. Unfortunately there is no direct evidence of any long-range accumulation. In the case of the 1985 Chile earthquake, for example, the region began to tilt at least six months before the shock (Fig. 4.7). Moreover, in a system that is convecting near stationarity, it is difficult to imagine that any stress can accumulate anywhere. The plate boundaries should be spring-loaded at a near-constant tectonic stress that equals the rate of convection times the viscosity. There are only two ways to strain a boundary: through aseismic creep or through seismic slip.

This discussion could go on forever, since the observed plate motions may be interpreted in many different ways. But we have to go ahead with prediction. A practical approach is to sidestep the issue. This is precisely what we do when we define a hypothetical process called *healing*.

Suppose that an earthquake of seismic moment M_0 occurs at time $t = 0$. Since M_0 equals the displacement times the area of rupture (and since we lack direct measurements of either), it is best to imagine an equivalent area of rupture that equals M_0 numerically. Let us call this area the *scar*. Now as the scar heals, its size decreases exponentially with time:

$$m_0\,(t) \,=\, M_0\,e^{-0.69315\,t/\tau}, \tag{5.3}$$

where M_0 is the initial size of the scar, τ is the half-life of the scar, and m_0 is called the *residual moment* of the rupture t years after the event. It may be thought of as the size of the scar after t years of healing. If preferred, you may think of m_0 as a seismic moment that is still "sitting" on the rupture area and impeding its being ruptured again; or alternatively, if you must think of something accumulating at the boundary, you may think of $M_0 - m_0$ as the "moment deficiency." Anyway, we shall always assume that wherever the boundary is scarred, it cannot rupture: A scar must heal first before it can break again.

Eq (5.3) says that the residual moment of the earthquake is halved every τ years; this is the purpose of the numerical constant in the exponent. The purpose of this exercise is to show that monitoring the residual moment is useful for purposes of earthquake prediction. Is this physically plausible? In a previous paper (1985) I showed that a rupture must first heal before it can break again. Even in the case of two successive earthquakes in the same region, such as the 1981 and 1985 Michoacán, Mexico, earthquakes, the scar of the 1981 event was not reruptured in 1985. The area of the 1981 scar was

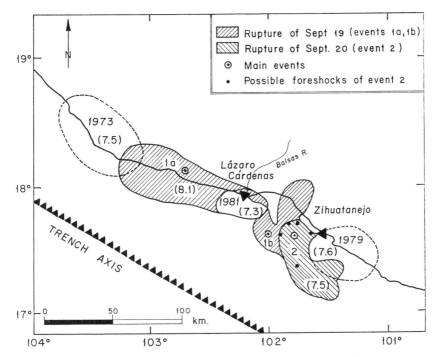

Fig. 5.15 *Time sequence of ruptures in the Mexico subduction zone. The sequence was 1a-1b-2. Dashed lines, scars from adjacent earlier earthquakes. From C. Lomnitz (1988). The Mexico earthquake. Natural and Man-made Hazards, M. El-Sabh and T.S. Murty, Eds. Published by D. Reidel, Dordrecht, The Netherlands.*

clear of aftershocks: Thus the 1985 rupture must have bypassed the existing scar by propagating around the edges (Fig. 5.15).

By calculating the cumulative residual moments Σm_0 in each segment along the boundary, we should be able to monitor the process whereby a high in residual moment becomes a low in relation to neighboring plate segments. In practice we accumulate the seismic moments M_0 for each of the events as they occur and the accumulated value is iteratively multiplied by $\exp(-0.69315 \, \Delta t/\tau)$ for every time step Δt (Fig. 5.16). The same procedure is carried out for each region. Thus we obtain graphs of the residual moment m_0 along a plate boundary.

For my data source I use a list of seismic moments of large earthquakes since 1900, compiled by Pacheco and Sykes (1992) (see Appendix 2). The half-life of a rupture was provisionally taken to be $\tau = 20$ years. The residual moments m_0 were calculated according to Eq (5.3) and graphed in various ways. An example is shown later in Fig. 5.19.

Notice that the 90-year list by Pacheco and Sykes totals 698 events of magnitude 7 and above, which makes an average of 7.75 events per year. This represents well over 90% of the world moment release in earthquakes.

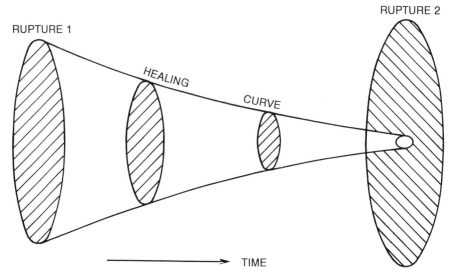

Fig. 5.16 *Diagram of the healing process.*

The 1960 Chile earthquake alone released about half the moment of all other earthquakes combined since 1900.

For imaging purposes I merged all three space coordinates *(x, y, z)* into a single number $\mathscr{F}$, where $\mathscr{F}$ is the Flinn–Engdahl region number. Ted Flinn and Bob Engdahl (1965) compiled this useful empirical regionalization of earthquakes with no particular theory in mind. They divided the world in 729 different geographical regions, in such a way that most seismic ruptures fell within the confines of one single region. There are serious theoretical doubts that this can always be done, but for purposes of demonstration of the method it is adequate. Actually there is enough coherence between adjacent regions as to be able to use them as if they were a geographical grid.

EVOLUTION OF EARTHQUAKE SCARS

Consider now the evolution of the residual moment in time. In other words, how do rupture areas turn into gaps? Using the Chile Plate boundary as a test case we may fit all major shocks since 1822 to the healing hypothesis. As Fig. 5.17 shows, the fit is excellent. The half-life is $\tau = 20.8$ years. There are no overlaps, and the nucleation of each event tends to occur at the edge of a scar. Lengths of rupture are assumed to decay as

$$L(t) = L_0 \, e^{-0.69315 \, t/\tau}, \tag{5.4}$$

where L_0 is the initial length of the rupture and $L(t)$ is the residual length of the scar.

According to the original gap criterion, McCann et al. (1979) proposed that ruptures turn into gaps on their 30th birthday. This allowed for no overlaps, no partial ruptures, no precession of rupture zones along the plate boundary. It left the healing process undefined. Some ruptures require much longer than 30 years to heal, especially when they coalesce with adjacent ruptures. This was the case of the 1906 and 1928 ruptures, both of about equal size. After 1928 the two contiguous scars formed a single scar that slowly healed as a unit (Fig. 5.17).

The 1822 scar had shrunk to a diameter of less than 40 km—about the half-width of the contact zone for large subduction earthquakes in this region—when the 1906 event occurred (Fig. 5.17). The scars of the 1851 and 1873 events were practically gone. Thus the 1906 rupture was ready to break: The 1822 scar was now small enough to be outflanked by the propagating rupture. In 1985, on the other hand, major scars persisted both to the north and to the south of the rupture. They were too large to be outflanked or broken. This explains why and where the rupture stopped.

Nishenko had noticed that the areas and lengths of rupture of the 1822, 1906, and 1985 earthquakes were different and unequal but no one could find

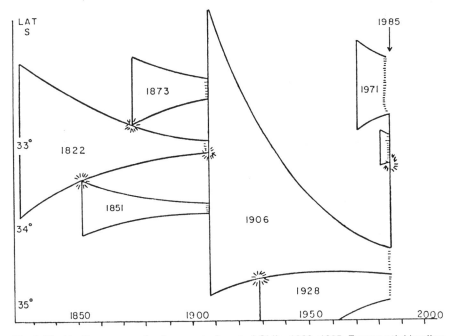

Fig. 5.17 *Healing process for the coast of central Chile, 1822–1985. Exponential healing at constant rate is assumed. From C. Lomnitz (1985). Tectonic feedback and the earthquake cycle,* Pageoph, 123, 667–682. *Reprinted with permission of Birkhäuser Verlag, Basel.*

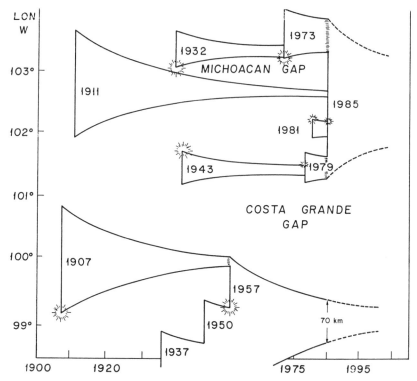

Fig. 5.18 As in Fig. 5.17, but for the coast of central Mexico. From C. Lomnitz (1985). Tectonic feedback and the earthquake cycle, Pageoph, 123, 667–682. Reprinted with permission of Birkhäuser Verlag, Basel.

any good explanation for this. It was puzzling that the rupture stopped short of rerupturing the Talca segment and that areas of successive earthquakes overlapped significantly at the edges. The healing hypothesis shows why this had to be so. No overlaps took place.

The sequence of southern Mexico can be explained in a similar manner (Fig. 5.18). The half-life of the ruptures is again about $\tau = 20$ years. As noted above, the 1981 Playa Azul scar was not ruptured again in 1985 (Fig. 5.15).

More than 80 years ago, Omori showed that aftershocks form a rate process:

$$n(t) = a/(b + t) \tag{5.5}$$

where n is the rate of occurrence of aftershocks t days after the earthquake. The number of aftershocks decays as a sum of exponential rate processes—and the total area covered by aftershock activity shrinks with time. As a logical extension of the healing hypothesis, we may assume that the aftershock process is actually an expression of healing. This is the reason why the aftershocks occur only within the scar. Other postseismic transients (notably groundwater transients) are also correlated with the healing process.

MOMENT-RATIO IMAGING (MRI)

Residual moments Σm_0 may easily be graphed along a plate boundary (Fig. 5.19). Unfortunately, this way of visualizing the earthquake process is confusing because the moment ordinate is strongly time-dependent.

A more practical way of imaging residual-moment anomalies is by means of graphs of

$$\mathcal{R}(t) = M_{0tot} \bigg/ \sum_{t=0}^{t} m_0(t), \qquad (5.6)$$

called the *moment ratio*. Here M_{0tot} is the total accumulated seismic moment released by the region over the time spanned by the catalog. The sum in the denominator is the residual seismic moment in the region updated to time t (i.e., the sum of the updated residual seismic moments from all preceding

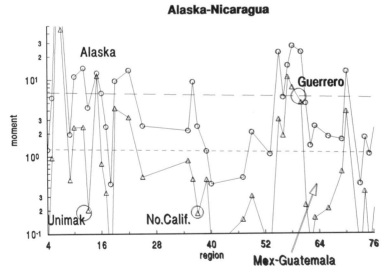

Fig. 5.19   *A graph of residual moments along the northeast Pacific from the Aleutians to Central America. Upper curve, 1980; lower curve, 1990. Note the moment deficiency before the 1992 northern California earthquake (M = 7.1). From C. Lomnitz (1993). Published by the American Geophysical Union.*

earthquakes). Thus, $\mathcal{R}(t)$ is the reciprocal of the normalized residual moment for the region (Lomnitz, 1993).

Starting with the origin of the catalog, taken as $t = 0$, we compute $\Sigma m_0(t)$ for every region. Each time an event of moment M_0 occurs Σm_0 is increased by M_0. After every time step Δt, the value of Σm_0 is multiplied by $\exp(-0.69315\Delta t/\tau)$. Thus $\Sigma m_0\ (t)$ looks like a sequence of exponential step functions (Fig. 5.20). In a system of stationary seismicity this function is long-term stationary.

Consider now what happens during a seismic cycle. Immediately after an earthquake occurs, the denominator of $\mathcal{R}(t)$ is increased by M_0. The net effect is a drop in $\mathcal{R}(t)$, while the values of $\mathcal{R}(t)$ in neighboring regions continue to increase. The depleted region becomes a valley. The result is a jagged curve (Fig. 5.21). In time the value of $\mathcal{R}(t)$ rises again, since the numerator stays constant while the denominator decays. As neighboring regions rupture in succession, the value of $\mathcal{R}(t)$ eventually peaks again and the next earthquake occurs. Because $\mathcal{R}(t)$ is normalized against the total accumulated moment M_{0tot} in each region, the relative state of depletion can be detected independently of whether the region is one of high or low activity.

Thus, in Fig. (5.21) we find two new *moment-ratio imaging (MRI)* gaps in Alaska, one old but increasing gap in northern California (which eventually ruptured in 1992, after the figure was made), a gap in Nicaragua (also broken in 1992), and two gaps in Mexico, one near the Rivera Plate and one in the Chiapas-Guatemala region. There is no premonitory peak in the area of the

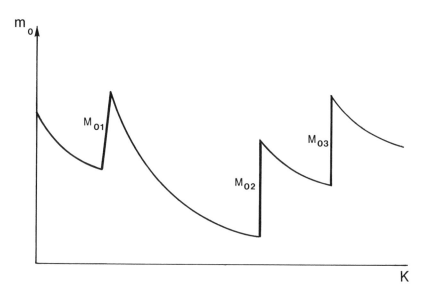

Fig. 5.20   *The concept of residual moment M in an exponentially healing segment of plate boundary.*

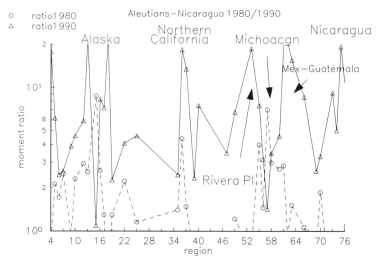

Fig. 5.21 *Moment-ratio imaging (MRI) for the northeast Pacific (Aleutians to Central America), for 1980 (dotted line) and 1990 (solid line). From C. Lomnitz (1993). Published by the American Geophysical Union.*

1992 Landers, California, earthquake because there was no earthquake of magnitude 7 or greater in this general area during 1900–1990.

Procedures for imaging strains and stresses along active faults have become popular recently, in order to attempt determining what segments have been loaded or unloaded by a specific earthquake. Hudnut et al. (1989) imaged seismic slips along cross-faults in California (Fig. 5.22), and attempted to predict the occurrence of main events on the fault proper. Detailed work of this type is being done for the 1992 Landers earthquake. However, the indeterminacy of the problem of estimating stress changes from data on relative slip is such that predictions for the location and magnitude of the next earthquake are unreliable.

The MRI method does not depend on such interpretations. The seismic moment deficiency is taken as a scalar assumed to be distributed over the region. This assumption appears to hold reasonably well, as the following preliminary results suggest.

(*a*) Japan. Since about 1980 a large earthquake, the Tokai earthquake, has been expected to occur in the Suruga Bay region of east-central Japan. This earthquake threatens the larger cities on the eastern seaboard, including particularly the Tokyo Metropolitan Area. In order to verify the present situation we may analyze the MRI plots for $t_1 = 1980$ (dotted) and $t_2 = 1990$ (solid line), for all regions of the western Pacific between Kamchatka and Java (Fig. 5.23). There was indeed a major maximum of $\Re(1980)$ in the central

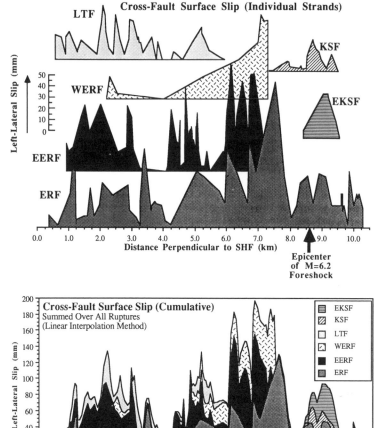

Fig. 5.22 *Triggering of earthquakes by slip from foreshocks on cross-faults. From Hudnut et al. (1989). With permission from the Seismological Society of America.*

Honshu region (including the Tokai area), but the earthquake did not occur. The region has now become a trough. Thus the hazard has shifted to the northern and southern parts of Honshu. There is a large peak in $\mathscr{R}(1990)$ forming off the coast of northern Honshu, possibly near Miyako. It appears that northern Honshu is now more hazardous than central Honshu. Other interesting peaks are off Chiba Prefecture and near Taiwan. Note also the prominent Java gap which forms an important MRI peak.

(*b*) South America. Here I present moment ratios for 1970 and 1980, merely in order to demonstrate the evolution of the MRI peak corresponding to the epicenter of the 1985 Chile earthquake. The central Chile region appeared as a clear single peak in $\Re$ already in 1970. It still persisted in 1980. The earthquake occurred in 1985. Presumably it could have occurred in 1970 but didn't. If MRI procedures had been in use, the preparations for the earthquake could have started in 1970. By the time the tilt anomaly developed (eight months before the earthquake) and the foreshocks started, everything would have been ready for the shock.

Another major gap, in Ecuador, may correspond to the destructive earthquake of March 5, 1987 (M = 7.3). This event occurred in the interior of Ecuador, along a major range fault on the flank of Tronador Volcano. It is a region of complex tectonics and the earthquake may have been on a neighboring plate boundary that connects the coast of Ecuador to the Boconó fault along the Colombia-Venezuela border.

The gap corresponding to the 1970 northern Peru earthquake is less impressive, again because the mosaic of Flinn–Engdahl regions is too complex in this area, causing the moments to spread out on the graph. But the peak is there. There is a suggestion that another Magellan Straits earthquake may be due soon. As for the much-feared northern Chile earthquake, believed to be overdue since 1868, the moment ratio is not very threatening. The earthquake potential is certainly there, but the region is "working off steam" at a good rate.

(*c*) The West Coast of North America. Here several fascinating features can be seen (Fig. 5–21, 5.25). The 1985 Michoacán, Mexico, earthquake (M = 8.1) was preceded by a clear peak in $\Re(1980)$. The approaching hazard could have been recognized in time. If MRI had been available, it would

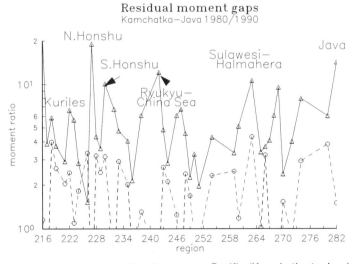

Fig. 5.23 *Moment-ratio imaging for the western Pacific (Kamchatka to Java), for 1980 (dotted line) and 1990 (solid line). From C. Lomnitz (1993). Published by the American Geophysical Union.*

have afforded a positive prediction and ample warning: The 1981 earthquake ($M = 7.3$) didn't work off enough moment and might have been recognized as a precursor.

The Guerrero gap, believed to be next in line to rupture, did not stand out in 1980 and does not stand out now. The moment ratio has not risen appreciably since before 1980. However, if an earthquake were to occur off the coast of Oaxaca, Chiapas, or Guatemala, the Guerrero peak might immediately stand out. This is something to watch for. There is a logic in the sequence of earthquakes progressing along a plate boundary.

A peak can be seen in northern California (Mendocino Fracture Zone), where the Petrolia earthquake ($M = 7.1$) occurred on April 25, 1992. On the other hand, the 1989 Loma Prieta, California earthquake was just below 7 and its effect was invisible on this scale. For earthquakes of this size one ought to look at a more detailed catalog, say of magnitudes down to 6.5, in order to detect the precursory moment deficiency. The case of the Landers earthquake of June 28, 1992 ($M = 7.4$), has already been mentioned. The seismic-moment status of the southern California region was pegged at zero: Thus one would hardly expect to find an MRI anomaly.

The graph (Fig. 5.21) suggests future events in the Alaska Peninsula, off Nicaragua (the event actually occurred in 1992, after the graphs had been prepared), and in the Mexico-Guatemala border region. A large event on the Rivera Fracture Zone also seems likely.

This brief discussion should help clarify the potential of moment-ratio imaging in earthquake prediction. The examples were purposely kept at a simple level; MRI is still in a very early stage of development. As a diagnostic tool it may eventually provide very useful leads in terms of where the next large earthquakes may be expected. Important events such as the 1985 Mexico earthquake might have been diagnosed by this method.

How reliable is it? By testing all events in the 1900–1990 catalog it is found that the reliability increases significantly above magnitude 7.8. When a peak extends over an area of five adjacent regions, as was the case for the 1985 Mexico earthquake, the significance of the anomaly is increased (Fig. 5.24). The negative correlation of *smaller* earthquakes ($M < 7.9$) with broad MRI maxima suggests that when the peak is too narrow to be imaged on a region-wide basis, the surrounding region may be significantly depressed. In this case the V-shaped peak is missed, but it should be detectable with a finer regionalization grid.

The amplitude of the anomaly (when detected) is always highly significant. In Fig. 5.25, the moment drop is scaled to the mean moment in the adjacent regions; thus, for a moment drop of 60% the MRI value is more than doubled. The relative amplitude of the precursor is not strongly dependent on magnitude; only the width of the anomaly is.

While the method is admittedly crude in its present stage, I would hazard a few specific predictions for $M > 7.8$ earthquakes in the next decade or so:

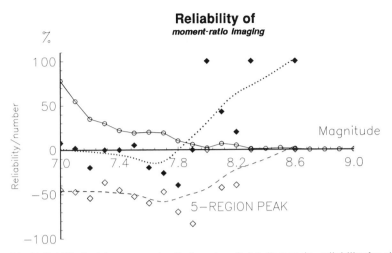

Fig. 5.24 *Reliability test for moment-ratio imaging.* Solid diamonds, *reliability for single MRI peak;* open diamonds, *for five-region wide peak;* open circles, *relative magnitude frequency. From C. Lomnitz (1993). Published by the American Geophysical Union.*

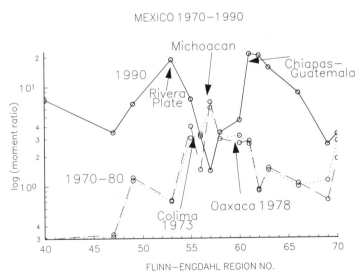

Fig. 5.25 *Moment-ratio imaging for the Michoacán, Mexico gap. Symbols as in Fig. 5.21. Small dots, 1970. From C. Lomnitz (1993). Published by the American Geophysical Union.*

(a) off Northern Honshu, (b) off Chiapas-Guatemala, (c) eastern Java, (d) Ryukyu Islands, (e) western Aleutians or Alaska Peninsula, (f) Sulawesi or Halmahera. These MRI forecasts (made in early 1993) are limited to the northern and eastern Pacific area; I have not yet worked out any MRI plots for South America or the South Pacific. As for California, as Kanamori suggested, a more detailed data set may be required in order to improve on the present coarse gridding based on the Flinn–Engdahl regions. Earthquake prediction work in California should require a complete and accurate catalog down to magnitude 6 or less.

In conclusion, peaks in moment ratio $\mathcal{R}$ point to specific regions about to rupture (usually within a decade or two). An MRI peak does not occur automatically when a segment of plate boundary remains unruptured for 30 years or longer. Rather, there must be a *saddle* of moment deficiency between adjacent relative highs. For example, in northern California the residual moment began to lag behind the total moment release for adjacent regions around 1980 (Fig. 5.21). The MRI peak became much more prominent in 1990, and eventually the earthquake occurred in 1992. Along the Guerrero coast, there has been a seismic gap for decades, yet the large Michoacán anomaly nearby and the lack of moment release to the south have prevented a moment-ratio peak from developing. Thus the seismic hazard in a region depends on the state of energy release and healing in adjacent regions.

AN ANNOUNCED EARTHQUAKE: OAXACA 1978

No statistical validity may be claimed for case histories: Every case is different. The case of the Oaxaca prediction may not be typical, but at least I can vouch for its factual correctness.

In 1975 I received a phone call from a colleague at the University of Texas at Galveston. It seems that several colleagues in Texas were predicting a large earthquake to occur on the coast of Oaxaca, Mexico, on the strength of a remarkable absence of small earthquakes recorded by teleseismic networks in this area since June 1973 and wanted to know whether I'd object to the publication of this prediction in a scientific journal "not likely to be seen by nonseismologists or to cause public concern in Mexico." I saw no reason to object at the time.

The paper was published two years later (Ohtake et al., 1977). It contained some dramatic figures, showing a total blank in a broad area of Oaxaca for earthquakes of magnitude $M > 4.5$ since 1973. The area was located between the rupture zones of the 1965 and 1968 earthquakes and had previously been described as a seismicity gap (Fig. 5.26). In Mexico we had not noticed any quiescence in the area, but then our data had not been used by the Texas group. We had neglected to report our data in time for inclusion in the world center catalog. This embarrassing omission was later corrected. On the other hand, our data had always been available to colleagues on request.

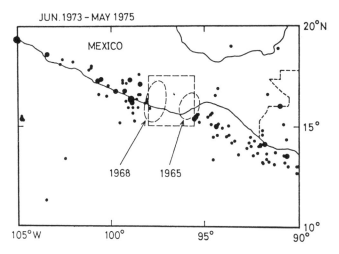

Fig. 5.26   *The Oaxaca quiescence area as a possible earthquake precursor. After Ohtake et al. (1981). In* Earthquake Prediction, *D. Simpson and P. Richards, Eds., Maurice Ewing Series vol. 4, pp. 617–628. Published by the American Geophysical Union.*

In January 1978 a Mexican government official telephoned to inquire whether an earthquake was due anywhere in Oaxaca State in April of that year. The reason for this unusual query was a letter addressed to the governor of Oaxaca by two citizens of Las Vegas, Nevada, predicting that the coastal town of Pinotepa Nacional would be destroyed on April 23, 1978, by an earthquake accompanied by severe tidal flooding. I was later shown a copy of the letter and realized that it qualified for Richter's "nut file," so I just told the official that earthquakes could not be accurately predicted. Neither, unfortunately, could I give assurances that no earthquake would occur in Pinotepa on April 23, as the area was known to be seismic. I also mentioned the Texas forecast and I agreed that the letter should be traced.

The official promptly visited Las Vegas and turned up a pair of unemployed croupiers who had formerly worked at one of the big casinos. They had invented a strategy at roulette that failed to make them rich but had apparently driven them insane. Among other eccentricities they had taken to predicting earthquakes and acknowledged having written the warning letter. Their awareness of the Texas prediction seemed unlikely. Why they had picked òn Oaxaca remains a mystery to this day.

The matter might have rested there but for the misplaced zeal of a secretary in the Oaxaca state government who referred a copy of the prediction letter to the mayor of Pinotepa Nacional with a slip "for your immediate attention". The result was a meeting of the town council and an ensuing surge of panic sales of land and cattle that soon had the coastal region in an uproar. This was the precise time the Texans chose to decide that they couldn't hold back any longer. As budget time approached in Austin they

Texas U Predicts Big Mexico Quake

AUSTIN, Texas (UPI) — University of Texas scientists, using space-shot technology to forecast disasters on earth, predict a massive earthquake will occur soon in the state of Oaxaca in southern Mexico and plan to be there to record it.

UT researchers expect the quake to be stronger than those that shook Managua, Nicaragua, and Guatemala City.

Dr. Creighton A. Burk,

director of UT's Marine Science Institute, said the evidence is based on statistics generated by the university's new computerized seismic monitoring system.

"We have discovered a large area in the state of Oaxaca, at the southern tip of Mexico, where no major earthquakes have occurred for more than almost five years," Burk said. "This is extremely unusual."

Fig. 5.27 Front page report of the Austin news conference on the Oaxaca prediction (from the Mexico City News, Monday, April 10, 1978.) With permission of UPI and the Mexico City News.

held a news conference and described the prediction in rather lurid terms (Fig. 5.27). The news item made the front pages in Mexico and was taken for a scientific confirmation of the doom of Pinotepa Nacional. The Texan forecast did differ from the Las Vegas version in essential details, but these subtleties were lost on the press and on the local ranchers.

Within hours, earthquake rumors spread all over the country and caused, among other damage, massive cancellations in Acapulco hotels. A local paper on the Guerrero coast offered a scoop (supported by "technical" sketches), claiming that the earthquake was to be triggered by a nuclear device planted offshore by the Americans (Sosa Ordoño, 1984). The idea was a land grab engineered by the Pentagon with the cooperation of the Marine Corps, because of the supposed discovery of uranium in Oaxaca. The earthquake was a cover: It all figured with the Texas "prediction". Why uranium? What else could give its black shiny patina to Oaxaca pottery—the very pottery American "tourists" were so eagerly buying!

Mass paranoia is contagious. The governor of Oaxaca, a retired general, was getting fidgety. In an effort to assuage the public anxiety, he let it be known that he intended to put in an appearance in Pinotepa on April 23 to preside over a public fiesta. He noted, in an aside to the press, that no earthquake was expected to spoil the fun.

The fateful day arrived and here were the representatives of press and television elbowing each other rather nervously in the modest town hall of Pinotepa. The Governor was taking his time. I took a stroll through the pleasant and picturesque tropical town, which I knew from a previous visit on the occasion of the 1968 earthquake (see next chapter). I couldn't help noticing that one out of five houses was shuttered, suggesting that the owners had fled. Some, it seems, never came back. The town seemed hushed though it was a lovely sunny day, promising a fine fiesta that evening.

The official helicopter arrived with the governor and staff on board. The politicians were promptly ushered into the town hall, where the Department of Public Works had mounted an exhibit of earthquake emergency measures. Just as the governor was being shown around the exhibition, the doors and windows rattled: an earthquake! There was a tremendous commotion in the hall, and the newsmen pounced upon the hapless seismologist, who was unable to keep a straight face. What did he think of the earthquake? Well, I ventured, perhaps Nature had perversely intended to serve notice that seismologists knew less about earthquake prediction than Las Vegas gamblers did. . . . The next day a major Mexico City daily ran a headline: "'Nature: perverse!,' complains earthquake wizard."

The shock had been slight (about magnitude 4.2) but perfectly loud and clear. It was one of the many local earthquakes that afflict the Oaxaca coast and which the Texans, for some reason, had not picked up. Now the newsmen surrounded the governor: Had he felt the earthquake? "What earthquake?" ruled the governor: "There was no earthquake!" Instantly the situation returned to normal, and the visit could proceed as planned. An hour later the officials took their seats on an open-air dais and the festival began. It was a fine fiesta with lots of singing and dancing, and everybody had a wonderful time. A few minutes past midnight the governor glanced at his watch and decided that April 23 was over and that he could safely return to the state capital, which he did.

Later that same year, on November 29, an earthquake of magnitude 7.6 struck the exact area of the alleged quiescence. It was about the right magnitude predicted by the Texas group. Three teams of seismologists (one Mexican and two American) were on the spot and made some first-rate recordings of foreshocks, main shock, and aftershocks. This was made possible, to a large extent, by the prediction. Seismologists everywhere greeted the Oaxaca prediction as an outstanding instance of successful earthquake prediction using *seismicity patterns*, in this case quiescence, as a precursor. The authors of the prediction, assisted by hindsight, claimed that the quiescence period had actually featured two distinct stages called α and β (Fig. 5.28). The α-stage was described by a total absence of small shocks, while the β-stage, beginning January 1978, was a stage of renewed local seismic activity. Thus the onset of the β-stage might have been used to predict the date of the earthquake.

R.E. Habermann of the U.S. Geological Survey, a supporter of earthquake prediction using seismicity patterns, now began to examine "manmade changes of seismicity rates," caused by the phasing in and out of seismic stations and networks. Such changes can be found in all earthquake

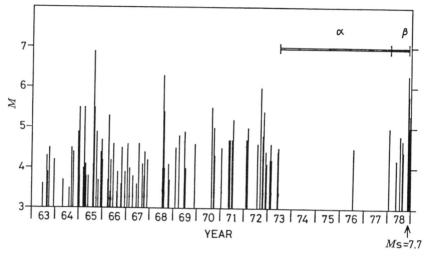

Fig. 5.28 Reinterpretation of the precursory quiescence in terms of "α and β stages." Ms = 7.7, time of occurrence of the predicted Oaxaca earthquake. After Ohtake et al. (1981). In Earthquake Prediction, D. Simpson and P. Richards, Eds., Maurice Ewing Series vol. 4, pp. 617–628. Published by the American Geophysical Union.

catalogs. For example, the closure of the VELA-Uniform seismic arrays in November 1967 produced a noticeable decrease in the number of small earthquakes reported from Mexico and Central America. Large earthquakes continued to be reported, however, since their detection hardly depended on the number and location of the recording seismic stations.

Eventually Habermann reexamined the alleged precursory quiescence in the area of the 1978 Oaxaca earthquake and reluctantly concluded that it might have been spurious as it coincided with the deactivation (α-phase) and subsequent reactivation (β-phase) of certain seismic stations. Thus the success of the Oaxaca prediction was short-lived. It had caused a flurry of optimism and expectation among geophysicists. Around 1982, disappointment and dejection prevailed. A curious detail was lost in the commotion: The 1978 Oaxaca earthquake had hardly caused any damage, yet damage had been an essential part of both predictions. Both the Texan scientists and the Las Vegas amateurs had forecast a tremendous amount of damage. The earthquake of November 29, 1978, was severe, but Puerto Escondido and other towns in the epicentral area were sited on hard rock and didn't suffer from earthquakes. The intensity barely reached VI on the Mercalli scale. Mexico City was too far away for any damage to occur there. In fact the only significant damage was caused by the prediction.

The unkindest cut of all, as far as the predictors were concerned, was the eventual realization that small earthquakes on the coast of Mexico cannot be located to better than 50 km with present teleseismic location methods. Recall that data from local Mexican stations had not been used for the prediction. A quiescent zone of 80–90 km length had been originally claimed, but an error circle with a diameter of 100 km drawn about each epicenter should have wiped this zone clear off the map. In conclusion, which was the more relevant achievement, the prediction of the Oaxaca earthquake of November 29, 1978 ($M = 7.8$), by a group of scientists in Texas, or the prediction of the smaller earthquake of April 23, 1978 ($M = 4.2$) by two unknown gamblers in Las Vegas? Both events occurred as predicted, but the gamblers had named a date while the scientists had not. Pinotepa Nacional was not obliterated by a tsunami on April 23, 1978, but neither did the coastal towns of Oaxaca suffer the predicted heavy damage on November 29 of that same year.

We may suspect the data the scientists worked on and the assumptions they used: Yet they were credited with doing a good job and being on the right track, while the gamblers were merely lucky. What data and assumptions did the gamblers use? We don't know and we don't care. Is this scientific?

6

The Best-laid Plans

What! not one hit?
—Merchant of Venice

INTRODUCTION

Early on a sunny Friday morning, August 2, 1968, a large earthquake (M = 7.2) severely damaged the small town of Pinotepa Nacional. A dozen people were killed. I was in my backyard in Mexico City, playing with Machi, a young female German shepherd. Suddenly the dog had a violent seizure and fell to the ground in a convulsive fit. I knew my dog was healthy. My first thought was that she might have been poisoned. I picked up the helpless animal and carried her indoors. I had barely come in when I felt the P wave of a strong distant earthquake. I put the dog down. The frequency was low as it usually is in Mexico City—a period of about 2 s. The intensity was fairly low too (about III–IV on the Mercalli scale), because the epicenter was some 370 km away and my house stood on hard ground. The strong motion lasted for nearly a minute. The moment it was over, the dog got up and frisked about as if nothing had happened.

I tried to remember how much time had passed between the dog's seizure and the beginning of the earthquake. Surely less than a minute. Thus the animal's reaction must have been coseismic, as it took about 50 s for the P wave to reach Mexico City from the epicenter.

This is the only instance of abnormal animal behavior in earthquakes of which I have firsthand knowledge. It refers to a specific animal which I knew well. By contrast, most descriptions of animal reactions in the literature are generic or statistical. In dogs, restlessness and loud whining or barking is reported from all countries, starting minutes to hours before the earthquake. Roosters are said to crow and birds to fly low as if before a storm. Cattle stampede and pigs bite each other. Rats and field animals tend to swarm together, as do bees. Fish jump out of the water or float motionless on the surface.

By far the largest number of cases of abnormal animal behavior is reported on the day of the earthquake, rarely several days before. Observations may come from anywhere. In China, as large earthquakes "occurred in densely populated urban and rural areas, the behavior of various kinds of animals

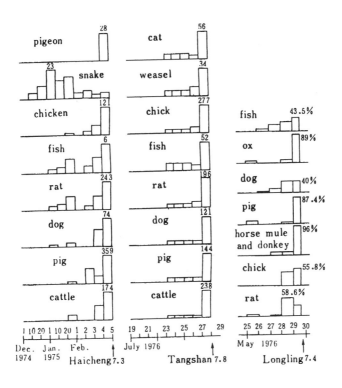

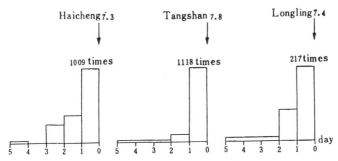

Fig. 6.1 *Summary of animal precursors observed in Chinese earthquakes. Reprinted by permission from* Earthquake Prediction, *Ma Zongjin et al., Eds. (1990), Springer-Verlag, New York.*

was observed continuously'' (Liu, 1990). It is easy to be sarcastic about such statements; yet there remains a core of real observations (Fig. 6.1). The question is: What are the animals trying to tell us?

For quite some time, Western scientists used to make fun of Chinese earthquake prediction by identifying it with the use of animal precursors. The Chinese became defensive. As a result, animal observations in China have been phased out. Today they are thrown in together with the "ugly ducklings" among the precursors: weather and climate change, earthquake sounds, earthquake lights, and other slightly disreputable effects. They are no longer carefully investigated. This change of attitude has paralleled a worldwide disappointment with earthquake prediction. Many seismologists have questioned the usefulness of an empirical search for operational precursors, and recommend more basic studies or research on disaster mitigation instead. Yet some countries, notably Japan, continue to invest a very considerable scientific and financial effort in collecting data on earthquake precursors.

REPORTING ANIMAL REACTIONS

Professor B.G. Deshpande (1987) complains that "premonition of earthquakes by animals does not normally appeal to most people's reason, perhaps because the subject is not very popular so far and not many wish to delve into it." True perhaps; but Prime Minister Zhou En-lai of China disagreed. He ordered farmers to watch animals in order to detect their abnormal reactions. There were many consistent reports. Could we be neglecting animals as informants because we are too citified and have become unaware of their potential as communicators?

Actually, animals are not very reliable subjects; their reactions to earthquakes are very much the same as to weather changes, particularly thunderstorms. If animals could detect an earthquake in advance, would they be good at signaling what they felt? Initially it was thought that people should be able to tell the difference between an impending earthquake and a weather change from a specific animal's behavior. In the Chinese People's Stations about 100,000 cowhands and stable attendants were enlisted for watching animal reactions. These experienced people turned out to be unable to distinguish between behavior changes resulting from different environmental changes. It never worked. One might think that this ambiguity in animal reactions should have been seized upon as a research opportunity. What exactly was it in earthquakes that made animals react as they do before thunderstorms?

Thunderstorms can generate fluctuations of the electric field of as much as 10,000 V/m. No electrical effects of this magnitude have ever been observed before earthquakes. On the other hand, dogs subjected to large experimental changes in the electric field showed no reaction whatsoever. Rats did not react to piezoelectric transients generated by rocks strained experimentally in compression.

One notable case of animal behavior anomaly was reported to have started as much as several months ahead of the earthquake. That was in Haicheng, in northern China. Twenty-three separate incidents of snakes prematurely coming out of hibernation were reported during a single week, in early January 1975. The snakes were found lying on the ground, frozen to death. Altogether 82 such findings were reported between November 1974 and February 1975. The Haicheng earthquake occurred on February 4, 1975. It was shown experimentally that a rise of 2° in ground temperature could interrupt hibernation in snakes. Temperatures measured at depths of 40 cm had shown a rising trend and had leveled off or exhibited some odd long-period fluctuations in January 1975. The case for a precursory rise in ground temperature having caused the anomalous behavior of the snakes seemed very strong.

Then it was realized that warm winters had been felt in Liaoning Province since about 1960. The winter of 1974–1975 was abnormally mild throughout China. In Liaoning the ground thawed and grass sprouted in early January even on shady hillsides. Surface temperatures climbed to 14.8°C (59°F) in the shade, which is unseasonably warm for a Manchurian winter. It seems likely that the snakes were fooled by the warm weather and had subsequently frozen to death in the evening. This was eventually recognized but too late: Too much publicity had been given to the case. In the end it was concluded that "the output of underground heat could not be ruled out." The case of the snakes continues to be cited in China as a prime example of "a reliable earthquake precursor."

According to Liu Defu (1990) the time of occurrence of animal precursors agrees roughly "with the sudden intense variations in the natural electric field, electromagnetic wave disturbance, ground water, escape of ground gas, geosound, earthquake light and existent conditions." If we discard water, gas, sound and "existent conditions" as unlikely to propagate with the speed of light to a distance of 400 km, the case of my dog must be attributed to electromagnetic effects. However, it is true that most animal precursors are reported within the immediate epicentral area or up to 100 km away. If my dog's seizure was not a precursor but a coseismic effect, the case is just as puzzling.

Thus we are essentially left with the possibility of electromagnetic waves. Electromagnetic precursors have been observed on the ground and on board satellites, but these transients have not been systematically investigated. The similarity of animal reactions to earthquakes and thunderstorms suggests the possibility that a precursory signal may be transmitted via the lower or middle atmosphere—though some kind of ionospheric signal cannot be ruled out.

A BASIC DIFFICULTY

The following problem with animal behavior seems to me basic. It appears that the scope of *normal behavior* in most animal species has been underrated. Human behavior covers a relatively narrow range compared with that of some animals. According to Kraemer et al. (1976), a classification of normal behavior in chimpanzees includes five kinds of walking (such as "tandem walk," "buddy walk," and "waltz"); 15 kinds of social play; nine types of sexual behavior; five kinds of "begging"; 17 "unclear cues" involving attack, display, threat, or play; and such puzzling activities as headstands and coprophagy. All this is supposed to be normal behavior. One wonders what a chimp would have to do in order to signal that an earthquake is approaching.

On the other hand, some life forms definitely react to changes in geophysical fields. I have watched magnetic bacteria swim in circles along the field lines of an external magnetic field. When the field around the microscope was reversed they instantly changed direction. With a little practice with the joystick one could get them to do figure eights and other circus tricks. Swarming bees and fishes in search of their annual spawning grounds can detect the rings of polarized ultraviolet light in the sky and easily find their way even on a cloudy day. Migratory birds seem capable of sensing the field lines of the earth's magnetic field. They are not thrown off by diurnal transients or annual fluctuations; they can detect field differentials on the order of 10 γ. They certainly ought to be able to sense anomalies caused by storms or earthquakes.

Among the Canadian tourists who habitually shuttle between homes in Canada and vacation spots in Mexico, none is more assiduous than the monarch butterfly. Every fall monarchs arrive in swarms at Monarch National Forest, in the state of Michoacán. Every spring, when the bare branches of the jacaranda tree in front of my window sprout sky-blue flowers, I know that these beautiful insects must be about to return north from their Mexican mating grounds. The air is thick with silent wings, and the tall pines flame up with butterflies.

Would the yearly monarch migration be thrown off course by an impending large earthquake? A few gammas should do the trick, but the butterflies never seem to miss. Perhaps they can navigate by sensing polarized light in the ultraviolet range. On the other hand, really large earthquakes are rare occurrences even in Mexico. The 1985 earthquake fell in September: too early in the year for testing an eventual butterfly precursor. The 1845 earthquake was in April, close to butterfly time; but I have been unable to find references to butterfly migrations in the natural history books of the time. Alexander von Humboldt, who visited the area around 1804, apparently hadn't heard of them. Neither are they mentioned in E. Trabulse's four-volume *Historia de la Ciencia en México*.

The mechanism of animal navigation remains mysterious. On the strength of what we know it seems entirely possible that strains developing before earthquakes could generate precursory effects that migratory or swarming animals, like bees or fishes, may be able to sense. They are among the creatures most frequently mentioned in connection with earthquake prediction. More research is needed.

At least 90 different animal species, ranging from ants to yaks, have been described as susceptible to earthquakes. But the descriptions are frustrating. In a peculiar way, the more specific one gets in terms of the animal the vaguer the reported anomalies tend to become.

The Haicheng earthquake is frequently mentioned as having been predicted with the help of animal precursors. A rundown of the references reveals that (beside the above-mentioned incident of the snakes) only a few isolated reports were retained by seismologists as worthy of mention. Within a period of 0–48 hours before the earthquake the following five occurrences were specifically quoted: (a) Some cows started fighting and scraping the ground in Yingkou county; (b) some pigs in Panjan refused to eat and started biting each other; (c) eight hours before the earthquake, as the foreshocks were going strong in Haicheng, some deer took flight in Anshan, far away from the epicentral area; (d) 20 min before the main shock a turtle "jumped out of the water and cried" in Dandong—more than 100 miles away; (e) just before the main shock a hen, also in Dandong, flew into a treetop. One wonders how an earthquake could have been predicted on the strength of such flimsy evidence.

In Japan, catfish in captivity are said to have "predicted" 17 out of 20 earthquakes felt between December 1977 and July 1978. The information seems worth investigating until it is realized that catfish *(namazu)* are traditionally believed to cause earthquakes. The fish had been kept for prediction purposes, and their "abnormal" behavior was detected with the aid of hindsight.

THE VAN GROUP

Humans should probably be included in the list of animals reacting strangely to earthquakes. The Greek philosophers of antiquity had no illusions about our position in the animal kingdom. They defined the human species as zoon politikon—the political animal—or even less complimentary, as a "featherless, two-legged creature." Predictably, this led to the exhibition of a plucked chicken as a counterexample.

Around 1980 three Greek physicists and natural philosophers, P. Varotsos, K. Alexopoulos, and K. Nomikos, began observing a series of "blips" on records of the earth's electric self-potential. They postulated that these transients (which could last from half a minute to several hours) might be generated by stress changes preceding strong earthquakes (Varotsos and Lazaridou, 1991). Eventually Varotsos, Alexopoulos and Nomikos became known by their initials as *the VAN Group*.

The electric potential of the earth is recorded as a voltage difference between pairs of electrodes implanted at intervals of 40–2,500 m. The electrodes were either affixed to or driven into the rock—or they were simply stuck into the ground. In the early 1980s the VAN Group presented a number of intriguing preliminary results of their research, which led to their proposal for an earthquake prediction system. This proposal was adopted by a branch of the Greek armed forces.

At present 18 VAN stations operate in Greece. Similar stations have been established by other groups in Japan (Uyeda et al., 1992), Bulgaria, and elsewhere. In the year 1982–1983 alone, 69 earthquake predictions were issued by the VAN Group, most of which were claimed to have been successful within a week or two. Rival groups immediately countered that 870 potential target earthquakes had occurred during that year and that the success of the VAN method should have been measured against this number. Predictions made at random would have been equally successful, they suggested, since any 69 dates in a year would always fall close to any 870 possible targets—more than one earthquake a day. The VAN Group was unmoved and continued to issue predictions: Thus a success rate of 15 in 17 predictions was claimed for the period May 1988-August 1989, including the two largest events ($M = 5.8$ and 6.0). These and other results have been disputed (see, e.g., Drakopoulos and Stavrakakis, 1991). As a result of the heat generated by the argument, the VAN Group became controversial. Comments of scientists ranged from "brave" and "remarkable" to "unbelievable" and "immoral." Greek seismologists finally quarreled over the date on which a certain prediction telegram had been mailed.

The scientific qualifications of members of this research group appear to be unimpeachable. Any group claiming to predict earthquakes of magnitude 5 (and sometimes as low as 4.3) in a region as seismic as Greece is bound to be controversial. The point is that blips are recorded at VAN stations. What are they?

Self-potential anomalies recorded at VAN stations are on the order of 20–100 mV, so they are at least an order of magnitude larger than the background noise. However, as far as we know, epicentral changes in the electric potential during strong earthquakes are on the order of 100 mV or less. The attenuation of a 100-mV anomaly in the crust should be such as to cause it to merge into the background noise at a distance of 20 km. How can we understand the propagation of these signals to much larger distances?

The VAN Group has proposed some fairly exotic explanations, one of them involving the existence of local amplification at so-called sensitive spots with linear dimensions as small as a few meters, due to hypothetical channels of high conductivity in the crust. Other scientists have suggested that the change in self-potential may be due to increased percolation of fluids as a result of precursory strain events. But such strain transients should damp out too, and at relatively short epicentral distances; in order to see an effect at a distance of 100 km the strain precursor would have to be 10 times larger than the strain drop of the earthquake!

Pascal Bernard (1991) has come to the rescue by arguing that a small precursory strain event might trigger a large number of small fractures and fluid-filled veins in the crust. His model would require "that the tectonically active crust is stuffed with small-scale, local metastabilities—fractures and nonhydrostatic fluid reservoirs.'' Bernard invokes the self-organized criticality of crustal structure in seismic regions in order to make this idea palatable. His model might also explain medium-term fluctuations in background seismicity—assuming that the seismic sources are located within the lower crust.

THE ROMANIAN EARTHQUAKE

Two Bulgarian researchers, T. Ralchovsky and L. Komarov, were sufficiently impressed by the work of the VAN Group to set up their own self-potential station on Vitosha Mountain, between Sofia and the Greek border. They used 10-cm-long steel electrodes that they hammered tightly into 1-cm-diameter holes drilled into the granite. They might not have bothered: The same recordings could have been obtained by laying the electrodes on the ground, or even by stringing them over the ground on insulators.

The preceding affirmation would be hotly contested by the authors. I never performed the suggested experiment; but neither did they. The point

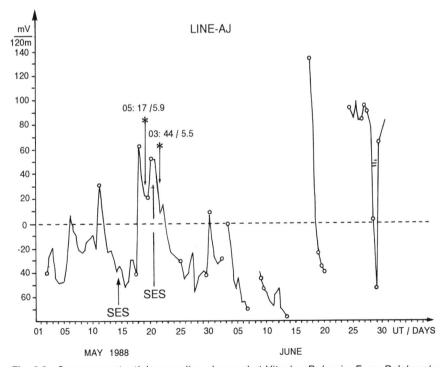

Fig. 6.2 *Some geopotential anomalies observed at Vitosha, Bulgaria. From Ralchovsky and Komarov (1991).*

is: We don't really know where the signal came from or whether it was transmitted via the atmosphere; induced by ionospheric transients; related to magnetic anomalies, telluric currents, earthquake lights, radio frequency disturbances; or whether it propagated inside the earth.

Ralchovsky and Komarov (1991) detected a sequence of 26 strong blips on their array, starting on August 19, 1986. After August 24 the rate slowed down to once or twice a day. The amplitude of the blips was about 60 mV. They stood out clearly against the background noise. The researchers thought that the appearance of this sequence of disturbances was decidedly anomalous. For comparison, the electric potential recording at Vitosha for two Greek earthquakes off the Straits of Corinth is shown on Fig. 6.2). Anomalous electric potentials for these two shocks ($M = 5.9$ and 5.5) were also recorded by the VAN Group.

On August 30 the destructive Vrancea earthquake ($M = 7.0$) occurred deep under the Carpathian Mountains north of Bucharest, about 400 km from the Bulgarian station. It was the largest European earthquake in decades. At 6:45 P.M., less than three hours before the earthquake, a large blip (amplitude 60 mV) developed on the Vitosha array (Fig. 6.3). It peaked at 21:28, exactly at the time of the earthquake. The recorded anomaly had a total

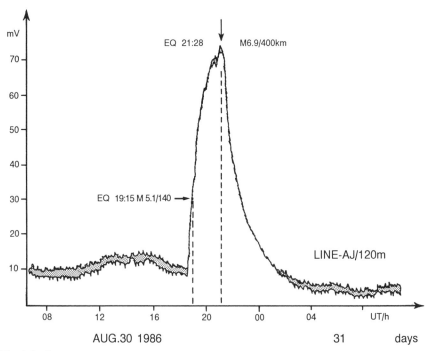

Fig. 6.3 *Precursory geopotential anomaly of the Vrancea, Romania earthquake recorded at Vitosha, Bulgaria. The precursor started half an hour before the foreshock and three hours before the main shock. From Ralchovsky and Komarov (1991).*

duration of seven hours. No further blips were recorded until September 5 even though several aftershocks took place before that date. Altogether seven further blips were recorded between September 6 and 16, all with amplitudes of 40 mV or less. Then the sequence stopped.

The following interesting features stand out in this sequence of events: (a) The frequency of occurrence of the blips decayed from about 6 per day to 0.5 per day as the earthquake approached; (b) the critical blip began two hours and 45 minutes before the earthquake; (c) the earthquake occurred at the peak of the signal, which decayed rapidly afterwards; (d) the rising and falling limbs of the signal were antisymmetrical and looked like the loading and unloading cycles of creep deformation in rocks (cf. Chapter 10); (e) there was a gap or quiescence immediately after the Vrancea earthquake, during which no further blips occurred.

SKY LUMINESCENCE

A significant detail is often omitted in the discussion of the Romanian earthquake prediction. The earthquake did not occur in the earth's crust. It occurred in the mantle, at a depth of 144 km below the earth's surface. The Vrancea seismic source is a well-known subcrustal perturbation. It is a localized and isolated nest of earthquake activity that spans a vertical range from 60 to 200 km depth: no events originate in the earth's crust proper, which has a thickness of less than 40 km in this area. Thus a triggering mechanism such as the one proposed by Pascal Bernard would not apply. Any precursor would have to propagate through the upper mantle and across 400 km of a stable crust to reach the Bulgarian station.

Sky luminescence was observed in an earlier destructive Vrancea event (on March 4, 1977). The 1986 shock may have occurred too early in the evening for sky luminescence to be observed. Earthquake lights are a well-established phenomenon known since antiquity. They were referred to as "strange eruptions" or "portents in the heavens" by Shakespeare and other writers. They have often been observed in deep earthquakes, such as a destructive earthquake under the coastal plain of Veracruz, Mexico (August 28, 1973, $M = 7.1$, focal depth about 100 km). During this event, sky luminescence was observed by many informants in the city or in the countryside: they would often omit mentioning it because they took it for granted that it was a part of the seismic phenomenon.

Photographs of earthquake lights are available from Japan, where many people have a camera at the ready. There are such photographs for the shallow Matsushiro swarm in 1965. The phenomenon resembles a low-latitude aurora; dominant colors are white and red. During the subcrustal Veracruz earthquake, observers in Mexico City mistook it for shorts in the street lighting system. The mechanism has not yet been determined. Electron bombardment was suggested by Brady and Rowell (1986), but this seems unlikely as streams of electrons would have to reach the atmosphere from depths on the order of 140 km in the case of Romania.

J.M. Meunier (1991) proposed a mechanism involving the triggering of earthquakes by strong electromagnetic field anomalies in the ionosphere; these anomalies are supposed to cause the sudden expulsion of ionized hydrogen from deep cracks. Again, this mechanism seems to require dry open channels to reach the surface from depths of a hundred kilometers or more.

Other explanations include regional effects of percolation (electrofiltration), caused presumably by large strain events or by the whole lithosphere being bent. Diffusion of porosity caused by strain transients has also been mentioned as a possible mechanism. There are difficulties with each of these explanations. Yet electromagnetic events are common enough to have persuaded a group of European scientists under J. Achache (Paris) to propose a satellite-borne experiment for detecting regional anomalies of the earth's electromagnetic field within a radius of $5°$ and a time interval of ± 5 hours to the occurrence of earthquakes of magnitude $M > 5$ anywhere on earth. The experiment has not yet been financed, as far as I know.

After the 1989 Loma Prieta earthquake it was discovered that the amplitude of electromagnetic signals had increased from a base level of about 50 picotesla (pT) to 6,700 pT before the main shock. The anomaly was recorded at a single station (Corralitos) located 7 km from the epicenter, and only in the range of frequencies of 0.01–0.02 Hz. Other magnetic stations or strain recorders failed to show a corresponding precursor (Fraser-Smith et al., 1993). The instrument had been installed just four months before the earthquake. Thus there is little background informtion and no conclusive evidence about the observed anomaly being significantly related to the earthquake. However, the rise in amplitude of ultralow frequency electromagnetic fluctuations started 12 days before the earthquake and increased very strongly two days before (from 210 to 6700 pT). No similar episode has been recorded in the three years that followed the earthquake. It seems possible that the observed effect was a true precursor, even though it only occurred in the immediate epicentral region.

PEER REVIEW

In 1989 the International Association of Seismology and Physics of the Earth's Interior decided to elicit the consensus of the scientific community about the validity of earthquake precursors in general, and about their eventual application to earthquake prediction. A project for the evaluation of earthquake precursors was proposed by the Subcommittee on Earthquake Prediction, and a call for nominations from the floor was circulated. Scientists were encouraged to propose specific instances of "precursor, method, or case history". Each nomination was to be backed by supporting documents intended to strengthen the "case," as if for a trial by jury.

Each nomination, as it was received, was sent out to four anonymous reviewers who were asked to qualify, not the scientific soundness of the nomination but their personal belief in the existence of the proposed precursor. The reviews were then judged by a panel of seven experts. Essentially, the question asked of the reviewers was, "Is this phenomenon convincing to you as an earthquake precursor?" About 20 initial nominations were received: only three were accepted (Wyss, 1991).

In view of the large number of rejections, the Subcommittee hastened to explain that the decision of the panel did not imply anything about scientific merit—as indeed it didn't. Acceptance (or rejection) was mostly a measure of the degree of credulity (or skepticism) of the reviewers. Considering the fact that they had not been selected among known skeptics about earthquake prediction, the high rate of rejections was alarming.

The Subcommittee tended to share the view that rigorous verification of earthquake precursors was impossible because precursor observations (rare and difficult at best) were not reproducible under different geologic conditions. In other words, the phenomena were elusive and differed from one place and time to another. This seemed to prevent anyone from ever being sure about the existence of any given earthquake precursor. Yet, as the Subcommittee put it, "it would be a disservice to earthquake prediction research to reject all claims of significant precursors at this time because independent verification is lacking." In other words, it would not be fair to the researchers in the field if the same rules of evidence were applied to precursor research as to other fields of science.

But science is sublimely indifferent to considerations of fairness. Its main ingredient is truth; and truth can be unfair, especially to scientists. Besides, the standards of fairness differ from one court of law to another; and those of the Subcommittee were certainly debatable. Ordeal by water was once considered a fair fact-finding procedure. The subject was bound to a chair and water was trickled down his throat until he either choked to death or gave up. This method is not fashionable anymore. Truth by ordeal went out with the Middle Ages. Or did it? Some day we will shudder to think that a trickle of anonymous peer opinion down our throats could have been mistaken for a fair method of reaching a scientific judgment.

Consider the well-known procedure followed for promoting someone to sainthood. The candidate is resurrected (so to speak) and arraigned before a special court of law, where a plea is made on his behalf. A "devil's advocate" is then appointed to find loopholes in his defense. This feature was lacking in the case of the trial for earthquake precursors; or rather, it was left to the reviewers. As it happened, one of the three cases validated by the Subcommittee on Earthquake Prediction was that of the 1975 Haicheng foreshocks; and in this case, no one was willing to play devil's advocate. All members of the panel shared the belief that the Haicheng earthquake had been scientifically predicted. Their endorsement may have done a disservice to earthquake prediction.

Not everyone in China was agreed on Haicheng. Some colleagues had reservations, based perhaps on an unreasonable commitment to scientific truth. This attitude would have made them politically suspect. Those who took a stand on the issue were sent to the "farms." Their peer reviews had been terrible.

CODA Q AMPLITUDES

Keiiti Aki (1965) pioneered the use of coda-wave decay as a measure of attenuation in seismology. Technically, the coda is the final part of the seismogram, which contains an incoherent mixture of body and surface waves. The rate of decay of the coda amplitude is a measure of attenuation (Fig. 6.4). On comparing coda waves in regions of different tectonic activity Aki noticed that there are systematic regional changes of attenuation in the earth. The question arose as to whether there might not be temporal changes too, and whether these changes might not be used to predict earthquakes.

Regions adjacent to plate boundaries (e.g., California and Japan) are highly attenuated, while intraplate regions (e.g., the central United States and the Baltic Shield) feature low attenuation. In general, a seismic signal will propagate farther across the Sahara or Australia as across the Mexican Volcanic Belt. The correlation of the attenuation with the degree of tectonic activity was found to be excellent. Thus it seemed natural to investigate coda-wave attenuation as an earthquake precursor.

The theory used by Aki and his students was based on the hypothesis that the coda is mainly backscattered energy from the middle crust. If the attenuation in the middle crust changes in time, the coda-wave amplitude should vary too. On the other hand, the origin of the coda as backscattered energy from crustal inhomogeneities has not been fully established. The effect of attenuation is difficult to separate from the source process itself. As Lomnitz-Adler and Lund (1992) have shown, source complexity alone can generate a fairly realistic coda without any need for assumptions about scattering along the path.

A. Jin and K. Aki (1988) favored the idea that the attenuation of seismic waves in the crust is largely due to backscattering from fluid-filled cracks. In 1989 they submitted a version of their work to the Subcommittee on Earthquake Prediction for its evaluation. It was rejected for the following reasons: (a) Data purporting to show differences in Q-values between fore- and aftershocks "cannot be considered relevant to the precursor problem"; (b) no quantitative definition of the anomaly was provided; (c) false alarms and failures to predict were not evaluated.

Jin and Aki had presented to the Subcommittee a list of 12 large earthquakes in which changes in coda Q were claimed to have occurred either before, during, or after the event. The reviewers doubted that the changes in Q had been adequately documented. The fact that coda Q was not yet

Fig. 6.4 Codas of small local earthquakes.

sufficiently well understood was stressed by all four reviewers. The fundamental paper (Aki and Chouet, 1975) claiming a relationship between amplitude decay of the coda and attenuation in the crust was now 18 years old, and still the misgivings on the nature of the coda had not been allayed.

The question seems to be, in this case, whether Jin and Aki intended to claim a specific *prediction* (by hindsight) of 12 large earthquakes or whether they rather intended to document a new *procedure* to be tested by others on future earthquakes. It seems to me that the latter interpretation applies. The reviewers did not dispute the possibility that measurements of Q might provide a valid earthquake precursor. Thus rejection of the method may have been premature.

TWILIGHT PHENOMENA

We shall now consider some examples of specific reports of earthquake precursors which fall in the twilight zone between the natural and the esoteric.

Changes in the earth's magnetic field relating to earthquakes have occasionally been reported in the range of 10 to 1000 γ; occasionally, however, extremely large effects have also been reported. Consider the following report of a magnetic effect in Mexico City some 150 years ago:

> In those days I was busying myself with my meteorological observations carried out on behalf of the Society. . . . The earthquake [of 1845, severely destructive in Mexico City] was barely over when I read the thermometer again and to my great surprise noticed that the column of mercury was divided in the middle in two large portions; and toward the lower reservoir sixteen droplets that could only be counted with the aid of a magnifying glass. . . . But there were more surprises. The penknife I had on my desk turned out to be absolutely magnetized, with the peculiarity that none of the other three blades that had remained folded in the handle during the earthquake were [magnetized]; and the magnetization was strong enough to be transferred to other iron objects by rubbing; furthermore, the position of the penknife was from north to south, with the blade pointing in the first-named direction. A graduated steel ruler or nonius that happened to lie on the desk in the same direction and at a distance of over one vara [83 cm] from the penknife was magnetized too; but not a large pair of scissors that lay near the ruler in the east-west direction, even though the scissors were uncovered while the ruler was in its leather case. These findings spurred my enquiries, so that I desired to examine other iron artifacts including the knives of the table set; but they had already been removed from their place during the earthquake and I was unable to ascertain their position. Yet I found one that was sufficiently strongly magnetized to attract steel needles and to gather a trail of iron filings (De Gómez, 1859:53–54, 58, 60, B. My translation).

This discussion is reproduced in full to demonstrate some features of historical accounts. Any ancient description can be cropped to such an extent that what is left makes no sense or sounds ridiculous. If the story about the disturbance of the thermometer had been left out, we might not have appreciated the meticulous mind of the observer. Of course the observation about the column of mercury can be easily accounted for by seismic vibrations while the magnetization of iron objects cannot.

In the 1986 Tangshan earthquake some effects suggestive of strong electromagnetic radiation were observed close to the fault trace. In one vegetable patch a number of bell peppers showed external burns. The bell peppers were sent to a laboratory, and the report suggested radiation damage. The matter was reported to me in full during my 1977 visit, but it was dropped from later reports and I believe cannot be found in English.

By comparison with earthquake reports of a century ago, recent reports seem impoverished. Some scientific journals have decided to reject descriptive accounts of great earthquakes. Earthquakes are enormously complex events, yet a misguided fastidiousness impels us to reject whatever we feel may be irrelevant or strange and to preserve only those data we think we can understand. How boring and presumptuous our papers must seem to scientists a century hence!

TANGSHAN RESISTIVITY ANOMALIES

Resistivity observations have been routinely carried out in China since shortly after the 1966 Xingtai earthquake. Background resistivity measurements were available at many stations in the Tangshan area since about 1970 (1972 in the case of the Tangshan station). The standard equipment consisted in a symmetrical quadrupole array (north-south and east-west lines) with a spacing of up to 1km between electrodes. The pattern is known in the West as a *Wenner array*.

Fig. 6.5 shows the resistivity background for 13 of the 14 stations located within a radius of 200 km from the epicenter of the Tangshan earthquake of July 28, 1976. The relative amplitudes of the Tangshan precursory anomalies $\Delta\rho/\rho$ for the same 13 stations were contoured as shown in Fig. 6.6.

There are some inconsistencies in the data. For example, the anomalous record at Tangshan station is not shown, though it was reportedly the largest with -4.4% relative amplitude. Xiaotangshan ("Little Tangshan") is shown with an anomaly of only -2.6%, which, if it is anywhere near Tangshan, should have changed the contours of Fig. 6.6 rather drastically. The Baodi station is shown with an anomaly of -3.2%, yet elsewhere it is stated that it *did not record* any anomalies (Zhang, 1990). Changli, at an epicentral distance of 75 km, with a reading of -5.6%, which is larger than Tangshan's, is shown as less than -4% in Fig. 6.6. The NS anomaly corresponding to station Heze appears to be significant (0.3 Ω-m or -2.6%), but unfortunately the EW component is missing and the background noise is not shown. The record starts just before the anomaly. Station Xiji has a *positive* anomaly of

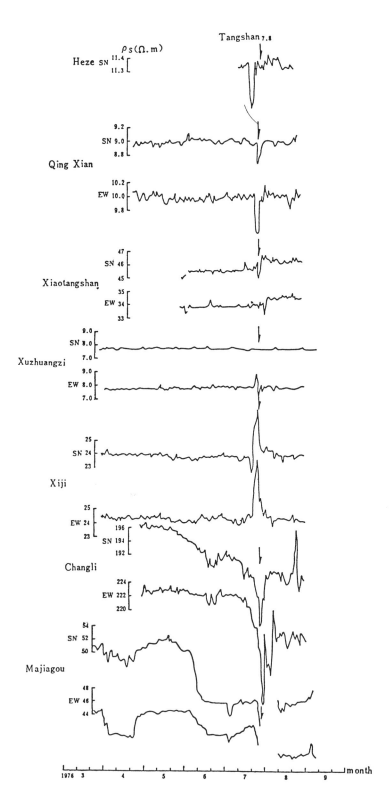

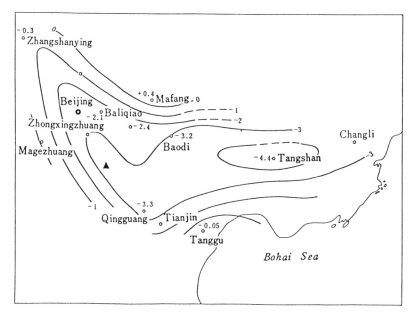

Fig. 6.6 *Contours of precursory resistivity anomalies for Tangshan. Reprinted by permission from* Earthquake Prediction, *Ma Zongjin et al., Eds. (1990), Springer-Verlag, New York.*

16.6%, the largest by far in absolute terms; but it is not shown in the contour map of Fig. 6.7 even though Xiji is less than 200 km from Tangshan.

These discrepancies should normally suffice to reject the observations as a whole. Yet they are representative of precursor observations in general (not necessarily in China). The reported resistivity anomalies are important even though they may not seem consistent from station to station. The anomaly began up to 8 hours before the earthquake, and the resistivity returned to normal within another eight hours or so. Resemblance with the self-potential anomaly found at station VTS for the Vrancea earthquake (see above) is quite suggestive. It seems plausible that the resistivity anomaly at Tangshan may have been caused by atmospherics, as G.A. Sobolev suspected. In that case, however, the huge reversed anomaly at Xiji would be difficult to explain.

The resistivity anomaly cannot be attributed to a rising water table. While the water table did rise in the Tangshan region some hours before the earthquake, it kept rising steeply after the earthquake. But the resistivity reversed. The immediate anomalies are particularly convincing in three cases where

←

Fig. 6.5 *Resistivity precursors recorded at various stations prior to the 1976 Tangshan earthquake. Reprinted by permission from* Earthquake Prediction, *Ma Zongjin et al., Eds. (1990), Springer-Verlag, New York.*

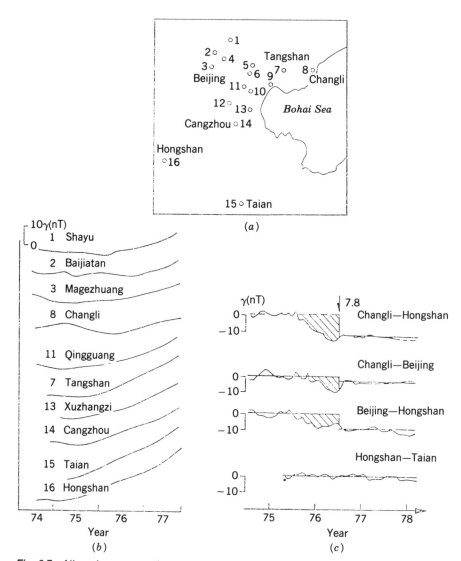

Fig. 6.7 *Alleged geomagnetic precursors recorded around Tangshan. Reprinted by permission from* Earthquake Prediction *by Ma Zongjin et al. (1990), Springer-Verlag, New York.*

background records were also provided, namely at Qing Xian, Xiji, and Changli. As for the medium-term resistivity anomalies claimed to be visible in Fig. 6.5, I cannot see them.

Variations in the geomagnetic field were also claimed to have preceded the Tangshan earthquake, on the grounds of a fluctuation with an amplitude of -11γ measured in early 1976 at Changli, 75 km east of Tangshan. The fluctuation looks like a sine wave of period T = 2 years for a total record length of less than 4 years. It might equally well have been interpreted as a *rise* of 11 γ one year before, depending on what is taken as the baseline (Fig. 6.7). Extrapolations of annual variations from other stations suggested to Chinese scientists that "the corrected geomagnetic anomalies before the Tangshan earthquake occurred principally in the Changli area" (Zhang, 1990, p.111).

THERMODYNAMICS OF EARTHQUAKE PRECURSORS

The question is the following: Can there be an objective way of detecting earthquake precursors? Otherwise the matter is beyond the jurisdiction of science. Up to the present, precursor research has lacked a theoretical framework that might serve as a general basis for discussing the available evidence. There have been *ad hoc* explanations for precursors but no common theory.

Consider the earth as an open system in stationary convection. The entropy production per unit volume is (Lomnitz, 1961)

$$S = (\mathbf{J}_q \cdot \mathbf{X}_u)/T \tag{6.1}$$

where $\mathbf{J}_q$ is the heat flow per unit area, T is the temperature, and $\mathbf{X}_u$ is the conjugated force corresponding to $\mathbf{J}_q$:

$$\mathbf{X}_u = -(\text{grad } T)/T. \tag{6.2}$$

Suppose that we introduce a perturbation in some state variable (say, the pressure P). The result is an *excited state*. Suppose, in fact, that an earthquake generates a stress drop anywhere in the earth:

$$\Delta\sigma = C^{-1}\mu D L^{-1}, \tag{6.3}$$

where $\Delta\sigma$ is the stress drop on the fault, C is a factor related to the geometry of faulting ($C = \pi/2$ for strike-slip faults), μ is the rigidity, D is the total displacement on the fault, and L is the half-width of the fault rupture. As a rule, D and L cannot both be determined from seismograms. Thus, unless D is independently known from the surface rupture, the stress drop must be estimated in other ways, for example, by assuming that the displacement on the fault was about $D \cong 10^{-4}L$, or in terms of the empirical relation

$$\Delta\sigma \cong M_0/(2.3 \ L^3), \tag{6.4}$$

where M_0 is the seismic moment. Most stress drops in earthquakes fall in the range of $\Delta\sigma = 10$ to 100 bars (1 bar = 0.1 MPa = 10^5 N/m^2). Since the atmospheric pressure equals 1 bar and the lithostatic pressure at the focal depth is on the order of thousands of bars this represents a small yet significant perturbation of the earth's steady-state pressure field.

Any convecting system is self-organized into surface regions of convergence and divergence, or downwelling and upwelling. In the earth these correspond to compressional and extensional tectonic regimes. At subduction zones the regime is convergent and compressional, while at spreading ridges it is divergent and extensional. The pressure drop ΔP caused by an earthquake must be of opposite sign for either regime.

The fault displacement D is not recovered after the earthquake. It generates a residual stress (as referred to the preseismic state), which is superimposed on the regional stress distribution. As the region gradually returns to the steady-state stress distribution, this residual stress is released in the form of aftershocks. We suggest that this "homeostatic" reaction of steady-state systems may have to do with self-organization.

The flows generated as a result of a seismic perturbation ΔP may be of different kinds: (a) flows of matter $\mathbf{J}_k$—particularly of groundwater and electrons; (b) differentials in heat flow $\mathbf{J}_q$; (c) chemical reaction rates $\mathrm{J_c}$. The entropy balance of the system may be stated as follows:

$$\rho \frac{ds}{dt} = - \operatorname{div} \mathbf{J}_s + S \tag{6.5}$$

which says that the change of specific entropy s in the system is caused by the negative divergence of an entropy flow

$$\mathbf{J}_s = \left(\mathbf{J}_q - \sum_k \mu_k \mathbf{J}_k \right) \Big/ T, \tag{6.6}$$

plus an entropy production

$$S = \left(\mathbf{J}_q \cdot \mathbf{X}_q + \sum_k \mathbf{J}_k \cdot \mathbf{X}_k + A \mathrm{J_c} \right) \Big/ T, \tag{6.7}$$

all per unit volume. The derivation follows De Groot (1952). The vectors $\mathbf{X}_q$ and $\mathbf{X}_k$ are called the *conjugate forces* corresponding to the vector flows $\mathbf{J}_q$ and $\mathbf{J}_k$. In the case of a chemical reaction of rate $\mathrm{J_c}$ the chemical affinity A plays a role similar to an $\mathbf{X}$ as a conjugate force. The μ_k are chemical potentials per unit mass for each phase k of the material. Thus the conjugate forces are

$$\mathbf{X}_k = \mathbf{F}_k - T \operatorname{grad} (\mu_k/T) \tag{6.8}$$

where the $\mathbf{F}_k$ represent the external accelerations, and

$$A = - \sum_k \mu_k \, v_k, \qquad (6.9)$$

where the v_k are the stoichiometric coefficients of each component.

Now suppose that the system is isothermal, that is, the temperature T remains constant at every point of the system. This is approximately true for time intervals on the order of a seismic cycle. Let ΔP be the pressure drop generated by the earthquake. This pressure drop must extend over the entire system; it is a function of the coordinates and of time. As an example, let us calculate the transient flow of water $\mathbf{J}_H$ induced by this perturbation. This recovery flow may be represented by an Onsager equation of the form

$$\mathbf{J}_H = \sum_n L_{iH} \mathbf{X}_H + L_{iq} \mathbf{X}_q, \qquad (6.10)$$

where the coefficients L_{ij} are known as Onsager's coefficients. The summation is over all types of flows in the system: Any perturbation of stationarity generates flows of every possible kind. For example, a pressure drop generates water flows but also electromagnetic flows and chemical flows. Each Onsager coefficient L_{ij} denotes the intensity of the specific cross-effect induced by phase i on phase j. Onsager showed that in the linear case (i.e., for small perturbations), the flows are symmetrical so that $L_{ij} = L_{ji}$ for all pairs of different phases. Thus the piezoelectric effect equals the electrostrain effect.

In the steady state there are no flows in the system, except for the heat flow $\mathbf{J}_q$. If we now introduce a pressure perturbation ΔP, the transient forces will be

$$\Delta \mathbf{X}_k = - v_k \, \mathrm{grad} \, \Delta P, \qquad (6.11)$$

where v_k is the specific volume of phase k. (Note that "phase" in this context may include flows of electrons.) In the present example the rate of flow of water towards the hypocentral region will be, according to Eq (6.10),

$$\mathbf{J}_H = - \sum_k L_{iH} v_H \, \mathrm{grad} \, \Delta P, \qquad (6.12)$$

since $\Delta \mathbf{X}_q = 0$ in an isothermal system. This takes account of all other phases i that may also change as a result of the earthquake. The negative sign of the vector $\mathbf{J}_H$ means that the water flows in the direction of the negative pressure gradient. Similar equations may be written for other transient flows.

In conclusion, the dynamic stationarity of the system requires that every stress gradient be countered by flows directed in such a way as to reduce the perturbation. In conclusion, after a stress drop the water table in the epicentral region must rise.

But the pressure transient may begin well before the earthquake. The earthquake is embedded in a strain transient that exceeds the time-space frame of the seismic transient by an order of magnitude at least. Beyond the region of rupture the time function of the strain step is spread over a period of up to a year or more, and the offset due to the earthquake proper may not even be visible (Fig. 4.7). The flows that occur before the earthquake are designated as precursors, while those that occur during or after the earthquake are coseismic or postseismic. In a similar manner the earthquakes generated by the pressure step before the earthquake are known as foreshocks, while those that are generated after the earthquake are aftershocks. From the shape of the pressure anomaly we may infer that the precursors may be of different sign inside or outside the locked region, and that the coseismic anomaly (and some related precursors and aftereffects) may only be detectable in the locked region.

AFTERSHOCKS AND PRECURSORS

A consequence of the existence of positive Onsager coefficients is the fact that any transient, of whatever nature, generates all kinds of flows in the system. Each flow is directed along the field lines of the perturbation. Because earthquakes are mainly mechanical perturbations, they generate chiefly flows of fluids (e.g., water), but also chemical reactions, electromagnetic currents, and increased heat flow (if the isothermal restriction is lifted.) The flow corresponding to the main perturbation is dominant because $L_{ii} > > L_{ij}$ ($i \neq j$).

The plate boundary always deforms in such a way as to minimize the resulting entropy production. From Eqs (6.7), (6.11), and (6.12) this entropy production is proportional to $(\text{grad } \Delta P)^2$. The slip along the boundary is irreversible: Thus some permanent tilt will remain in the region. Otherwise there would be no mountain building.

Aftershocks are decay processes that may be described by a Pólya process of the form

$$P(t) = \frac{\lambda (1 + \alpha)}{1 + \alpha \lambda t} \Delta t, \qquad \alpha > 0 \qquad (6.13)$$

where $P(t)$ is the probability of 1 event occurring at time t during an interval Δt. For $\alpha = 0$ a Poisson process is obtained. Prigogine has given a more general expression for the decay of the entropy production in rate processes:

$$S(t) = S_0 + \frac{\alpha_1}{t+\beta} + \frac{\alpha_2}{(t+\beta)^2} + \cdots, \tag{6.14}$$

where $t = 0$ is the time of the perturbation. Thus the recovery rate slows down approximately hyperbolically with time. In seismology a first-degree approximation is normally used:

$$\lambda(t) \cong \frac{\alpha}{t + \beta}, \tag{6.15}$$

known as Omori's Law, where $\lambda(t)$ is the rate of occurrence of aftershocks t days after the occurrence of the main shock. The higher-order terms in Eq (6.14) may be neglected when $t \gg \beta$. For relatively short times Utsu (1969–1970) has proposed the approximation

$$\lambda(t) = \alpha/(t + \beta)^p, \tag{6.16}$$

where p falls between 1 and 2 and may vary from one aftershock sequence to another.

The energy transient in aftershock sequences is

$$\Delta E(t) = \int_V dV \int_0^t T \, dS , \tag{6.17}$$

whence introducing Eq (6.14) and neglecting higher-order terms one finds that ΔE increases as $\log (t + \beta)$ in agreement with Omori's Law. Note that Omori's Law assumes that the magnitude distribution of aftershocks remains time-invariant during the sequence; but this is indeed observed as a rule. It may be taken as one indication of the ergodicity of the system.[1]

The following picture of the aftershock process now begins to emerge. The main shock suddenly deforms the region as referred to the steady state. The residual strain pattern is due to fault displacement and may be imagined as superimposed on the steady-state pattern. It causes stress concentrations to arise on the rupture plane itself as well as on its locked prolongation and on numerous small faults scattered throughout the region. As energy (i.e., water, etc.) flows back into the region from the surrounding system, it powers these stress concentrations, causing them to rupture randomly. Each after-

---

[1] This is perhaps the most telling argument for the steady-state theory. It was first proposed in Lomnitz (1966).

shock removes a small part of the residual strain pattern. Eventually the state of stress in the region returns to the steady-state level.

If this picture is correct, there should be a similarity between the residual stress field induced by an earthquake and the pattern of spatial distribution of aftershocks. This resemblance indeed exists and it can be very striking (Fig. 6.8). In the case of strike-slip faulting the aftershock activity may concentrate first at one end of the rupture and then at the other. It may generate a "butterfly pattern," as found in model experiments of shear cracks in homogeneous media (Fig. 6.9).

Aftershocks seldom extend beyond the fractured region because the coseismic strain anomaly is of local extent. In other words, the large-scale, mainly aseismic strain anomaly is much larger and is spread over a broader region than the seismic slip. Depending on when the earthquake occurs (early

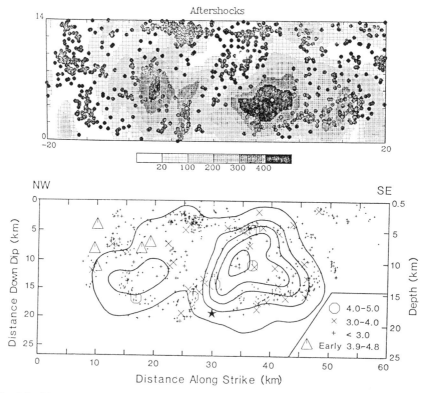

Fig. 6.8 *Distribution of aftershocks in space, on the fault plane of the 1989 Loma Prieta, California, earthquake. There appears to be a negative correlation with the amount of slip during the main shock (contours). From G.C. Beroza (1981), near-source modeling of the Loma Prieta earthquake: evidence for heterogeneous slip and implications for earthquake hazard,* Bull. Seismol. Soc. Am., *81, p. 1617. By permission of the Seismological Society of America.*

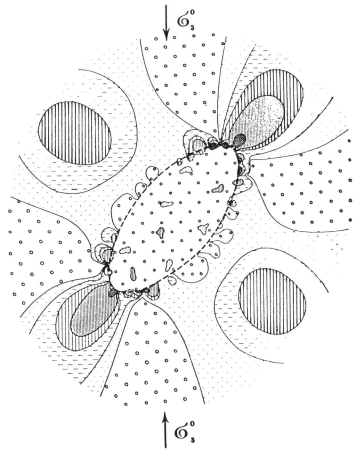

Fig. 6.9 *"Butterfly" patterns generated experimentally by straining optically active materials. From Mjachkin et al. (1984).*

at the beginning, towards the middle, or near the end of the anomaly), there may or may not be any precursors (including foreshocks).

We should expect some symmetry between the causes of foreshocks and aftershocks. While aftershocks are caused by residual strains due to fault slip, foreshocks are caused by the strain lag in the earthquake region, due to the fault being locked while deformation of the surrounding region has already begun.

7

Earthquake Hazard

Hindsight is twenty-twenty.
—American saying

THE TUNNELING EFFECT

In the present chapter we deal mainly with the distribution of earthquakes in time. A separate discussion of statistical behavior in space and in time is a concession to our weak capacity of imagining or representing four-dimensional objects such as the earthquake process, which is actually a single time-space process.

One basic question is the following: To what extent can earthquakes be modeled in time-space as independent events? If they can, the prediction of earthquake hazard boils down to studying the mean rate of incidence of earthquakes at one place relative to another.

Consider first the independence of earthquake occurrence in space. Let p_{ij} be the probability that an earthquake in region i will be followed by one in region j. This is called a *transition probability*. If the transition probabilities of earthquakes between two regions are independent, we have

$$p_{ij} = p_{.j}, \tag{7.1}$$

meaning that the probability of an earthquake in region i being followed by another in region j equals the probability of earthquakes occurring in j. Suppose an earthquake occurs in Mexico; if the transition probabilities are independent, the probability that the next earthquake will occur in Afghanistan will simply be the probability of occurrence of Afghan earthquakes (except for the aftershocks of the Mexican earthquake, of course). This was actually what I reported back in 1967, when I used extremely large regions, namely the 30-odd regions Gutenberg and Richter (1954) used to classify world earthquakes. If instead we use a finer grid, say the 700-plus smaller regions of the Flinn-Engdahl regionalization scheme (see Chapter 5), a strikingly different pattern emerges.

Fig. 7.1 shows a histogram of the number of transitions *versus* the distance between Flinn–Engdahl regions, for earthquakes of magnitude 7 and above that occurred during 1900–1990. The distance is given in regions: thus "0" means the same region, "1" an adjacent region, "2" a next-to-adjacent region and so on. Note that the histogram is bimodal, with transition probabilities highest for distances of zero to two Flinn–Engdahl regions. This effect might have been foreseen: It is caused by the occurrence of aftershocks.

But there is a second peak at a distance of seven regions; and this peak is separated from the aftershock peak by a distinct *minimum*! The pattern of transition probabilities is shaped like a Mexican hat. Thus during 1900–1990 there was not a single instance of an earthquake being followed by another just five regions away. This is a significant effect. The size of the Flinn–Engdahl regions is not constant; it is tailored to the seismicity. This result suggests that after any large earthquake there is a zone of silence around the epicentral region, followed by enhanced activity some seven to nine regions away. We call this the *tunneling effect*.

The tunnelling effect was first proposed by Charles Darwin (1860). He pointed out that the volcanic eruptions that followed upon the Chile earth-

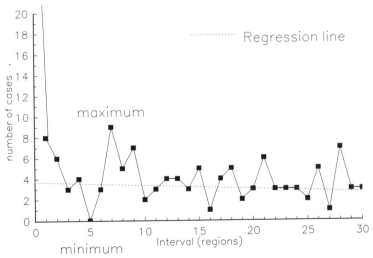

Fig. 7.1 *Histogram of transition frequencies between successive events as a function of distance in Flinn-Engdahl regions. The large maximum at zero regions corresponds to aftershocks. From C. Lomnitz (1993). Published by the American Geophysical Union.*

quake of February 20, 1835, did not occur in the epicentral region, which was off the coast of Concepción, but much farther south in the Reloncavi Straits. Apparently the influence of the earthquake extended over a much larger area than the seismic rupture. The tunneling effect thus represents an essential feature of the earthquake process. It explains why ruptures do not simply propagate sequentially up and down the plate boundary.

Experiments with moment-ratio imaging (Chapter 5) suggest that the tunneling effect must be a result of geometry. The stress drop lowers the probability of rupture to a distance measuring up to six times the rupture length on either side, depending on the magnitude of the moment release. The central energy peak is transformed into a trough. At the same time, the influx of recovery energy into the region raises the stress over a much broader region, thus fueling the aftershock process. Beyond the zone of lowered seismic hazard the probability of rupture is increased. The resulting strain pattern is shaped like a Mexican hat.

The existence of the tunneling effect means that large earthquakes cannot be independent events. Large earthquakes in South America tend to be followed by large earthquakes in South America, and large earthquakes in eastern Asia by large events in eastern Asia—but not too close to each other. There is a quiet zone or "donut pattern" around the epicentral area in which the probability of occurrence of an earthquake is near-zero, as Fig. 7.1 suggests. Similarly, as Lomnitz-Adler (1989) has pointed out, there is a "dead time" after the occurrence of a large earthquake in which the probability of another large earthquake is negligible.

The space-time dependence of large earthquakes on the preceding events represents the theoretical basis of statistical earthquake prediction. The probability of occurrence becomes time-dependent (Fig. 5.3). On the other hand, the dependence between one earthquake and the next is not strong—and it becomes weaker at very long times or for very large events. If we use the regression line in Fig. 7.1 as a criterion, the deviation from randomness is not very striking. For many practical purposes we may adopt the assumption of independent intervals as an approximation and use different interval distributions. These various options are the subject of the present chapter.

BASIC CONCEPTS OF RISK AND PREDICTION

Risk is hazard times cost. It is often defined as the seriousness of an event times the likelihood that it will happen. For instance, the risk of dying from a mosquito bite equals the incidence of mosquito bites times the mortality from the same. Similarly, earthquake risk (in dollars) equals the earthquake hazard (the probability of incidence of an earthquake of a given magnitude) times the expected loss, evaluated for each magnitude level and integrated over all magnitudes.

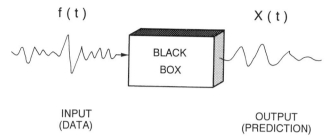

Fig. 7.2 *Diagram for Wiener prediction of time series.*

In the next chapter we argue that this model can be applied to small earthquakes ("mosquito bites") much better than to large ones ("epidemics of mosquito bites"). The problem is nonlinearity. But first let us describe (with a critical eye) what is commonly being done.

Basic structural models for predicting earthquake risk may be derived from the fundamental work of Norbert Wiener (1956) on the linear extrapolation of time series. The basic ideas are due to Alan Turing. Wiener's model is shown in Fig. 7.2. The time series on the left is called the data input. To the right is the predicted time series. In the case of earthquakes, the input series is a point process. The *black box* is a mathematical model capable of generating an output that resembles the future time series in some optimal way.

In Wiener's treatment, future values are assumed to be linear functionals of the input f:

$$X(t) = \int_{-\infty}^{t} f(t - u)\, \xi(du), \tag{7.2}$$

where $f(t)$ is a one-dimensional univariate process along the time axis. If the axis is not time but some other variable, the prediction is called an *extrapolation*. Extensions to marked and multivariate processes are possible.

Wiener's approach was initially used for steering antiaircraft fire during World War II. The input $f(t)$ represented the visual positions of the enemy aircraft as sighted by the gunner. The predicted time series $X(t)$ stood for the future positions of the aircraft; this function controlled the aiming mechanism of the gun. Since the shell had to rendezvous with a target that was also taking evasive action by seemingly random deviations from its expected course, the function $X(t)$ had to take into account the ballistic path of the shell plus a spectrum of frequency components of $f(t)$ that included the observed behavior of the pilot. In the special case of a stationary input, Wiener showed that the optimal linear prediction is based on the Fourier amplitude spectrum of the path of the aircraft.

Also, in the linear case there is a tradeoff between the input data f and the model ξ. The more input data we have, the fewer parameters are needed for defining the model. Conversely, the better the theoretical model the less input data would be required for a good prediction. For example, if we were personally acquainted with the pilot we might be able to foresee the pilot's evasive tactics, and we could dispense with sophisticated mathematical models for predicting them (but in this case we might not feel like shooting the pilot down).

More generally, if a complete data set were available the black box would become expendable or could be replaced by a passive filter, since a "complete" data set would contain all future states of the system as well. Conversely, if the black box were all-knowing, we would merely need a set of initial conditions to predict the future. If one had a reliable model of the human mind and its reactions under ground fire, one would not need to follow the plane's position in the gunsight. Taking aim and pulling the trigger would do. In fact, the gunner might be replaced by a robot. *All-knowing* is here equivalent to *deterministic*. Thus randomness becomes a measure of missing information, and the uncertainty principle becomes a reminder that all-knowing black boxes don't exist.

For purposes of earthquake prediction, a few decades' worth of data is all we have, let alone records of all earthquakes since the beginning of time. We chanced upon the scene as the experiment was already in progress—several billions of years after it all began. Therefore we are obliged to rely on statistical models.

THE SAFE SHUTDOWN EARTHQUAKE (SSE)

As a specific example of earthquake risk assessment, let us consider *critical facilities* such as dams, hospitals, military command posts and nuclear power plants. A nuclear power plant has a lifetime on the order of $D = 30$ years, which is dictated by the obsolescence rate of the equipment. It is an expensive and frail contraption. This was not ordained by nature; rather, it is a result of a peculiar way of looking at risks.

It is a standard assumption that nuclear plants must be zero-risk installations. Regardless of their actual operational life they are conceived to outlast the planners who designed them and the entire civilization of technicians and users. This is one possible attitude toward risks. At the opposite end of the spectrum of risk attitudes is the automobile. Cars are rugged, lightweight, economical, and expendable. They tend to become disposable. Their lifetime is not expected to exceed about $D = 5$–10 years. They are among the most hazardous devices of modern technology; yet, on the whole, they perform much better than one would expect given the kind of operators allowed to handle them. For example, cars are engineered to sustain large horizontal and vertical accelerations. They can be operated under a wide range of critical conditions, and they can be repaired by the user. They perform exceedingly well in earthquakes. Could critical facilities be designed with a similar approach in mind?

There is some evidence to the effect that nuclear power plants (NPPs) are overengineered against earthquakes. Since earthquake risk is highly site-specific and practically determines the design of the plant, every NPP is nonstandard. As a result, the introduction of design improvements is slowed down since the experiences gathered at one plant are not directly applicable to other plants. On the other hand, no NPP has ever gone through an earthquake large enough to require a power shutdown, though some have come close. The earthquake of April 13, 1992, on the Rhine graben ($M = 5.9$) tripped the seismic switch (but not the shutdown mechanism) at the *Biblis A* nuclear power plant in Germany. But a perfect safety record is an untested record. It is equivalent to marketing a new car model without a test drive on a bumpy road.

Incidents involving human operational error are frequent in NPPs. These accidents can be quite serious, as in the Three Mile Island plant, Pennsylvania, or even catastrophic as in the Chernobyl plant, Ukraine. Excessive complexity of operation is often responsible. The frequency of accidents involving human error, as we shall see, might be part of the price we pay for the absence of earthquake emergencies. Ironically, hazardous operation is to some extent the result of a peculiar philosophy of seismic safety.

The main specification for the seismic design of a nuclear power plant is a scenario known as the *Safe Shutdown Earthquake* (SSE). It is the largest possible imaginary earthquake which still allows the facility to be safely shut down. The shutdown procedure is critical: The nuclear reaction must be gradually moderated and reduced to zero. This takes time. The safety doctrine proposed decades ago by the Atomic Energy Commission of the United States recognized that a strong earthquake at the wrong time might interfere with a safe shutdown procedure. This risk is judged inadmissible. Therefore the SSE must be specified as the largest earthquake that can conceivably occur at the site. In practice, the SSE is an earthquake with a return period of $T = 36,000$ years.

Other critical facilities such as dams use a design concept called the *Maximum Credible Earthquake* (MCE), which is similarly defined as the largest earthquake that can believably be expected to occur at the site. Since human credulity may fluctuate between rather wide extremes, the value adopted for the MCE depends on whatever takes place in people's minds during the period of design. At times the term *Minimum Incredible Earthquake* would be more appropriate!

Once the SSE (or the MCE) has been ascertained, the next step is to determine the *Operating Basis Earthquake* (OBE). This is defined as a smaller (but also imaginary) earthquake such that the facility can be kept running normally, for example, without a power failure. The reason why *two* design earthquakes (SSE and OBE) are needed is simple. The reactor is the part of the plant actually involved in the shutdown procedure; but it is a small part of the plant. It would be fussy to design, say, the water purifying plant or the generator housing to the same exacting standards as the primary cooling system, or the graphite rod assembly which must drop into the core in order to moderate the nuclear reaction. Power distribution lines can take damage and the plant can still be shut down safely. The main thing—in terms of safety—is *scramming the reactor* so the core temperatures stay below the melting point.

Thus the OBE is used for designing all parts of the plant not vitally involved in the shutdown operation. This includes parts of the secondary cooling system and other failsafe devices. In practice the value of the OBE is taken as half the SSE. If the SSE is specified as a horizontal design acceleration of 0.40 g the OBE would be taken as 0.20 g.

Other critical installations also feature this split-level approach to seismic safety. In a hydroelectric power plant, for example, the dam itself is designed against the MCE while the penstocks and the power house are specified for half the MCE—called, in this case, the *Design Basis Earthquake* (DBE). Failure of the penstocks or generators would produce a power failure, which is bad enough but acceptable in an emergency. A dam break, on the other hand, might flood the valley downstream and endanger human settlements in the path of the flood. Such accidents have occurred. Between the Puentes, Spain, dam break in 1802 and the Fréjus, France, disaster of 1959 there have been about a dozen major dam failures with casualties totaling nearly 10,000 dead. The worst accident occurred in Johnstown, Pennsylvania, in 1889. None of these accidents, however, was caused by an earthquake.

THE ROLE OF THE HAZARD CONSULTANT

The regulatory agencies specify approaches and procedures to be used by consultants for estimating the minimum design parameters of a power plant. In the case of hydroelectric power plants it is often the utility that makes up its own rules and regulations, which are normally stricter than those required by the state.

In the case of a nuclear facility, consultants are normally required to produce:

(a) a geologic map containing all recognized active faults within a radius of 200–300 km from the site;

(b) a more detailed geologic map describing the position, extent, and rupture potential of all active or suspected active faults within a radius of 100 km of the site;

(c) a catalog of earthquakes recorded at the site or that might have been recorded if the site had been occupied, together with the estimated magnitudes and accelerations at the site;

(d) estimates of maximum magnitudes and *b*-values (explained below) for each source or source area that might affect the site;

(e) a tectonic model supporting the above estimates and capable of integrating the hazards computed for each source region into a coherent picture of earthquake risk for the site;

(f) a statistical and/or deterministic evaluation of the above, to produce an estimated value of the design acceleration corresponding to the SSE.

Safety reports should also spell out the uncertainties involved in complying with each of these steps. Not all consultants are thorough in this regard. Fault mapping is particularly critical and uncertain. Thus many recent destructive earthquakes have occurred on faults previously unknown or not recognized as active. Some active faults have been unexpectedly discovered during site investigations, to the dismay of the planners; others are never found until they rupture. Until it ruptured in the June 23, 1992, earthquake ($M = 7.4$), the Landers fault had not been recognized as a major active fault in Califor-nia. The Northridge, California earthquake of January 17, 1994 was caused by an unknown fault. The Tangshan fault, though perfectly mapped, was not thought to be active prior to the 1976 earthquake ($M = 7.8$).

Extrapolation of magnitudes for long return periods is made on the basis of the *b-value*, which multiplies M in

$$\log_{10} N = a - b M, \tag{7.3}$$

where N is the expected number of earthquakes exceeding a magnitude M, and a is the logarithm of the sample size for $M \geq 0$. Beno Gutenberg and Charles Francis Richter (the authors of this empirical formula) cautioned against its extrapolation. They knew that statisticians frown on prognostications carried beyond a time period equivalent to the span of the data. Projections can be affected by many errors; some of them cannot be foreseen at the time the projection is made. A projection made in the 1850's about the expanding use of the horse carriage predicted, on the basis of a statistical extrapolation, that by 1950 European cities would be knee-deep in horse manure.

Tectonic models can also be quite controversial. In general, tectonic interpretations do not age well. As likely as not, they will have changed by the time the facility is ready to be built. Seismic safety cannot rely on estimation procedures, however refined, for the probability of future extreme earthquakes.

The above discussion is meant to make explicit some of the basic pitfalls behind volumes of safety regulations. Much of this is common knowledge among specialists. One basic point, however, seems to have escaped the attention it deserves: The requirement of estimating an earthquake with a return period of 36,000 years confronts the seismologist with an impossible task. He or she is requested to extrapolate a few decades worth of data to a time period that exceeds the recorded history of mankind.

The total period of human settlement on the American continent spans only 14,000 years. Thus by evaluating the Safe Shutdown Earthquake we are implicitly estimating the size of an event that may have occurred when North America was ruled by mastodons and saber-tooth tigers.

On the principle "Ask a stupid question and get a stupid answer", the solution to the SSE dilemma is often unsatisfactory. C. Northcote Parkinson (1960) once pointed out that unreasonable taxation can turn honest men into habitual criminals. So can unreasonable safety regulations. The attempt to circumvent irrational risk specifications has turned some honest geophysicists into liars and squanderers of public funds.

Consultants are hired by utilities for their prestige with the regulatory agencies, the agencies who are ultimately responsible for issuing construction clearances. Financial institutions who advance the cash for building the facility follow the same guidelines of risk evaluation laid down by the regulatory agencies. The consultant is aware of his client's predicament: Both would prefer the least costly design compatible with safety standards. Yet the consultant cannot afford to be accommodating. His safety report might be turned down, and he might acquire a reputation of being lenient. This is the kind of "black eye" no consultant can afford. It could mar his professional record. On the other hand, excessive cost of a facility due to compliance with complex or unreasonable regulatory requirements has never harmed a reputation and is eventually passed along to the consumer.

This situation has nearly ruined the consulting profession. A geophysical consultant, like a lawyer or a doctor, enjoys a position of trust. Consultants must be public-minded, otherwise their expertise cannot be trusted. This is true regardless of whether the client is a public utility or a private business. I have been a consultant to a state-owned public utility in South America for a number of years. I was retained for interpreting the seismic safety recommendations issued by regulatory agencies and the safety reports of consulting firms. Essentially I was hired by the man in the street to make sure that the people's tax money was well spent.

For this it was necessary to wade through the double-talk in reams of reports. One consulting firm recommended excavating a deep tunnel that would cross an active fault. The tunnel was to feed the penstocks of a power plant. The consultants proposed insuring the tunnel for a sizable sum of money, and to gamble on the odds that no earthquake would occur. This would be cheaper (they maintained) than the alternate solution, which involved a tunnel along the other bank of the river. Such insurance would have been readily available in the consultants' home country, but not in a developing country. Eventually the taxpayer would have been saddled with the liability. Thus the best solution turned out to be the one the consultants thought was too expensive. I soon learned the lesson: The poorer you are, the more you have to pay. This is *Matthew's Law*: "Unto every one that hath shall be given, and he shall have abundance; but from him that hath not shall be taken away even that which he hath'' (Matthew 25:29).

Consulting practiced on behalf of the public can be rewarding, but it carries a lot of responsibility. When such a consultant flies First Class his or her heart travels in the steerage section, where the people who actually paid for the consultant's ticket are sitting.

Similar dilemmas confront the geophysicist who works for a regulatory agency. Nuclear power regulation is a two-tiered system, with national agencies voluntarily submitting their designs to the International Atomic Energy Agency (IAEA) in Vienna for approval. Most national agencies would rather be known for their toughness on safety than having their safety reports picked to pieces by roving teams of IAEA experts.

Excessive safety may take the form of (a) unreasonably massive or unwieldy equipment or construction; (b) too many complicated failsafe devices such as duplicate piping, valves, circuits and gadgets; (c) procrastination and technological lag. All three factors tend to increase the cost, hasten the obsolescence, and heighten the vulnerability of a nuclear power plant. Examples:

(a) Mexico's Laguna Verde nuclear power plant was ordered from the manufacturer in the mid-1960s. Due to protracted clearance procedures it was put on stream in 1989. By that time the original design was 30 years old. Who needs a 1960 Chevy for the price of a new Ferrari?

(b) The Three Mile Island, Pennsylvania, accident produced a small yet inadmissible amount of radioactive atmospheric pollution. The accident occurred in 1979 and was the result of a chain of human errors. It all began with a routine housecleaning operation. The operators shut down the plant in order to clean the water purifying plant, then forgot to open the water intake gates again. When the plant was turned on, it was starved for water and automatically switched the backup cooling system on, but by the time the operators realized their mistake the core had begun to melt. A safety valve in the backup circuit had gotten stuck in the open position and bled steam into the containment shell causing the core to overheat. This valve was one of many so that its existence was unknown to the operating crew. It was rated as having a low safety priority. It took experts flown into Pittsburgh eight hours to figure out what was wrong. All that time radioactive steam continued to escape into the containment, and some of it eventually leaked out—even though the reactor had been scrammed for hours.

The complexity of a nuclear power plant is daunting and, to some extent, unnecessary. The split-level safety concept was at the root of the Three Mile Island accident. The valve that got stuck represented an insignificant fraction of the total cost of the plant, but since it belonged to a backup circuit it did not have to be designed according to the same specifications as the components of the primary circuit. If the overall specifications had been more reasonable, the entire plant could have been built to a uniformly high safety standard. In previous tests the faulty valve had shown a reliability of 90%, that is, it got stuck once in every 10 operations. This was Russian roulette but it satisfied the rules. The safety bulletin had been duly received and filed away at Three Mile Island. So the valve got stuck on the first try—tough luck. Such double standards of quality would be unthinkable in a quality automobile.

Russian-built plants of the Chernobyl type have fewer frills than American plants—but also fewer safeguards in case something goes seriously wrong. They are to a Western plant what the old East German "Trabi" is to a West German Mercedes. They lack a containment shell around the reactor. This may have been a fatal flaw in the 1986 Chernobyl (rhymes with *noble*, not with *automobile*) disaster. The accident itself was caused by human error. In terms of ease of operation the Russian plants are just as cumbersome as the Western designs. Power plants were never meant to be user-friendly.

(c) The Bodega Bay nuclear power project, north of San Francisco, was scuttled by environmentalist opposition in the 1950's. Experts hired by the Sierra Club went on TV to claim that the plant, if built, would jump 30 feet up in the air as a result of an earthquake. The utility gave up and decided to concentrate on fossil-fuel power generation instead. For more than 30 years irreversible pollution damage to the environment occurred in San Francisco Bay as the price of energy inched up. Finally a kind of energy starvation, in the form of urban blight, set in. Meanwhile, the Bodega Bay site just sits there: It remains one of the safest solid-rock sites in the state in terms of actual earthquake activity.

(d) Sensible seismic safety guidelines were proposed as early as 1962 for the American Nuclear Regulatory Agency, then called the Atomic Energy Commission:

- "The probability of an area experiencing an earthquake of a given intensity is *impossible* to establish";
- "it is impractical to build earthquake resistance onto an existing design";
- "the general arrangement of the plant should be such that different components of the plant do not vibrate independently in a manner that they will damage each other";
- "long pipes that are not supported on a monolithic foundation structure are particularly dangerous";
- "the center of gravity of the plant and major components should be near the ground";
- the structures of *small reactors* usually have sufficient strength and rigidity for earthquake resistance if properly mounted" (Moore, 1962).

Thus experts had recognized as early as 1962 that some gambles were not worth pursuing. Asking geophysicists to estimate the future maximum acceleration at a site was the kind of game we should never have gotten into. Also, people realized back in 1962 that "small is beautiful" and that seismic design must be fully integrated into any plant, as a standard feature, no matter where the plant is located. *All power plants* should be able to resist earthquake vibrations. Cars can, so why not power plants?

(e) Having been occasionally involved in seismic safety clearance procedures of critical installations, including nuclear power plants, I strongly feel that the public deserves to be informed about the real issues. Seismic safety is but one aspect of nuclear clearance; yet it is the one aspect that never fails to get top billing. Why? Earthquakes are dramatic events that fire the imagination and that lend themselves to grandstanding. The subject of earthquakes will rivet the attention of any dinner party for five minutes. There are usually plenty of other reasons for opposing a power project to be built upstream of one's community; yet the earthquake issue is the one to bet on. It is the rare opponent who has the wit to enquire whether the alarm buttons in the control room can be seen by the operator. People naively assume that such trivial matters have been taken care of. At the time of the Three Mile Island accident one-third of all warning lights on the control panel were concealed by dangling tags with messages such as "MAINTENANCE." Not that it made any difference: the offending safety valve had no panel light.

There are special-interest groups for and against anything. This is a fact of life. But some groups will announce in advance that they won't listen to opponents. Thus there is no reason for listening to them. Their arguments become irrelevant, no matter how sensible they may often be. This situation invites the kind of double talk called "technical" language. A loss-of-coolant accident in the primary water piping is described as a "Primary LOCA". Why not just call it a pipe break? Euphemisms are rampant where plain English would serve the interest of the public better.

EARTHQUAKE CYCLES AND RESCALED RANGE ANALYSIS

Issues in earthquake risk estimation for critical facilities are important: They may affect entire industries. But in the long run, the more important problems are found in risk estimation for average urban construction. Let us examine some of the procedures by which ordinary risk estimation is carried out. Nearly all damage and loss of life due to earthquakes actually occurs in "noncritical" facilities such as apartment buildings, which are designed according to standard building codes.

Earthquake risk being a highly nonlinear phenomenon, we'll begin with a discussion of nonlinear risk estimation and leave the linear methods for the end of the chapter.

Geophysical time series include earthquakes, rainfall, floods, groundwater fluctuations, and variations in river discharge. They are neither linear nor, strictly speaking, stationary; rather, they commonly exhibit aperiodic trends and fluctuations. We commonly speak of *cycles* of rainfall, floods, droughts and so on, even though it is mostly understood that no real cyclic phenomena are involved. Seismologists or engineers are fond of denying that earthquake cycles exist: What they mean is that no single spectral line dominates the spectrum of the time series of earthquakes. Of course earthquakes are not produced by a clockwork. But earthquakes do come bunched together in cycles of 10, 20, or 30 years' duration separated by long intervals of quiet. Such cycles can be observed in California, China, Mexico, Italy, and many other regions.

Specific models for predicting nonlinear clustering processes began to be developed in the 1930s, but their intimate connection with fractality and self-organization processes was only recognized much later. Pioneers like H.E. Hurst were merely interested in developing simple procedures for predicting the evolution of nonlinear geophysical systems.

A process is said to be *first-order stationary* when the mean number of events within some time interval $[t, t + \tau]$ is independent of t, provided that the interval τ is fairly long. Systematic fluctuations in the mean (or the *intensity*) are attributed to memory effects in a system endowed with self-similarity (Mandelbrot and Wallis, 1969a). Consider a river system made up of a main stream with many affluents and subaffluents. We may assume that the primary catchment basin was partitioned into smaller and smaller catchment basins by a random process of self-organization (Fig. 7.3). The partition is generated by features of relief, and relief may be generated on a featureless plain by a random combination of rainfall and erosion. The drainage pattern is hierarchically self-organized and so are the catchment basins. The sizes x of catchment basins scale according to

$$\Pr[ax] = a^H \Pr[x], \tag{7.4}$$

where a is a scale factor. The exponent H is called the *similarity index* or *Hurst index*. This type of hierarchical self-organization is quite common in nature; it is also known as *self-similarity* because the pattern is similar at all scales a.

Note that x could be any variable related to the size of the basin: the length of streams, the annual rainfall over a catchment, the size of the largest annual flood on a tributary, and so on. A similar scheme may be applied to geologic faulting (Fig. 7.4). Every tributary fault is associated with a master fault, and faults are organized hierarchically like streams in a hydrographic basin. Strain is channeled through faults as rainfall is through streams, and so on.

H.E. Hurst, one of the more inventive minds of contemporary engineering, spent a lifetime looking for a way to estimate the optimum capacity of a reservoir on the Nile. This involved predicting the largest and the smallest

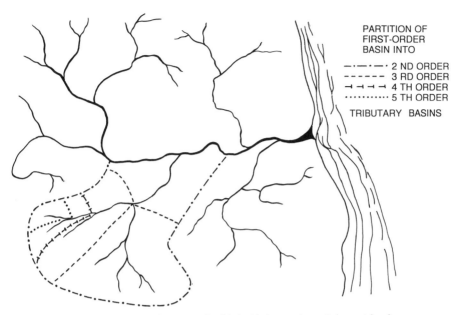

Fig. 7.3 *Self-organization of a watershed into higher-order catchment basins.*

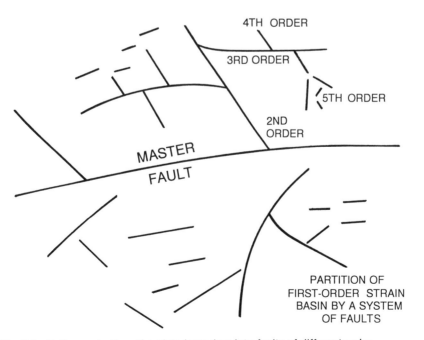

Fig. 7.4 *Self-organization of a plate boundary into faults of different order.*

annual floods. Eventually he discovered *rescaled range analysis*, a form of statistical analysis that anticipates some famous results which would be rediscovered much later by Benoit Mandelbrot, the inventor of fractals. One of the crucial insights provided by Hurst was his explanation of wet and dry "cycles." In a rainy year (Hurst suggested) some part of the total rainfall is stored in the ground. The next year the ground will absorb less water and more water will flow on the surface. Therefore a year of high runoff should be followed, as a rule, by one or more years of higher-than-average runoff, just because of the delayed contribution of the underground storage. Similarly, an unusually dry year would tend to dry out the basin to such an extent that part of next year's rainfall would be used up in replenishing the subsurface reservoir to its former level: thus a year of low runoff should be followed by several years of low runoff. This memory effect leads to pseudocyclical clustering. Similar effects may be at work in many geophysical variables including earthquakes. Quiet years tend to be followed by quiet years and active years by active years.

For example, the years 1966–1976 were unusually active in northern China, leading up to the severe Tangshan earthquake. After this event the activity quieted down. The years 1973–1985 were extremely active in Mexico, up to the destructive Michoacán earthquake. Cycles of high activity began in Turkey in 1939, and in California in 1989.

If every fault or subfault may be imagined as "draining" a specific tributary area, one may define a "strain regime" that has its analogy in the hydrologic cycle. Consider a marked point process $P[t_i,e_i]$, where e_i is the energy of an earthquake occurring at time t_i , and let us fit a straight line to the cumulative step function $E(t) = \Sigma e_i$ (Fig. 7.5). The *deviation* of the cumulative energy function from its average trend tells us something about the "cycles" of high (or low) seismicity.

Following Hurst, let us call this deviation $D(t)$ and note that $D(t)$ can be positive or negative. For every time interval $[t_1 ,t_2]$ one obtains a *different* straight-line fit, and for every straight-line fit a different set of $D(t)$ and therefore a different maximum value max(D) and minimum value min(D). Thus the Hurst statistic will depend on the length of the available interval of record.

For simplicity, let us consider the yearly energy release so that the process is evenly spaced in time. The *range R* of the deviations *D* is defined as

$$R(t) = \max(D) - \min(D) \tag{7.5}$$

for the given time interval t; and the standard deviation of the yearly energies is

$$S(t) = \left(\frac{1}{t} \sum_{\tau=1}^{t} \left[e(\tau) - \langle e \rangle_t\right]^2\right)^{1/2} \tag{7.6}$$

where $e(\tau)$ is the energy release for the τ-th year and $\langle e \rangle_t$ is the average yearly

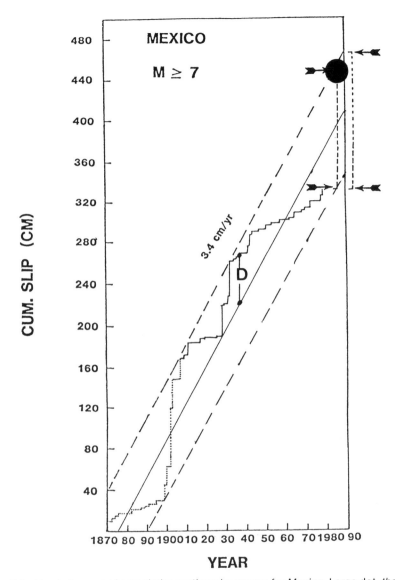

Fig. 7.5 *Hurst diagram of cumulative earthquake energy for Mexico.* Large dot, *the 1985 Mexico earthquake. See text for meaning of D.*

energy in *t* years. Hurst called $R(t)/S(t)$ the *rescaled range*—that is, the range of the deviations rescaled or renormalized by the standard deviation.

He found that this rescaled range obeyed a unique relation, shared by many natural phenomena:

$$R(t)/S(t) = (at)^H. \tag{7.7}$$

The value of H for most natural processes (including rainfall and runoff) was found to be clustered around 0.72 ± 0.1, with $a \cong 0.5$. This enables us to predict the maximum deviations for different time spans t.

Power laws such as Eq (7.7) are typical of fractality. If the events were independent, the value of H should be exactly 0.5, and a should be exactly $\pi/2$. The difference between 0.5 and 0.72, and between $\pi/2$ and 0.5, measures the degree of dependence between the values of the variable in successive years. To Hurst's surprise this approach worked well for many different "earth variables": river discharges, levels of rivers and lakes, rainfall, the thickness of varves in lake deposits, temperatures, atmospheric pressures, sunspot numbers, tree-ring indexes, and many others.

One recent "failure" of rescaled range (R/S) analysis is instructive. Ogata and Abe have applied R/S analysis to the magnitudes of earthquakes in Japan and the world; they obtained surprisingly low Hurst exponents, on the order of 0.56 for Japan and 0.57 for the world. Hurst had pointed out that short records with low values of H cannot be distinguished from records produced by an independent process ($H = 0.5$). Thus the result seemed to suggest that the earthquake process was independent and that cycles were absent.

But the seismic magnitude should not have been used as a variable in the first place. Magnitude is not a physical variable. It was intended by Richter as a classification index based on the logarithm of the amplitude of a standard seismogram; and logarithms are not additive. Three earthquakes of magnitude 7 do not add up to one earthquake of magnitude 21. Thus the deviation D lacked any physical interpretation and so did the R/S statistic. Furthermore, the R/S statistic should not have been applied to large complex regions such as all Japan or the world. For example, we should not expect a world rainfall statistic to exhibit any consistent cycles since dry and rainy years are not the same for, say, Europe and South America. The correlation decays rapidly with distance between individual watersheds; the larger the distance, the less long-term dependence is to be expected. If Hurst had studied all of Africa, he might never have found the R/S statistic. In conclusion, it is important to use appropriate additive variables such as seismic moment or energy, and the area or region for application of rescaled range analysis must be carefully defined.

I have used rescaled range analysis as a simple, effective and elegant tool for estimating the design magnitude at a given site. First one determines the Hurst exponent H for the given earthquake record. It is usually around 0.72. The range R is next computed as a function of the span t of the prediction:

$$R(t) = S(t)(at)^H, \tag{7.8}$$

which estimates the total energy that can be released in any given time period t. If $S(t)$ is assumed constant, this provides a conservative estimate for the upper bound $\mathcal{M}$ of the maximum magnitude:

$$\mathcal{M}(t) = 0.75 \log_{10}R(t) - 3, \tag{7.9}$$

where R is in joules. A similar procedure can be applied for the seismic moment instead of the energy. I have used Eq (7.9) successfully for a quick estimate of maximum credible earthquake magnitudes. As a first approximation one may safely assume $H \cong 0.72$ and $a \cong 0.5$. Thus for $t = 10$ years one finds $R/S \cong 3$, and for $t = 50$ years, $R/S \cong 10$. Hence the expected maximum magnitude rises by $0.75(\log 10 - \log 3) \cong 0.4$ as one goes from a design period of 10 years to one of 50 years. The horizontal design velocities should at least be doubled. Those are useful first guesses for risk assessment in engineering applications.

In building codes no mention is made of the design period of the structure; yet it is evident that a building expected to last for a century or more should be built to different specifications than one expected to be torn down in at most 30 years. Instead, the building code in effect applies a cost surcharge on the order of 15–20% in order to make the building earthquake-resistant. In some cases this approach works well; in others, such as Mexico City, it does not seem to be optimal. We shall have more to say about this topic in Part II.

THE POISSON PROCESS

Processes with positive memory (Hurst index $H > 0.5$) are called *persistent*. Similarly, processes in which $H < 0.5$ are called *antipersistent*. Fig. 7.6 shows examples of synthetic records for persistent, independent, and antipersistent processes using an identical algorithm. Note that persistent processes look less "noisy" than antipersistent processes; this is a result of self-organization. Actually there is no noise present in any of these records.

Mandelbrot and Wallis (1969b) were curious about the reasons why the R/S statistic works. They found that normalizing the range R by the standard deviation S has the effect of stabilizing the rescaled range when the time series is non-Gaussian. To some extent, this accounts for the robustness of R/S analysis and its success at characterizing long-range dependence for such a wide range of different processes.

It is time to reconsider the familiar linear approach to risk estimation. To what extent is a traditional linear treatment still useful and aceptable? This is a complicated question. Engineers or geophysicists who equate linearity with simplicity may be disappointed by what we have to say.

The basis of linear treatments of earthquake risk is a stochastic process named after Siméon Denis Poisson (1781–1840). Because it is so basic, it is often called "randomness" for short. The classical Poisson process is based on three fundamental assumptions:

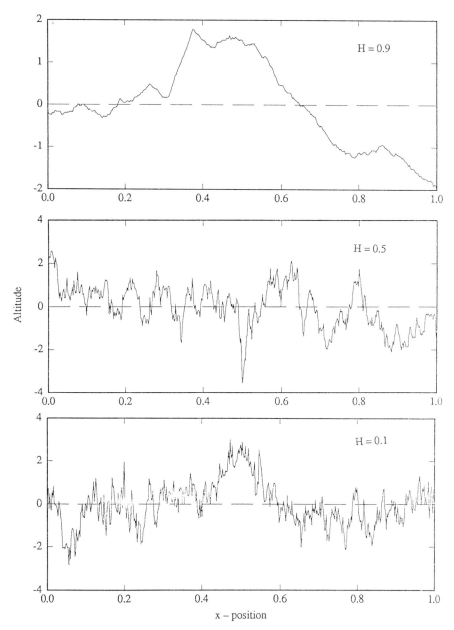

Fig. 7.6 *Persistent* (top) *and antipersistent* (bottom) *versions of a process with otherwise identical parameters.* Middle, H = 0.5. *From Feder (1988). Reprinted by permission of Plenum Press, New York.*

(a) *Independence:*

$$\Pr[A|B] = \Pr[A] \qquad (7.10)$$

where A and B are any two events in the process. This equation is to be read "the conditional probability of A given B equals the marginal probability of A". In other words, as far as the occurrence of event A is concerned, it makes no difference whether any other event B occurs or not—much less when it occurs, how large it is, and so on.

(b) *Stationarity:*

$$p_k(x) \equiv \Pr[N(t,t + x) = k] \qquad k = 0,1, \ldots \qquad (7.11)$$

where k is the number of events in $(t,t + x)$ and the probability $p_k(x)$ depends on both k and x but not on the time t.

(c) *Orderliness.* This means that the probability of two or more events occurring in a time interval Δt tends to zero as Δt vanishes. Thus simultaneous events are ruled out.

Any point process that features these three properties is a Poisson process. But the converse is not true, that is, any Poisson-distributed sequence of events has not necessarily been generated by a Poisson process. Actually the point processes most frequently encountered in nature are superpositions of processes with *dependent* intervals. These wolves in sheep's clothing are the ones we must deal with in earthquake risk evaluation; the overall distribution tends to the Poisson distribution.

Daley and Vere-Jones (1988, p. 269) explain the situation as follows:

> In a loose sense, each of the operations of superposition, thinning, and random translation is entropy increasing; it is not surprising then that among point processes with fixed mean rate, the limit Poisson process is that with maximum entropy.

This somewhat cryptic statement may be explained as follows. The Poisson process is often a result of any of a number of random operations performed on a set of non-Poisson processes. It is a limiting case to which other point processes converge in some statistical sense; yet each of the individual point processes bears no resemblance to a Poisson process. This is not as strange as it appears. If the truth be told, none of the ideal properties of independence, stationarity, and orderliness is to be found in the real universe. Why then should the Poisson process be so ubiquitous?

Until the work of C. Palm (1943) and A. Ya. Khinchin (1960) the Poisson process was treated as an ideal case. Enter Khinchin, who proved the following theorem first enunciated by Palm.

The Palm–Khinchin Theorem

Let N be a simple stationary process on the real line with finite intensity λ (i.e., having λ events per unit time). Let S_n be the point process ΣN_i obtained by superposition of n independent processes of the N type with finite random intensities independently distributed about the mean λ. Then as $n \to \infty$, S_n converges weakly to a Poisson process with mean $n\lambda$.

Note that the processes N are not specified: They could be anything. The theorem as paraphrased above (a more rigorous version is given in Daley and Vere-Jones, 1988) is enormously general. The events don't have to be independent. For example, the intervals could be lognormally distributed or even constant. Yet the merged data always tend to a Poisson process. By *superposition* we mean an operation such that each component process is laid alongside the others parallel to the time axis and all processes are then added to form a single process (Fig. 7.7).

As an example, suppose that California contains n active faults and that each fault generates an earthquake process of unknown type and rate λ_1, $\lambda_2, \ldots, \lambda_n$. If the λ's have a joint distribution, the pooled output for the entire system ($\lambda = \Sigma \lambda_i$) tends to a Poisson process. We assume that the seismicity of California is approximately stationary over the time period to be considered. This explains why the catalog of California earthquakes fits a Poisson process rather closely, as there are so many active faults of different sizes in California. I tested the Palm-Khinchin property both for California earthquakes and for world earthquakes as a whole; in both cases the fit was very close.

The larger and the more complex the region, the more sources are included and the closer is the resemblance of the pooled seismic output to a Poisson process.

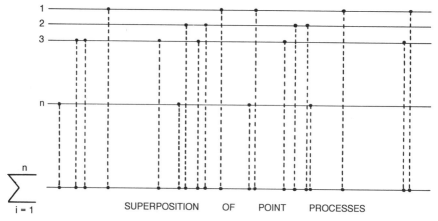

Fig. 7.7 *Superposition of renewal processes with identically distributed random source strengths yields a Poisson process.*

THE POISSON MODEL AND ITS EXTREME-VALUE VERSION

The well-known Poisson equations are:

$$\Pr[N = x] = \frac{\lambda^x}{x!} e^{-\lambda}, \qquad x = 0, 1, \ldots \qquad (7.12)$$

$$\Pr[T < x \le T + \Delta T] = \lambda e^{-\lambda x} \Delta T. \qquad (7.13)$$

Here N is the number of events in any interval of length unity, and T is the interval of time between two consecutive events. The parameter λ is called the *rate* or *intensity* of the process. Also, λ^{-1} is called the *mean interval* or the *recurrence time* of the process. In our case λ is the mean number of earthquakes per year and λ^{-1} is the mean interval between earthquakes in years. Note that either of the two equations interchangeably defines the process: one equation can be derived from the other. However, Eq (7.12) represents a discrete distribution (for values of the abscissa $x = 0, 1, 2,$ ...), while Eq (7.13) defines a frequency distribution in continuous x:

$$f_T(x) = \lambda e^{-\lambda x}. \qquad (7.14)$$

We shall be working mostly with the latter as it is particularly easy to simulate on a computer.

An asymptotic Poisson model of seismic risk for large earthquakes was proposed some years ago along these lines (Epstein and Lomnitz, 1966). It is widely used among engineers for assessing the earthquake hazard at a specific site. The model works best when many different potential earthquake sources contribute to the hazard. The basic structure of the model is as follows.

(a) Magnitude Distribution

The magnitudes of earthquakes are assumed to be independently distributed as

$$f_M(x) = \beta e^{-\beta x}. \qquad (7.15)$$

This is the well-known empirical result by Gutenberg and Richter though it can also be derived from a number of theoretical assumptions. The inverse of the parameter β estimates the mean magnitude $E[x]$ of the process. If x is defined as $M - M_t$ (where M_t is the threshold magnitude of whatever catalog is being used), then $M_t + \beta^{-1}$ is the estimated mean magnitude of the process.

The *b*-value originally defined by Gutenberg and Richter is more familiar than β. Gutenberg and Richter had written Eq (7.15) as follows:

$$\log_{10} N = a - bM, \tag{7.16}$$

where N is the expected number of earthquakes of magnitude exceeding M, and a is the sample size for $M \geq 0$. Hence b is related to β as

$$\beta = b \ln 10 \cong 2.3 \, b. \tag{7.17}$$

Thus when we say that the b-value rises we mean that the mean magnitude β^{-1} is falling, and vice versa.

(b) Interval Distribution

The time intervals T between earthquakes are assumed to be independently distributed with constant hazard function

$$h(x) = \lambda , \tag{7.18}$$

where λ is the mean number of events per unit time. Here the hazard function $h(x)$ is defined as

$h(x)dx = Pr[$an earthquake occurs in x, $x + dx$ given it does not occur before time x].

Thus $1/\lambda$ is the mean interval, or *interoccurrence time*, of the process. This is a standard or "pure" Poisson distribution. The interval distribution is exponential:

$$f_T(x) = \lambda e^{-\lambda x}. \tag{7.19}$$

The two distributions (7.15) and (7.19) define the model. They happen to be symmetrical: The magnitude and interval distributions are formally the same. This is the simplest two-parameter model of seismicity, and it agrees amazingly well with many data sets. The larger the size of the event to be predicted the better is the agreement.

This might have been expected. In a list of large earthquakes it takes time to find two events repeating on the same fault. Thus large earthquakes on a given fault are likely to be widely spaced in time; conversely, large earthquakes occurring one after another are likely to be far apart in space. In either case the physical dependence between events is likely to be weak. The *extreme-value approach* makes use of this fact. Let y be the largest event in any year. Suppose that only y is listed instead of all events greater than some threshold magnitude. Then we obtain a much shorter catalog. This has a number of advantages. First, it is much more reliable, since the larger events are better recorded. Second, the Poisson fit is bound to improve since only large events are used. Third, the loss of information incurred by discarding the smaller events is more than compensated by the possibility of going farther back in time.

Old historical earthquake records are only reliable for the largest events, since small earthquakes were not routinely recorded. This is also true for the earlier instrumental lists. Before 1960, for example, the world list is definitely incomplete for earthquakes of magnitude smaller than about 6.5. It makes little sense to include the records for relatively small earthquakes, especially if we are interested in predicting the risk from large events, since we know that the small shocks are merely going to introduce a bias in the statistics. This bias, by the way, leads to unconservative risk estimates.

Magnitudes of large earthquakes are available for historical periods, thanks to the patient researches of expert historians who have been able to reconstruct the intensity distributions of earthquakes for centuries before seismographs were in use. Reconstructed or inferred magnitudes are often surprisingly reliable. In China, a well-organized bureaucracy has been keeping written records at least since the Tang Dynasty. The extreme-value approach enables one to use data that go back up to two millennia in history. Information of this kind is invaluable: It cannot be replaced by a few decades of instrumental records.

E.J. Gumbel (1958) showed that for a Poisson variable with exponentially distributed intervals (as in Eq 7.19), the annual maximum magnitudes y have a survivor function

$$S(x,y) = \exp[-\alpha x \exp(-\beta y)], \qquad (7.20)$$

which is bivariate Poisson in the magnitude y and the sampling interval x; it is independent of the magnitude origin. If we have a reliable list of largest annual earthquakes ($x = 1$) in a region, we may estimate the return periods and the hazard function from this list. The same procedure may be used for the largest earthquakes in a decade ($x = 10$) or in a century ($x = 100$). Only large events are used; thus the only part of the distribution that matters is the tail, and the tail of one distribution resembles another's for broad categories of distributions. For instance, the normal and the exponential distributions have near-identical tails. This accounts for the robustness of extreme-value methods.

The cumulative distribution function of y is

$$F_M(y) = \exp(-\alpha e^{-\beta y}), \qquad (7.21)$$

where α is the mean annual number of earthquakes ($M \geq 0$) and β is the reciprocal mean magnitude as defined above. Eq (7.21) can also be derived from first principles in various ways (cf. Lomnitz-Adler and Lomnitz, 1978). The cumulative probabilities F are computed directly from the data. The parameters α and β are estimated by regression, noting that

$$\log [-\log F] = \log \alpha - \beta y , \qquad (7.22)$$

from Eq (7.21). In the case of California earthquakes it turns out that $\log \alpha = 11.43$, meaning that California has on the average $e^{11.43}$ or roughly 100,000 earthquakes ($M \geq 0$) per year. The value of β for California is 2.0, or equivalently the b-value found from extreme values is $2.0/2.3 = 0.87$, in agreement with values found by other authors.

Let us now estimate the mean magnitude of earthquakes in California. It is $1/\beta = 1/2.0 = 0.5$. This is the expected mean magnitude for a sample of California earthquakes above magnitude 0. For a magnitude threshold $M_t = 4.0$ the mean sample magnitude would be $4.0 + 0.5 = 4.5$; for $M_t = 5.0$ it would be 5.5, and so on. This result is easily verified.

We now calculate mean return times for different magnitudes:

$$T(y) = \alpha^{-1} \exp (\beta y). \qquad (7.23)$$

Thus a shock of magnitude $y = 8$ should occur on the average every 100 years in California. Note, however, that this is the result of an extrapolation: Our sample was less than a century long.

The probability that a maximum annual earthquake of magnitude y will occur in any D-year period is the *earthquake hazard:*

$$R_D(y) = 1 - \exp (-\alpha De^{-\beta y}). \qquad (7.24)$$

As an exercise, let us estimate the hazard for a maximum annual earthquake of magnitude 7.1 (similar to the 1989 Loma Prieta earthquake) to occur in any 10-year period in California. From Eq (7.24) one obtains, setting $D = 10$,

$$R_{10} (7.1) = 1 - \exp (-e^{11.43} \times 10 \times e^{-2 \times 7.1}) = 0.5, \qquad (7.25)$$

thus suggesting that there is an even chance for an earthquake of this size to occur in any 10-year period. The fact that three such events have occurred in 1989–1992 may seem remarkable. Perhaps we better switch to the rescaled-range method?

The mean recurrence period for maximum earthquakes of magnitude 7.1 in California may be found from Eq (7.23):

$$T(7.1) = \alpha^{-1} \exp (\beta y) = \exp (2.0 \times 7.1)/\exp 11.43, \qquad (7.26)$$

which yields $T(7.1) = 15.8$ years, which is close to the interval between the San Fernando and the Loma Prieta earthquakes.

CLUSTERING

The preceding brief discussion will serve to introduce the important statistical concept known as *clustering*. This refers to the property of the intervals *T* in a point process, which causes small intervals to be more frequent than large intervals. As a result the events occur in batches called *clusters*. The concept of clusters is similar to what is popularly known as *cycles*: the events come bunched together, and the bunches are separated by relatively long intervals. But those are not Hurst cycles. The typical example is the classical Poisson process: Since the distribution of intervals is exponential, the probability of intervals decays monotonically with increasing *T*. This means that long intervals are infrequent and appear like long empty spaces between bunches of events separated by short intervals.

The occurrence of three large events in three years in California (1989–1992) would be nothing unusual in a Poisson process. Clustering in itself is not opposed to randomness. Consider two point processes A and B, such that the interval distribution of A is more peaked than an exponential while B has a mode at some interval $T_{mod} > 0$ (Fig. 7.8). In process B the events are more regularly spaced since many intervals fall around T_{mod}. On the other hand, process A has a greater tendency to cluster, as long intervals are rare. As referred to the Poisson process, process A is said to be *overclustered* and process B is said to be *underclustered*.

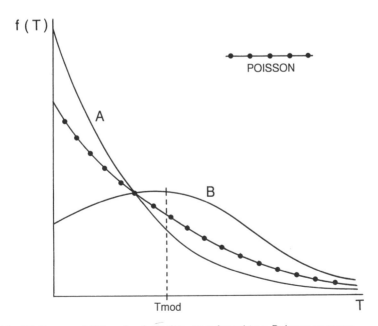

Fig. 7.8 (A) Over- and (B) underclustering, as referred to a Poisson process.

Finally, an important class of point processes is composite processes such that one sub-process is generated by the other, for example, beetles and beetle larvae, or earthquakes and aftershocks. These are called generically *cluster processes*. In the old days it was thought that earthquakes and aftershocks could be objectively distinguished and separated in a sample, but of course this is impossible. In the statistical treatment of cluster processes one may distinguish between the process of cluster *centers* and the daughter processes: but the question of separation of the composite process does not arise.

BENIOFF-SHIMAZAKI MODELS

Consider the following simple generalization of the Poisson model of Eq (7.18):

$$q_T(x) = n\lambda x^{n-1}, \tag{7.27}$$

where n is called the *Weibull index*. The resulting process is called a *Weibull process of index n*. We might define the Poisson process as a special case of the Weibull process, namely the one for which $n = 1$.

There are infinite ways of generalizing the Poisson process in order to obtain other point processes; this is just one example. As far as earthquakes are concerned, various other generalizations have been proposed, but the Weibull process is of particular interest. An important special case is $n = 2$, which we shall discuss presently.

The seismologist Hugo Benioff loved to build things that worked: seismographs, musical instruments, geophysical theories. In 1935 he invented the most accurate measuring instrument ever built, the Benioff strain meter. It consisted of 25 yards of quartz tubing welded together with cesium cement and fiberglass tape and suspended from piano wires. Before welding, each segment was separately fine-tuned with a tuning fork. Thus he got an accuracy of one part in a billion: in other words, he could resolve an eighth of an inch in 200,000 miles. The sun shining on a hillside was enough to drive the instrument offscale. It had more accuracy than anyone could use on this wobbly planet.

Benioff invented (or coinvented) the "Benioff plane," which dipped under the continents and was later to be called a subduction zone. He also invented cumulative graphs similar to Hurst's deviation plots and used them for earthquake prediction. In 1950 he predicted an earthquake of magnitude 7.5 in the Indian Ocean—at the risk of ending up in Richter's nut file. Fortunately the earthquake did take place about a year later, on December 8, 1951, at the same spot in the Indian Ocean where Benioff had predicted it and with

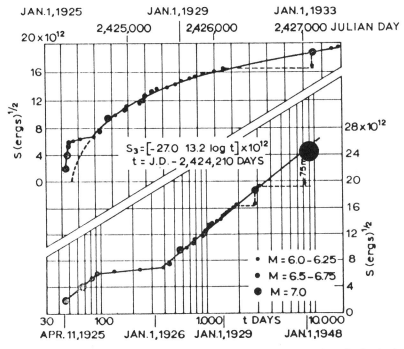

Fig. 7.9 *Successful prediction by Benioff of a magnitude 7.5 earthquake in the Indian Ocean* (large dot). *Logarithmic time decay is assumed.*

the predicted magnitude (Fig. 7.9). No earthquake prediction made by Benioff was ever successful again. However, a similar prediction made for a large earthquake to occur in Mexico before 1986 was successful (Fig. 7.5).

Benioff's model was eventually rediscovered by Shimazaki and Nakata (1980), who called it the *time-predictable model*. Suppose a segment of plate boundary accumulates strain at a constant rate k (Fig. 7.10a). Consider the

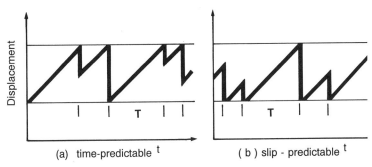

Fig. 7.10 *The Shimazaki-Nakata process, showing that the time-predictable and slip-predictable versions may be obtained from each other by reflection at both axes.*

interval *T* between two consecutive earthquakes. If the probability of rupture depends linearly on the accumulated strain the plate boundary will always rupture at the same critical strain. Then the interval is $T = kJ$, where J is the strain release (or *strain drop*) of the previous earthquake. If the strain drop *J* is selected at random from some distribution $f(J)$, the interval between events is a random variable distributed independently as $f(kJ)$. This process belongs to a class known to statisticians as *renewal processes*: that is, point processes with independently distributed intervals.

There has been some confusion among seismologists as to whether the time-predictable model does actually lead to a renewal process in time. Since the interval *T* equals the preceding strain release *J* times a constant, they must be identically distributed. Nevertheless, the process in time is a renewal process since the intervals are independent of each other.

Now suppose instead that the strain is released at a variable critical level but drops always to the same constant base level (Fig. 7.10b). Shimazaki and Nakata called this version the *slip-predictable model*, because the amount of slip *J* in the next earthquake may be inferred from the value of the preceding time interval *T*. The two models are closely related: one version may be obtained from the other by reflection at both axes. In other words the time-predictable model is the upside-down mirror image of the slip-predictable model and vice versa.

Since the time scale remains invariant during reflection at any axis, the same interval distribution $f_T(x)$ must be shared by both versions. Let us derive this interval distribution. Consider, for example, the slip-predictable version (Fig. 7.10b). If the probability of rupture is proportional to the accumulated strain and if the previous earthquake occurred at $t = 0$, the probability that exactly one earthquake occurs at time *t* is

$$\text{prob } [N(t, t + \Delta t) = 1] = kt\Delta t + o(\Delta t), \tag{7.28}$$

supposing that no event has occurred in $(0, t)$. Then the probability $P_T(x)$ that the interval *T* to the next earthquake will be greater than *x* is

$$P_T(x + \Delta x) = \text{prob } (T > x + \Delta x)$$
$$= P_T(x) \cdot \text{prob } [\text{no event occurs in } (x, x + \Delta x)]$$

or, from (7.28),

$$P_T(x + \Delta x) = P_T(x) \cdot [1 - kx\Delta x + o(\Delta x)], \tag{7.29}$$

and, setting $P_T(x + \Delta x) - P_T(x) = dP_T(x)$:

$$dP_T(x) = -kx \, P_T(x) \, dx. \tag{7.30}$$

The solution of this differential equation is $P_T(x) = P_T(0) \exp(-kx^2/2)$ or, since $P_T(0) = 1$,

$$F_T(x) = 1 - \exp(-\xi x^2), \tag{7.31}$$

where $\xi = k/2$. This is a Weibull distribution with exponent $n = 2$. As we have just shown that the Shimazaki model leads to a Weibull distribution, the resulting process may be called a *Benioff–Shimazaki process*. For $n = 1$ we obtain the Poisson process, as pointed out above.

The Benioff–Shimazaki process is the only such process where the probability of rupture is a linear function of the strain accumulation. It occupies a special position for this reason. The hazard function of the Benioff–Shimazaki process is linear:

$$h(x) = 2\xi x. \tag{7.32}$$

Thus the probability of occurrence is proportional to the time transcurred since the previous earthquake. Every cycle is decoupled from earlier cycles, and the process has no memory. The forward recurrence time is proportional to the mark (see also Daley and Vere-Jones, 1988, p. 377). Equivalently, the Benioff-Shimazaki process can also be derived from a Poisson process by assuming a variable intensity function $\lambda(x) = \xi x$, where x is the *backward recurrence time*, that is, the time measured from the last event.

The magnitude distribution for the Benioff–Shimazaki process,

$$F_M(x) = 1 - \exp(-\xi x^2), \tag{7.33}$$

features a mode at some finite nonzero magnitude value. This mode corresponds to large complex ruptures at plate boundaries. Eq (7.33) may be superimposed onto the Gutenberg–Richter distribution for small events in order to yield the total magnitude distribution for events of all sizes.

Consider now a further generalization. Suppose that the loading rate k is not constant. Instead, suppose that it fluctuates during each cycle, from a maximum value right after an earthquake to zero right before the next event (Fig. 7.11). Thus we assume that there is a feedback between the state of stress and the loading rate. Such a model is intermediate between a Shimazaki model ($k = $ constant) and a Poisson model ($k = 0$). The resulting Benioff–Shimazaki process must therefore be intermediate between $n = 1$ (Poisson) and $n = 2$ (Shimazaki):

$$F_T(x) = 1 - \exp(-\xi x^n), \qquad 1 < n \le 2. \tag{7.34}$$

This model is physically more plausible than either: The rate of strain accumulation should probably be higher during the postseismic transient (Fig. 7.11), when the region is depleted of strain, than during the last stage of the seismic cycle when the region is approaching instability. This is also consis-

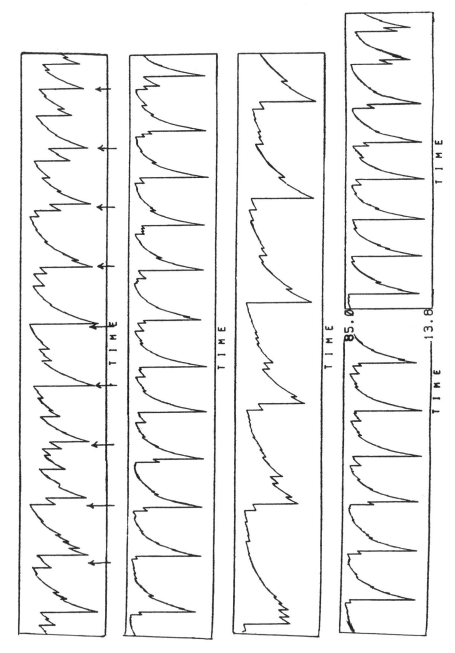

Fig. 7.11 A generalized Shimazaki-Nagata process, where the loading rate decays during the seismic cycle. Computer simulation by the author.

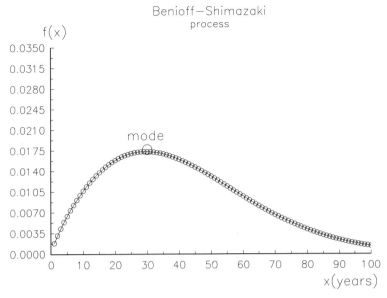

Fig. 7.12   *The Benioff-Shimazaki process with $\alpha = 2$, adjusted for a modal interval of 30 years.*

tent with a model of healing. The aftershock activity is precisely caused by the high rate of influx of strain energy at the beginning of the cycle. As the seismicity dies down, the rate of energy influx is reduced.

The probability density function for this new variant of the Shimazaki model is

$$f_T(x) = n\,\xi\,x^{n-1}\,\exp(-\xi x^n). \tag{7.35}$$

A realization of this distribution is shown in Fig. 7.12. The parameters were chosen so that the mean recurrence interval $T_{\mathrm{mean}} = 21.8$ years, as in the Parkfield, California, sequence. The mean recurrence interval is

$$T_{\mathrm{mean}} = \int_0^\infty x f(x)\,dx = \xi^{-1/n}\,\Gamma\!\left(1 + \frac{1}{n}\right), \tag{7.36}$$

and the variance

$$\begin{aligned}
Var(T) &= \int_0^\infty x^2\,f(x)\,dx - T_{\mathrm{mean}}^2 \\
&= \int_0^\infty \xi^{-2/n}\left[\Gamma\!\left(\frac{n+1}{n}\right) - \Gamma^2\!\left(\frac{n+1}{n}\right)\right]
\end{aligned} \tag{7.37}$$

while the mode may be found from the condition $f'(T_{\mathrm{mode}}) = 0$:

$$T_{mod} = \xi^{-1/n} \left(1 - \frac{1}{n} \right)^{1/n} \tag{7.38}$$

For $n = 2$ the ratio T_{mod}/T_{mean} is $(\pi/2)^{-1/2} = 0.7979$, so that the modal interval is only about 20% shorter than the mean interval. This process is underclustered as compared to the Poisson process: the mode is only about four years shorter than the mean. The Parkfield sequence, though cited as an extreme example of underclustering, might easily have been generated by this process.

The lower the value of n the more clustered is the process. For $n = 1.5$ we obtain $T_{mod}/T_{mean} = 0.532$. For $n = 1.33$ the ratio goes down to 0.385. For the Poisson process, of course, we should have $n = 1$ and $T_{mod} = 0$. In conclusion:

(a) The time-predictable model proposed by Shimazaki and Nakata (1980) implies that the probability of rupture is a function of the accumulated strain, since rupture occurs always at the same strain value for any given fault independently of the starting point.

(b) In this case the distribution of intervals or magnitudes is no longer arbitrary but leads necessarily to a Weibull distribution. Here we have shown the Weibull exponent to be $n = 2$ when the probability of rupture is linear in strain, but it is easy to generalize this result for any continuous function.

(c) When the assumption of constant strain rate is relaxed, one obtains a family of processes ranging from the Poisson process ($n = 1$) to the Benioff–Shimazaki process ($n = 2$). Any particular data set of great earthquakes fits a member of this family of processes, and predictions of recurrence times can easily be obtained.

These predictions (and not the Poisson prediction) represent more plausible estimates on the assumption of statistical independence between successive earthquakes.

IS THE POISSON MODEL CONSERVATIVE?

The relevance of the preceding section to the practice of earthquake prediction is considerable, because a statistical dependence between successive earthquakes is extremely difficult to prove. Even in the case of aftershocks only the functional form $\lambda(t)$ of the rate of occurrence is known. The events themselves appear to be independent; in fact, the magnitude distribution is stationary so aftershock sequences might be simulated by a nonstationary Benioff–Shimazaki process.

Some argument can be found in the literature, especially in the engineering literature, about whether the Poisson estimation of earthquake hazard is conservative. The following discussion applies also to other processes of independent increments, including the Benioff–Shimazaki process.

If we are looking at earthquakes generated by a specific structure, say a segment of the San Andreas fault, the Poisson hypothesis will always be a poor assumption to make. The reasons were clear to Hurst and represented the motivation for his search of nonlinear models featuring dependence between successive events. Yet the Poisson assumption may still be useful when an upper-bound estimation of the largest credible earthquake is required.

The tails of the Poisson and the Weibull distributions are quite similar, and so are their extreme-value distributions. As far as the extreme values are concerned it should make little difference in practice whether we use Poisson or Weibull even though these distributions differ substantially for small time intervals. Cornell and Winterstein (1988) have pointed out that the Poisson hypothesis is conservative when the average duration of the seismic cycle is long, or rather when we are still in the early part of a cycle. This suggests that the Poisson or Benioff-Shimazaki approximations can be very useful in many applications when the hazard corresponding to very large distant events is needed.

Let t_0 be the time elapsed since the last event up to the present. Then the probability of the next event occurring at some future time greater than x is the survivor function of x, normalized to the survivor function of t_0:

$$\Pr[t \geq x|t_0) = \frac{S(x)}{S(t_0)} = \exp[-\lambda(x^2 - t_0^2)], \; x > t_0 \qquad (7.39)$$

assuming $n = 2$. This probability decays more rapidly than $\exp(-\lambda x)$ for $x \gg t_0$. In other words, for times t greater than the mean interval the event tends to occur sooner than would be expected from using the Poisson model. This means that the Poisson model becomes unconservative once the mean interoccurrence time has been exceeded.

In practice I have found that rescaled-range analysis yields more reliable results when the plate boundary is believed to be near rupture. However, since rescaled-range analysis is still comparatively little known it is often important to be able to evaluate estimations made with renewal models such as the Poisson process.

In engineering practice the hazard from earthquakes at a specific site is routinely estimated by means of computer programs that assume a combination of line sources and area sources, and translate the resulting waveforms into accelerations at a target. This is the bread and butter of damage prevention. It is done by using transfer functions $a = f(R,h)$ which estimate the ground acceleration a of an earthquake of focal depth h at an epicentral distance R (e.g., Joyner and Boore, 1981). The functions f are nonlinear, but the procedures of estimation are basically linearized.

KLONDIKE MODELS

In this section we are concerned with linear, dependent models that have been derived in recent decades in connection with accident statistics, the clustering of beetle larvae on a patch of ground, or the spread of contagious diseases. The common feature of these models is the following: The occurrence of an event is assumed to be enhanced (or retarded) by the occurrence of an earlier event. Important research in this field is associated with the names of Markov, Yule, Greenwood, Pólya, Neyman, Bartlett, Cox, and Lewis. An application to earthquakes was suggested as follows (Lomnitz, 1974):

> Suppose that the energy of earthquakes is likened to the occurrence of gold in the Klondike. Prospectors search the area at random. Whenever a strike is made the news spreads and many prospectors swarm to the new area, with the result that many new strikes (mostly "after-strikes" in the same lode) occur. Gradually the area is exhausted, the number of strikes is reduced and their distribution returns to a random pattern—until the next major strike. Often a major strike may be preceded by medium-sized "fore-strikes".

This model decouples the spatial distribution of energy from the spatial distribution of strikes (assumed random with some feedback due to information). The lodes are assumed to be replenished by some suitable "healing" mechanism after each strike.

One statistical model which includes the main features of a Klondike process is the self-exciting infectivity model proposed by Hawkes (1971). This model was originally proposed to describe the spread of an epidemic. Suppose that some infected individuals enter a population at random times and infect other people, so that the process of immigration of cluster centers (i.e., initiators of a chain of infections) may be treated as a Poisson process in time. The intensity of the process at time t is given by

$$\lambda(t) = \nu + \int_{-\infty}^{t} \mu(t - u)\, dN(u), \tag{7.40}$$

where N is the number of events and the function $\mu(t)$ is called the *infectivity*. As we can see, the intensity λ (i.e., the number of events per unit time) depends in a linear fashion on the occurrence times of all previous events.

For practical purposes the infectivity function $\mu(t)$ may be parameterized in various ways, such as

$$\mu(t) = \begin{cases} \displaystyle\sum_{k=0}^{K} \alpha_k L_k(t)\, e^{-bt}, & (t > 0) \\[2mm] 0, & (t \le 0) \end{cases} \tag{7.41}$$

where the $L_k(t)$ are Laguerre polynomials. If one has a list of earthquakes starting at $t = 0$ one may set $K = 0$ in Eq (7.41) so that the contribution from the unknown past can be parameterized as a single exponential term (Vere-Jones and Ozaki, 1982):

$$\lambda(t) = \nu + \int_0^t \mu(t - u) \, dN(u) + A_0 e^{-bt} \tag{7.42}$$

where $A_0 = \alpha_0\nu/(b - \alpha_0)$. A detailed application may be found in Vere-Jones and Ozaki (1982).

In the Klondike model, as a cluster phases out, the "prospectors" abandon the depleted area. They scatter over the general region, and some eventually strike a new lode. This accounts for the tunneling effect whereby the next earthquake often occurs in areas six or seven regions removed from the original "strike." In other words, most prospectors remain in Alaska though some immediately embark for Australia after the Klondike lode has been depleted.

Part II

The Spiral of Theory

8

Disaster Theory

> GLENDOWER: . . . At my birth
> The frame and huge foundation of the earth
> Shak'd like a coward.
> HOTSPUR: Why, so it would have done
> At the same season, if your mother's cat
> Had but kitten'd.
> —Henry iv, Part i, Act iii

INTRODUCTION

In their introduction to a workshop held at the U.S. Geological Survey, seismologists K. Aki and W.D. Stuart (1987) remarked that "we need social scientists who would study objectively the behavior of physical scientists working on earthquake prediction."

Aki and Stuart may have expected that the strange behavior of physical scientists would come under the immediate scrutiny of the social sciences. In this they were disappointed. Nothing of the kind happened. Except for an interesting discussion of politics and public relations by R.S. Olson (1989), little has been heard about the sociopolitical aspects of earthquake prediction.

I was born into a time of changing paradigms in the earth sciences. My teachers believed in a fixed earth. Earthquake prediction was taboo. Professor Charles F. Richter had a "nut file" where he preserved, among other oddities, letters and documents pertaining to earthquake prediction. As a special treat he would allow graduate assistants to peek into it.

One of my early papers was docked because it mentioned convection in the earth's interior. When I removed the offending reference to convection, the paper was published. Today it could not be published unless convection was mentioned.

Beno Gutenberg, the tiny giant of seismology, laid down the law at Caltech. Stringy-haired, bike-riding Sir Harold Jeffreys and mighty, bigger-than-life Maurice Ewing helped build the foundations of modern geodynamics; yet they themselves thought of the earth as basically static. Ewing was a survivor of the extinct race of South Seas adventurers. He flew the Jolly Roger from the top of his research schooner *Vema*—a present from an oil magnate. The captain of the *Vema* sported a peg leg. I recall a memorable week spent on board, off the coast of Chile. Ewing never slept. A fierce workaholic, he affected a deceptively mild manner, but actually he drove his associates and students as well as himself to the limit. He saved his considerable charm for admirals and millionaires who underwrote his research voyages. He had been born in a small town in the Texas Panhandle where electric light had somehow forgotten to arrive.

I owe it to Dick Jahns (who was then in charge of the Field Geology course at Caltech) to have shown me that any backyard geology can be as challenging and intellectually stimulating as the mode splitting of the eigenvibrations of the earth.

Of course, social scientists must deal with tremendous complexities, surpassing even those of geology. In this chapter I introduce some considerations on disaster theory and some related ideas on instability and chaos, with considerable reservations as I am not a specialist in either field.

METAPHORS OF KNOWLEDGE

We have already encountered two different metaphors related to the acquisition of knowledge. One began with "We are like scared children . . . ," and appeared to represent knowledge as the cumulative result of a series of random forays in the dark. The other was Mao's parable of knowledge as an ascending spiral, which represented knowledge as an orderly, purposeful, and progressive quest. Such contradictory *métarécits* (Barthes) can be elaborated further, and many different ones can be added.

The close relationship between disaster theory and epistemology was first noticed by Dombrowsky (1987). The incidence of earthquake disasters began to decrease after the introduction of modern brick-and-concrete housing, then it increased again after 1950. The expectation that earthquake hazard would be definitely vanquished was disappointed. Similar developments occurred in other kinds of disasters. Dombrowsky suggested that "disasters are the only phenomena in the world that require an explanation," as they seem to fly in the face of our idea of progress. The power and knowledge of humankind can hardly be rated very high as long as millions remain exposed to sudden tragedy because of various kinds of natural phenomena. Carrying this idea a bit further, he concluded that

> disasters are the only falsifications we can find in reality that will prove the truth, the empirical correctness, of our practical knowledge as well as of our epistemologies. . . . Disasters are the missing link between theory and praxis, between appearance and essence.

Epistemologies are basically metaphors of the human mind. One Indian metaphor pictures the mind as a layered structure, where insight proceeds in an upward direction across seven layers. Each layer has a name (the Physical Body, the Emotional Body, the Astral Body, the Intellect, and so on), and a polarity (Pleasure and Pain, Love and Hate, Positive and Negative Biorhythms, Male and Female Intelligence, etc.). Another such layered model was proposed by Freud.

Mao's metaphor sees the Mind climbing a spiral road. Each half-turn of the spiral is alternately labeled "theory" or "praxis." If science is a laborious process of climbing the spiral road to knowledge, we must traverse alternating stages of theory and praxis. It brings us back to our starting point at every turn. But it will not be the same point, since we gain altitude and perspective with every turn of the spiral.

However, experiment does not always precede theoretical insight: often an intuition may guide us to new results more reliably than any experiment would. Szent-Györgyi used to abstain purposely from visiting the library for months at a time. He would repeatedly perform the same experiment and try to visualize the phenomena like a child ("We are like scared children . . . "), until eventually he had an inspiration.

Some epistemologies are based on religious ideas. The Cabalists of medieval France and Spain believed that knowledge had a *structure* that was identical with the structure of the universe, of the Bible, and of God. The Bible contained coded messages that had to be arranged according to a certain dynamic pattern which constituted the key to knowledge.

Their idea of the universe somewhat resembled the architecture of a computer. It was like a set of 10 parallel processors (called *sephiroth*) connected by logical switches. The structure had a hierarchy (up-down) and a gender polarity (left-right). The top and bottom *sephiroth* ("Godhead" and "World") were connected both through a right-hand or "active" path (theory), and a left-hand or "passive" path (practice). Theory led through the *sephiroth* of "Intuition" and "Freedom," while practice led through "Tradition" and "Discipline." This entire structure was called the "Tree of Life."

Thus the process of creation (artistic or otherwise) moved downward from the Godhead to the World (bottom), while knowledge moved inversely up from the World toward the Godhead. To know is to retrace the steps of creation.

This particular metaphor represents scientific research as fundamentally opposite to artistic creation. Art is to science as convolution is to deconvolution. Artistic creation moves down toward the world: Scientific research moves up toward the source. Theory and practice are combined in either case.

Some Eastern metaphors of knowledge are both simpler and more radical. The basic model of a Shinto mind is the shrine: A raised empty stage on which spirits are welcome to play or dance. There are ropes tied around trees and knots of straw, like the *malinalli* of the Aztecs. All this is meaningless to the European mind though it should be familiar to a Mexican. This metaphor is fundamentally skeptical of the acquisition of new knowledge. Knowledge has always been around, and all we have to do is open our minds and wait. We cannot penetrate beyond the mystery.

We might try to construct our own metaphor of knowledge on the analogy of the double helix. In this metaphor "theory" and "practice" are helicoidal strands of matching coded information. This information is carried within every cell of the social structure. The code is knowledge—and it is used to generate more knowledge. Each cell carries a blueprint of the entire social organism and can be used by the social organism to replicate (or reproduce) itself.

The spiral of theory carries the same code as the spiral of practice, yet both are required for replication. Local "errors" in the code may arise from time to time. These genetic variants are responsible for innovations, which may be advantageous or dysfunctional from the point of view of the society. With the help of such models it might become possible to predict social change in terms of changes in the information content that is transmitted within a society.

DISASTER AND DISORDER

But what are disasters? The worldwide risk of dying from a natural disaster is about 0.1% of the total mortality. This is to say that about one death in 10,000 is attributable to an earthquake, a volcanic eruption, a flood, a hurricane, or a landslide. This is far from negligible: It comes to more than 100,000 deaths in an average year.

Some countries are more disaster-prone than others. Italy has a disaster casualty rate about five times the world average; this has been attributed to the high incidence of earthquakes and volcanic eruptions. Peru is today the most disaster-prone country in Latin America—but this was not always so. In Japan the disaster casualty rate has decreased over recent decades: yet the rate of incidence of earthquakes and other natural hazards has not changed. The explanation is simple. Natural hazards are primarily technological, and technology changes. Where industrial disasters are common, the casualty rate from natural disasters is also high.

The human perception of disasters may change from culture to culture. In Latin America the interpretation of the Mercalli scale of earthquake intensity is different from that in the United States. One and the same earthquake may be rated at intensity V by Latin American engineers and VI by Americans. How can this be explained? The Mercalli scale is applied by humans: the assessment of intensity is based on an engineer's perception of damage in certain types of structures. One crack in one home rates VI for the entire locality—to the American engineer. Breakage from an overturned stack of soft-drink bottles in a supermarket rates as damage—again to the American.

The Latin American engineer is apt to shrug it off. His or her mental picture of damage is different.

Cultural differences in hazard perception have been recognized in the social sciences since about 1960. At the University of Chicago, geographers led by Gilbert F. White began introducing the idea that disasters cannot be explained in terms of geophysical causes alone. White proposed to distinguish between a geophysical *event* and the *character* of the resulting disaster. The latter (he claimed) depended almost entirely on human actions or omissions. The important work of White and his co-workers (e.g., White and Haas, 1975) eventually led to specific proposals that tended to treat earthquake prediction as an "emerging technology" whose implementation, however necessary, might also exact a high economic and social price.

Some social scientists rebelled against White's emphasis on action. They claimed it was *ethnocentric*—a cardinal sin in the social sciences. Unlike the underdeveloped South, the West is supposed to be action-oriented, but most disasters occur in non-Western societies. White had defined *hazard* as the risk encountered in occupying a location exposed to extreme geophysical phenomena—as if people lived in exposed locations by choice.

When economics became recognized as a major factor in the causation of disasters the field of disaster research was thrown wide open. Disasters were attributed to poverty in general and were assumed to be implicit in the everyday condition of the exposed populations. Governments were accused of perpetuating disasters in the form of poverty and of increasing the vulnerability of the population through doles, the introduction of a market economy, and misguided actions of disaster relief.

Not all of this critique was necessarily rooted in dissident models of society. Much of it led to the uncovering of examples of disaster mismanagement, causing governments to tread more softly. On the other hand, it led to the realization that many traditional societies had found ways to cope with their environment, including disasters. The changes induced by modernization could modify these compensating mechanisms and thus cause a traditional society in transition to turn extremely vulnerable to disasters. Awareness of these and other socioeconomic factors of disaster causation became widespread among United Nations experts and among officials of nongovernmental organizations dedicated to disaster mitigation. The word *relief* was out!

An influential paper by M. Watts (1983) proposed that disasters ought to be studied from the point of view of the relations of production, since vulnerability to disasters was "redefined by the transformation in the social relations of production," and that the response of the rural poor to threats from their environment was "contingent upon their situation in the productive process." The implication was that disasters should be redefined in terms of the ordinary, day-to-day situation of people rather than for some exceptional time of crisis. In other words, disasters don't exist as discrete events; rather, entire populations tend to live in a permanent disaster.

These views may seem compassionate on the surface, but they actually promote a certain insensitivity to the specific problems of people in disaster areas. Disaster or no disaster, the mass of humans everywhere lead lives of quiet desperation:

> Some of you, we all know, are poor, find it hard to live, are sometimes, as it were, gasping for breath . . . are unable to pay for all the dinners which you have actually eaten . . . always on the limits, trying to get into business and trying to get out of debt . . . always promising to pay, promising to pay, tomorrow, and dying today, insolvent (H.D. Thoreau).

This was America in 1846, and is still true of most of the world today. In the meantime, who will tell us what disasters are, in order to deal with them? The more we equate disaster with our everyday lives, the less we are likely to learn about them.

K. Hewitt (1983) has argued persuasively that we should not yield to the callous reflexes of bureaucrats in whose view "natural hazards, like disease, poverty, even death, become simply the unfinished business of our endeavors." This is rather well said. Hewitt scorned the efforts of the state to control disasters by applying technical equipment, expertise, forecasting techniques, prevention, public education, central controls "and if all else fails, organizing relief on a grand scale." The alternative, according to Peter Winchester (1992), would be to

> change the bias of programs from physical protection and over-reliance on technology and administration, to building up the resources of the most vulnerable sections of the society through long-term credit, health and educational improvement programs, based on a wider definition of the term vulnerability, so that it applies to a much wider field than an exclusive relationship to the probability of a natural phenomenon occurring.

Such proposals eventually became absorbed into the official policies of Third World governments. In the 1985 Mexico earthquake all foreign assistance was turned down, and the government relented only when the international impact of the disaster sank in. A Disaster Management Office was subsequently created in the Ministry of Governance, which handles internal security. In 1992 a Ministry of Social Development was created with aims and philosophies very similar to those advocated by Winchester.

In our political systems the interference of high-powered foreign technology or massive outside relief is rarely appreciated, particularly in areas of the society as politically sensitive as the urban and rural poor. This partly accounts for the unpopularity of ventures such as the 1990–2000 International Decade of Natural Disaster Reduction. Should we welcome the contributions of First-World social critics? They are socially literate men and women, who fancy themselves our allies; and perhaps they are. They can afford to assume that technology is evil, since they enjoy its benefits. Guilt is more bearable than want. But technology actually cuts both ways. Where technology is high, the quality of life may be low, and vice versa. Many Americans deplore their quality of live, yet I suppose that they would rather do without Mexican technical assistance and relief—as some of us would without theirs. Disasters are sometimes in the eye of the beholder. The incidence of disasters in developing countries could not be as high as it appears from Western statistics, at least in terms of social awareness of the threat they represent. For example, a recent paper on "Natural hazards and disasters in Latin America" (Stillwell, 1992) cited 59 references, only four of which were Latin American.

We must find better explanations of disasters, in the framework of a different view of society. If disasters were purely technological—or purely geophysical, or purely economical—we should be better able to prepare an appropriate response. At present, however, we don't seem to know exactly what disasters are.

DISASTER AS INSTABILITY

Disastrous earthquakes are caused by freak instabilities in the environment-society system. This may be seen as follows. Society is embedded in nature; it cannot be viewed as separate from its environment. This system is nonlinear; the effects of a disastrous earthquake cannot be extrapolated from the effects of smaller events. For example, the seismicity of a region, measured in terms of the number of earthquakes of magnitude 3, is a poor indicator of earthquake risk.

Modeling the future behavior of complex nonlinear systems, such as the nature-society system, is beyond our present capacity. However, the conceptual description of such a system is within the scope of recent developments in modern physics (see, e.g., Nicolis, 1989). In this approach the interaction between society and nature is characterized by *flows* (such as the yearly production of grain or petroleum, or earthquakes, or the yearly output of carbon dioxide or fluorocarbons), and each state variable X_i (e.g., the gross national product of a given nation) is related to all other state variables by an equation of the form

$$\frac{dX_i}{dt} = F_i (X_1, \ldots, X_n; \lambda_1, \ldots, \lambda_m), \qquad i = 1, \ldots, n \qquad (8.1)$$

where F is a rate function and the λ are parameters. The problem is that the rate function is strongly nonlinear in the state variables: therefore there are always several solutions of Eq (8.1). The asymptotic solutions, or *attractors*, depend on how far the nature-society system is from equilibrium. For example, in a society such as the Aztec, large earthquakes did not cause disasters because the system was closer to equilibrium (e.g., people lived in low huts made of light materials). Instabilities arise in the system mainly because of the devices that regulate the flows between the society and its environment. These devices are collectively described as "technology." As an example, consider the case of China.

China cannot be considered a country of high seismicity. Except for Tibet, it borders on none of the world's major plate boundaries. Yet it suffers from extremely severe disasters caused by intraplate events. The world's most destructive earthquakes have occurred in China. The Huaxian disaster of January 23, 1556, killed 820,000 people in the Xian area. It may have been the worst seismic disaster in history. On a visit to Xian in 1977 I ventured to ask the local seismologists how they had arrived at this incredibly high casualty figure. They replied, "we have the names."

This reply aroused my curiosity. It turns out that the Wei River valley around Xian has been densely populated since prehistoric times. It is the heartland of China and the cradle of Chinese civilization. The earthquake occurred in the Jiajing Reign (1522–1567) of the Ming Dynasty, when Xian was the capital of China. According to Tang (1988), the Jiajing Annals state that "more than 820,000 people known by name" plus countless unknowns (people belonging to the lower classes) died in the earthquake. This statement is the origin of the erroneous claim that a list of casualties must exist somewhere. The figure quoted in the Annals may actually include victims of epidemics and starvation as a sequel to the disaster.

At the time many people lived in caves carved out of loess cliffs facing the Wei River. Loess, an aeolian cemented sand not unlike the Merritt Formation in San Francisco Bay, is stable in vertical cuts—*under ordinary conditions*. It is stiff, smooth, homogeneous, easy to carve, an excellent thermal insulator—in short an ideal material for human dwellings, except for its vulnerability to earthquakes. In the 1556 earthquake, slides in steep loess slopes took hundreds of thousands of lives. Housing technology (as represented by cave dwellings) set up an instability at the interface between Chinese society and its environment.

In Mexico City, earthquake disasters are caused by the vulnerability of reinforced concrete-frame high-rise structures sited on soft lake mud. Large damaging earthquakes hit the Mexico Valley at least once a century, but the casualty rate began climbing when high-rise buildings were introduced around 1945 as a response to skyrocketing real-estate values. These structures have been systematically damaged in strong earthquakes ever since; yet society cannot or will not do without them.

In the 1970 Peru earthquake the town of Yungay was obliterated by a mudslide from Mt. Huascarán. An estimated 25,000 people were buried alive by the slide. A combination of coupled instabilities of different orders caused this disaster. First, tropical glaciers such as Mt. Huascarán are basically unstable even under ordinary conditions. Previous mudflows or *huaycos* had been frequent and damaging. Second, the earthquake broke off a huge block of ice from the upper ledge of the glacier. The ice tumbled nearly vertically for about 1,000 m and formed a mixture of rock and ice fragments. Third, owing to a little-understood instability (see Chapter 9), the dynamic mixture of solid fragments *liquefied*, and the slurry went down a steep glacial valley at high speed. The town of Yungay was sited on a plain separated from this valley by a lateral moraine, at the point where the valley made a sharp turn. At this point the avalanche banked and overtopped the ridge so that a mass of slurry spilled over the sloping plain beyond. The mudflow covered the town and solidified rapidly. The tops of four lone palm trees protruding from the mud signaled the location of the main square. Fourth, the town of Yungay was the historical site of a famous 1880 battle in the Chile-Peru war. Eventually, it became a resort that attracted local tourists because of its delightful climate.

Instabilities in the environment-society system thus can be traced simultaneously to social and environmental factors. They are the result of some inadequate technological response to a social or environmental challenge. As a rule it is extremely difficult to say whether a disaster is "natural" or "human-made"; usually it is both. My Oxford English Dictionary defines a *natural disaster* as one "not caused by human beings"—but there is no such thing. Earthquake disasters in particular are normally caused by the collapse of dwellings made by human beings.

IRRATIONALITY OF EARTHQUAKE DISASTERS

Panic is one response of humans to disasters that is often described as irrational. But so is the kind of spontaneous solidarity we have witnessed after the 1985 Mexico earthquake. About a million people, many of them middle-class youths, converged on the downtown area in order to try and help the people entombed under the collapsed buildings. Many youths heroically risked their lives by squeezing into cracks and narrow openings in the ruined structures to bring relief to trapped victims. Thousands of housewives prepared meals to feed the distraught and the homeless. No government agency had told them to do this. Doctors and nurses went straight to the collapsed hospitals, without waiting for instructions. It took three days for an organized administrative response to develop; in the meantime, the spontaneous assistance of the citizenry had done their share. Fortunately, solidarity is the rule and panic the exception.

Irrationality may be seen as a response to instability. The assessment of a risk is seldom rational. A driver may voluntarily take much higher chances on the road than he or she would be willing to tolerate from, say, consuming food additives or living next door to a nuclear power plant. This irrational behavior persists in the face of evidence of accidents; it has been attributed to the fact that drivers tend to feel more confident of their own driving skills than of the authorities' ability to enforce rules for the good of society.

Insurance companies know that assigning a money value to the only life we've got is something we'd rather not leave to others. We can assess a price tag on our own life, but we hate others doing it for us. When we buy life insurance, we rarely experience trouble deciding the precise amount of coverage we can afford, but we hate spending taxes on enforcement of controls which would abridge our freedom to endanger others.

In the Tokachi-Oki, Japan earthquake of May 16, 1968 ($M = 7.8$) a number of reinforced concrete-frame buildings collapsed in the Tohoku District. The region was less than prosperous, and in some cases the only reinforced-concrete building in town collapsed while less substantial houses remained standing. Professor Umemura, the admired dean of a generation of Japanese earthquake engineers, publicly took the blame. His students rallied around him and took charge of reconstruction, ignoring the student protest movement that had closed down their faculties. Their attitude saved the honor of Japanese engineering and made possible the subsequent and sweeping reform of the building code (1971–1981).

After the 1985 Mexico earthquake Professor E. Rosenblueth, dean of Mexican earthquake engineers, followed Umemura's example. He stepped forward on TV and accepted personal responsibility for the shortcomings of the Mexico City building code. His courageous attitude deflected the blame from the engineering profession and buttressed his own moral authority. But the reform of the Mexico City building code fell short of the Japanese reform. Some experts estimate that the current code requirements for soft ground are perhaps four times less stringent in Mexico City than in Tokyo. This may or may not reflect different valuations of human life, but it certainly has to do with social and economic considerations. I am aware that comparisons are difficult to make because of different cultural backgrounds and economic conditions.

In conclusion, nonlinearity pervades the field of disaster theory and response to disasters. The effect of nonlinearity may be detected in two ways: (a) as the presence of instabilities in the environment-society system; (b) as a lack of "rationality" in many features of a disaster, including the response of governments and populations.

STABILIZING EFFECT OF EARTHQUAKE PREDICTION

Consider the following operational definition: *Disaster is an instability in the nature-society system that may be induced or prevented by societal or natural inputs.*

Technology is at the interface between society and nature. It is the set of humanmade bridges constructed from a society to nature (including human nature). Caves in loess or high-rise buildings on soft mud are examples of building technologies that may enhance the disaster potential. The examples could be multiplied indefinitely. The present rather vague idea of *vulnerabil-*

ity could thus be replaced by specific instances of inadequate technological response leading to instability.

Gerhard Berz, a mild-mannered, unassuming scientist, has been a frequent visitor to Mexico. Beginning in 1976, as chief geophysicist to a major international reinsurance corporation, he expressed his concern about the next Mexican disaster. He made a detailed assessment of the potential damage, and this assessment became company policy for Mexico.

When the earthquake occurred, Berz was on the spot in a matter of hours. We had breakfast at his hotel and I learned some essential details about the extent of damage. His information was substantially accurate even in the light of more thorough investigations over the following months and years.

But Dr. Berz was not just well informed. His mission went beyond fact-finding. This time he was in Mexico strictly on business, to meet with his clients and to settle insurance claims. In a few days he worked out settlements and flew back to Europe. This had been his company's policy ever since the 1906 San Francisco earthquake. Quick cash after a disaster was of the essence.

It was also good business. What turns an earthquake into a disaster is to a large extent its suddenness and our lack of preparedness. Thus, weeks before the Mexico earthquake a major currency devaluation had taken place. Insurance policies lost nearly half their real cash value. This was a windfall to my friend's company: they only paid out $30 million, substantially less than the amount they had budgeted for this emergency. Their share represented 11% of the total insured damage, which in turn was about 7% of the actual damage. Lulled by a feeling of false security induced by faith in the building code, no official had warned the Mexican public to adjust their policies in time. In the event, the insurance industry was let off lightly by the seismic disaster. A hailstorm that had struck Munich the year before, damaging mostly windshields, had cost the insurance business $1,000 million, substantially more than the worst natural disaster in Mexican history.

Gerhard Berz feels that the 1985 Mexico disaster was by no means as damaging as a worst-case estimate. It did not even reach the probable maximum loss estimated by the insurers. The data used by Berz were available to Mexican officials who could have prepared a response as swift and effective as that of the insurance business. But damage prediction was a part of the long-range strategy of the insurers, not of the Mexican government. Disasters were the insurers' business; they could not afford to make mistakes. Their policy of routine predictions was successful in stabilizing the part of the system they are concerned with.

Gerhard Berz has been modestly, consistently, and accurately predicting earthquakes (as well as hailstorms!) for years. The secret of his success? His shareholders. His job depends on their satisfaction.

Science is an attempt to explain the world as a whole and to seek unity behind the diversity of phenomena, with the aid of principles based on reason rather than on the whim of deities seated on top of Olympus or beyond the physical world. The Greek philosophical tradition had in common with modern science that it attempted to think the existence or unity of the world by making explicit the experience of reason in dealing with itself (Habermas, 1985). But this tradition is now being threatened from within. Science no longer aims to refer to the *whole* world (nature, history, and society) in the sense of a total knowable entity. The theoretical substitutes of our world views have been undermined by the very progress of empirical science, and particularly by the self-conscious reflection that this progress has brought about. Scientific thought steps behind itself and gazes critically at its image. It doesn't like what it sees.

Progress in science has been from the complex to the simple, from the multiplicity of species and elements to quantum chromodynamics and the Big Bang. Today's science is much more unified and much simpler than the science of the 19th century. Yet this unity and depth has been achieved at the cost of breadth and generality. Many scientists live in a rational, nonfalsifiable universe of constant and knowable properties. It is the world of *mundane reasoning* (Gouldner, 1976), which we presume to share with everybody around us. If we compare ourselves with the scientists of Darwin's age, we must concede that we have become parochial.

The 1985 Mexico earthquake was the worst natural disaster in the history of Mexico. It killed at least 10,000 people—not barefoot peasants but urban apartment dwellers whose lifetime savings were suddenly turned into lethal rubble. Yet the broken windshields of Munich were more valuable. They mattered more to the world.

Nobody was hurt in Munich. Munich could afford a hailstorm. Precisely because it was not a disaster it cost the world more money. Natural hazards cause instabilities in the nature-society system *only when they are not foreseen.*

INSTABILITY

The ancient Mexicans attributed the emergence of order in the universe to a divine creation at the origin of time. They believed the gods assembled in Teotihuacan to create the world from chaos. The 17th day of the sacred 20-day month commemorated Nanahuatzin throwing himself into the sacred fire to become the sun. Thus the early priest-philosophers explained the order of the world through powerful primal myths and symbols.

Only since about 1960 did physicists begin to recognize that order emerges out of disorder. The creation of the world never stops and never ends. Philip W. Anderson describes this as the ascendancy of a new approach to physical reality. Dynamic chaos and self-organized criticality have become the hallmarks of the new frontier of physics:

It is one of the universal miracles of nature that huge assemblages of particles, subject only to the blind forces of nature, are nevertheless capable of organizing themselves into patterns of cooperative activity (Davies, 1989).

The idea, however, is not altogether new. Heraclitus (535–475 B.C.) used to teach that "the fairest order in the world is a heap of random sweepings." Along the ages, many thinkers have reflected on order emerging from disorder. Some have watched more closely than others. Consider this description of what happens when a frozen soil layer melts at the edge of a pond in spring:

> Innumerable little streams overlap and interlace one with another, exhibiting a sort of hybrid product, which obeys half way the law of currents, and half way that of vegetation. As it flows it takes the forms of sappy leaves or vines, making heaps of pulpy sprays a foot or more in depth, and resembling, as you look down on them, the laciniated, lobed, and imbricated thalluses of some lichens; or you are reminded of coral, of leopards' paws or birds' feet, of brains or lungs or bowels, and excrements of all kinds.

This is H.D. Thoreau describing a phenomenon known today as viscous fingering (Homsy, 1987). Let us see what happened the next morning at Walden Pond:

> When the sun withdraws the sand ceases to flow but in the morning the streams will start once more and branch and branch again into a myriad of others. You see here perchance how blood vessels are formed. If you look closely you observe that first there pushes forward from the thawing mass a stream of softened sand with a drop-like point, like the ball of a finger, feeling its way slowly and blindly downward. . . . It is wonderful how rapidly yet perfectly the sand organizes itself as it flows. . . . You find thus in the very sands an anticipation of the vegetable leaf. No wonder that the earth expresses itself outwardly in leaves, it so labors with the idea inwardly. . . . Thus it seemed that this one hillside illustrated the principle of all the operations of Nature. The Maker of this earth but patented a leaf. What Champollion will decipher this hieroglyphic for us, that we may turn over a new leaf at last? (Walden, p. 203–205).

Thoreau's idea of self-organization fully anticipates those of contemporary physicists Per Bak, Kurt Wiesenfeld, and Chao Tang. Many phenomena of nature exhibit the same scaling laws determined by self-organized behavior, related to the phase transition of liquefaction. What Thoreau calls "the principle of all the operations of Nature" is in fact nothing but a power law at work. The study of chaos and self-organization has been fed by contributions of many thinkers over the centuries.

Social systems are self-organizing too. We fancy that we are making history when we merely happen to be at a "drop-like point . . . feeling its way slowly and blindly downward."

Earthquakes can be modeled as clusters or avalanches of small shear fractures propagating along a plate boundary. This approach leads to important predictions regarding the distribution of time intervals between events. The theory is being developed by J. Lomnitz-Adler (1989), Sornette and Sornette (1989), Lomnitz-Adler et al. (1991), and others. Self-organization is being recognized as a general feature of steady-state, conservative complex systems.

A "SMALL PAPER" BY KOLMOGOROV

Order is a fact. Chaos is also a fact. The point is how to explain order as emerging from chaos.

The challenge was taken up, among others, by Andrei N. Kolmogorov. He was a fascinating personality. After a brilliant and eventful career he withdrew from science and spent the last decades of his life working as a schoolteacher.

In a number of papers in 1941, Kolmogorov took up Einstein's often-misunderstood remark that "God does not play dice." He showed, for example, that self-similarity can arise from homogeneous fragmentation or subdivision—a mechanism already encountered in connection with rescaled-range analysis. The proof is simple. Suppose that we have a big rock and plenty of time to watch it over the centuries as it crumbles into sand. There is really no other possibility of explaining soils such as sand except as the result of the grinding down of rocks. If the environmental stresses are the same whatever the size of the rock, we may imagine that the probability that a given piece of rock is fragmented into n_i smaller rocks is independent of the stage i of the fragmentation process. In other words, if we start out with a single rock ($n_0 = 1$), in the next stage we have n_1 smaller rocks, in the next stage each of these smaller rocks is fragmented into n_2 still-smaller rocks, and so on. If the n_i are independently distributed random variables, the number of grains at the kth stage of fragmentation must be

$$N_k = \prod_{i=1}^{k} n_i = n_1 n_2 \cdots n_k, \tag{8.2}$$

or

$$\log N_k = \sum_{i=1}^{k} \log n_i. \tag{8.3}$$

But the grain sizes S_k are inversely proportional to the number of grains N_k. By applying a variant of the Central Limit Theorem Kolmogorov found that the logarithms of the grain sizes are normally distributed: that is to say, the distribution of grain sizes in sand is lognormal.

The amazing generality of this proof (greatly simplified here) is the reason for the ubiquity of the lognormal distribution: grain sizes, sizes of watersheds, topographic contours, tree rings, species of animals or plants in Linné's classification, sizes of stars and galaxies, incomes in a society, even characters by number of strokes in a Chinese dictionary. The world originated in a process of fragmentation: the Big Bang. One may wonder whether Kolmogorov realized the universality of his fragmentation process (probably yes). For one thing, he prevailed on one of his friends to translate the little paper into German. Unfortunately it seems, however, that it was mistaken for one of those "little" papers that geniuses like to toss off for the fun of it. Lognormality of grain sizes had long been a well-known property of sands and aggregates. Kolmogorov had provided the beginning of an answer to the implicit question posed by Einstein.

The basic feature of lognormality is the power law. Let X and Y be two random variables. Then if X is lognormal and if

$$Y = aX^d, \tag{8.4}$$

Y is also lognormal. The parameter a is called the *scale factor* and the exponent d is the *fractal dimension*. Power laws such as (8.4) are known as *self-similarity relations*. Conversely, if both X and Y are known to be lognormal, there must exist a self-similarity relation such as Eq (8.4) between them. Kolmogorov invoked this property to deduce that, if the grain sizes of sand are lognormal, so are the grain volumes and (by inference) the fractions by weight retained in sieves of different mesh size.

Aitchison and Brown (1957), who rediscovered Kolmogorov's paper, pointed out that the same fragmentation process can also be applied to many homogeneous branching processes (governing, for example, the distribution of leaves, rivers, and faults), a finding which appears to justify Hurst's results as well as Thoreau's grand intuition. Indeed *the Maker of this Earth but patented a leaf!*

DISASTERS AS INSTABILITIES

Now we have begun defining a disaster as an instability in the nature-society system. We may now make our meaning more precise. *Instability* in a nonlinear system is the uncertainty about the path to be followed by the system in phase space when it is far from equilibrium. There is a *bifurcation* when the system can take at least two different paths except continue in the direction it has been going (which has become unstable). Once the bifurcation has been traversed the system becomes again predictable: At the bifurcation itself it is essentially unpredictable.

When a system drifts away from equilibrium (i.e., the frozen ground begins melting, the soil softens in an earthquake, or a society starts modernizing), new phenomena of self-organization appear. At every instability (disaster), new patterns may appear.

In conclusion, self-organization is a result of nonequilibrium dynamics in a strongly nonlinear system. The nonlinearity causes the system to fluctuate and to *change*, while the continuity properties want to stabilize the system. The dialectics between continuity and change create a synthesis that represents a new kind of *order*. Self-organization is itself a kind of equilibrium, or rather a *compromise* with instability. When such a compromise is denied, the system becomes either erratic (totally disorganized) or dead (totally organized).

When the environment is highly unpredictable (e.g., when a nature-society system is exposed to frequent large earthquakes), the society responds by raising the level of random behavior of the individuals. Nicolis (1986) has shown that the logistic equation

$$dX/dt = aX(N - X) - bX \qquad (8.5)$$

can be used to describe the behavior of colonies of ants. Here X is the number of ants at a source of food, and N is the total number of ants. The parameter a measures the recruitment rate per individual ant, while b measures the frequency of ants coming and going between the food source and the nest. When the food sources are predictable as to location and availability, the ant society responds by a regulated strategy: Permanent trails are developed to each food source. But when the food supply is unpredictable or random, the best strategy is one of random foraging. The differential equation governing the social behavior is the same in both cases, but the strategy is adaptive to the specific situation. Experiments in other insect societies or biological systems (Martiel and Goldbeter, 1987) tend to confirm that the selection of a route in phase space depends on the predictability of the environment.

We may conclude that the most effective strategy for the control of earthquake hazard leads through prediction. Dynamical systems theory affords a practical approach for monitoring the effect of earthquake prediction on disaster control. Even if we don't know how to predict earthquakes at this time, we should not stop enquiring for the regularities of the process so as to gradually learn to anticipate them.

PREDICTABILITY

A self-organizing system evolves from some initial state. As it wanders away from equilibrium it may drift into some typical behavior or attractor. A periodic attractor is a closed loop in phase space. There may be several such attractors in different regions of phase space and a system may fall into one or the other depending on its path in phase space.

Because of the fractality of the underlying system, the attractors are chaotic, or "strange." The future of such a system can be predicted only in a limited sense. Strange attractors arise in common phenomena such as turbulence or climate change. In plate tectonics, a plate boundary is generated by a continuous process of attrition and fragmentation: After a time it is composed of an organized system of small fracture planes of different sizes. Small earthquakes break one or a few of such elementary faults at a time, but complex propagating ruptures are large-scale instabilities on the order of the size of a plate boundary, involving thousands of elementary faults.

A plate boundary is approximately steady-state and conservative, because all seismic activity is embedded in a process of global quasi-stationary convection. Thus, every earthquake is part of a larger strain transient that features patterns and regularities. Earthquake prediction is likely to be feasible in the same sense, and to the same extent, that weather prediction is feasible. If we succeed in imaging the shifting energy patterns along plate boundaries, we can begin making sense of precursors.

Deformation of plate boundaries occurs largely through aseismic creep; only a smaller part corresponds to seismic fault slip. As a rule the aseismic phase, which starts earlier than the earthquake, generates precursors that can be detected.

Even if earthquakes were essentially chaotic and unpredictable, the effects of earthquakes on society might still be largely predictable. The occurrence of the 1992 Landers, California earthquake ($M = 7.5$) increased the public concern over weaknesses that were detected in the level of preparedness of the San Francisco Bay region during the 1989 earthquake. Society still depends on destructive earthquakes to provide the needed impulse for controlling earthquake risk. Earthquake prediction programs can represent a rational approach in this direction.

Where the nature-society system is more closely integrated, as in Japan, earthquake prediction has become a prime consideration and the risk due to earthquakes can be more closely controlled. This is reflected in many aspects of social life: an ordered lifestyle, long-range planning, interpersonal relations of trust that pervade all social interactions, technological innovations including unitized and standardized housing systems, and high standards of reliability and safety. Thus the earthquake risk can be gradually made independent of the type of geological environment. In order to prevent disasters the entire nature-society system must be made more predictable.

9

Theory of Strong Motion on Soft Ground

The earth hath bubbles, as the water has.
—Macbeth

INTRODUCTION

Soils are highly nonlinear. It remains unclear, however, exactly what role nonlinearity plays in wave propagation and how this is expressed in the behavior of systems of soils.

The nonlinear behavior of soils is not altogether unexpected. Soils are hybrids between solids and liquids. The softer the soil, the more its behavior resembles that of a liquid. After the 1923 Tokyo earthquake, T. Matuzawa (1925) observed the residual or "frozen" waveforms found on the ground surface and suggested that they were due to hydrodynamic waves. These waveforms are now known as *jinami* or earth waves in Japan. A decade later, the founders of soil mechanics, Karl von Terzaghi and Arthur Casagrande, discovered the liquefaction of some natural soils subjected to strong vibrations.

In 1967 Freeman Gilbert developed a linear theory of Rayleigh wave propagation in soils; he showed that the type of propagation is governed by the dimensionless ratio

$$\mathscr{L} = \rho g/\mu k \tag{9.1}$$

where ρ is the density, g is the acceleration of gravity, μ is the modulus of rigidity, and k is the wavenumber. Since $k = 2\pi/\lambda$ (where λ is the wavelength), the shorter the wavelength the larger is $\mathscr{L}$ and the softer is the mate-

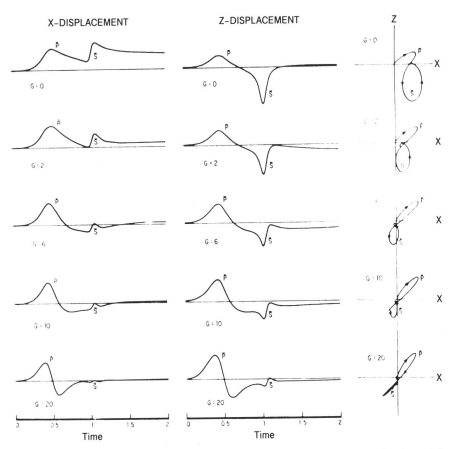

Fig. 9.1 *Particle motion of Rayleigh waves for different values of* $G = k\Delta\mathcal{L}$, *where* Δ *is the epicentral distance. Note that the motion becomes prograde at* $G > 6$, *which means* $\mathcal{L} > 1$ *for distances of the order of one wavelength. After Gilbert (1967). By permission of the Seismological Society of America.*

rial. When $\mathcal{L} > 1$, the particle motion turns prograde (Fig. 9.1), and the Rayleigh wave slows down and increasingly resembles a water wave.

In 1941 A.N. Kolmogorov discovered that the distribution of grain sizes in soils could be explained by a mechanism of homogeneous stagewise fragmentation, of the type known today as *fractality* (see Chapter 8). Starting with a rock of any size and assuming that the number of fragments is an independently distributed random variable at any stage of fragmentation, he obtained the lognormal distribution in agreement with observations.

This result is of great generality. It suggests that power laws may occupy a central position in the theory of soils. For example, from the theorem of the lognormal distribution it follows that any variable B is lognormal if it is a power function of a lognormal variable A, i.e.

$$B = kA^n. \tag{9.2}$$

Thus the lognormality of the grain sizes of soils means that the grain surfaces, the grain volumes, and any other variables which are proportional to any of the preceding, must also be lognormal variables.

We may extend this result to the stress-strain behavior of soils. Suppose that we subject a unit section of a soil to a unit simple shear strain. We find that the shear forces applied to each grain must be lognormally distributed, since they are proportional to the grain surfaces. By this reasoning it turns out that the shear modulus G and the rigidity μ should both be related to the grain surfaces by power laws; therefore they must be related to each other by a power law:

$$G = c\mu^d, \tag{9.3}$$

or, replacing G and μ by their definitions in terms of shear stress σ and shear strain ϵ:

$$\frac{d\sigma}{d\epsilon} = c\left(\frac{\sigma}{\epsilon}\right)^d, \tag{9.4}$$

which is the constitutive equation of soils in shear, derived from first principles.

LIQUEFACTION AS A PHASE TRANSITION

Soil engineers B.O. Hardin and V.P. Drnevich (1972) had empirically proposed a constitutive equation of soils. From hundreds of laboratory tests in all kinds of soils they found the hyperbolic stress-strain relation in shear:

$$\sigma = G_0 \frac{\epsilon\gamma_r}{\epsilon + \gamma_r}, \tag{9.5}$$

which can be obtained by integrating Eq (9.4) and setting $d = 2$. The exponent d is usually called the *fractal dimension*, and the parameter γ_r was called *reference strain* by Hardin and Drnevich. Eq (9.5) is strongly nonlinear. It may be interpreted as saying that the shear modulus $G = \sigma/\epsilon$ of a soil decays inversely as $1 + \tau$, where $\tau = \epsilon/\gamma_r$ is the normalized strain. The curvature of the stress-strain curve is largest near the origin and smallest at approaching failure. This behavior is the opposite of what we expect to observe in rocks,

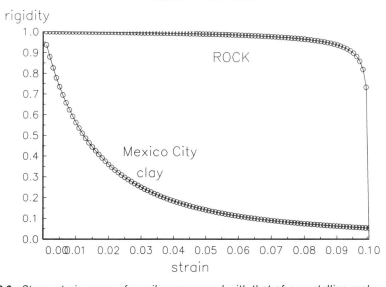

Fig. 9.2 *Stress-strain curve of a soil as compared with that of a crystalline rock.*

metals, and other polycrystalline solids (Fig. 9.2). Strictly speaking, the stress-strain behavior of soils cannot be linearized at small strains.

Soils continue to be treated as essentially linear materials within the range of seismic strains. However, evidence of nonlinearity has increasingly been reported in large earthquakes. Nonlinearity breeds instability. A soil is an assemblage of solid grains in a fluid matrix. At what amplitude will the properties of the matrix begin to dominate over those of the solid skeleton? Such a phase transition would be rather similar to the observed liquefaction in soils (Fig. 9.3).

Richard Feynman once told his students that a box full of ball bearings could propagate waves similar to water waves along its free surface. The ball bearings stand for the solid grains of a soil. A transition from solid to liquid behavior may or may not be implicit in the constitutive equation. Instabilities can arise in many different ways. Yet solids cannot gradually turn into liquids: The transition must be sudden and discrete. Liquefaction is a phase change.

An example of such a phase change may be demonstrated in a material which obeys Eq (9.5). Consider a Rayleigh wave propagating over a deep, flat horizontal layer of soil. If A is the amplitude and k is the wavenumber, the energy per unit volume is

$$E = \int_{\epsilon=0}^{Ak} \sigma d\epsilon, \qquad (9.6)$$

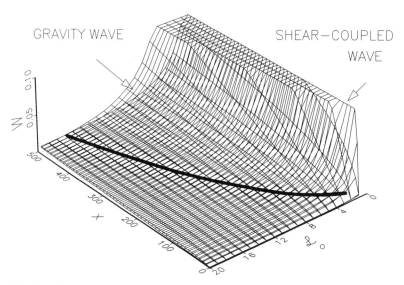

Fig. 9.3 *$\mathscr{L}$-x diagram of the energy W per unit area, showing that the critical amplitude (crossover of the two surfaces) depends on the $\mathscr{L}_0$ -number (i.e. on the initial rigidity of the soil). The lower the initial rigidity, the lower is the critical amplitude x.*

since Ak equals the maximum shear strain in a cycle. Let us now introduce the dimensionless peak strain $\tau = Ak/\gamma_r$. Integrating Eq (9.5) we find, for $d = 2$,

$$E = G_0\gamma_r^2 [\tau - \ln(1 + \tau)] \qquad (9.7)$$

per unit volume. The energy per unit area W_s is obtained by dividing E by the average depth of the strained surface layer, which is pproximately $1/k$ (Gilbert, 1967). Thus we may write

$$W_s = G_0\gamma_r^2 k^{-1} [\tau - \ln(1 + \tau)] \qquad (9.8)$$

per unit area. In the case of a gravity wave, on the other hand, the energy per unit area is $W_g = A^2 \rho g$, where ρ is the density. It increases more steeply than W_s (Eq 9.8) when $\tau > 1$. In other words, for a given amplitude, the restoring force of gravity waves becomes larger than that for Rayleigh wave at large strains. The crossover (i.e., the transition) is found approximately by equating W_s with

$$W_g = \rho g\gamma_r^2 k^{-2}\tau^2. \qquad (9.9)$$

We find

$$\rho g k^{-1} G_0^{-1} \tau^2 = \tau - \ln(1 + \tau). \qquad (9.10)$$

at crossover. Eq (9.10) has always a real positive root since the right-hand side is positive for all $\tau > 0$. Thus there is a phase transition. Above the instability the gravity wave represents the more economical mode of propagation, because its amplitude is lower for a given input energy than the amplitude of the Rayleigh wave. Thus as soon as the critical amplitude τ is reached, the rigidity μ drops, the wavelength shortens and the strain rises chaotically until the Rayleigh wave is shear-decoupled.

Eq (9.10) says that the transition depends on the parameter

$$\mathcal{L} = \rho g / \mu k \qquad (9.11)$$

since $G_0 = \mu_0$. Thus the left-hand side of Eq (9.10) becomes $\mathcal{L}\tau^2$. A parameter such as $\mathcal{L}$, which governs a phase transition, is called an *order parameter*. The process may be pictured as follows. As the strong motion begins, the soil is relatively rigid ($\mu \gg 0$) and $\mathcal{L}$ is small. But as the amplitude of the seismic motion rises, the shear velocity $\beta = \sqrt{(\mu/\rho)}$ decays. Since

$$\mathcal{L} = g/(k\beta^2), \qquad (9.12)$$

(from 9.11), we see that $\mathcal{L}$ rises as β decreases. At the critical value of $\mathcal{L}$ given by Eq (9.10) the phase transition takes place. Conversely, as the earthquake wanes, $\mathcal{L}$ traverses the critical value in the opposite direction and the surface "freezes"—that is, the gravity wave is shear-coupled and the soil solidifies.

The preceding *stability analysis* is not exact for several reasons. First, it assumes the validity of a specific constitutive equation; and, while this equation has been extensively tested and confirmed in all kinds of soils, the phenomenon of liquefaction may depend on mechanisms of an entirely different nature, for example, on surface friction at grain level. Second, our analysis assumes linearity in the region of the transition. As a rule, the critical values of τ are overestimated by Eq (9.10). For our purpose (which is, understanding the phenomenology of the phase transition) the present stability analysis will do. I hope it convinces the reader that liquefaction is likely to be a general feature of soils at large cyclic strains.

PLANE SOLITON IN TWO DIMENSIONS

Now the wave equation for a gravity wave in shallow water is

$$\omega^2 = gk \tanh kh, \qquad (9.13)$$

where h is the depth of the water. In the case of Mexico City the soft soil layer has a depth of $h = 20\text{-}50$ m, which would be borderline between deep and shallow water. Introducing a wave period of 2 s we find a wavelength of the order of 10 to 15 m.

What would a nonlinear solution be like? Consider the following wave equation, known as the Kadomtsev–Petviashvili equation (Infeld and Rowlands, 1990):

$$u_{tx} + 12(uu_x)_x + u_{xxxx} + 3u_{yy} = 0 \qquad (9.14)$$

where u is the vertical displacement for a wave propagating in the x direction, the subindices stand for partial differentiation, and the length dimension has been renormalized to get rid of coefficients in the velocity ratio β/α. For positive dispersion the term in u_{yy} should be taken as negative. The velocity potential $\phi(u = \phi_x)$ is

$$\phi_t + 6\phi_x^2 + 3\int_{-\infty}^{x} \phi_{yy}dx = 0, \qquad (\phi = 0 \text{ at } x \to -\infty). \qquad (9.15)$$

Consider a formal expansion of the potential $\phi = \phi^{(1)} + \phi^{(2)} + \cdots$ such that all terms vanish at minus infinity. Eq (9.15) suggests a linear operator L such that

$$L\phi^{(1)} = (\partial_t + \partial_x^3 + 3\partial_x^{-1}\partial_y^2)\phi^{(1)} = 0. \qquad (9.16)$$

Then we have

$$L\phi^{(2)} = -6(\phi_x^{(1)})^2 \qquad (9.17)$$

$$L\phi^{(3)} = -12(\phi_x^{(1)}\phi_x^{(2)}) \qquad (9.18)$$

$$\cdots\cdots\cdots\cdots\cdots\cdots\cdots\cdots\cdots$$

$$L\phi^{(n)} = -6\sum_{l=1}^{n-1} \phi_x^{(l)}\phi^{(n-1)} . \qquad (9.19)$$

Let us now introduce the following functions:

$$f_l(x) = \exp(q_l x), \qquad (9.20)$$

$$g_l(x) = \exp(q_l x)\, C_l(y,t), \qquad (9.21)$$

$$C_l(y,t) = C_l(0)\, \exp[-(p_l^2 - q_l^2)y - 4(p_l^3 + q_l^3)t] \qquad (9.22)$$

where p and q are related to the wavenumber as

$$k_x = \frac{1}{2}(p_1 + q_1), \qquad k_y = \frac{1}{2}(q_1^2 - p_1^2),. \tag{9.23}$$

for $l = 1$ (a single soliton). It can be shown that

$$\phi^{(1)} = \sum_{l=1}^{N} f_l(x)g_l(x, y, t) \tag{9.24}$$

$$\phi^{(2)} = -\sum_{l=1}^{N}\sum_{m=1}^{N} \frac{1}{p_l + q_m} f_l(x)g_l(x,y,t)f_m(x)g_m(x,y,t) \tag{9.25}$$

satisfy the operator for any finite number N of solitons. Thus, if we introduce a matrix **B** of $N \times N$ elements such that

$$B_{lm} = \frac{1}{p_l + q_m} f_l(x)g_m(x,y,t), \tag{9.26}$$

then

$$\phi^{(1)} = \mathrm{Tr}\left(\frac{\partial \mathbf{B}}{\partial x}\right), \quad \phi^{(2)} = -\mathrm{Tr}\left(\frac{\partial \mathbf{B}}{\partial x} \cdot \mathbf{B}\right), \tag{9.27}$$

and more generally,

$$\phi^{(n)} = (-1)^{n-1}\,\mathrm{Tr}\left(\frac{\partial \mathbf{B}}{\partial x} \cdot \mathbf{B}^{n-1}\right). \tag{9.28}$$

This is the origin of the term *trace method* for this particular approach, first applied to the Korteweg–de Vries equation by Wadati and Sawada.

Finally, from Eq (9.28) we obtain the velocity potential

$$\phi = \mathrm{Tr}\left(\frac{\partial \mathbf{B}}{\partial x} - \frac{\partial \mathbf{B}}{\partial x}\mathbf{B} + \frac{\partial \mathbf{B}}{\partial x}\mathbf{B}^2 - \cdots\right)$$

$$= \frac{\partial}{\partial x}\,\mathrm{Tr}\,\ln(\mathbf{I} + \mathbf{B}). \tag{9.29}$$

For any square matrix we have $\det(\exp \mathbf{A}) = \exp(\mathrm{Tr}\,\mathbf{A})$. Thus if we introduce $\mathbf{A} = \ln(\mathbf{I} + \mathbf{B})$, the preceding equation yields

$$u = \frac{\partial \phi}{\partial x} = \frac{\partial^2}{\partial x^2}\,\ln \det(\mathbf{I} + \mathbf{B}), \tag{9.30}$$

which is the desired solution. It may be shown to include the soliton solution for surface waves found by Lord Rayleigh in 1876:

$$v = 3\eta\,\mathrm{sech}^2\,[0.5\,\eta^{0.5}\,(x - \eta t) \tag{9.31}$$

where v is the velocity of the soliton in the x-direction and η is a constant amplitude. In conclusion, the velocity of a soliton is roughly proportional to its amplitude.

Solitons are stable phenomena. A single soliton consists of one pulse that propagates with little dispersion. Well-known examples are the *tsunami* waves generated by large earthquakes, which can cross the Pacific Ocean though their amplitude in deep water may be of the order of 1 m or less. In shallow water and especially in funnel-shaped bays or estuaries they can grow to heights of 30 m, as in the destructive 1960 Chile earthquake.

Solitons interact with other solitons as if they were particles: two rectilinear solitons crossing at right angles go clear through each other without interference. Other nonlinear wave effects shown in Fig. 9.4 include the so-

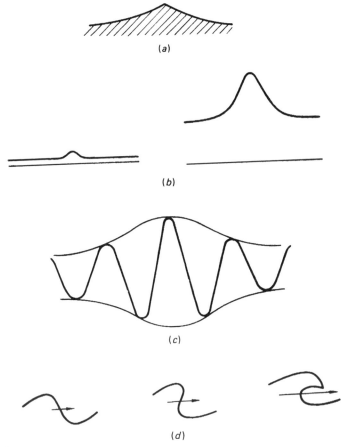

Fig. 9.4 *Some nonlinear wave phenomena. (a) a 120° cusp forming on a water wave; (b) two different solitons; (c) an envelope soliton (the envelope behaves as a soliton) (d) Shoaling and breaking. From E. Infeld and G. Rowlands,* Nonlinear Waves, Solitons and Chaos. *Copyright Cambridge University Press, 1990. Reprinted with the permission of Cambridge University Press.*

called envelope solitons, in which the envelope of a wave packet behaves as a soliton. When several solitons of different amplitudes are generated, the packet spreads out as it travels with the largest amplitude in front, since the velocity depends on the amplitude. J. Scott Russell (1844) was the first to observe an actual soliton propagating in a canal near Edinburgh in 1834. Similar solitons (as well as standing waves) can be generated in sedimentary basins during large earthquakes.

SOLITONS IN CRATERING

In 1968 Bill Van Dorn, a hydrodynamicist at the Scripps Institution of Oceanography, published a small paper on the ringlike structures observed around impact craters on the Moon (Fig. 9.5). He was able to show that the diameters and elevations of the rings fitted exactly (to within 3%) the pattern of propagating solitons. It was as if the surface of the moon had liquefied under the impact and had later frozen to preserve the shape of the wave. He calculated that liquefaction of the moon's surface should have lasted for about one hour, during which successive solitons propagated outward from the center of the disturbance. The solitons looked like tsunamis, or waves generated by earthquakes in the ocean. He called the phenomenon a "lunar tsunami".

This work represented a verification of an earlier suggestion made by Ralph Baldwin (1972). As a hydrodynamicist, Van Dorn found his explanation natural and convincing: but it flew in the face of accepted theories of surface wave propagation in soils. Lunar soils are bone-dry. The idea that liquefaction can occur in dry soils contradicted the prevailing dogma that soils liquefy because of a sudden rise in pore pressure in a liquid matrix. Besides, the parameter $\mathscr{L}$ in lunar sediments was supposed to be very small, and it was not realized at the time that it would have to rise as a result of the excitation. In conclusion, the idea of tsunamis in the Moon was dismissed. They could not exist—*under assumptions of linearity*.

Van Dorn persisted with his ideas long enough to suggest that seismic damage to engineering structures on soft ground could be caused by gravity waves. This was pure heresy at the time. He finally gave up and the ring pattern around lunar craters was explained in other ways—though the observed ratio of the radii makes sense only if the surface of the Moon and other planetary bodies liquefies under impact (Melosh, 1989).

I picked up the trail of Van Dorn's observations around 1970. By then I realized (as a few engineers also did at the time) that he was probably right. I had observed ground waves similar to water waves on soft sediments during the 1960 Chile earthquake. Waves resembling water waves had been reported by witnesses during practically every large earthquake on soft ground. C.F. Richter had agreed that these observations must be real, but other seismolo-

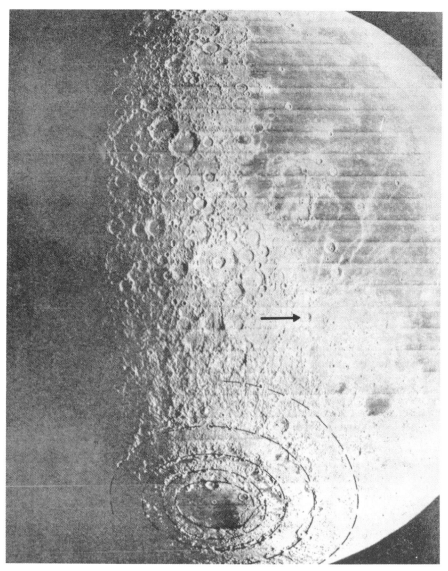

Fig. 9.5 Tsunamis *on the Moon: the historic Orbiter IV image used to infer impact-gener-ated gravity waves from the Orientale crater (lower left). The arrow signals the outer limit of ejecta. Radii of rings* (dashed) *increase as* $\pi(2n - 1) - \omega t$, *where* n *is the crest order number; this relation can be explained from hydrodynamics. Reprinted with permission from* Nature *(Van Dorn, W.G., Tsunamis on the moon? Vol. 220, p. 1102–1107). Copyright 1968 Macmillan Magazines Limited.*

gists tended to shrug them off as "optical illusions." The question was: How could water waves propagate on solid ground?

The answer was that the ground was no longer solid.

LINEAR AND QUASI-LINEAR APPROACHES

The prevailing theory of strong motion prediction on soft ground underwent a shock treatment at the hands of the 1985 Mexico earthquake. It emerged a different theory. Prior to 1985 it was generally thought that soft ground "deamplified" strong ground motion. Soil was often preferred to hard rock as a foundation material. Nuclear reactors were built on soil even though hard rock was available next door—or a layer of sandy fill was purposely emplaced on top of the rock surface to "improve" foundation conditions.

The difference between soil and rock was thought to run in favor of sites on soft ground even more strongly at high ground accelerations (above 0.1 g). This illusion was brutally dispelled when 371 high-rise buildings collapsed on soft ground in downtown Mexico City. Many engineers had regarded these buildings as poor risks in case of an earthquake; but the same buildings remained standing on hard ground a few city blocks away. The Mexico City disaster claimed an undisclosed number of victims (10,000 is a minimum figure), but no casualties were reported on hard ground. Similar differences in vulnerability of structures on hard and soft ground were observed in the 1989 Loma Prieta, California, earthquake, where 41 people were squashed to death in the collapse of a reinforced concrete freeway on soft ground in Oakland. The freeway had been built in 1957 and had been retrofitted in 1978. It had not been singled out as a poor risk in case of an earthquake.

Fig. 9.6 reveals the watershed in engineering predictions that developed as a result of these two earthquakes. Both curves were proposed by the same author, one before the 1985 Mexico earthquake and the other one year after the 1989 Loma Prieta earthquake. Notice how the estimated amplification in the range of rock ground accelerations of 0.1–0.2g doubled from one prediction to the other. This is the range of accelerations where most moderately damaging earthquakes occur. The peak acceleration in the Mexico City earthquake was above 0.2g. In the Loma Prieta earthquake it was 0.44g in the epicentral region and around 0.29g in the Bay area.

Soft ground is now generally acknowledged to *amplify* strong motion at all amplitudes up to a level of about 0.4g. At higher accelerations a deamplification is still expected. Some recent data suggest that amplitudes may tend to saturate around 0.4g. Yet theory suggests that amplitudes of up to 2g should occur in sediments, and amplitudes of up to 1.5g have actually been recorded near active faults.

Low resonant frequencies of the soil layer and low shear-wave velocities are common on soft ground (Fig. 9.7). Since tall buildings tend to have large lateral dimensions and low natural frequencies of oscillation, they are more

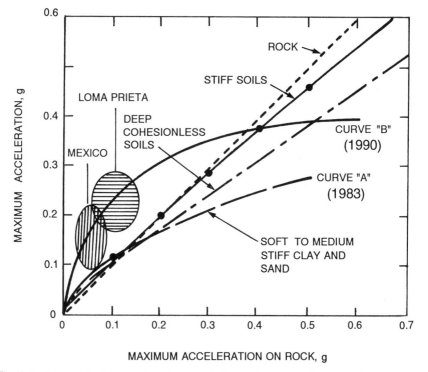

Fig. 9.6 *A watershed for engineering predictions of amplification on soft ground. The two curves correspond to predictions by the same author (Idriss, 1990), (A) before, and (B) after the Mexico and Loma Prieta earthquakes. From Finn (1991). With permission from the Association for Earthquake Disaster Prevention, Tokyo.*

Fig. 9.7 *Example of overturned building due to foundation failure in the 1985 Mexico earthquake. Here the piles were pulled out together with the intervening soil. Author's photograph.*

vulnerable on soft ground than on hard ground. Nonlinearity of soils involves much more than just amplitude saturation. Eventually it will be recognized that soil sites are more hazardous than rock sites for all structures at all seismic amplitude levels.

STANDARD PREDICTION TECHNIQUES FOR STRONG GROUND MOTION

These insights have been coming the hard way. Even after the 1985 Mexico earthquake many engineers continued to insist that the combination of strong resonant periods with high amplifications on soft ground in that earthquake was "very unusual" and "a very special case which would not be duplicated elsewhere" (Green, 1987). Two years later the Loma Prieta earthquake produced severe damage in the San Francisco Bay area. Underlain by soft bay mud, this region was 100 km distant from the epicenter. Damage in the immediate epicentral area was minor, but reinforced concrete-frame structures tumbled down on bay mud—even though the earthquake had been much weaker than the Mexican event.

Linear methods still retain their popularity with engineers. Often they can lead to suggestive and intellectually stimulating results. Two major ground-motion prediction experiments, one in Japan and the other in the United States, have been carried out on the proposal of an international working group of engineers and seismologists; other similar experiments are currently being proposed. The idea of the experiments (one at Turkey Flat, California, and the other in Ashigara Valley, Japan) was to have different numerical approaches tested by groups from different countries, in order to improve the prediction of earthquake ground motion on soft ground. The predicted strong-motion seismograms were compared with actual seismograms that were not made available to the predictors until after the predictions were received. This simple idea of a "blind" procedure represents a bold step to do away with the *a posteriori* forecasts that have plagued the field of earthquake prediction.

The two test sites are: (1) Turkey Flat, California Test Area, U.S.A., established by the State of California Division of Mines and Geology less than five miles southeast of Parkfield, California, where a major earthquake was expected to occur before the end of 1992; (2) Ashigara Valley, Kanagawa Prefecture, Japan, including the coastal city of Odawara on the north shore of Sagami Bay, on a deep alluvial plain. The "blind predictions" consisted in asking participants to identify methods for the optimal estimation of synthetic seismograms, peak amplitudes, and spectra of strong or weak ground motion in moderate-sized earthquakes. The submissions were compared with actual records that had not been made available to the participants beforehand.

The prediction techniques used in these two experiments fall into two large groups: (a) techniques for investigating the relevant parameters of ground geology; (b) techniques for obtaining actual ground-motion predictions.

(a) Geotechnical Procedures

The following techniques were used generally both in Japan and in the United States:

SOIL PROPERTIES DETERMINATION
  Surface geology
  Drilling logs (*stratigraphy*)
  Borehole lateral loading (*elastic moduli*)
  Caliper logging (*determine diameter of borehole at depth*)
  Electrical logging (*apparent resistivity*)
VELOCITY PROFILING
  Downhole velocity logging (*P and S velocities*)
  Suspension velocity logging (*P and S velocities*)
  Vertical seismic profiling (*S-wave velocities*)
  Shallow seismic reflection (*S-wave velocities*)
  Shallow seismic refraction (*P and S velocities, Q*)
LABORATORY TESTS
  Specific gravity
  grain size
  moisture content
  unit weight
  Attenberg limits
  resonant column and torsion cyclic shear
  tests for rigidity and damping
  triaxial ultrasonic wave velocity determinations

On the basis of the data from these tests, a standard model was constructed for each site. This standard model was a synthesis of the total geological and geotechnical information: it was intended to be used by all participants, although any group was free to use additional models of their own. The input from geology was perhaps somewhat perfunctory. Little information was available (or required by the participants) as to the geological setting and the tectonic history of the two sites. Some groups optionally conducted their own geotechnical investigations or prepared their own synthesis in the expectation of improving their predictions by using a nonstandard geological model.

(b) Mathematical Approaches

The following techniques were used singly or in combination by different groups:

EQUIVALENT LINEAR ESTIMATION
  Computer programs (*SHAKE, LAYSOL, DESRA2, DYNA1D, SIREN, EQLM*)
  Linear viscoelastic methods

SPECTRAL METHODS
  Semianalytic (*plane/antiplane wave calculations*)
  Stochastic (*Boore*)
  Stochastic with SH-wave propagators

HASKELL METHODS
  Haskell
  Discrete wavenumber boundary elements
  Hybrid ray theory (*Sánchez Sesma*)

WAVE PROPAGATION
  Finite difference
  Frequency/wavenumber
  Propagator matrix with source effect

TWO-DIMENSIONAL METHODS
  Finite-element methods (*elastic, viscoelastic, elastoplastic, nonlinear hysteretic*)
  Wave propagation (*discrete wavenumber, Haines*)
  Boundary-element methods

THREE-DIMENSIONAL METHODS
  Wave propagation

The variety of numerical methods is representative of the rich development of recent methods for strong ground motion simulation. Some other methods were also used; however, most groups preferred equivalent linear, one-dimensional treatments. This preference proved to be well founded. While only a single group bothered to use a three-dimensional method, no significant difference in the results were found to exist between three-dimensional, two-dimensional, or one-dimensional methods. In fact there was a wider scatter between different one-dimensional approaches, and the more sophisticated methods were not necessarily better than the simpler ones. Unfortunately the organizers of the experiments were reluctant to identify the individual contributions, in order not to hurt feelings, and it is difficult to determine who did better than whom. Only the statistics were published. But these statistics are adequate for comparing the results of the various methods: They tend to show a broad agreement in terms of amplitude predictions and a wide scatter in almost everything else.

This may mean that we are not looking at the damage problem in the right way. Either all methods and approaches are equally poor, or we are not considering all causes of damage. In Turkey Flat as in Ashigara the experts were asked to predict gound motions on open flat terrain, but damage occurs in sedimentary wedges along the edges of valleys or lakes and around bay-shore waterfronts. We seem to excel at predicting amplitudes in all situations where damage does not occur.

The structural integrity of a building is (like virginity) a strictly nonlinear affair. It is lost under rather peculiar and extenuating circumstances. Reasons for blaming the building (or the maiden) can always be found. But, rightly considered, it is always due to local inputs that vastly exceed ordinary linear calculations.

A HYBRID METHOD FOR SEISMIC RESPONSE

As an example, let us briefly dwell on a specific computational method that has the advantage of being relatively simple, straightforward, and economical. Other methods can obtain synthetic seismograms at the cost of a relatively large effort in terms of supercomputer time, at least for realistic geological models, even though the basic mathematical approach may be simpler (cf. Aki and Richards, 1980). But, as we have just seen, this effort does not seem to pay off.

The hybrid approach developed by Francisco J. Sánchez Sesma and his group in Mexico has the advantage of running on a personal computer with no severe loss of accuracy as compared to more exact calculations. The approach is termed *hybrid* because the solution is obtained by fitting together one-dimensional and normal-mode solutions (Calderón et al., 1992). Suppose that a sedimentary valley is modeled as a sandbox embedded in a flat one-sided homogeneous plain that goes to infinity, that is, a *half space* (Fig. 9.8). The material in the sandbox can be layered, with different seismic velocities for each layer. We wish to predict the time history of the ground motion at any point on the surface of the sandbox. All materials are assumed to be elastic so that the approach will be linear. We assume that the earthquake excitation consists of plane SH waves coming from below at some arbitrary angle θ. Damping is considered for all propagating terms.

The desired displacement v_E^{left} at the left side of the sandbox may be written

$$v_E^{\text{left}} = v^{(0)} + v^{(\text{dleft})} \tag{9.32}$$

where $v^{(0)}$ is the free-field displacement for the half-space by itself and v^{dleft} is the diffracted wave field. A similar expression may be written for the right

SURFACE

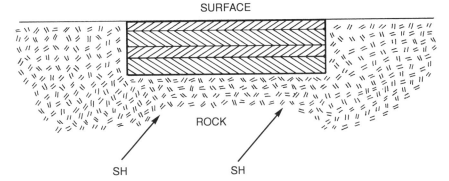

Fig. 9.8 *Model of an alluvial valley, Redrafted after Calderón et al. (1992). By permission of the Association for Earthquake Disaster Prevention, Tokyo.*

side. We assume that the two sides are sufficiently far away from each other that the exterior effect of one edge on the other may be neglected.

Consider first the displacements on the right-hand side of Eq (9.32). Writing the spatial part only (i.e. omitting the term in $e^{i\omega t}$ for brevity), we have

$$v^{(0)} = 2 \cos (\omega z \cos \theta/\beta) \exp[-i\omega x \sin \theta/\beta], \tag{9.33}$$

$$v^{(d)} = \sum_{n=1}^{N} A_n G_n, \tag{9.34}$$

where ω is the frequency, θ is the angle of incidence, β is the shear-wave velocity in the half-space, N is the number of sources, A_n are source coefficients to be determined, and G_n are the Green's functions given by

$$G_n = -i/4 \, [H_0^{(2)} \, (\omega/\beta r_n) + H_0^{(2)} \, (\omega/\beta r_n')] \tag{9.35}$$

where $H_0^{(2)}$ is the zero-order Hankel function of the second kind, r_n is the distance to the source, and r_n' is the distance to the image of the source with respect to the surface. Expressions such as Eq (9.35) appear quite commonly in seismology when the treatment is one-dimensional: that is, we are considering cylindrical SH waves that propagate radially from the source.

Now the refracted field is the sum of the one-dimensional solution and the contribution of the modes:

$$v_R = v_{1D} + \sum_{m=0}^{M} v_m(z) \, [B_m \exp(ik_m x) + C_m \exp(-ik_m x)], \tag{9.36}$$

where v_{1D} is the one-dimensional solution (which may be obtained separately, for instance by Haskell's method), M is the number of modes to be considered (as small as possible), and B_m and C_m are the modal coefficients to be determined.

Finally, we introduce the variation of displacements with depth due to surface waves in the sandbox:

$$v_m(z) = \ell_1(k_m, z, \omega), \tag{9.37}$$

which shows the displacement as a function of the depth z, the frequency ω, and the wavenumber k corresponding to each mode m. Since the excitation is assumed to contain only SH waves we consider only Love wave modes associated with the frequency ω for the given layered structure.

Now the unknown coefficients A, B, C can be calculated by introducing the boundary conditions, notably continuity of displacements and of tractions at the edges of the sandbox:

$$v_E = v_R, \tag{9.38}$$

$$\mu_E \frac{\partial v_E}{\partial \mathbf{n}} = \mu_R \frac{\partial v_R}{\partial \mathbf{n}} \tag{9.39}$$

where $\mathbf{n}$ is the normal vector of the interface directed into the sandbox. The unknown coefficients are evaluated by regression as the number of equations of condition is larger than the number of coefficients.

Fig. 9.9 shows a comparison between results obtained by this hybrid method and by a complete two-dimensional boundary-element method, which involved a much more expensive calculation. The sandbox was a shallow rectangular basin of 1,000 m depth and 8 km width, with a flat horizontal bottom. The S-wave velocities were 1,000 m/s for the basin and 2,500 m/s for the half-space. The angle of incidence was vertical. Only two normal modes (the fundamental and the first) were used in the hybrid calculation in spite of which the agreement is good. Even better agreement is obtained with more realistic models, such as sloping interfaces and oblique incidence.

The general level of mathematical sophistication that is required in seismological work has risen over the past 15 years but remains modest compared with other fields of physics. It requires an operational familiarity with elastic wave propagation in one or more dimensions. The preceding example shows, however, that little may be gained from refining these techniques over and above a certain level.

In the case of the problem of soft-ground response this is due to the geometry of sedimentary valleys, which is very shallow and flat, with an aspect ratio on the order of 1:50 or more. Little difference between one-dimensional and three-dimensional treatments would be expected. But there is a more fundamental reason. Soils are nonlinear, and the amplitudes are strongly affected by nonlinearity near an instability. At low amplitudes one finds a comfortable margin of convergence between all linear methods and the field data. But at large amplitudes anything might happen. And the large amplitudes are the ones of practical interest.

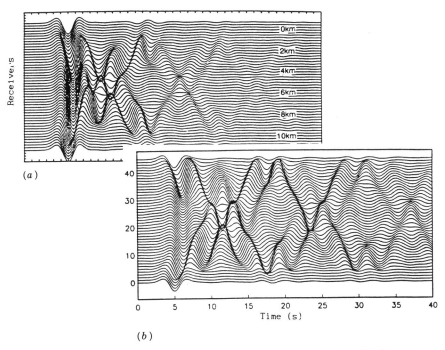

Fig. 9.9 *Comparison of (a) one-dimensional method described here with (b) complete two-dimensional method. From Calderón et al. (1992). Reprinted by permission of the Association for Earthquake Disaster Prevention, Tokyo.*

NONLINEAR EFFECTS AND AMPLIFICATION

The nonlinear behavior of soils in shear has come to be widely acknowledged by engineers and seismologists alike. Yet, in what looks like a rearguard action, the shadow zone where seismic effects take place is claimed as a special preserve in which the linear elastic approach is still claimed to be approximately valid. All soils are nonlinear, but some are supposed to be more nonlinear than others.

Mexico City clay forfeits 20% of its rigidity at cyclic strains of 0.1%. San Francisco Bay mud loses up to 60% of its rigidity for the same level of excitation. Hence Mexico City clay is claimed to be "less nonlinear" than Bay mud even though both are clearly nonlinear. S.K. Singh was able to show that seismograms from large earthquakes recorded in Mexico City do not scale with those of smaller earthquakes, especially the famous surface-wave coda that looks so much like a water wave and which is believed to be responsible for the damage in the earthquake. In Fig. 9.10 the seismograms for the 1985 main shock ($M = 8.1$) and the large aftershock that occurred the next day ($M = 7.5$) are compared. On hard ground (station CUIP) the amplitudes scale 1:4, as they should. The magnitude difference was 0.6 and

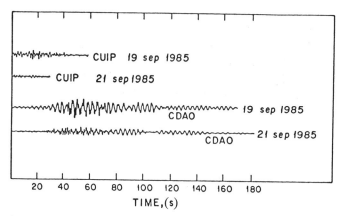

Fig. 9.10   *Comparison of 1985 Mexico main shock and main aftershock at two Mexico City stations, one on hard ground (CUIP) and one on soft ground (CDAO), showing the effect of nonlinearity. Body waves are scaled 1:4 as they should be, since the magnitude difference was 0.6 = log 4. The late, large-amplitude surface waves on soft ground are only scaled 1:2. After S.K. Singh et al., 1988. By permission of the Seismological Society of America.*

log 4 = 0.6. But on soft ground (station CDAO) the late surface waves were almost the same for both earthquakes. At 80 s into the earthquake the amplitude ratio was only about 1:2. This is interpreted as evidence that the amplitudes of surface waves in very large earthquakes are smaller than what we might expect from linear theory. The energy goes into shortening of the wavelength. The nonlinear amplitude reduction in the San Francisco Bay area was comparatively smaller, as Chin and Aki (1991) have shown. Yet many engineers still believe that the response of Mexico City clay to ground motion was essentially elastic up to amplitudes of 0.2g. Whatever nonlinear effect there was tended to *reduce* the amplitude of surface waves in large earthquakes, which sounds like good news.

W.D. Liam Finn (1991) disagrees. He insists that almost any soil would be better than Mexico City clay for engineering purposes.

EFFECTS OF PROGRADE AND RETROGRADE SURFACE WAVES

Elastic surface waves are of two kinds: Rayleigh waves and Love waves. Both propagate at velocities approaching the speed of shear waves. Soft sedimentary layers have shear-wave speeds above 50 m/s or so. Thus at a period of 1 s the wavelength of surface waves should be at least half a city block long. Buildings would have to be longer than a city block to actually feel this kind of deformation. But the collapsed Mexico City buildings were between 10–15 m wide. Visible waves have wavelengths of 5–20 m and move at speeds of only 5–10 m/s since they can easily be followed with the naked eye.

This is possible because the soil begins to lose rigidity as soon as the strong motion starts. The shear velocity goes down and the wavelength of surface waves decreases during the earthquake. We cannot monitor this decrease because we do not actually know what happens in the wavenumber domain during an earthquake. The rotational components of ground motion are not recorded.

The motion of a surface element has six independent components: three translations and three rotations. At present only the translations are recorded by strong-motion instruments. Consider a surface wave propagating from left to right in one dimension (Fig. 9.11). If u is the displacement in the direction of propagation and w is the vertical displacement, the motion of a Rayleigh wave may be described as

$$u = A \cos (\omega t - kx), \tag{9.40}$$

$$w = B \sin (\omega t - kx), \tag{9.41}$$

and

$$\xi = dw/dx = -Bk \cos (\omega t - kx), \tag{9.42}$$

where ξ is the tilt in the x-direction. If the amplitudes A and B are both positive, the particle motion is retrograde (or counterclockwise). The tilt ξ

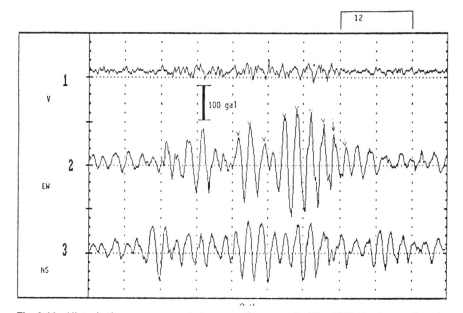

Fig. 9.11 *Historic three-component strong-motion record of the 1985 Mexico earthquake on soft ground, showing prograde surface waves. The direction of propagation is to the northeast. Notice that the vertical component (V) is a quarter-phase in advance of the east-west component (EW).*

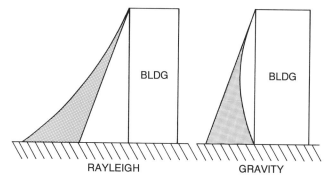

Fig. 9.12 *Static comparison of the effect of retrograde* (left) *and prograde* (right) *surface waves on tall buildings. The rotational contribution* (shaded) *is either added to or subtracted from the translational contribution* (triangle). *Retrograde motion tends to make the building behave as if it were broader at the base, while prograde motion decreases the base shear and increases the overturning moment.*

is out of phase with the horizontal displacement u. Notice also that the tilt increases with the wavenumber k.

Consider now the case of gravity waves. The particle motion is now prograde, that is, the amplitude B in Eqs (9.41)–(9.42) is negative. The tilt ξ is now in phase with the horizontal translation u (Fig. 9.12). The translational and rotational accelerations are in opposition. The base shear is reduced, but there is a net overturning moment due to the shear forces concentrating in the middle stories. This causes wider and wider oscillations with every cycle.

The destabilizing effect of gravity waves is familiar to anyone who has tried to stand up in a small boat on a lake or in a bay. The cause is prograde particle motion. The wave pushes the boat to the right and tilts it to the left. As one attempts to steady oneself, one tends to lean into the direction the boat is tilting. The effect on a tall structure is rather similar. This is why naval engineers attempt to lower the center of gravity of ships.

If the building is rectangular, like an upright slab, the horizontal force due to the earthquake is the same at all levels. Then the static loading diagram is triangular with the largest force at ground level (Fig. 9.12), and an equivalent concentrated load should be applied at one-third the height. The rotational acceleration, on the other hand, increases with elevation: the loading diagram is a parabola. When the two accelerations are additive, as in the case of a Rayleigh wave, the total loading diagram is more squat and the centroid is lowered. The effect is as if the building were broader at the base than it is at the top; the stability is increased. But when the two accelerations are in opposition, as for gravity waves, the centroid is raised and the structure becomes more unstable with every swing (Fig. 9.12).

Most apartment buildings in Mexico City have a height of 8–15 stories.

Their resonant period is around 1 s. The dominant period of the earthquake is about 2 s. If the building stands on hard ground, it will be subjected to the action of Rayleigh waves and the natural period will tend to drift away from resonance. If, on the contrary, it stands on soft ground, the action of gravity waves will tend to increase its natural period with every swing. A building of 7–15 stories is barely on the edge of resonance; but on soft ground it tends to drift into resonance and into the collapse mode. This is the reason why tall buildings are generally safer on hard ground (Fig. 9.13).

The engineer is in a bind. If he or she anchors the structure very firmly at ground level the upper floors will tend to collapse. As soon as collapse occurs, the effective height of the structure is reduced and the natural period is abruptly shortened. The structure snaps out of resonance. This occurs at the expense of the upper floors, but the lower half of the building often

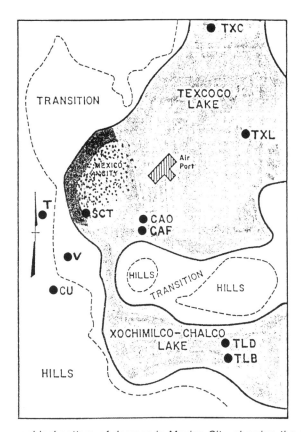

Fig. 9.13 *Geographical pattern of damage in Mexico City, showing the correlation between damage and soft ground. Locations of accelerograph stations are shown with their code abbreviations* (black dots). *Most collapsed buildings* (dotted and shaded areas) *stood on former beaches or wedges of soft material surrounding the shallow lake and the island on which Mexico City was originally built.*

Fig. 9.14 Collapse of the 15-story Nuevo León structure, an apartment building in the Tlatelolco Housing Project (built around 1963). The building was on piles. It had three independent sections of 50-m length each; one remained standing (background). The basement was shallow. (Photo courtesy of Aarón Sánchez (Unomasuno).

remains intact and serviceable. On the other hand, when the building is light or has shallow foundations, it may capsize like a ship (Fig. 9.14). Both modes of failure are observed in Mexico City high-rise buildings on soft ground. It is an unpleasant dilemma the engineer has to face.

The experience of Mexico City suggests that the best solution is to have the building lie as deeply as possible in the soil, like a ship. In the 1985 earthquake the worst collapses were in buildings with extremely shallow basements—like the Nuevo León Building (Fig. 9.14), which extended barely 10 ft below grade. The best performance was of buildings that had two or more levels of underground garages.

THE EFFECT OF DAMPING

According to Hardin and Drnevich the stress attenuation in a soil may be represented by

$$D = D_{max} - \frac{\epsilon}{\epsilon + \gamma_r}, \tag{9.43}$$

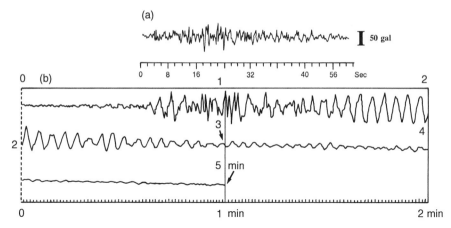

Fig. 9.15 *Long duration of strong-motion accelerogram on soft ground (b, station CDAO) as compared with one for a nearby station on hard ground (a, TAC). Both records were written in Mexico City for the same event (Sept. 19, 1985), and the recording instruments were the same. After S.K. Singh et al. (1988). By permission of the Seismological Society of America.*

where ϵ is the shear stress and D is the *damping ratio* (also known as the *damping factor h*), defined as the proportion of energy lost by internal dissipation to total wave energy. Seismologists are more familiar with the *quality factor Q*:

$$Q = 2\pi/D. \tag{9.44}$$

Thus, a damping ratio of 4% is equivalent to a Q-value of 157. The low damping ratio of Mexico City clay (about 4%) contributes to the long-lasting reverberations of surface waves in the valley floor, which should otherwise damp out very quickly. In the 1985 Mexico earthquake, one strong-motion record on soft ground had a total duration of more than 5 min (Fig. 9.15). The total measured duration of strong motion in the great Acapulco earthquake of March 28, 1784, in Mexico City was over six minutes.

The saturation damping ratio D_{max} may attain up to 31% in some clays; that is, up to 31% of the energy per cycle may be dissipated. The transition from solid-like to liquid-like behavior in soils should take place long before such high values of damping are reached.

THE EFFECT OF ROTATION

Charles Darwin (1860) experienced the great 1835 Chile earthquake near the seashore, on deep sediments at a distance of about 300 km from the epicenter. He describes the motion as follows:

The rocking of the ground was very sensible. . . . There was no difficulty in standing upright, but the motion made me almost giddy: it was something like the movement of a vessel in a little cross-ripple, or still more like that felt by a person skating over thin ice, which bends under the weight of the body.

. . . The earth, the very emblem of solidity, has moved beneath our feet like a thin crust over a fluid. (*Voyage of the Beagle*, February 20, 1835).

Darwin was a discerning and exceptionally gifted observer of nature. In the course of fieldwork on this same 1835 earthquake he intuitively recognized the connection between geodetic uplift, faulting, and earthquakes, an insight that would take another century to be confirmed.

In the paragraph above Darwin describes the effect of gravity waves on soft soils in large distant earthquakes. The inference of prograde ground motion that may be drawn from this observation is still resisted by seismologists and engineers. How can we account for a lag of a century and a half? Didn't other scientists experience what Darwin felt and might they not have drawn their own conclusions? The fact is, however, that very few scientists have actually experienced a large earthquake.

I have lived through several, and I can attest that there is a qualitative difference in the ground motion between a major earthquake and a moderate one. The difference, as Darwin perceived, is that between a solid and a liquid. Small earthquakes shake and rock the ground: large earthquakes liquefy it. There is a phase transition between the two.

After the Mexico earthquake, engineers had no trouble spotting flaws in design, detailing, and construction. Every single collapsed building had failed for some good reason. Yet the same buildings were still standing a few miles away on hard ground. I do not dispute the fact that the buildings were inadequate. They had not been designed against gravity waves. But they were not flawed. They were up against a different kind of earthquake than their brethren that stood on hard ground.

About a century ago, Count Fernand de Montessus de Ballore collected material on the connection between geology and damage in earthquakes. Damage on soft ground was asymmetric: It always seemed to occur close to the edges of valleys, where the sedimentary layer thinned out, and rarely near the center of a valley where soils were deepest. Some of this can be seen in linear simulations (Fig. 9.16), but the effect during large earthquakes is far worse: Darwin compared strong motion on soft ground near the edge of the Valdivia, Chile coastal plain to the motion of "a vessel in a little cross-ripple."

Consider the situation around Lake Chalco, a subdivision of the great Mexico Lake. The lake is today a huge swampy flat and the soft layer is 25–40 m thick (Fig. 9.17). It is as soft as butter and contains around 90% water by volume. The solids are represented mostly by organic matter. There is a paleo-beach zone about 200–300 m wide all around the lake, where the soft lake sediment has developed a hardened "crust" (as Darwin would say).

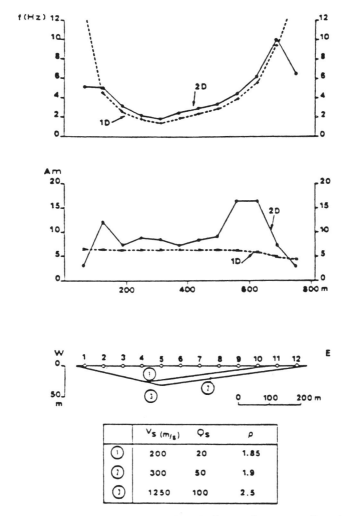

Fig. 9.16 *Linear simulation of edge effects in a shallow sedimentary valley of triangular cross-section. Both amplitude (Am) and frequency (f) rise near the edges. From Jongmans and Campillo (1989). By permission of Société Géologique de France.*

The most likely cause of this mineralized top layer is seasonal wetting and drying due to the fluctuations of the lake level. Every time the beach dried out, brackish water would rise to the surface by capillarity and the salts would accumulate near the surface (Alvarez, Lomnitz, and Chávez, in preparation).

Thus a shallow wedge of soft soil is sandwiched between two harder layers everywhere around the former lake. We found that this geological situation was quite common along the rim of lakes or bays. In an earthquake, the surface waves are trapped in this wedge and large local amplification effects

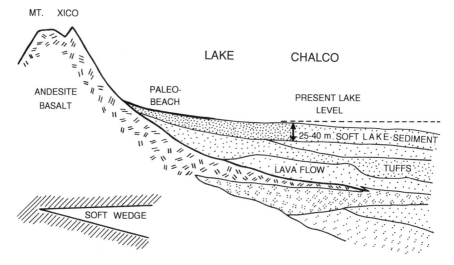

Fig. 9.17 Lake Chalco, a surviving (now largely dry) outlier of the original lake that covered Mexico Valley during the Pleistocene. Paleo-beaches formed around the lake. Note the top crust of hardened soil due to seasonal wetting and drying. Seismic waves are trapped and amplified in the soft wedge.

are produced. This accounts for the damage distribution in several recent large earthquakes on soft ground, including Caracas, Oakland, and Mexico City.

SOME NONLINEAR EFFECTS

(a) Visible Surface Waves

On Saturday morning, May 21, 1960, a large destructive earthquake caused about 100 deaths in Concepción, Chile. I flew down from Santiago with an American colleague, Dr. Pierre St. Amand, and we reached Concepción shortly before 3 P.M. on Sunday afternoon.

The airfield was on the alluvial plain of the Bío-Bío River, not far from the city. We were walking along the wire fence outside the airfield when we noticed some aircraft rolling forward a few feet, then stopping and rolling backward. This was repeated at intervals of two or three seconds. Next we noticed some parked cars (evidently parked in neutral gear) rolling back and forth. Suddenly Pierre exclaimed, "It's an earthquake!"

We had felt nothing because we were walking, and because the motion was so slow. We looked at a row of trees ahead of us. They were sturdy shade trees; their natural periods were probably well below one second. Yet we could clearly see the trees leaning back and forth, tilting into and away from each other with a period of perhaps two seconds. The trees were some

5 m apart. We didn't know the angle of incidence of the wave front; but the wavelength couldn't have been more than 20 m.

The aircraft were parked on unpaved ground. The rolling motion should have required a tilt of at least $\delta = 1°$, perhaps more. This should have implied a vertical amplitude of at least $\delta/k = 1 \times 20 \times \pi/(2\pi \times 180) = 0.0055$ m, about the amplitude of vertical ground motion in Mexico City during the 1985 earthquake. Actually it was probably quite a bit more: This was the largest earthquake in the world in centuries. We were about 200 km away from the epicenter of the great Chile earthquake ($M_w = 9.5$, where M_w is the moment magnitude).

Elastic surface waves should have had a wavelength of at least 2 km: the resulting tilt would have been a few hundredths of a degree at most. Hence our observations could not be explained by linear theory.

The German missionary priest, Rev. Juan Bautista Wevering, was taking his lonely Sunday afternoon walk in the hills east of the Lake Budi mission. The Araucanian reservation was well within the epicentral region. He was overlooking the coastal plain, enjoying the clear view, when the earthquake struck. He felt the violent shaking but he was unafraid. Seconds later he watched the landscape turn into a kind of seascape, with countless waves slowly rolling inland across the open countryside. He thought it was a beautiful and awesome sight. Father Wevering (a tough, sober man of about 40) told me he could not take his eyes away. Nothing seemed to move in the sunlight but the propagating furrows sweeping across the ground. Some trees standing on a ridge bent and swayed as in a strong wind. The waves looked and behaved for all the world like water waves. He naturally assumed that these were the seismic waves he had read about. Until I told him otherwise, he had been convinced that he had seen nothing out of the ordinary.

The geological setting of Lake Budi is in Tertiary to Quaternary sediments with a thick soil cover. The lake occupies an old meander of the Imperial River. The coastal plain is narrow and has been downfaulted against the coast range. Father Wevering was standing on top of the eastern (upper) block of the Budi fault (Lomnitz, 1969, 1970).

In the 1985 Mexico earthquake (and in previous Mexico City earthquakes) many observations of visible waves were reported. One resident saw a wave moving down the street and tilting the large cement tiles of the sidewalk back and forth like planks floating in a marina. The Nuevo León Building was seen "wriggling like a snake" before capsizing and killing 472 residents (Fig. 9.14). A similar snake-like propagating deformation of the old Chapultepec Aqueduct (now demolished) was described for the earthquake of June 19, 1858:

The author . . . was on Chapultepec Road traveling toward the capital, when a strong high-frequency shaking was felt at a quarter past nine in the morning. It was followed by strong oscillations that changed direction abruptly and which finally became a wave-like motion. The fields of Hacienda La Condesa [present-day Colonia Condesa in Mexico City—C.L.] heaved and subsided by stretches and alternately, so that the water in the ditches would collect by being constrained to flow in opposite directions or cascading into ditches at right angles, due to the sudden tilts caused by the terrifying and uneven ground motion. The trees along the avenue were whipping against each other making confused sounds as their leaves collided; and the long series of arches leading to Salto del Agua [end point of the old aqueduct—C.L.] took on the undulating movements of a snake winding on the ground. And upon springing leaks all at once, in many places it began to spout abundant jets of foaming water that shone in the sunlight (García Cubas, 1904; my translation).

This fine description of a gravity wave refers to an area of present-day Mexico City sited on soft lake sediments, where much damage also occurred in 1957 and 1985. Chapultepec Avenue runs roughly at right angles to the old lakeshore. The aqueduct was repaired after the 1858 earthquake.

The susceptibility to vibrations of the soft ground of Mexico City has been known for centuries; for example, after large earthquakes all carriage traffic in the city was banned to prevent further damage to buildings (Fig. 9.18).

Another observation of a gravity wave was made in the Loma Prieta, California, earthquake according to *Time* magazine (October 30, 1989, p. 14).

AVISO

Se Suspende, hasta nueva orden, el uso de todo carruaje, bajo la multa de cien pesos, Interin los arquitectos de Ciudad reconocen los estragos que haya ocasionado el movimiento de tierra habido el día de hoy.

Solo el coche del Divinisimo recorrerá libremente la Ciudad.

Y De orden del Exmo. Sr. Gobernador, lo hago saber al público.

Méjico, Junio 19 de 1858.

Francisco de P. Tabera.

Fig. 9.18 *Public ordinance barring the use of all carriages (except the carriage of the Divinísimo for the administration of the last rites) in Mexico City after the 1858 earthquake, on account of possible damage caused by vibrations on soft ground.*

Lisa Sheeran, a public relations manager, picked up a rental car in Colma, just off the San Andreas fault. As she opened one of the doors, the vehicle bounced up and down. "What's wrong with this car?" she asked. The rental agent shrugged and said, "I don't know." Then both watched a wave of undulating earth approach them from a graveyard down the hill.

Interestingly, this observation was shared by two independent witnesses. It was made at a time when neither had identified the phenomenon as an earthquake. The low phase velocity and short wavelength, which enabled the witnesses to follow the progress of the wave on the ground, excludes the possibility of Rayleigh waves.

(b) Matuzawa Waves

Observations of visible waves are apt to be dismissed by seismologists who have never been in a strong earthquake. In particular, waves seen on pavement are not credited because no cracks are visible afterwards in the pavement.

Yet permanent wavy deformations with wavelengths on the order of 5–20 m are frequently found in asphaltic or other pavement or on open ground *after* a large earthquake. These "frozen" waves were first investigated after the 1923 Tokyo earthquake, notably by Matuzawa (1925), who attributed them to gravity waves.

A gravity wave is a wave driven by gravity as a restoring force, in opposition to an elastic wave, where the restoring force is provided by elastic energy. Surface waves in water are examples of gravity waves. So are many wave phenomena in the atmosphere and in plasmas. Around 1490, Leonardo da Vinci observed that, when a wind wave moves across a field of corn, the ears do not move bodily across the field. Each ear stays in its place: what propagates is some kind of energy. This is what happens when gravity waves propagate on the surface of a fluid, except that the restoring force is provided by the weight of the water rather than by the bending resistance of the stalk.

Today Leonardo's corn wave would be called a Kelvin-Helmholtz instability. It is a nonlinear phenomenon, like a water wave. Matuzawa tentatively suggested that the permanent ground waves in Tokyo streets might have been produced by a special rheology of soils similar to that of pitch or resin, which made them capable of flowing under their own weight. Though there was no physics on which to base this idea in 1925, the great Japanese theoretician recognized that the effect could not be attributed to elastic waves.

Hisashi Nirei made observations of permanent ground deformations in the 1987 Chiba earthquake and in the 1990 Philippines earthquake (Fig. 9.19). He called the phenomenon *jinami*, or earth wave. The implied analogy with *tsunami* was intentional. The existence of *jinami* strongly suggests that the phenomenon must involve a solid-liquid phase transition. If the transition were gradual, the amplitudes would die down together with the signal and would not remain imprinted on the surface of the soil layer.

Fig. 9.19 A jinami or "frozen" gravity wave photographed on soft ground after the 1987 Chiba, Japan earthquake. Photo courtesy of H. Nirei.

(c) Liquefaction

In this section we introduce the phenomenological concept of liquefaction in soils.

Jinami, tsunamis-in-the-Moon, and visible earthquake waves have this much in common: they require soils to behave like liquids under certain special circumstances. Terzaghi and Casagrande, the founders of soil mechanics, had discovered such a transition for soils in 1936: they called it *liquefaction*. Today liquefaction is considered a major cause of earthquake damage.

Unfortunately, the phenomenology of liquefaction in soils is plagued by paradoxes. In physics, every transition must be associated with a transition in the reverse direction. Melting is associated with freezing, boiling with condensation and so on. Yet liquefaction in soils is assumed to destroy the structure of the soil by a sudden violent increase in pore pressure.

If liquefaction occurs at a critical value of the shear stress, solidification must take place at the same stress value. Thus the explanation of the observations must be different. First the soil is subjected to a large external excitation (earthquake, impact of planetesimals). The critical strain is exceeded and the material "liquefies." But this does not necessarily mean that the soil flows like water. It suffices that it forfeits its ability to transmit elastic surface waves. The wavelength of the surface wave shortens and a gravity wave propagates on the ground instead of an elastic surface wave.

As the excitation dies down the gravity wave continues to propagate until its amplitude drops below the threshold strain value. Then the reverse transition occurs. The wave "freezes," and from this point on only elastic surface waves can propagate.

This explanation seems to account for all observed seismic effects. The question is: Does it fit in with current ideas on soil liquefaction?

All soils behave according to the same constitutive equation (9.3). This

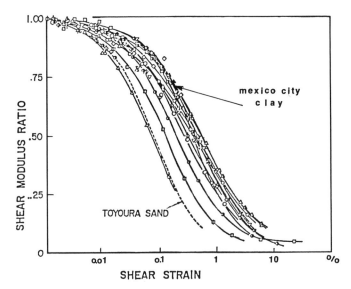

Fig. 9.20 *The stress-strain equation of soils is self-similar with respect to the logarithm of strain. All soils have the identical constitutive equation in terms of the normalized strain* ϵ/γ_r *. After Kokusho et al. (1982). By permission of* Soils and Foundations, *Tokyo, Japan.*

fact is remarkable in itself. Still more remarkable is the form of this equation, for its nonlinearity is such that the rigidity drops very quickly—in fact, faster than the amplitude can rise. The result is that surface waves become unstable at a critical amplitude. But in this case liquefaction should be observed in all soils. Why should only wet sands liquefy? And what about the dry soils which liquefied on the surface of the Moon?

This paradox can be resolved in a simple way. Liquefaction is not caused by rising pore pressures in saturated noncohesive materials. Liquefaction occurs in all soils, because of the mathematical shape of the constitutive equation (Fig. 9.20). The moment a soil loses its capacity to transmit shear waves, it has liquefied. Some soils flow like water; others don't. Clays retain some internal cohesion; sands have none. Saturated soils may show a rise in pore pressure at liquefaction; lunar soils may not.

The point is that all soils behave the same way: At some point they stop transmitting Rayleigh waves and start transmitting gravity waves.

AN EXAMPLE: THE CYPRESS STRUCTURE

Auto mechanic Richard Reynolds . . . ran out of his shop to find "the whole goddam ground lifting up." He grabbed a telephone pole as the sidewalk buckled beneath his feet, and looked up at a horrifying sight. A mile-long section of the freeway's upper deck began to heave then collapsed onto the lower roadway, flattening cars as if they were beer cans. "It just slid. It didn't fall. It just slid," said Reynolds.

This quote from *Time* magazine (October 30, 1989, p. 10) is an accurate description of what happened in Oakland, California, during the Loma Prieta earthquake of October 17, 1989. The Cypress Structure of Interstate Freeway 880 collapsed over a stretch of 50 bents, from Bent 62 (south) to Bent 112 (north), or from Eighteenth Street to about Thirty-fourth Street. The upper deck fell on top of the lower deck, killing 41 motorists and passengers.

It was 5:04 P.M. and most people were at home watching TV. The World Series ball game at Candlestick Park was about to begin. Traffic on the freeway was light: about one car every 40 meters going each way. Suddenly the drivers felt a slight steering problem, as if one of the tires was developing a flat. They didn't slow down. None of the witnesses identified the problem as an earthquake. A few instants later there was a tremendous lurch and within 1 s the upper deck crashed onto the lower roadway. Most motorists on the lower deck were instantly killed.

The witness Reynolds described the instant of liquefaction as a sudden "lifting-up" and "buckling" of the ground. The initial part of the seismic signal (which made him run out of his shop) was felt as a "flat-tire effect" by the motorists. The huge lurch that made the ground and the freeway buckle occurred while the earthquake had been in progress for several seconds.

The 1989 Loma Prieta earthquake caused unexpectedly high horizontal accelerations, up to 0.29g, along the Oakland, California, waterfront. These high accelerations were recorded both on Bay mud and on adjacent sections of Oakland sited on Merritt sand, a compact aeolian sand of Wisconsin age. Thus the accelerations were about the same on hard and soft ground. However, the double-decked, reinforced concrete-frame viaduct collapsed only along the section sited on Bay mud. Identical sections of the viaduct founded on Merritt sand did not collapse.

Careful studies of the Cypress Structure were made after its collapse (Bertero, 1990; Moehle, 1989; Nims et al., 1989; Rogers, 1991). Liquefaction was ruled out as a possible cause: Muds were not believed to be capable of liquefying. Instead, failure was attributed to transverse lateral forces exceeding the shear resistance of the upper columns. Why the adjacent sections sited on Merritt sand did not fail was less clear. Presumably it had something to do with the soil properties. The characteristic dimensions of the Cypress Structure were as follows:

Width of bents	16 m
Height from ground to upper deck	15–16 m
Span between bents	16–20 m

Notice the similarity of the dimensions—all around 16 m. A resonance of

Fig. 9.21 *The Cypress Structure, an elevated two-level viaduct which collapsed over a stretch of one mile on soft ground during the 1989 Loma Prieta earthquake. Notice a hole in the pavement made by an ejected column. Photo courtesy of J. David Rogers.*

the structure in the longitudinal direction with a ground wave having a wavelength of around 16 m seems more than likely. In fact this is what Mr. Reynolds saw.

On the other hand, it is unlikely that the Cypress Structure collapsed in transverse motion. The upper deck nowhere fell off the lower deck. Everywhere it came to rest squarely on top of the lower deck (Fig. 9.21). Mr. Reynolds was standing on Bay mud, facing the viaduct. He watched the upper deck beginning to "heave" then to slide (not fall) onto the lower roadway. Thus the failure occurred in a single cycle of ground motion. The witness did not report any transverse motion from east to west.

This story was substantially confirmed by witnesses driving on the upper deck. They described a loss of steering control ("flat-tire effect"), which is typical of body waves shaking the vehicle in a transverse direction. They saw intermittent puffs of concrete dust at the supporting bents, suggestive of spalling. But the viaduct did not collapse. No motorist attempted to stop; the steering difficulty was not recognized as being of seismic origin. The actual collapse began and ended in a second, precisely when the upper deck began to heave. The cars had no time to stop.

The reinforced-concrete column shown in Fig. 9.22 was bodily ejected from between decks at Bent 72 (Rogers, 1991). It landed upside down on the pavement, at a distance of more than 7 m from its original emplacement. The picture shows the column lying on its side after it was removed. The base had stood 8 m above street level. It was one of several columns that were ejected in the same manner. The reinforcing rods were pulled straight

Fig. 9.22 *This reinforced-concrete column (shown after removal) was ejected from the second level of the structure and landed upside down on the pavement. The reinforcing bars in the base were pulled out straight. Photo courtesy of J. David Rogers.*

out of the base, not bent or twisted off. How could these columns have been "blown off" (as some engineers called it)? The heave that tore out these columns must have been directed upward, not sideways.

All along the destroyed section of the freeway one single frame survived: the portico over the Thirty-second Street crossing (Bents 96 and 97). Survival of this single frame (Fig. 9.23) was due to the fact that Bents 96 and 97 had been oriented at a slant of 27.5° with respect to the axis of the structure, to allow for a railroad crossing under the freeway at this particular angle. These bents were spared because they could not rotate about their baseline together with the rest of the structure.

Fig. 9.23 *Single surviving frame on soft ground. It was preseved because the bents were slanted almost 30° to the axis of the freeway, in order to allow for a railroad crossing at ground level. Photo courtesy of J. David Rogers.*

The collapse skipped the railroad crossing and continued on the other side; yet there was no structural continuity as the crossing remained standing. Hence the collapse must have been carried by a ground wave propagating longitudinally along the axis of the structure.

A bulge in the upper deck could have arisen by buckling against some immovable object. This object was the undamaged section of the Cypress Structure south of Eighteenth Street. This section was founded on Merritt sand (Fig. 9.24). The original contractor of the Cypress Structure had "experienced some problems with driving the pipe piles through the partially saturated Merritt sands south of Eighteenth street, as these materials were found to be quite stiff" (Rogers, 1991). The ground wave coming from the section on Bay mud was unable to propagate on Merritt sand because of its stiffness. Merritt sand did not liquefy. The section of the freeway founded on Bay mud tilted and smashed itself to pieces against the section on Merritt sand.

When the bents rotated southward, they caused the upper deck to buckle at Eighteenth Street. Bertero (1990) found that the rupture must have started at this spot, more exactly at Bent 73 where the layer of Bay mud pinches out and the first upper column was ejected. The height of the bents increased from north to south toward Bent 62.

In conclusion, the moving structure bumped into Bent 62 with the energy of a swinging baseball bat. As the deck buckled, it heaved and uprooted the upper columns with explosive force. To make sure that it did, the sections of the upper deck had been attached together with restrainer cable some time in 1978, under the CALTRANS Phase 1 retrofitting program. The upper

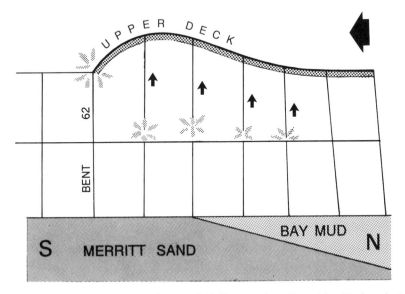

Fig. 9.24 The upper deck of the freeway initially moved south and buckled against the "immovable object" (i.e., the section of the freeway sited on solid Merritt sand).

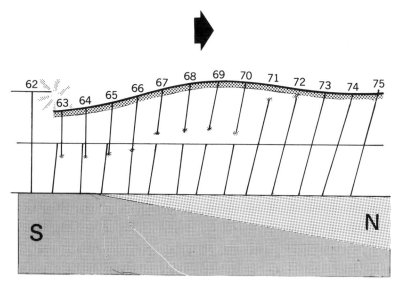

Fig. 9.25 *Once the upper deck tore itself free, the resulting bulge traveled north and snapped the upper columns serially as it propagated.*

deck had no problem transmitting stresses lengthwise. As the motion changed direction, the deck tore itself free from Bent 62, thus decoupling the southern part of the structure, which survived. The bulge in the upper deck propagated northward at shear-wave speed, snapping the upper columns serially at one swoop (Fig. 9.25).

This was not the work of a Rayleigh wave. For a Rayleigh wave the wavelength should have been around 100 m at a frequency of 1 Hz, which was six times the spacing between bents. Thus the bents should have tilted against each other, and no resonance could have resulted. In order to propagate a coherent bulge down the structure, the wave must have been able to induce spatial resonance; this was only possible if the wavelength of the surface wave was of the same order as the spacing between bents.

There is a layer of artificial fill shown as Qf on top of the layer of Bay mud (Fig. 9.26). This compacted crust turned the Bay mud layer into a waveguide, that is, the energy of the surface wave was trapped and channeled toward the Oakland shore. As the layer of Bay mud pinched out, the amplitude increased catastrophically and the material liquefied.

This is similar to the nonlinear phenomenon of shoaling. A gravity wave rolls up the beach; its amplitude increases until it breaks. In the case of a soil we would not expect any breakers, but phenomena of surface rupture suggestive of extremely large local amplitude were also observed in Mexico City.

The collapse of the Cypress Structure could not have been due only to the fact that it was double-decked, or that it was poorly designed. The Bay

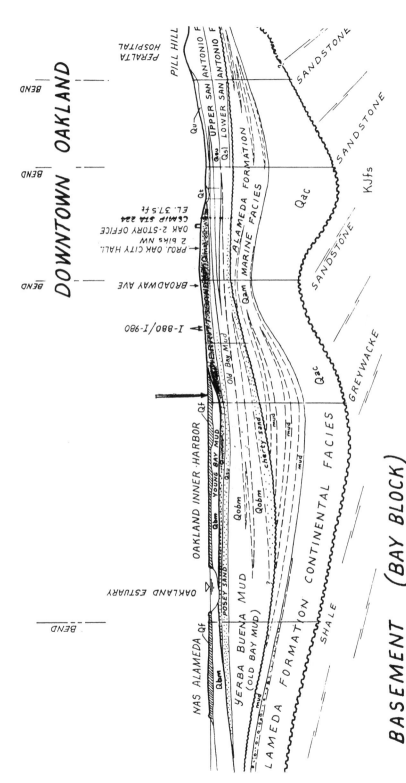

Fig. 9.26 Geology of San Francisco Bay showing the mud layer (Qbm) which caused the disaster. Arrow, position of the collapsed section of the Cypress structure. From Rogers (1991).

249

mud pinched out at both ends of the collapsed section. The identical structure did not collapse a few bents away on hard ground, though the accelerations were about the same on Merritt sand and on Bay mud (Rogers, 1991). Collapse must have been caused by a type of surface wave that could not propagate on Merritt sand as it did on Bay mud.

Collapse of reinforced concrete-frame structures on soft ground can be prevented by increasing the depth of foundation footings to below the reach of gravity waves, that is, at least 5–10 m. Spatial resonance of the structure with wavelengths of 10–20 m should be avoided. Finally, and most importantly, nonlinear failure modes should be considered. In the case of the Cypress Structure, lengthwise resonance over stretches of 50 bents at a time was not thought to be possible, nor was dynamic buckling of the upper roadway. Liquefaction of soils creates entirely new structural situations.

It is our job to predict the occurrence of such situations wherever possible. As important as forecasting when the earthquake will occur and how strong it will be, and just as challenging, is predicting what the effect will be at a given site. In order to address this question successfully, earthquake prediction must begin to consider seriously the problem of nonlinear phase transitions on soft ground.

10

Science in Ashes:
A Theory of Coincidence

The shoe is on the other foot.
—Cinderella

A STEADY-STATE EARTH

This chapter is about model dependence and some related questions of earth-quake prediction that arise in hypothesis testing. These questions may occur in all branches of science and also—particularly—in the interface between science and society.

Suppose, for example, that we wish to test for the possibility that a set of earthquakes in a region was triggered by a previous large earthquake. We divide the region into annular segments according to epicentral distance, and we compute the number and the expected magnitude of events in each segment. In the actual example, as the observed magnitudes or numbers consistently exceeded the expected values, we computed the probability that a particular configuration of exceedances would turn up at random; this turned out to be a ridiculously small number.

Should we conclude from this that the hypothesis of triggering is proved beyond the shadow of a doubt? No, because the particular test is only one among a large number of possible tests. Thus the result of the test depends on the number n of annular segments. If n is doubled, the observed rate of exceedances usually drops to half, because the segments were selected to coincide with the events. We should actually have used a large number of models instead of one model, and the result of the test should reflect the number of possible models—including the possibility that the null hypothesis (i.e., random independent occurrence) is incorrect.

Consider now a lava pool in the crater of a volcano (Fig. 10.1). The solid, rugged crust of black lava drifts away from the center of the crater toward

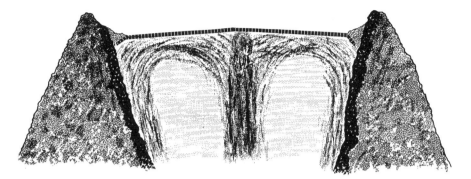

Fig. 10.1 Convection and "plate tectonics" in a lava pool.

the edges, driven by unseen convection currents. On the surface, a pattern of long linear structures develops. Plates of lava drift apart as molten material seems to be upwelling to fill the cracks. Transform faults, hot spots and scars of older ridges can be observed, too.

The banks of the lava pool are made of chunks of frozen lava. The hot lava current dips under the banks, and there is a complicated give-and-take of underthrusting and accretion as thin slivers of crust are constantly being shored up against the margins. The top of the lava crust breaks in brittle fracture or slides jerkily, while the lower crust yields and deforms.

Is this a good model for predicting earthquakes? The process is very much like subduction, and the whole picture of convection in a lava pool resembles plate tectonics. Might we perhaps describe plate tectonics more easily by means of self-organized flow in a lava pool than by appealing to the abstract idea of rotating plates on the surface of a sphere?

The question is more a matter of good sense. Geological models can be useful as metaphors if there is nothing better to be had. They cannot replace a detailed physical description of the system. A lava pool is not necessarily more familiar to an earth scientist than the model of plate tectonics. Moreover, the modeling of such a complex system would require truly gigantic computing facilities. Models of self-organized criticality have begun to make progress only recently, with the availability of fast supercomputers such as the CM-5 connection machines, running at the rate of over 4 billion floating-point operations per second.

The decisive theoretical breakthroughs in the theory of self-organization were made in the early 1940s independently by Alan Turing and (in a different direction) by the Belgians Prigogine, De Groot and their students. A new discipline, nonequilibrium thermodynamics, which deals with perturbations in steady-state dynamic equilibrium, was created around 1950. The prime example of a self-organizing system is thermal convection. Bénard discovered many years ago that any homogeneous fluid will spontaneously organize itself into a number of small cells revolving about their centers. Above a certain critical temperature, any small random perturbation in the system is enough to determine the pattern of the cells; once the system has organized itself it is dynamically stable. It is a *steady-state* system.

Tectonic theories and models must somehow fit into this broad general framework. But many older concepts still remain current among earth scientists. Their compatibility with physics has never been seriously tested or examined. In this chapter we provide a random sampling of such theories, and we discuss some broader implications of earthquake prediction in terms of the world situation of scientific research in general.

THE DILATANCY-FLUID DIFFUSION HYPOTHESIS

Around 1972 a new hypothesis about the origin of earthquake precursors emerged on the basis of observations of volume increase in rocks before compressive failure. Diffusion of fluids into the dilated region around the focus was perceived as a possibility and was assumed to be a critical part of the seismic process. It was believed to account for the existence of precursors and to determine the earthquake magnitude and the dimensions of the focal region (Nur, 1972; Scholz et al., 1973).

The volume increase was observed in samples of rock subjected to very large loads. The cause is crack formation. A similar process, assumed to take place in the focal region of an earthquake, could explain the peculiar signature observed by Soviet and Chinese scientists in earthquake precursors (Fig. 10.2). The question is: Does dilatancy actually occur in the focal region of an earthquake?

Dilatancy should have the effect of initially lowering the velocity of seismic waves, because of the increase in void ratio. Then water would begin

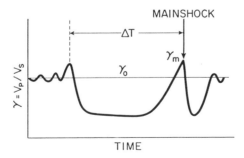

Fig. 10.2 *"Standard" signature of earthquake precursors, according to Soviet theorists. The precursor γ (here the ratio between the velocities of compressional and shear waves) begins to drop some time ΔT before the earthquake and recovers when the earthquake is imminent.*

flowing into the dilated regions thus causing the velocities to rise again. This would account for the first-down-then-up pattern of some reported earthquake precursors. The earthquake itself might be attributable to a combination of dilatancy followed by fluid diffusion.

Whether the volume of rocks can dilate or contract at great depths in response to seismic strains remains a mystery. However, the field evidence eventually failed to confirm the hypothesis of dilatancy at shallow depths. Decreases in the velocity of seismic waves were indeed reported before large earthquakes, both in the Soviet Union and in the United States, but could not be confirmed by more careful measurements. No significant velocity changes were detected either before or after an earthquake. A particularly fastidious experiment was run between 1968 and 1978 by the Geographical Survey of Japan. They used controlled explosions over lines fanning out over the entire Izu Peninsula and beyond. In spite of the bulge in the center of the Izu Peninsula, which kept rising during this decade, no change was detected before the 1978 Izu-Oshima earthquake; no coseismic change in velocity corresponding to the earthquake was recorded either. Anomalies of the ratio v_S/v_P between the shear and compressional body-wave velocities were frequently reported at the time and were still widely credited by many geophysicists.

The most likely explanation for these observations is the fact that any fashionable hypothesis will generate a proliferation of experimental confirmations when the reported effect is of marginal size, as it often is. The interpretations of the experimental evidence tend to be colored by the expectations of the experimenter. The v_S/v_P effect found by different researchers was always around 5%, which was within the noise level of the observations. Perhaps the most important single piece of evidence ever submitted in support of the model was the geodetic uplift preceding the 1964 Niigata earthquake. This uplift was attributed to dilatancy: its pattern in time seemed to agree with the hypothesis of fluid diffusion. Eventually the case was reexamined by Mogi (1984), who concluded that "there is a possibility that the precursory uplift is not real, and even if this uplift is real, their space-time pattern cannot be explained reasonably by the dilatancy model."

THE "STEP-BY-STEP" THEORY

"Step-by-step" is a peculiar approach to earthquake prediction, believed to be especially suited to the present pretheoretical stage of development of the field. A progressive approximation is believed to optimize the search process and to lead to the eventual capture of the "earthquake enemy"—even when the scientist remains essentially ignorant of the enemy's strategy.

The step-by-step strategy proposes to divide the campaign against earthquakes into four stages: long-term, medium-term, short-term, and imminent.

Aside from the fact that the number 4 is magical in China, the cumulative effect of finding earthquake precursors can lead to more precursors being found—even when no real effect is present.

The step-by-step approach has often been connected with the idea of the *earthquake field* (Zhang, 1990). As discussed in Chinese texts the concept of an earthquake field that extends over a vast region and eventually concentrates on the epicentral area seems to have been borrowed from T. Matuzawa, who in turn may have been inspired by Buddhist ideas. At any rate, the earthquake field idea seems to underlie the following explanation provided by Professor Fu Chenyi, influential elder statesman of Chinese geophysics and founder of the first Chinese chair in theoretical seismology:

> Before an earthquake occurs, part of the earth medium has been subjected to an accelerating stress buildup: this is the seismogenic area which we may call the "inflamed" area. Rock deformation and migration and other movements of matter in the seismogenic area modify the medium in the upper crust on a large scale. This might involve changes in mechanical properties, electric properties, magnetism, thermal properties and other physical or chemical changes. Earthquake precursors are but reflections of these changes (Fu Chenyi, 1976).

This is known as the *inflammation hypothesis*. The earthquake field contains an "inflamed" area. But what causes the inflammation? And what exactly is an inflammation? Is it an alteration of the rock? In medicine the term is gradually being abandoned in favor of more specific terms. The hypothesis of inflammation seems vague enough to be compatible with a dozen different ideas about the origin of earthquakes—not excluding the Aristotelian hypothesis of a buildup of air pressure in underground cavities.

Professor Fu confided in 1977 that he didn't think the pattern of Chinese seismicity could be explained by plate tectonics. "We don't know what goes on in the focal area," he told me, "but in order to be successful at earthquake prediction we must find out what happens *before* an earthquake, not afterwards." If I understood Fu's ideas correctly, he seemed to agree that the elastic-rebound model which involves a stress accumulation over a long time period needs revising. Such comments strike me as illuminating. It is a fact that we still lack a serviceable model for the larger deformation process that the seismic event is imbedded in—or for the insertion of the earthquake in it.

However, models unsupported by data are of limited use. Geologists once enjoyed inventing such models for volcanoes. One was constructed in Mexico in the 1890s. It featured a sand box containing an underground bag filled with sand slurry. As air was pumped into the bag the liquid slurry was forced out and something like a miniature eruption occurred. It must have looked rather interesting, but what could be learned from it?

A recent non-Chinese publication defines a precursor as "a quantitatively measurable change in an environmental parameter that occurs before mainshocks, and that is thought to be linked to the preparation process for this mainshock.'' Does everybody know and understand what is meant by the "preparation process"? Is the distinction between a "mainshock" and foreshocks clear beforehand, or isn't it rather defined after the event has occurred? After the destructive Concepción, Chile, earthquake of May 21, 1960 I told some local reporters that the occurrence of an even larger earthquake was unlikely. The next day the giant Chile earthquake occurred. It was the largest earthquake to occur in the world for centuries, yet it took the trouble to make one seismologist look foolish.

ELASTIC REBOUND

The theory of elastic rebound was the brainchild of geologist Andrew C. Lawson and seismologist Harry F. Reid, who conceived the idea right after the 1906 San Francisco earthquake. The two men were the main investigators on the California Earthquake Commission appointed after the earthquake; they also became close friends. Ideas resembling elastic rebound had been proposed before, in particular by Professor G.K. Gilbert. Reid as chairman of the Commission lent quantitative rigor to the idea by introducing the fruitful though somewhat misleading analogy between the earth's crust and a flexed cantilever beam. Some of the shortcomings of the analogy were eventually recognized by Reid and Lawson.

However, the main insight proved to be astoundingly correct. It boldly anticipated plate tectonics. It consisted in the idea that two "blocks" (eventually to be called the Pacific and North American plates) ride past each other at a constant and uniform mean velocity. The Pacific block moves to the north in relation to the North America block. All available evidence confirms this remarkable intuition. Large oceanic plates are strongly coupled to the moving mantle; for all intents and purposes, they may be treated as geological units. They are driven by viscous coupling and therefore the stress remains constant in the plate—at least near the center. The plate boundaries are, as it were, spring-loaded.

Thus the Pacific Plate rides past San Francisco at a near-constant rate. The thin crusty slag has no bulk strength and cannot accumulate stresses over large distances. The San Andreas fault is the main plate boundary—a narrow strip vertically as well as horizontally between the two plates. Earthquakes occur within the upper 25 km of the crust but are absent further downward, which suggests that the two plates can move past each other unimpeded at depth. Even in the upper contact zone creep deformation is the rule and brittle fracture the exception. As the plates move against each other the boundary is increasingly deformed until it ruptures.

Andrew Lawson did not stop at outlining this model. He attempted to translate his insight into a blueprint for earthquake prediction. ''If the amount of strain," he wrote in 1922, "which the earth will endure has been ascertained, and the rate at which the earth's crust is creeping toward the breaking point has been learned, when and where the break will occur is a mere matter of calculation." Being an excellent geologist, Lawson was mainly concerned with strains rather than with stresses. He essentially disregarded the shear strength of earth materials.

Whenever a "slowquake" occurs on the San Andreas fault, the deformational episode may or may not be followed by earthquakes. Radon anomalies were detected before a strain event that occurred in late 1979 near Palmdale, California, and before an earthquake of magnitude 5.0 that occurred on January 1, 1979, near Malibu, California (Savage et al., 1981; Shapiro et al., 1981). If the strain event in Palmdale had led to the occurrence of an earthquake, the radon anomaly would have been termed a precursor. Actually no earthquake resulted—or so it was believed until the 1992 Landers earthquake near Palmdale caused some geophysicists to have second thoughts.

Elastic rebound might more properly be called *elasto-plastic rebound*. A creep event on the San Andreas fault may have the same *signature* in terms of groundwater anomalies as an earthquake. T. Rikitake expected that this ambiguity might be removed by using a variety of different precursors simultaneously and/or by observing the region over a long enough period of time. This may be wishful thinking, as the fault itself may not always "know" in advance whether it will ultimately yield in a slow strain event, in a series of small earthquakes, or in a major shock.

What remains of the theory of elastic rebound is essentially a grand intuition, now superseded by plate tectonics. The idea that stresses build up along segments of plate boundaries over long periods of time is probably inconsistent with self-organization or with a stationary earth model. We should rather expect the stresses to remain stationary and the boundaries to be creeping and yielding more or less at random.

A HANDLE ON Q

Americans say "getting a handle on something", for gaining insight into some elusive problem. Understanding the concept of Q is such a slippery problem in seismology. Everyone agrees that it is crucial to earthquake prediction. Getting it into focus is another matter.

Q originated in circuit theory. A complicated electrical circuit has certain bulk properties: When a potential is applied across it, there is a DC lag; when it is excited by an alternating current, there is power consumption. This may be described by the loss factor $Q^{-1} = \Delta W/2\pi W$, where W is the total energy and ΔW is the energy loss per cycle. Since rheological models (composed of springs and dashpots) are perfect analogs of electrical circuits (composed of resistors and condensers), the concept of Q can be directly transferred to stress wave attenuation in materials.

Consider a small stress step σ_0 applied to a linear solid at time $t = 0$. The resulting strain at time t will be

$$\epsilon(t) = \frac{\sigma_0}{\mu} [1 + \phi(t)] \tag{10.1}$$

where σ_0/μ is the elastic strain and $\phi(t)$ is called the creep function (Lomnitz, 1956; 1957). Polycrystalline materials such as rocks or metals have long been known to exhibit logarithmic creep:

$$\phi(t) = q \log (1 + \omega_0 t), \tag{10.2}$$

where q is a material constant called the *creep modulus* and ω_0 is a characteristic frequency.

Let now a small-amplitude stress wave $\sigma_0 e^{i\omega t}$ be applied to a rock and let the strain response be $\epsilon(t)$. Because of attenuation the strain response lags behind the stress input:

$$\epsilon(t) = \mu^{-1} e^{i\delta} \sigma(t), \tag{10.3}$$

where μ is the dynamic modulus and δ is the lag. We set

$$Q^{-1} \equiv \tan \delta, \tag{10.4}$$

where Q^{-1} is a function of frequency ω. Each spring-dashpot couple forms an elementary circuit that has an eigenfrequency $\omega = 2\pi\mu/\eta$, where μ is the rigidity of the spring and η is the viscosity of the dashpot. Let $f(\omega)$ be the probability density function of ω. Then the response rate $\dot{\epsilon}$ to a step input σ_0 to the system at time $t = 0$ may be represented as

$$\dot{\epsilon}(t) = \dot{\epsilon}(0) \int_0^\infty f(\omega) e^{-\omega t} \, d\omega, \tag{10.5}$$

where $\dot{\epsilon}(0) = \sigma_0 \omega_0 q/\mu$ is the initial creep rate, from Eq (10.2). If the eigenfrequencies $\omega_i = 2\pi\mu_i/\eta_i$ of the elementary circuits are exponentially distributed as

$$f(\omega) = \omega_0^{-1} \exp(-\omega_0/\omega), \tag{10.6}$$

we find

$$\dot{\epsilon}(t) = \frac{\sigma_0 \omega_0 q}{\mu} (1 + \omega_0 t)^{-1}, \tag{10.7}$$

which is the derivative of the logarithmic creep equation. Thus the logarithmic creep function can be derived from the distribution of grain sizes or "resonators" in the rock structure.

More generally, we may write the strain response to an arbitrary stress input as the convolution of the input with the step response (which is known from creep measurements):

$$Q(\omega) = \frac{1 + \int_0^\infty \dot{\epsilon}(t) \cos \omega t \, dt}{\int_0^\infty \dot{\epsilon}(t) \sin \omega t \, dt}. \tag{10.8}$$

Introducing Eq (10.2) we find (Fig. 10.3):

$$Q^{-1}(\Omega) = \frac{q\left[\left(\dfrac{\pi}{2} - \text{Si } \Omega\right) \cos \Omega + \text{Ci } \Omega \sin \Omega\right]}{1 + q\left[\left(\dfrac{\pi}{2} - \text{Si } \Omega\right) - \sin \Omega - \text{Ci } \Omega \cos \Omega\right]} \tag{10.9}$$

where $\Omega = \omega/\omega_0$ is the normalized frequency, and Si x and Ci x are the sine and cosine integral functions:

$$\begin{aligned} \text{Si } x &= \int_0^x \frac{\sin u}{u} \, du, \\ Ci \, x &= 0.577215 + \ln x + \int_0^x \frac{\cos u - 1}{u} \, du. \end{aligned} \tag{10.10}$$

On a logarithmic scale Eq (10.9) features a flat-topped maximum over more than three orders of frequency, in agreement with reports that Q is constant and independent of frequency for body waves. Results for other frequency ranges showed that Q^{-1} may decay with frequency as the right limb of the theoretical curve of Fig. 10.3. As with the proverbial elephant, depending on where we are located in the frequency domain, Q may either seem to increase, decrease or remain constant with frequency. The right-hand corner frequency occurs at about $\Omega = q$.

Thus the function (10.9) fits all available experimental data on attenuation of seismic waves in the earth. This is as it should be, since the zero-frequency response is known and the amplitudes are small. Thus at small amplitudes all observations conform to the simple linear theory. For seismic wave propagation the wave-length is on the order of kilometers, and the attenuation depends on structures of the same order of magnitude; yet because of self-similarity the same creep function applies. Aki and Chouet (1975) have suggested that inhomogeneities in the middle crust may be responsible for the attenuation of body waves; in this case the value of ω_0 may be as low as 1–10 Hz. In fact, corner frequencies of around 0.02 Hz with ω_0 around 1–10

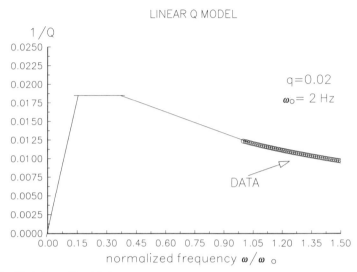

Fig. 10.3   *Variation of Q with frequency (standard linear model), showing the region where seismic data exist*

Hz yield excellent agreement with the available data for coda Q. Thus the systematic differences in Q found by Aki and his collaborators for Q in different tectonic environments must be due to fluctuations in the creep modulus q.

There are other intriguing applications of the linear Q theory. The unusual self-potential anomaly detected at the Vitosha observatory in Bulgaria before the Vrancea earthquake of August 30, 1986 (see Chapter 6) fits Eq (10.2) quite well. This represents an additional piece of evidence in favor of attributing certain electromagnetic precursors to strain effects in the earth.

THE DINARIC CAPER

Let us now consider the specific problem of independent verification of earthquake precursors and the evaluation of possible coincidences in the occurrence of such precursors.

A proposition, advanced by a group of Italian researchers, held that large earthquakes in the southern Dinaric Alps are precursors for large earthquakes in southern Italy. The proponents of this hypothesis stated that there is a lead time of less than 10 years for earthquakes in the Dinaric Alps over earthquakes in southern Italy. The study was evaluated by Rhoades and Evison (1989).

The authors proceeded by staking out two regions—D (in the Dinaric Alps) and I (in southern Italy)—in such a way that the seven largest events in region D preceded the seven largest events in region I by less than 10 years each. The fact that such a data presentation was possible was submitted as proof of the validity of the proposed hypothesis. Since the correlation between the two sequences of seven events each turned out to be extremely high, it was suggested that the proposed pattern was not the result of a random coincidence, and that this conclusion could be sustained with an extremely high probability.

But this conclusion was perfectly reasonable on quite another basis. The selection of earthquakes had been performed because of a prior hypothesis, and in an extremely unrandom, purposeful manner. For example, if the selected number of events had been six or eight instead of seven, or if the boundaries of the regions had been traced in any other way, the alleged precursory effect between Dinaric earthquakes and Italian erthquakes would have been destroyed or even reversed, as Rhoades and Evison showed.

Rhoades and Evison clearly understood the situation. As a test they tentatively modified the selection criterion by shifting the magnitude threshold by one decimal point in the upward or downward direction. The alleged precursory effect was destroyed. Sometimes an event in the Dinaric Alps followed an event in southern Italy, and sometimes it followed another event in the Dinaric Alps or vice versa, as one might expect for any two uncorrelated series of random events.

Such a test should have been conclusive, and the proposed precursor would have been rejected without further consideration. Instead, Rhoades and Evison (1989) voiced some concern that this logic might be unfair to the authors. They concluded that "the very interesting ideas [of the Dinaric earthquakes being precursors of Italian earthquakes] are in practice untestable," because in their opinion it might take the earth about 150 years to duplicate a run of seven events in each of the regions, similar to those observed by the authors. Only by duplicating the original situation, they claimed, could a fair test be conducted.

This incident raises the complex issue of fairness in the evaluation of scientific work. Were Rhoades and Evison justified in withholding their judgment when they had shown rather conclusively that the authors' hypothesis didn't hold water? Was this in the interest of science? Luckily for Rhoades and Evison, scientific opinions are not subject to legal procedure. For it seems to me that their case would not stand in court. Scientific work is not conducted for the benefit of scientists. The advancement of science is in the public interest. Thus if the proponents of the Dinaric prediction method had explicitly stated that their prediction was only valid for the seven events used in their sample, they should have been given the benefit of the doubt; otherwise the objections raised by Rhoades and Evison were in force. Since no such reservations were made, all considerations of fairness were out of place.

But a subtle point may be lost here. By bending over backwards to be fair to their colleagues, Rhoades and Evison succeeded in demolishing their hypothesis much more thoroughly than if they had subjected it to a frontal attack. For it was quite clear to everyone, the authors included, that scientific activity cannot be brought to a halt for a century or more while we wait for an experimental confirmation of some earthquake precursor to come through. Scientific research must be evaluated on its own merits, now, using the rules of evidence, and earthquake prediction cannot claim an exception.

The Italian authors thoroughly revised their work; this time they included data all the way back to 1800. They found instead of the claimed Dinaric precursor that there was a strong periodicity in central Mediterranean earthquakes (Mantovani et al., 1992). The periodicity appeared to be around 40 years and periods of high and low activity were simultaneous in the Dinaric Alps and in Italy. A cross-correlation between the two regions showed that the phase lag was zero (Fig. 10.4). This effectively undermined the initial claim of a precursory effect. But it showed the much more interesting possibility of alternating cycles of activity and quiescence in the central Mediterranean. The authors still cling to their belief that cycles of activity start earlier in the Balkans than in Italy, but the evidence is clearly marginal.

The idea of a strict periodicity can probably be dismissed, as only four complete cycles were recorded. But a rescaled-range analysis might yield some interesting predictions for the maximum earthquake size. It appears that the entire Adriatic region may represent a single strain catchment basin in the Hurstian sense. Thus an initially flawed and unpromising research on precursors did finally come up with prime evidence on clustering of the earthquake process. Science works in devious ways.

The other issue raised by the Dinaric caper concerns the rules of evidence

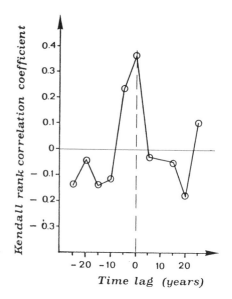

Fig. 10.4 *Cross-correlation between earthquakes in Italy and in the Dinaric Alps, suggesting that the average time lag is near zero. By permission of Il Cigno–Galileo Galilei, Rome.*

to be used when attempting to draw inferences from data. When should a positive correlation be dismissed as "coincidence"? According to Wittgenstein (1918) "there is nothing accidental in logic. . . It would seem a coincidence, as it were, if some state of affairs could be attributed *a posteriori* to a thing that can exist by itself."[1] In other words, a coincidence is merely another data point. It should not be privileged by a retroactive assignment of special meaning.

Does this mean that all conclusions based on a limited set of observations should be branded as coincidental and dismissed as naive? This is absurd. One is reminded of the scene in Eugene Ionesco's play *La cantatrice chauve*, in which a lady repeatedly marvels *"Quelle coincidence!"* on finding out that the man sitting next to her has taken the same train, traveled in the same compartment, gone to the same hotel, slept in the same bed, and so on. The audience knows that the man is her husband, though the couple on the stage seems to have forgotten all about each other.

Consider the following real-life example. A few years ago the President of Mexico instituted a National Sports Prize to be shared every year by one male and one female competitor. The prizes, awarded for the first time in 1988, went to two people having the same last name: *Torres*. Was this a coincidence, or would it afford a method for predicting the names of future winners?

Using the same method as in the case of the Dinaric earthquakes I went to the Mexico City telephone book and found at least 10,000 different family names. Thus the probability that the Presidential Sports Commission would have selected the name *Torres* twice was less than 10^{-8}, on the assumption of independent random trials. But the entire population of Mexico (men, women and children) is less than 10^8. Thus a coincidence can be ruled out and we must believe that the selection of two people named *Torres* was intentional.

Now one might conclude one of two things: either (a) all events are due to conspiracies, or (b) nothing can be learned from whatever happens. But there is a third possibility, namely that our reasoning was faulty. Indeed, a moment of reflection should convince us that sports prize winners are not selected by random trials. They are not meant to be. A prize is not a lottery. On the contrary, the winners are supposed to be selected on the basis of stringent criteria. The problem is how to interpret these criteria and the whole mechanism of the selection. If we favor the conspiratorial theory, we must believe that the actual criterion was different from the one that had been publicly announced, namely excellence in sports. But once we accept this possibility, there is no stopping at developing further "clues" based on a more detailed study of the two winners. It turns out, for example, that

---

[1] *"In der Logik ist nichts zufällig. . . . Es erschiene gleichsam als Zufall, wenn dem Ding, das allein für sich bestehen könnte, nachträglich eine Sachlage passen würde"* (Logisch-philosophische Abhandlung, Propositions 2.012 and 2.0121).

they were not relations (which seems to exclude nepotism as a motive); but on the other hand, Mr. Torres was a mountaineer who had conquered Mount Everest while Miss Torres was a champion of Tae Kwon Do, a Korean martial art. Thus there is indeed a secret link between the winners, namely "Asia." Come to think of it, didn't the remote forebears of both winners cross the Bering Straits into the American continent—from *Asia*?

Such "strange coincidences" can be found in any limited data set. The more they are looked for, the more such coincidences appear and can be recognized by human or by computer. "Pattern recognition" is in the eye of the beholder.

But there is a correct way to look at the problem. If the null hypothesis of random trials is unrealistic, which is better? Since no one could have guessed in advance that the name of the two winners would be *Torres*, the degree of astonishment depended on the fact that the names of the two winners *was the same*. In terms of the situation at hand, it would have made no difference if the name of the two winners had been *González* instead of *Torres*. Thus the null hypothesis to be tested is that of *any two last names* drawn at random being the same. Now we find that the name *Torres* takes up more than 10 pages in the Mexico City phone book; but there are many other family names (such as *González*) that take up a lot more space. Adding up all the probabilities for repeated names to turn up in two random trials we find that the chance for any two Mexican last names picked at random being the same is nearly 5%, a great deal higher than 10^{-8}. Now the problem boils down to this: Can we reasonably believe, on the basis of what we know about the awarding of sports prizes, that the Commission *intentionally* selected two winners with the same last name rather than two outstanding athletes? If we think the odds for this to occur to be higher than 5% we can probably believe anything.

The same method could have been used to analyze the case of the Dinaric earthquakes. In conclusion, if we can believe, on the strength of seven painstakingly selected examples, that there is a causal connection between earthquakes in a region of the Balkans and a region of Italy, we might as well start using tarot to predict earthquakes.

CERTIFICATION OF PRECURSORS

Let us immediately concede that the preceding discussion does not invalidate in the least the possibility that the occurrence of an earthquake in the Dinaric Alps might in fact increase (or decrease) the earthquake hazard in southern Italy. On the contrary, I have advocated such a "tunnelling effect" myself. But we are talking about a methodology for hypothesis testing.

This is related to the current discussion on whether the Palmdale uplift was a precursor of the 1992 Landers earthquake. Some scientists have used the null hypothesis of a "coincidence." Suppose that the uplift occurred independently of the earthquake; then why did the maximum occur *exactly* over the epicentral region of the Landers-Big Bear earthquakes? Granted that such a reasoning cannot disprove our null hypothesis, it is felt "intuitively", nevertheless, that a causal connection is more likely. There is a logical somersault involved in this conclusion. As Gertrude Stein might have said, a coincidence is a coincidence is a coincidence. It is improbable by definition. The fact that we may think other alternatives more likely is beside the point.

If earthquake precursors are to be objectively tested, there must be a general way of dealing with the null hypothesis of coincidence. Carl Friedrich Gauss (1823) addressed the problem in his classical dissertation on errors. He proposed to measure the length of a table. One way to do this is using a tape measure and jotting down the result. If we are correct, it is by *coincidence*. More likely, we may make a number of errors in placing or reading the tape and even in noting the result. The right way of going about this requires three previous assumptions. Gauss discusses each of these in turn.

(1) *Independence*. If we make a number of measurements, we may assume that each trial (i.e., each measurement) is independent of all other trials. This assumption can be made to hold more strictly, for example, by having the measurements made by different people.

(2) *Absence of Bias*. We assume that the true length of the object can be underestimated or overestimated with the same probability. Thus positive or negative errors are equally likely.

(3) *Regularity*. However many sources of error there may be, we assume that small errors are always easier to make, and hence more likely, than large ones. The larger the error the more unlikely it is.

If these three assumptions are realistic for a given situation, Gauss proves that the optimal method of estimation is the root-mean-square algorithm. This leads to the distribution of errors now known as the Gaussian or normal distribution.

But finally we can never be sure of the true length of the table. What if all our measurements had been *coincidentally* 2 inches short on the average? There is no way to rule this out except by repeating the measurements, preferably with another tape and another group of observers. Even then, the possibility of an influence between the groups cannot be ruled out. This sort of thing has often happened in the history of science. On the other hand, the assumptions of the test may be unrealistic; for example, the tapes may be biased. In the case of measuring the arrival times of seismic waves in the presence of noise, one is more likely to overestimate the arrival time than the reverse. Yet we still use least squares for epicenter location, simply because nonlinear regression is tricky and other errors are larger.

In the case of earthquake precursors, a major problem is the experimenter's bias. The seismologist is actively looking for earthquake precursors, so he or she finds them. One way to prevent this is by a variant of the double-blind test, a test often applied for purposes of certification of drugs or medical treatments. In the United States, this type of certification is regularly supervised by a government agency, the Federal Drug Administration. The rulings of this agency are seldom above controversy, but it is generally agreed that it performs a useful function on behalf of the general public.

The idea is to devise an objective procedure that depends as little as possible on the structure of the test or on the possible bias of the scientists. In the case of earthquake prediction, we may imagine that a set of unlabeled records of some geophysical variable (earth currents, water levels in a well, and so on) is presented for evaluation of the possible presence of a precursory effect. The records are divided into subsets of comparable length, all dates and other identifying labels are removed, and a *placebo set* (i.e., a set of computer-generated random records of the same character and frequency structure) is generated for each subset. Two groups of analysts are asked to read the records without knowing which is an actual record or a placebo and to single out anomalies as specified in the procedure to be tested.

As a variant, each group of analysts may be given a set of "target earthquakes," to be matched to a set of "precursors" (Table 10.1). Some may be actual earthquakes and some computer-generated random events. Each group would also be asked to identify any precursors not attached to events. Such a double-blind test was performed by Helen W. Friedman (1966) in order to detect bias in the procedure of reading seismograms. A set of unlabeled seismic records was distributed among professional and amateur seismogram analysts. It was found that the resulting readings were normally distributed.

This conclusion was unfortunately flawed, because of the inference that human error was unbiased and that the method of hypocentral location of

TABLE 10.1   A Search for Precursors

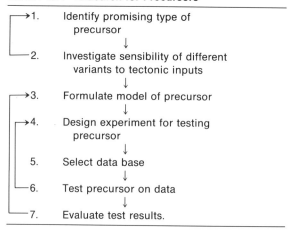

1. Identify promising type of precursor
   ↓
2. Investigate sensibility of different variants to tectonic inputs
   ↓
3. Formulate model of precursor
   ↓
4. Design experiment for testing precursor
   ↓
5. Select data base
   ↓
6. Test precursor on data
   ↓
7. Evaluate test results.

earthquakes by least squares was justified. But the mean of the distribution of readings was not compared with the true arrival times of the signals. If this had been done, it would have been realized that readings always tend to lag behind true arrivals. The bias in seismogram reading is not due to human error but to seismic noise in the earth. All signals emerge from noise; thus a real lag is introduced in attempting to read the beginning of a signal, no matter how carefully it is done. The lag is inversely proportional to the signal/noise ratio.

Errors may even be introduced by way of parameter definition. An example close to home is the evaluation of magnitudes in seismology. Wyss (1991) has shown that erroneous identifications of alleged precursors such as seismic quiescence may be due to bias in the regional magnitude determination caused by a single new station being enabled, or a single old station being disabled. For a related discussion on erors in the estimation of earthquake magnitudes, see Friedman (1967).

For years Gutenberg and Richter resisted the idea of calculating magnitudes to the nearest decimal. At most they would allow half- or quarter-values, say $5\frac{1}{2}$ or $7\frac{1}{4}$. They realized that the magnitude parameter was not a physical quantity. Eventually they gave in and proposed the present procedure of averaging the magnitudes M_i reported by individual stations:

$$M = n^{-1} \sum_{i=1}^{n} M_i, \qquad (10.11)$$

where n is the number of reporting stations. This procedure is biased, since M_i is defined as a logarithmic measure of the station amplitude A_i:

$$M_i = \log A_i + F(\Delta), \qquad (10.12)$$

where $F(\Delta)$ is a function of the epicentral distance, such that $F(100 \text{ km}) = 0$ on a standard instrument (the Wood–Anderson seismometer). And the mean of logarithms does not equal the logarithm of the mean. Introducing Eq (10.12) into (10.11) and assuming that Δ_n is some average epicentral distance we find

$$M = n^{-1} \sum_{i=1}^{n} \log A_i + F(\Delta_n), \qquad (10.13)$$

which is a biased estimator of the logarithm of the mean amplitude. This bias may easily lead to an underestimation of the seismic energy by more than 30%. The smaller the earthquake and the fewer the reporting stations, the worse is the bias.

Other biased parameters in seismology include the location as obtained by least squares (a sphere is not a linear surface, and the interior of the earth is not homogeneous), the focal depth (the azimuthal distribution of stations is strongly inhomogeneous, especially near plate boundaries), the travel time (late pickings of a signal that emerges from a noisy background are more probable than early pickings), and so on. In conclusion, the design of a testing procedure for earthquake prediction is by no means a trivial undertaking; yet it is critical to any evaluation process.

Meteorologists have weather balloons, satellites, ecosondes and weather stations; we seismologists have only our brains to get inside the earth. Precursor research has yet to find a useful signal that stands out clearly from the noise. Harold Jeffreys used to say that "if an effect is really there it shouldn't take a statistician to bring it out." He was not a statistician for nothing.

A DIAGRAM

A large earthquake is a transient embedded in a larger transient, which we may call the *creep transient*. The precursors are often generated by the creep transient, or by the difference in behavior between creeping and locked regions. The problem is to detect these precursors and to interpret them.

Consider the situation right after the earthquake (Fig. 10.5). The broad negative peak is the response of the system to a regional stress drop (cf. Chapter 6, *Thermodynamics of earthquake precursors*). In the case of the 1985 Chile earthquake this response would have covered the area of precursory tilt. The narrow positive peak in the center represents the aftershock area itself. Here the anomaly is caused by the coseismic strain due to fault displacement. The result is shaped like a Mexican hat.

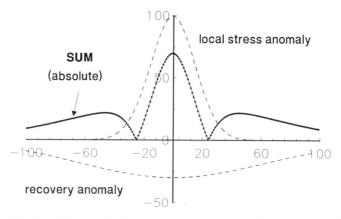

Fig. 10.5 *Diagram of the coseismic stress anomaly as a function of epicentral distance. The absolute value of the sum of the local effect from fault displacement* (positive dashed line) *and of the regional recovery from the stress drop* (negative dashed line) *is shaped like a Mexican hat.*

Note that the area of aftershock activity is surrounded by a ring of quiescence and an outer area of slightly increased activity. Exactly the opposite pattern would be expected to appear *before* the earthquake. The locked central area would be quiescent and would be surrounded by a ring of increased seismic activity, called a *donut pattern* by Mogi (1985). Tilt would also occur within the broad area of precursory stress accumulation. So would other precursors, such as groundwater flow, radon, and eventually foreshocks.

Current precursor research is mostly concerned with (a) the time of initiation of the precursor, (b) the lag or delay between the precursor and the earthquake, (c) the size of the earthquake. But while the present model accounts for most of the observed phenomenology of precursors, it appears that often the precursor does not yet "know" whether an earthquake will occur and when. The larger the locked area, the larger will be the tilt and other precursors which depend on stress differences. As for the occurrence and the exact time of the earthquake, they might depend more on the actual strain configuration, somewhat like thunderstorms which depend on the local ground topography. Take the case of the Chile earthquake. The MRI anomaly was there since the 1970s. Even if we had detected the onset of the tilt transient and correctly gauged the potential size of the earthquake, there would still have been an uncertainty of the order of at least one year as to the exact time of occurrence.

Scientific thinking may be defined as "the gradual realization that events do not happen in an arbitrary manner, but that they reflect a certain underlying order" (Hawking, 1988). The major orderly features detected so far in the earthquake process are foreshocks and aftershocks. Foreshock sequences rarely extend over periods of more than a few weeks or months. This is a very short time compared with the seismic cycle of decades, sometimes centuries, involving rupture, recovery, and quiescence. The foreshock period must correspond to the period of strain anomalies preceding a large earthquake. Nothing in the data suggests that periods of strain accumulation of years take place.

The Haicheng case suggests that even a lead time of less than 24 hours can be useful in saving human lives. If our reasoning is correct, we must find better and faster ways of imaging the shifting hazard patterns along plate boundaries. A comparison with weather prediction may be useful here. If we have a set of descriptive weather reports from a hundred different stations no useful prediction is possible. It takes too long to plot the data and to try making sense of it. By the time our weather report is ready the weather has changed. But if we have a satellite image, we can actually follow the weather as it changes in time, and even a layperson watching television can learn to anticipate it to some useful degree.

In Russia, V.I. Keilis-Borok had somewhat similar ideas. He proposed to let computers find out by themselves about the precursory patterns of seismicity that precede large earthquakes. For this purpose, he only required a large amount of seismic data. No particular model of the earthquake process would be needed.

But the learning algorithms were unstable and the results were doubtful. Meanwhile, the world's concern shifted. Earthquakes suddenly seemed less threatening than the ozone hole or the greenhouse effect. Earthquake prediction was not providing much excitement. Scientists yawned: So what if some Russian algorithm was marginally successful at predicting some earthquake in Armenia?

EARTHQUAKES, POLITICIANS, AND SCIENTISTS

In 1964 Japan inaugurated a major earthquake prediction program. Over the years it received sustained funding at the rate of $60 million per year, of which about one-fourth goes to university projects such as a network of telemetered ocean-bottom sensors in Suruga Bay. The program has steadily supported the research of 500 geophysicists and engineers all over Japan. Among its major achievements is a nationwide system of disaster preparedness unequaled anywhere in the world, as any casual visitor can testify. The program is also unique in being controlled, not by a state agency as in China or the United States, but by a committee of eight senior scientists who represent the main participating universities and laboratories. There is no lead agency for earthquake prediction.

After the Loma Prieta, California earthquake of 1989, the American seismological establishment flailed about aimlessly as earthquake after big earthquake hit California. The 1994 Northridge earthquake was the last straw. "'Many of us in the scientific community feel intuitively that the Landers–Big Bear quake sequence has increased the probability of large earthquakes over the next few years,'" said *EOS*, the news sheet of the American Geophysical Union, quoting a spokesperson for the U.S. Geological Survey, "'but we can't ask public agencies or individual citizens to make preparedness or emergency plans based on intuition'" (Bush, 1992). This came perilously close to admitting that official earthquake prediction has been guided by hunches.

Meanwhile, back in Japan, some business interests were becoming impatient with earthquake prediction for standing in the way of development of reclaimed land along the bayshore waterfront. On April 9, 1992, the weekly *Nature,* dean of the world's scientific press, lambasted the Japanese approach on earthquake prediction (Swinbanks, 1992). Citing two prestigious Tokyo University professors, Robert J. Geller and Seiya Uyeda, neither of whom had previously engaged in earthquake prediction, *Nature* charged that critics had been prevented from having a say on prediction by "small groups of powerful academics" who supposedly resisted "attempts to open up the system to outsiders."

There is no direct evidence that either Geller or Uyeda shared the position of the author of the note. Geller (1991) sounded a more careful (though no less critical) note. He wouldn't have said that "a handful of senior seismologists, who have been in the earthquake prediction business since the 1960s . . . have effectively bypassed external review". In this context, "external review" could only mean review by state agencies or by academic seismologists who claim (as Robert Geller does) that "earthquake prediction is beyond the present capabilities of science." One may easily imagine how the program would have fared under their ministrations.

Two days after publication of the article in *Nature*, the Tokyo metropolitan government canceled its earthquake prediction research program. This program had included the sort of empirical observations the journal had criticized, such as radon monitoring in groundwater and observations on the behavior of *namazu* eels (Küppers, 1992). As City Hall withdrew from earthquake prediction, it began to waver on earlier policies restricting construction along the waterfront. Bureaucrats saw a chance of striking a blow at one of the few programs that had eluded their control. The Earthquake Research Institute, flagship of Japan's research effort in seismology, was suddenly to be wrested from the University of Tokyo and "opened" to users nationwide. The attempt eventually failed, but regional observational networks (whose diversity had once been a source of scientific strength) were consolidated in Tokyo. At the same time, Mombushô, Japan's Ministry of Education, announced a shakeup of national universities.

The directorship of the Earthquake Research Institute had been traditionally occupied by senior scientists soon to retire. Every two years another senior scientist headed the institute by strict order of seniority. In this way, politicking was kept at a minimum since everyone's turn in power was perfectly predictable. Now the junior scientists, in order to forestall more sweeping reforms, changed the system. They brought in a director from the outside. Prof. Yoshio Fukao, a prestigious seismologist from Nagoya, was called to head the institute. Fukao was not near retirement age. The implications of the new policy are hard to foresee.

Japanese seismologists tended to endorse Professor Geller's appraisal of the dismal scientific quality of earthquake prediction research; but the cause of this perceived mediocrity was far from clear. It was not necessarily due to the closedness of the system. Actually the program was overly sensitive to peer criticism, as the response to the articles in *Nature* also suggests. Historically, peer criticism in Japan adopts subtle forms and channels of expression, which Professor Geller does not necessarily have access to. On the other hand, a research program can become conservative, stale, and unimaginative in the same way as in the West, and for similar reasons.

Actually *Nature* may have a point. Academic critics from the outside have never had much say in the distribution of research funds for earthquake prediction. Thus, in the United States, the program is exclusively managed by one government agency, the USGS. I have been asked to review USGS proposals; but I am under no illusions about my ever being able to break into the USGS club. Not that I haven't tried. I have been a critic of the Parkfield project since its inception; yet no one has ever asked me to state my point of view. If there was "external review", it must have been of a cozy sort.

I happen to find this normal. Over the years, no one has prevented other research groups from going ahead and generating the *"exciting new research"* we are promised from a *"fundamental reform of the earthquake prediction program"* (Geller, 1991). The proof of the pudding is in the eating. Should peer review substitute for the missing creativity?

The Japanese earthquake prediction program may look like a tightly restricted little club to Western critics; yet it allows for direct continuous participation by at least eight major universities. It provides 500 full-time jobs for research scientists all over Japan. In today's open world, Professor Robert Geller is happily teaching at a Japanese university while Professor Hiroo Kanamori, a distinguished Japanese seismologist, teaches just as happily at an American university. Both are people with a creative, independent and highly unconventional turn of mind; certainly no conformists. This too is as it should be.

Inevitably, the Japanese program will be taken over by state agencies, as it was in the United States. But one thing is certain: The moment prediction is hit, prevention goes out the window. One has only to compare the levels of disaster preparedness in Japan with those in the United States to realize the benefits that have accrued to the Japanese people from their prediction research program since 1964. Posters with instructions about what to do in case of an earthquake alert are prominently displayed everywhere in Japan (as Geller himself points out), thus making the population aware of the earthquake hazard. A casual visitor can see plenty of examples of earthquake preparedness all over the country.

Nature upbraids Japanese seismologists for refusing to acknowledge in so many words that earthquakes cannot yet be predicted. I wonder. Japan has never issued an official earthquake alert. California has issued several—all of them duds. The balance favors Japan.

Is earthquake prediction really beyond the present ken of science? How can anyone be sure? Three or four decades ago the conundrum of genetics was thought to be beyond the capabilities of science to unravel. Should one have pulled the funding from under the "handful of senior scientists" who insisted on deciphering the genetic code? Jim Watson and Francis Crick's work on the double helix might never have been performed, and the skeptics would have been proved correct.

It seems possible that accurate large-scale earthquake prediction may never be achieved. The universe may be basically unpredictable. Weather is, too: but this is no reason for abolishing the weather man. Synoptic short-term forecasts on a local scale are not to be sneezed or sniffled at. Millions use them every day to keep from catching nasty colds.

No mechanism of "external review" is both foolproof and fair to science;

no one has a crystal ball showing where the next discovery will come from. Not only that; "the fact is that we do not know what is going on" (Ralph E. Gomory). In 1918 Albert Einstein sensibly remarked that "the temple of science has many mansions"; but in the next breath he talked of "uniting quantum theory with electrodynamics and mechanics in a single logical system." This may have looked like a major priority of science in 1918, but actually it turned out to be one of those vexing philosophical quandaries that had better be left alone by active scientists. "Joining the classical to the quantum world is a deep and longstanding enigma" (Davies, 1989).

"Cast thy bread upon the waters" remains a plausible science policy, though it is admittedly difficult to enforce. During the Cold War years, American science enjoyed almost unlimited support for military research, and the overflow fed academic and industrial research as well. Science was doing great. Sure enough, as resources began to dry up, we started hearing from the politicians. It seems that we hadn't been doing our job after all. The earlier approach to funding was suddenly derided as "the linear one-dimensional model," as a Congressional report put it (Brown, 1992). "Basic research does not contribute directly or automatically to society's needs," the report sniffed. However, "this is not the fault of the scientists," it added as an afterthought. It must be the fault of the Japanese.

Ludwig Boltzmann, on a visit to exotic California back in 1905, reflected on the local research scene and noted the predilection of American scientists for well-advertised mega-projects involving big sums of money—for those days. He was impressed by some projects and dismayed by others—without any correlation with their eventual scientific worth, as it turned out. In his travelogue written for an Austrian daily, Boltzmann (1992) mused that "some things can be accomplished by large-scale efforts . . . But the truly great scientific advances (our Minister of Education mustn't hear this) are always made with the smallest means".

Poor Herr Professor Doktor Boltzmann, how right he thought he was! He killed himself a year later, largely out of despondency over the lack of acceptance of his work. Had he waited another year, Einstein's vision would have come to the rescue of his own. Boltzmann should have gone to see his Minister of Education, a sensible man who might have talked him out of it. I can imagine the conversation. The Minister would have said soothingly, "There, there, professor. As many ways of doing science exist as there are scientists. The wise man, if he is honest about his calling, expects no recognition. Come to think of it, why should a good scientist be more famous than a good dentist?"

We don't need politicians to tell us how lousy our work is. That is the job of peer review. Politicians are there to hold our hands. A Minister of Science who never stopped a professor from killing himself, or who never treated an aggravated research scientist to lunch, has not earned his keep.

We scientists certainly need to listen more carefully to what politicians are saying. But let's stop trying to teach them about one-dimensional models.

11

Conclusion

Vouchsafe to those that have not heard the story
That I may prompt them: and of such as have,
I humbly pray them to admit the excuse
Of time, of numbers, and due course of things.
—Henry V

IN DEFENSE OF EARTHQUAKE PREDICTION

If humans exist on earth for a purpose, it is likely to be for scientific research. It is the one urge that is exclusively human and distinctive of the race. Animals may be more perceptive than we are in the event of an approaching earthquake, but they are unable, unwilling, or too lazy to distinguish between it and a thunderstorm. They can't be bothered with the difference. As for us, rolling back the frontiers of knowledge is our species-specific specialty and our exclusive hangup and responsibility. If we fail there, we fail in everything.

In 1990 the State of California decided to implement a *Short-term Earthquake Prediction Response Plan*, to issue public warnings on the basis of eventual predictions cleared by the California Earthquake Prediction Evaluation Council. A similar plan had been in force in Japan for years, but unlike California, Japan never issued an actual warning. The journal *Nature* got on its white charger and suggested

> that the aim of the whole complex warning system [in Japan] is to diffuse responsibility among as many scientists, bureaucrats and politicians as possible in case it does not work. All seismologists know that earthquakes can seldom be predicted . . . but they cannot say that too loudly for fear that the ¥1,800 million ($14 million) a year in funds for earthquake prediction would dry up (Schaefer and Swinbanks, 1990).

Fancy being overheard. No one is listening. The quoted amount was not even the total Japanese funding for earthquake prediction; it was merely the

274

share of academic research. The share of government agencies was three times larger. Let us be loud and clear: Earthquakes cannot be predicted in the present state of our knowledge. Neither can economic recessions, hurricanes, virus epidemics, the outcome of Presidential elections, the popularity of rock stars, or a host of other disasters that may or may not carry a higher price tag than earthquake prediction research does. In Japan no warnings are issued for one reason: because it is widely understood that we are not capable of predicting earthquakes. In California public warnings are issued for the same reason—or perhaps in spite of it.

However strongly we may feel about earthquake prediction research being conducted by government agencies or by the scientific community, as scientists we must uphold the truth. When our motives are questioned, it is time to rally about earthquake prediction.

MITIGATION OR PREDICTION?

Even before the 1967 proposal to Congress there was some question in the United States as to whether public funds were better spent on earthquake prediction or on hazard reduction and prevention of earthquake damage.

This is an example of a false dilemma. There is no either/or proposition. Unless earthquake prediction research is actively pursued there will be no mitigation either. After the Frank Press proposal for earthquake prediction was turned down in 1967, no hazard reduction effort was carried out in America. A document entitled *Earthquake Prediction and Public Policy*, published by the National Academy of Sciences in 1975, took issue with the views that earthquake prediction research should be given up or postponed: "Such views," the report cautioned, "reflect a profound misunderstanding of the situation in which we find ourselves." It called earthquake prediction "an inescapable reality."

The 1978 proposal to predict the next Tokyo earthquake—sometimes dismissed by Japanese critics as "propaganda"—has finally resulted in positive action toward hardening the defenses of the Tokyo Metropolitan Area against earthquakes. Katsuhiko Ishibashi, the original proponent of the Tokai earthquake prediction, has written distinguished papers on plate motions in central Japan. He may or may not qualify for Nature's blacklist of "powerful academics" who "can exert enormous influence over government funding of research" in Japan. Frank Press has stepped down as president of the National Academy of Sciences in Washington, after many years of distinguished service to the academic community; Ishibashi is a researcher at an international institute near Tokyo. Is it credible that such men should deliberately conspire to hush up the well-known fact that earthquake prediction is a frontier subject that has not yet attained its ultimate aim? Should earthquake prediction be pilloried rather than, say, cancer research or AIDS research? Why not recognize the advances that have been made?

Hazard reduction is the aim and hazard prediction is the means. No strategy of risk abatement can do without earthquake prediction, any more than an effective strategy of public health can dispense with medical research.

As for the optimum strategy of earthquake prediction research, there is a wide scatter of opinions. Basic research on the earthquake process and on the mechanics of faulting is certainly essential. We need to know how strain accumulates at plate boundaries and how it is released. But pragmatic research on earthquake precursors is equally important. The Chinese approach I think is correct in stressing the need for a broad paradigm (the earthquake field, in this case), which can integrate the various research results into a coherent whole. In this book I have attempted to show how thermodynamic field theory could be used in a similar way to integrate observations on precursors.

I am sorry to see the neglect of animal earthquake prediction studies in China after the 1976 earthquake. We tend to see animals as second-rate citizens of our world, and we underestimate the help they could give us in solving problems at the interface between society and the environment. As a general observation, too much equipment and too little thought have gone into earthquake prediction programs. The symposia and workshops on earthquake prediction tend to reflect this situation. They consist in a series of disjoint individual presentations; good reviews or critical discussions are rare. Interpretations of seismic records (*seismology is the science of data called seismograms*—remember?) prevail over fundamental physics. We might adopt the format of some social science meetings, where a discussant is assigned to every presentation and round-table discussions are organized in advance. Instead, the trend in seismology is toward poster sessions. A poster may be excellent for presenting a geologic map or the results of a field study, but there is hardly any chance of an interaction or discussion between papers hanging on a wall. Those of us who have voices and love a good argument may feel deprived.

THE CASE OF MEXICO CITY

Foresight, meticulous planning, and careful management are the secret ingredients that have earned Japan its well-deserved prominence in the world. We in Mexico could do worse than heeding Japan's example. Mexico was an early admirer of Japan back in the 19th century: It was the first country to recognize Japan and to open an embassy in Tokyo on equal terms.

There is another, deeper link between the Mexican and Japanese cultures. The common ancestors of the Japanese and Mexican nations (not the good egg of Columbus) discovered America 14,000 years ago. They crossed the frozen straits between America and Asia on foot and undertook the settlement of a continent that no human being had ever set foot on. We of all people should be sensitive to this spectacular achievement and mindful of the depth and originality of Asian contributions to human discovery.

Well before the 1985 earthquake it was clear that local site conditions would play a decisive role in the next earthquake to hit Mexico City. The geology of the soft layer in the Mexico valley had been investigated for nearly a century (see, e.g., Felix and Lenk, 1890). Ground effects had turned out to be dominant compared with other effects, such as earthquake magnitude and epicentral distance, as reflected in the predictions of maximum ground acceleration (see, e.g., Esteva, 1970). The insurance people knew this. The 1976 version of the Mexico City Building Code was based on a predicted amplitude in downtown Mexico City that turned out to be right on the mark. The dominant frequencies of ground motion had also been accurately anticipated. Then why did 371 high-rise buildings collapse? What was the new and unexpected factor that emerged in the 1985 earthquake?

Foresight, meticulous planning, and careful management of risks were needed. Site conditions have traditionally been incorporated into hazard assessment through a site coefficient S in the specifications for estimating the design base shear. This site coefficient was obtained from a classification of soils—it typically ranged from 1 to 2. This meant that the specifications should be doubled if the soil was very soft. But peak ground accelerations on soft ground often were at least five times higher than on adjacent hard ground. This was known since the observations of Gutenberg and Richter in the 1940s. In California, average amplifications as high as 10 times were later found by Jack Evernden of the U.S. Geological Survey.

Seismograms on soft ground tend to be low in frequency, monochromatic, prograde, slowly beating, and of long duration compared with records on adjacent hard ground (see, e.g., Yamazaki et al., 1988). They are evidently largely surface waves. Yet the dominant type of analysis featured one-dimensional SH-wave excitation propagating vertically through the soft layer, using as input a strong-motion record from some nearby site on hard ground. This prediction method successfully duplicated the observed response spectrum on soft ground, but that was all. It failed to explain the seismograms or the observed behavior of the structures. The reason was that it tried to explain everything in terms of body waves.

Why dismiss the relevance of surface waves in strong ground motion? The answer is shown in Fig. 11.1. The large spectral peak corresponds to recorded ground motion at station SCT1 in the 1985 earthquake. The squat spectra belong to the 1976 and 1987 building codes. This is like trying to hide a mountain behind a molehill. If the ground motion was random, so that the excess spectral acceleration could reasonably be dissipated by nonlinear mechanisms in the joints and members of the structure, a lower design acceleration was allowable.

In conclusion, the ground motion had to be attributed to body waves. Otherwise high-rise buildings would have to be disallowed or thoroughly redesigned. Only high-rise buildings had collapsed in 1985.

DAMPING FACTOR= 5%

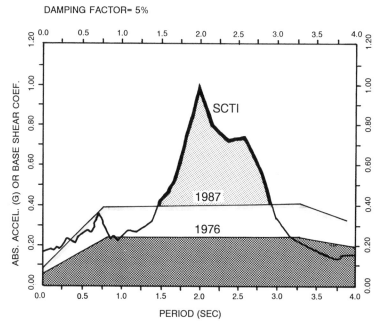

Fig. 11.1   *Response spectrum at station SCT1 (1985 earthquake) as compared with design spectra for the 1976 and 1987 versions of the Mexico City Building Code.*

A famous accelerograph record obtained in downtown Mexico City during the 1985 earthquake showed a long train of regular, slightly beating surface waves (Fig. 9.11). This wavetrain was the cause of the large spectral peak observed in Fig. 11.1. The direction of propagation was toward the northeast. The particle motion was found to be elliptical prograde, with the major axis elongated about 6:1 in the direction of propagation. Hadley et al. (1991) showed that the combination of forced oscillations with a long wavetrain of free oscillations could not be duplicated by any linear model.

The similarity of the long wavetrain with water waves was striking. A large body of descriptive literature referred to sightings of waves similar to water waves in large earthquakes. In the great 1960 Chile earthquake I had observed effects similar to those of water waves. Matuzawa had written about wavy deformations of the ground after earthquakes being caused by hydrodynamic waves. Bill Van Dorn had shown that the rings around moon craters were caused by solid *tsunamis*. Could it be that soils were capable of propagating hydrodynamic waves?

After the 1985 Mexico City disaster I began to entertain the idea that damage on soft ground was created not just by surface waves but by a different kind of surface wave. Apparently nature could sustain both elastic and gravity waves on soft ground. There was a gray area of insufficient knowledge between seismology, earthquake engineering, and soil mechanics, where the relevant three fields interface.

In 1970 K. Aki and K.L. Larner solved the seismological problem of scattering of SH waves by an irregular shallow slope, using a new mathematical technique. After the 1985 Mexico earthquake this procedure was applied in an effort to duplicate the observed duration of strong motion on soft ground. The solutions had in common the assumption of a basin of concave shape under the Valley of Mexico (Fig. 11.2). But there is no such basin under Mexico City. The "Valley of Mexico" is actually a closed shallow intramontane depression within the Mexican Plateau, at an altitude of about 2,300 m. It is underlain by 2 km of Tertiary and Quaternary volcanics on top of Cretaceous limestones lying flat at about sea level. Tectonism in the Mexican Volcanic Belt is largely tensional or transcurrent; there is little folding. No major river dissected this flat plateau.

The huge strato-volcanoes Popocatépetl and Ixtaccíhuatl pierce this flat sequence forming a high ridge that closes the Valley off to the east. Low hills, or *lomas*, of the Tarango Formation (tuffs and breccias) border it to the west. Some 50,000 years ago the Chichinautzin Volcanic Chain erupted along the southern edge of the valley. Its activity continues into the present: The most recent episode, the Xitle eruption, occurred about 1,500 years ago. Thus the southern exit of the depression was cut off, and a shallow swampy lake formed on the flat bottom of the valley. A unique ecological environment developed; it supported an abundant and highly diversified flora and wildlife and (after the discovery of America about 14,000 years ago) a large human population.

Consider now some of the great earthquake disasters in Mexico City, such as those in 1611, 1711, 1784, 1845, 1957, and 1985. The epicentral distance always fell between 300 and 500 km; within this range the location of the

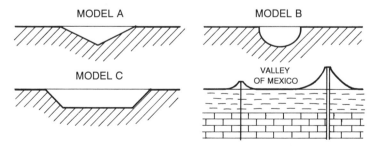

Fig. 11.2 *Simplified geologic cross-section under Mexico City (below, right), as compared to models used in simulations by different authors. The contact between the limestones and the volcanic overburden is approximately at sea level.*

epicenter made no noticeable difference. For earthquake risk estimation purposes, the entire stretch of coast between Colima and Oaxaca was a point source as far as Mexico City was concerned.

As soon as magnitude 6.9 was exceeded, the Mexico City valley floor began to behave in a notoriously nonlinear fashion. Accelerations along the edge of the soft layer got out of control. Solitons and other nonlinear hydrodynamic phenomena arose in localized areas, where the amplitudes were enhanced through wedge effects. These effects were easy to understand once the hypothesis of liquefaction on soft ground was accepted. But why did the soft layer behave like a liquid?

Mexico City clay is normally a soft solid. It contains around 90% of water by volume. When shaken it loses more than half its rigidity in a matter of seconds. Of course this rigidity is low to start with: The velocity of low-amplitude shear waves is only about 50 m/s—which is closer to zero than it is to the velocities recorded on hard ground. But such a rapid loss of rigidity can also be found in other soils.

Gradually we realized that the collapses of high-rise buildings have certain things in common. They occur near the flat edges of soft layers, where the amplitudes are very large. They happen in areas where the soft layer is topped by a crust of fill or other harder material, as in Mexico City or in the San Francisco Bay area. They occur when the structure has a shallow foundation. And they involve spatial resonance with wavelengths on the order of only 10–20 m.

There is a phase transition in soils called *liquefaction*, which suddenly lowers the rigidity of a soil to zero. This transition may also occur in powdered materials such as flour or plaster of Paris, where the grain size is uniform. The impact of meteorites on Mars causes a splatter that suggests to some astronomers that the surface is semi-liquid, but the same splatter can be produced in dry flour. Significantly, the sediments on Mars were generated by differential settlement in a deep ocean; the grain sizes are very uniform.

Thus it was realized that liquefaction in sediments is conditioned by the fractal distribution of the grain sizes, as in sands or other terrestrial sediments. Lunar sediments also liquefy, as Van Dorn (1968) discovered. Lunar sediments must also have a fractal particle structure. This cannot be due to erosion by water or atmospheric agents; it must be due to random fragmentation by external impacts.

Mitchell Feigenbaum had discovered that there are universal scaling relations that lead to phase transitions. Scaling relations of precisely this type produce the self-similarity in the structure of soils. Systems that are self-organized, like a sedimentary layer, also tend to undergo transitions to chaos, for example, liquefaction. Thus it seems likely that liquefaction in soils is a first-order phase transition.

During an earthquake the soil does not actually flow like a liquid except under rather special circumstances. More often we have a perfectly level layer, as in Mexico City, and the soil has nowhere to flow. It stays in place but loses its ability to propagate shear waves. The transition from elastic to gravity waves shortens the wavelength suddenly from about a mile to around 10–20 m, and the particle motion becomes prograde instead of retrograde. This instantly increases the overturning moment acting on tall buildings. Unless the building is specifically designed against gravity waves, it will fail.

EPILOGUE

Specialists in science policy may wonder why the connection between lique-faction and earthquake damage was not discovered earlier, and why it is still resisted by many engineers and geophysicists. The answer, I believe, is that some of these results refer to rather recent advances in physics. The basic paper by Kolmogorov on the particle distribution in sands was published in 1941, but it has not yet come to the attention of most earth scientists.

On the other hand, certain interests would prefer the analogy between high-rise buildings and ships to be kept under wraps. Design procedures on soft ground would have to be changed. Many designs that are acceptable under present codes or regulations would have to be altered. Civil engineers and seismologists would have to learn all about roll, pitch, and yaw. We would have to study naval engineering.

Should we perhaps encourage more interdisciplinary research on applied subjects such as these, that are relevant to societal needs such as the prevention of earthquake damage on soft ground? Most experts on science policy tend to agree. I have news for them. Japan has had interdisciplinary research centers on *disaster prevention* for many years. Precious little interdisciplinary research has come out of them. Instead, specialists of every stripe are busy erecting fences around their various disciplines, so that rival specialists cannot interfere.

One of the best among these research centers belongs to Kyoto University. On a recent visit I proposed a joint research project with the engineers on the effect of prograde ground motion on high-rise buildings. But I found that the earthquake engineers were mostly engaged in solving problems related to simulation of soil-structure interaction. This happens to be a hot subject in earthquake engineering at the moment. The trouble with "interdisciplinary" research is that everyone does his or her own thing anyway. Real interdiscipline can arise in applied research, where people are looking for solutions to specific problems. Even then, each specialized group tends to retain its identity and to follow the research lines that happen to be "hot" at the time.

We have it on Darwin's own authority that he nearly missed the crucial insight that there were as many species of Galapagos finches as there were islands in the Galapagos. Each species had originated on a different island. Once this insight was achieved, it proved more than sufficient for a lifetime: Darwin in fact spent the rest of his life organizing and studying his data collection and writing his book. He never felt the need of going back to the Galapagos. One data set—one insight: Plenty to keep a Darwin busy for a lifetime.

The euphoria over the Haicheng prediction was short-lived. Within a year, the giant Tangshan earthquake destroyed all illusions of the earthquake predictors. The Parkfield caper could have lasted longer if the scientists had taken a broader view, and especially a broader prediction window. Today Parkfield has become an albatross around Menlo Park's neck. There is not enough money for needed research elsewhere. In both cases the approach was simplistic, perhaps simple-minded. More to the point, it was motivated by political pressure.

Wine is allowed to decant and mellow in the dark. Most scientists are granted one insight per lifetime; but all too often, instead of maturing this insight to perfection, we let ourselves be rushed into conclusions and from there into publicity.

We need to develop what Campbell and Mayer–Kress at Los Alamos call *nonlinear intuition*. Here the word *intuition* is not used in a derogatory sense, like *hunch* or *guess*, but rather in the sense of overcoming the limitations of thinking along more traditional lines. Mathematical models such as the Haskell–Thompson scheme in wave propagation have their dangers. A mathematical model can cut both ways. It may predict what is likely to occur, but it can also limit our perception of what can or cannot occur.

There are essential limits to predictability, not only of earthquakes but of other more familiar phenomena (weather, the economy). New regularities remain to be discovered that have not been anticipated in linear models (critical seismic slip, liquefaction of soils). In short, nonlinear dynamics must become an essential component of our thinking about earthquakes.

The other component of thinking I would like to stress is imaging. There is one major difference between earthquake prediction and weather prediction, and that is satellite imaging. If we could visualize the strains along plate boundaries, in the same way that we actually watch the weather change nightly on the TV screen, we might begin formulating predictions. With a little practice, an assiduous viewer of weather programs can begin filling in the forecasts of the experts.

Perhaps we are unlikely to enjoy soon the imaging of an advancing strain front in the earth's crust on television. In fact we cannot yet measure stresses in the earth's interior directly. There are no satellites or weather balloons inside the earth. No Columbus ever traveled to the earth's core. No Marco Polo brought back samples of what is inside. All the more reason for inventing better methods of imaging what goes on in the earth's interior. The new method of space radar interferometry points the way.

Finally, we need to understand that earthquakes are transients embedded in a larger and slower transient. The word *slowquake* has been coined to describe a strain transient that generates no seismic waves: it develops over times on the order of minutes. In the case of large earthquakes, the slowquake may begin weeks or months before the earthquake. It may take one or more years to unfold. Effective short-term earthquake prediction depends on our ability to detect these transients or their effects on geophysical fields. We need more and better long-baseline geodesy (satellite geodesy, very-long-baseline interferometry, tilt measurements in lakes and reservoirs), more and better groundwater measurements, more and better strain and rotation measurements. We need to understand the thermodynamics of strain-coupled flows of water in a stationary system.

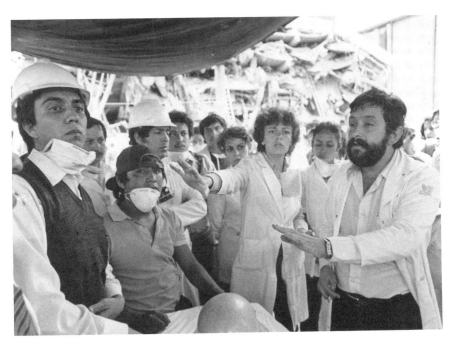

Fig. 11.3 *These medical students spontaneously set up a surgical emergency station using equipment and supplies borrowed from medical school. They worked around the clock with volunteer rescuers and stretcher-bearers for the first three days. Photo courtesy of Aarón Sánchez (Unomasuno).*

This brief enumeration may give but a small idea of the large number of scientific challenges that await those willing to engage in earthquake prediction. I stop here because I don't wish to give the idea that there is a rigid agenda to be followed. *Science should be fun*, as the physicist-seismologist Merle Tuve used to say. Fun but not a joke. "Science requires a higher supervision and surveillance: a hygiene of living" (Nietzsche). The misuse of earthquake prediction research as a convenient source of funding or personal promotion brings its own nemesis.

Disasters cut deeply into our experience of human life on this planet, but they cut both ways. A million volunteers poured onto the streets of Mexico City after the 1985 earthquake (Figs. 11.3, 11.4). It was their finest hour. Disasters are critical phenomena, caused by instabilities in the nature-society system. They bring out the best in humans as well as the worst. "Only what is thought, said or done at a certain rare coincidence is good," wrote Thoreau.

Fig. 11.4 *Everybody lent a hand in the rescue operations. Photo courtesy of Aarón Sánchez (Unomasuno).*

Something similar might be said about understanding. Rare moments of insight bring out the best in us. When the double helix of theory and practice clicks on itself, it is an eminently satisfying experience to a scientist. "As in music," Darwin wrote, "the person who understands every note will, if he also possesses a proper taste, more thoroughly enjoy the whole."

Appendix 1

Earthquake Disasters by Country

Compiled from *World Map of Natural Hazards,* Munich Reinsurance Company, 1988; updated list of natural disasters (same source, May 1993), and other sources.

Country	Date	Locality	*M*	Casualties	Damage (m$)
Afghanistan	1505 Jul 5–6	Paghman			
	1842 Feb 19	Alignar		1,000	
	1956 June 10	Kabul	7.6	2,000	
Albania	1851 Oct 12	Narta		2,000	
Algeria	1716 Feb 3	Médéa		20,000	
	1790 Sep 9	Oran		766	
	1825 Mar 2	Blida		7,000	
	1954 Sep 9	El Asnam	5.0	1,243	6
	1980 Oct 10	El Asnam	7.5	2,590	3,000
	1989 Apr 15	El Asnam	5.9	30	
Argentina	1861 Mar 21	Mendoza		18,000	
	1944 Jan 15	San Juan		5,600	100
	1977 Nov 23	San Juan	7.4	65	80
Armenia	1988 Dec 7	Spitak	7.0	25,000	14,000
Australia	1989 Dec 27	Newcastle	5.5	12	3,200
Austria	1348 Jan 25	Villach		5,000	
Azerbai jan	1667 Nov	Shemakha		80,000	
Bangladesh	1737 Oct 11	Bengal		300,000	

Country	Date	Locality	M	Casualties	Damage (m$)
Bulgaria	1928 Apr 14	Plovdiv		107	
Canada	1663 Feb 5	Saguenay			
	1732	Montreal	6		
	1872 Dec 14	Vancouver			
	1925 Feb	Charlevoix	7		
Chile	1647 May 13	Santiago		1,000	
	1730 Jul 8	Valparaiso			
	1835 Feb 20	Concepción			
	1868 Aug 13	Arica, Peru		3,000	
	1906 Aug 17	Valparaiso	8.6	3,800	260
	1928 Dec 1	Talca	8.3	220	
	1939 Jan 25	Chillán	8.3	28,000	38
	1960 May 21–22	S. Chile	9.1	3,000	880
	1965 Mar 28	La Ligua	7.3	400	80
	1971 Jul 9	La Ligua	7.5	85	137
	1985 Mar 3	Valparaiso	7.9	200	1,200
China	1038 Jan 9	Shaanxi		23,000	
	1057	Qili		25,000	
	1290 Sep 27	Qili		100,000	
	1556 Jan 23	Guanzhong; Huaxian		820,000	
	1662	Anhwei		300,000	
	1730 Sep 29	Qili		100,000	
	1850 Sep 22	Sichuan		300,000	
	1907 Oct 21	Tianshaan		12,000	
	1920 Dec 16	Gansu		77,000	
	1966 Mar 22	Xingtai	7.2	8,000	
	1969 Jul 18	Bohai	7.4		
	1970 Jan 5	Yunnan	7.7		
	1970 Dec 3	Ningxia Hui	5.5	100	
	1974 May 1	Yunnan	7.1	20,000	
	1975 Feb 4	Haicheng	7.3	1,328	
	1976 Jul 27	Tangshan	7.8	242,000	5,600
	1976 Aug 16	Songpan	7.2		
China (Taiwan)	1862 Jun 6	Tainan		1,000	
	1906 Mar 17	Kagi	7.1	1,266	
	1935 Apr 20	Taihoku	7.0	3,410	
	1951 Oct 21	E. Taiwan	7.3	100	
	1966 Mar 12	E. Taiwan	7.5		
	1972 Jan 25	E. Taiwan	8		
	1972 Apr 24	Dagangkou	7.3		
Colombia	1785 Jul 12	Bogotá		10,000	
	1906 Jan 31	Tumaco	8.9	400	
	1979 Dec 12	Tumaco	7.7	640	8
	1983 Mar 31	Popayán	6.0	250	380
	1992 Oct 17–18	Chocó	7.1		

Country	Date	Locality	M	Casualties	Damage (m$)
Costa Rica	1822 May 7	Cartago			
	1841 Sep 2	Cartago		6,000	
	1910 Apr 13	Cartago		1,750	
	1990 Mar 25	Nicoya	7.0		
	1991 Apr 22	Limón	7.5	76	
Cuba	1992 May 25	Off Oriente	6.3		
Ecuador	1645 Feb 12	Quito			
	1797 Feb 4	Ambato		6,300	
	1868 Aug 16	Ibarra		40,000	300
	1949 Aug 5	Pelileo	6.8	5,050	20
	1976 Apr 9	Esmeraldas			20
	1987 Mar 5	Napo	7.3	1,000	700
Egypt	1303 Aug 8	Cairo		10,000	
	1588 Apr 9	Cairo			
	1992 Oct 12	Cairo	5.9	561	300
El Salvador	1854 Apr 14	San Salvador		1,000	
	1859 Dec 8	Offshore			
	1873 Mar 4	San Vicente		800	
	1917 May 7	San Salvador			
	1951 May 6	Jacuapa	6.2	1,100	23
	1965 May 3	San Salvador		127	
	1986 Oct 10	San Salvador	6.2	1,200	1,500
Ethiopia	1969 Mar 29	Serdo		40	
France	1909 Jun 11	Haute-Provence		40	
Germany	1612 Nov 8	Bielefeld			
	1978 Sep 3	Swabian Alb			150
Ghana	1636	Accra			
	1862 Jul 10	Accra			
	1939 Jun 22	Accra		17	
Great Britain	1990 Apr 2	England–Wales	5.0		
Greece	1201	Aegean Sea		40,000	
	1384 Aug	Lesbos		500	
	1491 Oct	Cos		5,000	
	1750 Jun 7	Ionian Sea		2,000	
	1810 Feb 16	Crete		2,000	
	1881 Apr 3	Chios		7,886	
	1926 Jun 26	Rhodes	8.3		
	1953 Aug 12	Kephalonia	7.1	455	100
	1978 Jun 20	Salonika		50	160
	1981 Feb 24	Corinth		25	900
Guatemala	1773 Jul 29	Antigua		100	
	1902 Apr 18	Quetzaltenango		2,000	
	1918 Jan 3	Guatemala City		2,650	
	1976 Feb 4	Motagua	7.5	22,778	1,100
Guinea	1983 Dec 22	NW Guinea		342	
Haiti	1842 May 7	Cap Haitien		500	

Country	Date	Locality	M	Casualties	Damage (m$)
India	1819 Jun 16	Kutch		1,543	
	1827 Sep	Punjab		1,000	
	1828 Jun 6	Kashmir		1,000	
	1885 May 30	Kashmir		2,000	
	1897 Jun 12	Assam	8.7	1,425	
	1905 Apr 4	Kangra	8.6	18,815	
	1934 Jan 15	Bihar	8.4	10,653	
	1950 Aug 15	Assam	8.7	1,526	
	1967 Dec 11	Koyna	6.3	180	
	1991 Oct 20			2,000	100
	1993 Sep 29	Latur	6.4	30,000	
Indonesia	1674 Feb 12	Amboina		2,347	
	1815 Nov 27	Bali		10,253	
	1883 Aug 27	Krakatau Volcano		3,600	
	1899 Sep 30	Ceram	7.8	3,864	
	1917 Jan 21	Bali		15,000	
	1976 Sep 16	W. Irian		6,000	
	1992 Dec 12	Flores		2,080	100
Iran	1042	Tabriz		40,000	
	1641 Feb 5	Tabriz		30,000	
	1721 Apr 26	Tabriz		10,000	
	1727 Nov 18	Tabriz		77,000	
	1755 Jun 7	Kashan		40,000	
	1778 Dec 15	Kashan		30,000	
	1780 Jan	Tabriz		100,000	
	1824 Jun 25	Shiraz		20,000	
	1853 Apr 21	Shiraz		12,000	
	1853 Jul 11	Isfahan		10,000	
	1909 Jan 23	Boroujerd	7.7	5,000	
	1941 Feb 16	Qain	6.2	600	
	1960 Apr 24	Lar	5.7	450	
	1962 Sep 1	Boyin-Zara	7.2	12,225	
	1968 Aug 31	Dasht-e-Bayaz	7.2	12,100	
	1972 Apr 10	Ghir	7.0	5,400	5
	1978 Sep 16	Tabas		20,000	11
	1990 Jun 20	North Iran		36,000	7,000
Iraq	1007	Ktesiphan		10,000	
	1666	Mosul			
Israel	1034 Jan 4	Tiberias		70,000	
	1068 Mar 18	Ramla		25,000	
	1202 May 22	N. Jordan Rift		30,000	
	1759 Oct 30	N. Jordan Rift		20,000	
	1837 Jan 1	Safed		2,000	
	1927 Jul 11	Jerusalem	6.2	242	
Italy	1117 Jan 3	Monte Cassino			
	1169 Feb 4	Catania		14,000	
	1222 Dec 25	Brescia			
	1456 Dec 5	Napoli; Isernia		30,000	
	1627 Jul 30	Foggia		5,000	

Country	Date	Locality	M	Casualties	Damage (m$)
Italy	1688 Jun 5	Benevento		10,000	
	1693 Jan 11	Catania		60,000	
	1694 Sep 8	Irpinia		6,500	
	1703 Jan 14	Aquila		10,000	
	1783 Feb 4	Calabria		29,000	
	1805 Jul 27	Campobasso		5,573	
	1851 Aug 14	Melfi		700	
	1857 Dec 16	Basilicata		12,300	
	1883 Jul 28	Ischia		2,000	
	1887 Feb 23	San Remo		640	
	1908 Dec 28	Messina	7.5	83,000	116
	1915 Jan 13	Avezzano	7.5	29,978	60
	1930 Jul 23	Irpinia	6.5	1,883	
	1968 Jan 15	Belice	5.4	281	320
	1976 May 6	Friuli		978	3,600
	1980 Nov 23	Irpinia		3,114	10,000
Jamaica	1692 Jun 7	Port Royal		2,000	
	1907 Jan 14	Kingston		1,003	30
Japan	684 Nov 29	Nankaido			
	869 Jul 13	Oshu			
	887 Aug 26	Mino			
	1293 May 27	Kamakura		22,000	
	1498 Sep 20	Tokaido		41,000	
	1605 Jan 31	Nankaido		5,000	
	1611 Sep 27	Miyagi		3,700	
	1611 Dec 2	Hokkaido		4,000	
	1703 Dec 31	Tokyo/Odawara		5,233	
	1707 Oct 28	Nankaido (Hoei)		4,900	
	1711 Dec 20	Takamatsu		1,000	
	1751 May 20	Joetsu		2,100	
	1771 Apr 24	Ryukyu		11,700	
	1792 May 21	Shimabara		15,000	
	1847 May 8	Matsumoto		8,600	
	1854 Dec 23–24	Tokai/Nankaido		31,000	
	1855 Nov 11	Tokyo		10,000	
	1891 Oct 28	Mino-Owari		7,273	
	1896 Oct 28	Sanriku		27,122	
	1923 Sep 1	Tokyo	8.0	130,000	2,800
	1927 Mar 7	Tango	7.3	2,925	40
	1933 Mar 3	Sanriku	8.9	3,064	
	1943 Sep 10	Tottori	7.2	1,190	
	1944 Dec 7	Tonankai	7.9	998	
	1945 Jan 12	Aftershock	7.1	1,901	
	1946 Dec 20	Nankaido	8.0	1,330	
	1948 Jun 28	Fukui	7.3	3,895	1,000
	1952 Mar 4	Hokkaido	8.6	600	
	1964 May 16	Niigata	7.5	26	205
	1968 May 16	Tokachi-Oki	7.8	48	160

Country	Date	Locality	M	Casualties	Damage (m$)
Japan	1973 Jun 17	Hokkaido	7.4		
	1978 Jun 12	Sendai		28	865
	1983 May 26	Nihonkai-Chubu	7.7	104	560
	1993 Jan 15	Kushiro	7.8	2	125
Jordan	1202 May 22	Jordan Rift		30,000	
	1546 Jan 14	Nablus		1,000	
Lebanon	1201 Jun 2	Tripoli		10,000	
	1759 Oct 30	Bekaa		20,000	
	1956 Mar 16	Bekaa		136	
Libya	1183	Tripoli		20,000	
	1963 Feb 21	Al-Marj		290	
Marianas	1990 Apr 5	Marianas	6.9		
	1993 Aug 8	Guam	8.1	0	250
Martinique	1839 Jan 11	Fort-de-France		187	
Mexico	1611 Aug 25	Mexico City			
	1697 Feb 25	Acapulco			
	1701 Dec 21	Oaxaca			
	1711 Aug 16	Colima, Mexico City			
	1754 Sep 1	Acapulco; Mexico City			
	1784 Mar 28	Acapulco; Mexico City			
	1806 Mar 25	Jalisco			
	1845 Apr 7	Acapulco; Mexico City			
	1858 Jun 19	Michoacán; Mexico City			
	1875 Feb 11	Zapopan			
	1887 May 3	Bavispe, Son.		42	
	1899 Jan 29	Oaxaca	8.9		
	1907 Apr 15	Acapulco	8.3		
	1911 Jun 7	Michoacán	8	45	
	1928 Jun 17	Oaxaca	7.9		
	1931 Jan 15	Oaxaca	7.9		
	1932 Jun 18	Jalisco	7.9		
	1957 Jul 28	Acapulco	7.5	160	25
	1973 Aug 28	Veracruz	7.1	539	
	1985 Sep 19	Michoacán	8.1	10,000+	4,000
Myanmar	1930 May 5	Pegu		550	
Morocco	1757 Apr 15	Constantine		3,000	
	1960 Feb 29	Agadir		13,100	120
Netherlands	1992 Apr 13	Roermond	6.0	1	150
New Guinea	1976		7.1	6,000	
New Zealand	1855 Jan 23	Wellington			
	1931 Feb 3	Hawke's Bay		256	25
	1987 Mar 2	Bay of Plenty		0	350

Country	Date	Locality	M	Casualties	Damage (m$)
Nicaragua	1931 Mar 31	Managua	5.5	2,450	15
	1972 Dec 23	Managua	6	5,000	800
	1992 Sep 2	Offshore	7.0	170	
Pakistan	1935 May 31	Quetta		35,000	
	1945 Nov 27	Makran		4,000	
	1974 Dec 28	North		994	
Peru	1687 Oct 20	Lima		5,000	
	1746 Oct 28	Lima		18,000	
	1868 Aug 13	Arica		2,000	
	1946 Nov 10	Quiches		1,400	
	1970 May 31	Santa Valley	7.8	66,800	500
Philippines	1645 Dec 5	Manila		600	
	1863 Jun 3	Manila		300	
	1976 Aug 17	Mindanao		3,564	120
	1990 Jul 16	Dagupan	7.0	1,660	2,000
Portugal	1531 Jan 26	Lisbon		30,000	
	1755, Nov 1	Lisbon; N. Africa		30,000	
Puerto Rico	1918		7.5	116	
Romania	1940 Nov 10	Vrancea			980
	1977 Mar 4	Vrancea	7.0	1,387	800
	1986 Aug 30	Vrancea	7.0		
South Africa	1969 Sep 29	Ceres		9	
Spain	1428 Feb 2	Catalonia		1,060	
	1430 Apr 25	Granada			
	1749 Mar 25	Valencia		5,000	
	1829 Mar 21	Murcia		3,000	
	1884 Dec 25	Andalucia		745	
St. Lucia	1788 Oct 12			900	
Sudan	1990 May 20	Omdurman	7.4		
Switzerland	1356 Oct 18	Basel		300	
Syria	1042 Aug 21	Palmyra		50,000	
	1139 Oct 12	Aleppo		10,000	
	1156 Oct 5	Hama		20,000	
	1201 Jun 2	Aleppo			
	1796 Apr 26	Latakiya		1,500	
	1822 Aug 13	Aleppo		8,000	
	1872 Apr 3	Aleppo		1,800	
Tunisia	1757	West		3,000	
Turkey	1268	Kilikia		60,000	
	1458	Erzincan		32,000	
	1509 Sep 14	Izmit		13,000	
	1653 Feb 23	Izmir		8,000	
	1688 Jul 10	Izmir		17,500	
	1822 Aug 13	Antakya		20,000	
	1883 Oct 15	Izmir		15,000	
	1903 Apr 29	Malazgirt		6,000	
	1939 Dec 26	Erzincan	7.9	32,740	20

Country	Date	Locality	M	Casualties	Damage (m$)
Turkey	1943 Nov 27	Ladik		4,013	
	1944 Feb 1	Gerede		3,959	
	1966 Aug 19	Varto		2,500	35
	1970 Mar 28	Gediz	7.3	1,086	95
	1975 Sep 6	Lice	6.7	2,370	17
	1976 Nov 24	Muradiye	7.3	3,626	25
	1983 Oct 30	E. Anatolia	6.9	1,346	
	1992 Mar 13	Erzincan	6.9	677	
Turkmenia	1948 Oct 5	Ashkhabad	7.3	19,800	
United States	1811–1812	New Madrid, MO			
	1857 Jan 9	Ft. Tejon, CA			
	1886 Aug 31	Charleston, SC		60	5
	1906 Apr 18	San Francisco	7.8	2,000	524
	1933 Mar 11	Long Beach, CA		116	38
	1946 Apr 1	Alaska; Hawaii		173	25
	1952 Jul 21	Kern County, CA	7.4	14	50
	1957 Mar 9	Rat Islands	8.1		
	1964 Mar 28	Anchorage, AK	8.4	131	538
	1971 Feb 9	San Fernando, CA		65	535
	1987 Oct 1	Los Angeles		8	358
	1989 Oct 17	Loma Prieta, CA	7.1	68	6,000
	1992 Apr 25	Petrolia, CA	7.1		
	1992 Jun 28	Landers, CA	7.6	1	
	1994 Jan 17	Northridge, CA	6.6	55	
Uzbekistan	1902 Dec 13	Andijan		4,562	
	1907 Oct 21	Samarkand	8.1	12,000	
	1966 Apr 26	Tashkent	5.5		
Yemen	1982 Dec 13	Yemen		3,000	90
Yugoslavia	1963 Jul 26	Skopje	6.0	1,070	600
	1979 Apr 15			131	2,700

Appendix 2

Seismic Moments of Great Shallow Earthquakes 1900–1990 with Magnitude > 7

From Pacheco and Sykes (1992). Reprinted with permission of the Seismological Society of America.

Date (y-m-d)	Time	Lat.	Long.	Depth	M_s	M_{corr}	$\times 10^{20}$ Nm
19000120	0633	20.00	−105.00	0.0	7.4	7.3	1.23
19000621	2052	10.00	−85.50	0.0	7.2	7.1	0.62
19000729	0659	−10.00	165.00	0.0	7.6	7.5	2.45
19000917	2145	−5.00	148.00	0.0	7.1	7.0	0.44
19001009	1228	57.09	−153.48	9.0	7.7	7.6	3.47
19001029	0911	11.00	−66.00	0.0	7.7	7.6	3.47
19001225	0504	43.00	146.00	0.0	7.1	7.0	0.44
19010107	0029	−2.00	−82.00	0.0	7.2	7.1	0.62
19010118	0439	60.00	−135.00	0.0	7.1	7.0	0.44
19010405	2330	45.00	148.00	0.0	7.4	7.3	1.23
19010525	0032	−10.00	160.00	0.0	7.2	7.1	0.62
19010624	0702	27.00	130.00	0.0	7.3	7.2	0.87
19010809	0923	40.00	144.00	0.0	7.3	7.2	0.87
19010809	1301	−22.00	170.00	0.0	7.9	7.8	6.92
19010809	1833	40.00	144.00	0.0	7.5	7.4	1.74
19011008	0214	13.00	−87.00	0.0	7.1	7.0	0.44
19011209	0217	26.00	−110.00	0.0	7.1	7.0	0.44
19011231	0902	51.45	−171.02	0.0	7.1	7.0	0.44
19020124	2327	−8.00	150.00	0.0	7.2	7.1	0.62
19020419	0223	14.00	−91.00	25.00	7.5	7.4	1.74
19020822	0300	40.00	77.00	0.0	7.7	7.6	3.47
19020922	0146	18.00	146.00	0.0	7.5	7.4	1.74
19020923	2018	16.00	−93.00	25.00	7.8	7.7	4.90

Date (y-m-d)	Time	Lat.	Long.	Depth	M_s	M_{corr}	$\times 10^{20}$ Nm
19021212	2310	29.00	− 114.00	0.0	7.1	7.0	0.44
19030114	0147	15.00	− 93.00	0.0	7.7	7.6	1.37
19030201	0934	48.00	98.00	0.0	7.1	7.0	0.44
19030227	0043	− 8.00	106.00	0.0	7.4	7.3	1.23
19030429	0359	− 20.00	− 175.00	0.0	7.1	7.0	0.44
19031228	0256	7.00	127.00	0.0	7.1	7.0	0.44
19040120	1452	7.00	− 79.00	0.0	7.2	7.1	0.62
19040404	1026	41.75	23.25	0.0	7.1	7.0	0.44
19040625	1445	52.00	159.00	0.0	7.2	7.1	1.80
19040625	2100	52.00	159.00	0.0	7.4	7.3	3.10
19040627	0900	52.00	159.00	0.0	7.2	7.1	0.62
19040824	2100	30.00	130.00	0.0	7.1	7.0	0.44
19040827	2156	64.66	− 148.08	25.00	7.3	7.2	0.87
19041220	0544	8.30	− 83.00	25.00	7.2	7.1	0.62
19050214	0846	50.73	− 178.55	25.00	7.3	7.2	0.87
19050318	2356	− 10.00	168.00	0.0	7.2	7.1	0.62
19050404	0050	33.00	76.00	0.0	7.5	7.4	5.80
19050630	1707	− 20.00	− 175.00	0.0	7.1	7.0	0.44
19050706	1621	39.50	142.50	0.0	7.1	7.0	0.44
19050709	0940	49.00	99.00	35.00	7.6	7.5	55.00
19050723	0246	49.00	97.00	35.00	7.7	7.6	50.00
19050915	0602	52.06	171.45	0.0	7.4	7.3	1.23
19051217	0527	17.00	− 113.00	0.0	7.1	7.0	0.44
19060131	1536	1.00	− 81.30	0.0	8.2	8.1	80.00
19060219	0159	− 10.00	160.00	0.0	7.1	7.0	0.44
19060410	2118	20.00	− 110.00	0.0	7.2	7.1	0.62
19060418	1312	38.00	− 123.00	12.50	7.8	7.7	9.30
19060601	0430	− 1.30	143.80	0.0	7.1	7.0	0.44
19060817	0010	51.05	179.69	0.0	7.8	7.7	4.90
19060817	0040	− 33.00	− 72.00	0.0	8.1	8.0	66.00
19060830	0238	− 21.00	− 70.00	0.0	7.1	7.0	0.44
19060914	1604	− 7.00	149.00	0.0	7.5	7.4	12.70
19061002	0150	− 4.00	149.00	0.0	7.2	7.1	0.62
19061119	0718	− 22.00	109.00	0.0	7.2	7.1	0.62
19061219	0114	− 19.00	− 172.00	0.0	7.3	7.2	0.87
19061222	1821	43.30	85.00	0.0	7.2	7.1	0.62
19061223	1722	56.85	− 153.90	0.0	7.3	7.2	0.87
19070102	1157	− 21.06	− 175.06	0.0	7.4	7.3	1.23
19070104	0519	2.00	94.30	0.0	7.5	7.4	1.74
19070415	0608	16.70	− 99.20	25.00	7.7	7.6	8.34
19070418	2059	14.00	123.00	0.0	7.1	7.0	0.44
19070902	1601	52.59	169.73	0.0	7.4	7.3	1.23
19071016	1457	28.00	− 112.50	0.0	7.2	7.1	0.62
19071021	0423	38.00	69.00	0.0	7.2	7.1	0.62
19071230	0526	12.10	− 86.30	0.0	7.2	7.1	0.62
19080817	1032	− 60.00	− 40.00	0.0	7.2	7.1	0.62
19090427	1244	0.00	147.00	0.0	7.1	7.0	0.44
19090603	1840	− 2.00	101.00	50.00	7.3	7.2	0.87
19090608	0546	− 26.50	− 70.50	0.0	7.3	7.2	0.87
19090707	2139	36.50	70.50	0.0	7.2	7.1	0.62
19090730	1051	16.80	− 99.90	50.00	7.3	7.2	2.48
19100101	1102	16.50	− 84.00	60.00	7.1	7.0	0.44
19100331	1813	− 71.00	− 6.00	0.0	7.1	7.0	0.44

Date (y-m-d)	Time	Lat.	Long.	Depth	M_s	M_{corr}	$\times 10^{20}$ Nm
19100629	1045	−32.00	−176.00	0.0	7.3	7.2	0.87
19100906	1959	−25.00	−70.00	0.0	7.1	7.0	0.44
19101115	1421	−58.00	−22.00	0.0	7.2	7.1	0.62
19101126	0441	−14.00	167.00	50.00	7.3	7.2	0.87
19101210	0926	−11.00	162.50	50.00	7.3	7.2	0.87
19101213	1137	−8.00	31.00	0.0	7.6	7.5	2.45
19101216	1445	4.50	126.50	0.0	7.6	7.5	2.45
19110103	2325	43.50	77.50	0.0	7.8	7.7	4.90
19110218	1841	40.00	73.00	0.0	7.3	7.2	0.87
19110607	1102	17.50	−102.50	50.00	7.7	7.6	2.83
19110712	0407	9.00	126.00	50.00	7.5	7.4	1.74
19110816	2241	7.00	137.00	0.0	7.7	7.6	3.47
19110915	1310	−20.00	−72.00	40.00	7.1	7.0	0.44
19110917	0326	51.00	180.00	0.0	7.1	7.0	0.44
19111216	1914	16.90	−100.70	50.00	7.6	7.5	2.45
19120523	0224	21.00	97.00	0.0	7.7	7.6	3.47
19120707	0757	63.07	−146.14	0.0	7.2	7.1	0.62
19120809	0129	40.50	27.00	0.0	7.6	7.5	2.45
19120817	1911	4.00	127.00	0.0	7.3	7.2	0.87
19120929	2051	7.00	138.00	50.00	7.5	7.4	1.74
19121209	0832	15.50	−93.00	0.0	7.1	7.0	0.44
19130111	1316	1.50	122.00	0.0	7.2	7.1	0.62
19130314	0845	4.50	126.50	40.00	7.9	7.8	6.92
19130425	1756	9.50	127.00	0.0	7.2	7.1	0.62
19130530	1146	−5.00	154.50	0.0	7.7	7.6	3.47
19130626	0457	−20.00	−174.00	0.0	7.7	7.6	3.47
19130806	2214	−17.00	−74.00	40.00	7.8	7.7	4.90
19131221	1537	24.50	102.00	0.0	7.2	7.1	0.62
19140130	0336	−35.00	−73.00	0.0	7.5	7.4	1.74
19140411	1630	−12.00	163.00	50.00	7.2	7.1	0.62
19140526	1422	−2.00	137.00	0.0	8.0	7.9	9.77
19140625	1907	−4.50	102.50	0.0	7.6	7.5	2.45
19140804	1241	43.50	91.50	0.0	7.3	7.2	0.87
19141003	2207	38.00	30.00	0.0	7.1	7.0	0.44
19141023	0618	6.00	132.50	0.0	7.6	7.5	2.45
19150501	0500	47.00	155.00	0.0	8.0	7.8	6.92
19150731	0131	54.00	162.00	0.0	7.6	7.4	1.74
19151003	0652	40.50	−117.50	0.0	7.7	7.5	2.45
19151101	0724	39.00	142.50	0.0	7.6	7.4	1.74
19160101	1320	−4.00	154.00	0.0	7.8	7.6	3.47
19160113	0618	−3.00	136.00	0.0	7.5	7.3	1.23
19160113	0820	−3.00	135.50	0.0	7.7	7.5	2.45
19160124	0655	41.00	37.00	0.0	7.3	7.1	0.62
19160227	2020	10.70	−85.98	0.0	7.5	7.3	1.23
19160407	0926	−30.00	55.00	0.0	7.3	7.1	0.62
19160424	0802	10.00	−82.00	0.0	7.4	7.2	0.87
19160803	0130	−4.00	144.50	0.0	7.2	7.0	0.44
19160828	0639	30.00	81.00	0.0	7.3	7.1	0.62
19161031	1530	45.40	154.00	0.0	7.7	7.5	2.45
19170130	0245	56.50	163.00	0.0	7.8	7.6	3.47
19170220	1929	19.50	−78.50	0.0	7.3	7.1	0.62

Date (y-m-d)	Time	Lat.	Long.	Depth	M_s	M_{corr}	$\times 10^{20}$ Nm
19170501	1826	− 29.00	− 177.00	50.00	7.9	7.7	12.00
19170531	0847	54.79	− 159.12	0.0	7.9	7.7	2.00
19170626	0549	− 15.50	− 173.00	0.0	8.4	8.2	70.00
19170704	0038	25.00	123.00	0.0	7.3	7.1	0.62
19170729	2152	− 3.50	141.00	0.0	7.7	7.5	2.45
19170730	2454	29.00	104.00	0.0	7.5	7.3	1.23
19171116	0319	− 29.00	− 177.50	0.0	7.5	7.3	1.23
19180213	0607	24.00	117.00	0.0	7.4	7.2	0.87
19180520	1436	7.50	− 36.00	0.0	7.2	7.0	0.44
19180703	0652	− 3.50	142.50	0.0	7.4	7.2	0.87
19180708	1022	24.50	91.00	0.0	7.6	7.4	1.74
19180815	1218	5.70	123.50	0.0	8.0	7.8	25.00
19180907	1716	45.50	151.50	0.0	8.2	8.0	22.00
19181011	1414	18.50	− 67.50	0.0	7.5	7.3	1.23
19181027	1706	− 2.00	148.00	50.00	7.3	7.1	0.62
19181108	0438	44.50	151.50	0.0	7.7	7.5	2.45
19181204	1147	− 26.00	− 71.00	40.00	7.6	7.4	1.74
19190101	0133	8.00	126.00	0.0	7.2	7.0	0.44
19190302	0326	− 41.00	− 73.50	40.00	7.3	7.1	0.62
19190302	1145	− 41.00	− 73.50	40.00	7.2	7.0	0.44
19190430	0717	− 19.00	− 172.50	0.0	8.2	8.0	27.10
19190503	0052	40.50	145.00	0.0	7.5	7.3	1.23
19190506	1941	− 5.00	154.00	0.0	7.9	7.7	4.90
19200202	1122	− 4.00	152.50	0.0	7.7	7.5	2.45
19200605	0421	23.50	122.00	0.0	8.0	7.8	6.92
19200920	1439	− 20.00	168.00	0.0	7.9	7.7	4.90
19201210	0425	− 39.00	− 73.00	0.0	7.3	7.1	0.62
19201216	1205	36.60	105.40	0.0	8.6	8.4	30.00
19210227	1823	− 18.50	− 173.00	0.0	7.2	7.0	0.44
19210328	0749	12.50	− 87.50	0.0	7.4	7.2	0.87
19210911	0401	− 11.00	111.00	0.0	7.5	7.3	1.23
19211111	1836	8.00	127.00	0.0	7.5	7.3	1.23
19220106	1411	− 16.50	− 73.00	0.0	7.2	7.0	0.44
19220131	1317	41.00	− 125.00	0.0	7.3	7.1	0.62
19220901	1916	24.50	122.00	0.0	7.6	7.4	1.74
19220914	1931	24.50	121.50	0.0	7.2	7.0	0.44
19221011	1449	− 16.00	− 72.50	50.00	7.3	7.1	0.62
19221111	0432	− 28.50	− 70.00	0.0	8.3	8.1	140.00
19230122	0904	40.50	− 124.50	0.0	7.2	7.0	0.44
19230202	0507	53.50	162.00	0.0	7.2	7.0	0.44
19230203	1601	54.00	161.00	0.0	8.3	8.1	70.00
19230224	0734	56.00	162.50	0.0	7.3	7.1	0.62
19230302	1648	6.50	124.00	0.0	7.2	7.0	0.44
19230324	1240	31.30	100.80	0.0	7.3	7.1	0.62
19230413	1531	56.50	162.50	0.0	7.2	7.0	0.44
19230601	1724	35.75	141.75	0.0	7.2	7.0	0.44
19230622	0644	22.75	98.75	0.0	7.3	7.1	0.62
19230901	0258	35.40	139.20	16.00	8.2	8.0	7.60
19230902	0246	35.13	140.50	30.00	7.7	7.5	2.45
19231007	0329	− 1.75	128.75	0.0	7.4	7.2	0.87
19231105	2127	29.25	130.00	0.0	7.2	7.0	0.44

Date (y-m-d)	Time	Lat.	Long.	Depth	M_s	M_{corr}	$\times 10^{20}$ Nm
19240414	1620	6.50	126.50	0.0	8.3	8.1	19.50
19240626	0137	−55.00	158.40	0.0	7.7	7.5	30.20
19240703	0440	36.00	84.00	0.0	7.2	7.0	0.44
19240711	1944	36.50	84.00	0.0	7.2	7.0	0.44
19240830	0304	8.50	126.50	0.0	7.3	7.1	0.62
19250118	1205	47.50	153.50	0.0	7.3	7.1	0.62
19250322	0841	−18.50	168.50	50.00	7.2	7.0	0.44
19251110	1350	−1.00	129.50	0.0	7.4	7.2	0.87
19251113	1214	13.00	125.00	0.0	7.3	7.1	0.62
19260125	0036	−9.00	158.00	0.0	7.4	7.2	0.87
19260208	1517	13.00	−89.00	0.0	7.2	7.0	0.44
19260327	1048	−9.00	157.00	0.0	7.2	7.0	0.44
19260412	0832	−10.00	161.00	0.0	7.4	7.2	0.87
19261003	1938	−49.00	160.20	50.00	7.5	7.3	1.23
19261026	0344	−3.25	138.50	0.0	7.6	7.4	1.74
19270307	0927	35.60	135.10	10.00	7.6	7.4	0.46
19270522	2232	30.05	102.37	0.0	7.9	7.7	4.30
19270810	1136	−1.00	131.00	0.0	7.2	7.0	0.44
19271121	2312	−44.50	−73.00	0.0	7.2	7.0	0.44
19271228	1820	53.80	161.40	20.00	7.3	7.1	2.20
19280309	1805	−2.66	88.83	29.00	7.7	7.5	4.10
19280316	0501	−22.00	170.50	0.0	7.6	7.4	1.74
19280322	0417	15.67	−96.10	0.0	7.5	7.3	1.79
19280514	2214	−5.00	−78.00	0.0	7.3	7.1	0.62
19280617	0319	16.30	−96.70	25.00	7.8	7.6	10.20
19280804	1826	16.20	−96.76	0.0	7.4	7.2	0.87
19281009	0301	16.30	−97.30	0.0	7.6	7.4	1.74
19281201	0406	−35.00	−72.00	0.0	8.0	7.8	4.41
19281219	1137	7.00	124.00	0.0	7.5	7.3	1.23
19290307	0134	50.88	−169.71	50.00	7.5	7.3	6.70
19290501	1537	38.00	58.00	0.0	7.2	7.0	0.44
19290613	0924	8.50	127.00	0.0	7.2	7.0	0.44
19290616	2247	−41.75	172.25	0.0	7.6	7.4	1.74
19290627	1247	−54.00	−29.50	0.0	7.7	7.5	11.80
19290707	2123	52.00	−178.00	0.0	7.3	7.1	0.62
19291118	2031	44.00	−56.00	0.0	7.2	7.0	1.40
19291217	1058	53.67	171.46	0.0	7.8	7.6	3.47
19300505	1345	17.00	96.50	0.0	7.4	7.2	0.87
19300506	2234	38.00	44.50	0.0	7.2	7.0	0.44
19301125	1902	35.00	139.00	7.50	7.2	7.0	0.27
19301203	1851	18.00	96.50	0.0	7.5	7.3	1.23
19310115	0150	16.00	−96.75	40.00	7.8	7.6	5.00
19310127	2009	25.60	96.80	0.0	7.7	7.5	2.45
19310202	2246	−39.50	177.00	0.0	7.8	7.6	3.47
19310210	0634	−5.40	102.88	0.0	7.2	7.0	0.44
19310309	0348	40.50	142.50	0.0	7.8	7.6	3.47
19310807	0211	−4.00	142.00	0.0	7.2	7.0	0.44
19310810	2118	47.00	90.06	0.0	7.9	7.7	8.50
19310818	1421	47.00	90.00	0.0	7.3	7.1	0.62
19310827	1527	29.75	67.25	0.0	7.2	7.0	0.44
19310925	0559	−5.10	102.61	0.0	7.5	7.3	1.23

Date (y-m-d)	Time	Lat.	Long.	Depth	M_s	M_{corr}	$\times 10^{20}$ Nm
19311003	1913	− 10.50	161.75	0.0	7.9	7.7	6.30
19311003	2247	− 11.00	161.50	0.0	7.2	7.0	0.44
19311010	0019	− 10.00	161.00	0.0	7.8	7.6	3.47
19311102	1002	32.00	131.50	0.0	7.6	7.4	1.74
19320514	1311	0.50	126.00	0.0	8.0	7.8	13.73
19320603	1036	19.80	− 104.00	16.00	8.2	8.0	15.25
19320618	1012	18.95	− 104.42	16.00	7.8	7.6	7.30
19321221	0610	38.75	− 118.00	0.0	7.2	7.0	0.44
19321225	0204	39.25	96.50	0.0	7.7	7.5	2.45
19330223	0809	− 20.00	− 71.00	40.00	7.2	7.1	0.62
19330302	1730	39.25	144.50	30.00	8.5	8.3	43.00
19330618	2137	38.50	143.00	0.0	7.3	7.1	0.62
19330624	2154	− 5.50	104.75	0.0	7.5	7.3	1.23
19330825	0750	31.75	103.50	0.0	7.5	7.3	1.23
19330828	2219	− 59.50	− 29.00	0.0	7.4	7.2	0.87
19331120	2321	73.00	− 70.75	0.0	7.2	7.0	0.44
19340115	0843	26.50	86.50	20.00	8.3	8.1	11.00
19340214	0359	17.50	119.00	0.0	7.6	7.4	1.74
19340224	0623	22.50	144.00	0.0	7.3	7.1	0.62
19340228	1421	− 5.00	150.00	0.0	7.2	7.0	0.44
19340305	1146	− 41.70	172.00	0.0	7.5	7.3	1.23
19340415	2215	7.75	127.00	0.0	7.2	7.0	0.44
19340718	0136	8.14	− 82.38	0.0	7.6	7.4	2.79
19340721	0618	− 11.00	165.75	0.0	7.2	7.0	0.44
19350530	2132	29.50	66.75	20.00	7.6	7.4	17.50
19350904	0137	22.25	121.25	0.0	7.2	7.0	0.44
19350911	1404	43.00	146.50	60.00	7.4	7.2	0.87
19350920	0146	− 3.50	141.75	0.0	7.9	7.7	14.50
19351012	1645	40.25	143.25	0.0	7.2	7.0	0.44
19351018	0011	40.50	143.75	0.0	7.2	7.0	0.44
19351214	2205	14.75	− 92.50	0.0	7.4	7.2	0.87
19351215	0707	− 9.75	161.00	0.0	7.6	7.4	1.74
19351217	1917	22.50	125.50	0.0	7.2	7.0	0.44
19351228	0235	0.00	98.25	0.0	7.7	7.5	5.91
19360215	1246	− 4.50	133.00	0.0	7.2	7.0	0.44
19360401	0209	4.50	126.50	0.0	7.8	7.6	3.47
19360419	0507	− 7.50	156.00	40.00	7.4	7.2	0.87
19360630	1506	50.50	160.00	0.0	7.4	7.2	0.87
19360713	1112	− 24.50	− 70.00	60.00	7.2	7.0	0.44
19360822	0651	22.25	120.75	0.0	7.3	7.1	0.62
19360919	0101	3.50	97.50	0.0	7.2	7.0	0.44
19361102	2045	38.25	142.25	0.0	7.2	7.0	0.44
19370107	1320	35.50	98.00	0.0	7.7	7.5	2.45
19370221	0702	44.50	149.50	0.0	7.5	7.3	1.23
19370722	1709	64.75	− 146.75	0.0	7.2	7.1	0.62
19370820	1159	14.50	121.50	0.0	7.5	7.3	1.23
19371223	1317	16.57	− 98.53	18.00	7.5	7.3	1.63
19380201	1904	− 5.05	131.50	40.00	8.2	8.0	52.00
19380512	1538	− 6.00	147.75	0.0	7.5	7.3	1.23
19380519	1708	− 1.00	120.00	0.0	7.6	7.4	1.74
19380523	0718	36.50	141.30	40.00	7.6	7.4	4.00

Date (y-m-d)	Time	Lat.	Long.	Depth	M_s	M_{corr}	$\times 10^{20}$ Nm
19380610	0953	25.50	125.00	0.0	7.7	7.5	2.45
19380616	0215	27.50	129.50	0.0	7.4	7.2	0.87
19380816	0427	23.50	94.25	0.0	7.2	7.0	0.44
19381010	2048	2.25	126.75	0.0	7.3	7.1	0.62
19381105	0843	36.97	141.71	30.00	7.7	7.5	7.00
19381105	1050	37.24	141.75	45.00	7.7	7.5	4.80
19381106	0853	37.30	142.20	17.00	7.6	7.4	3.80
19381110	2018	55.48	−158.37	0.0	8.3	8.1	12.30
19381117	0354	55.45	−157.55	0.0	7.3	7.1	0.62
19390125	0332	−36.20	−72.20	0.0	7.8	7.6	3.47
19390130	0218	−6.50	155.50	0.0	7.8	7.6	3.47
19390430	0255	−10.50	158.50	50.00	8.0	7.8	6.92
19391010	1831	38.50	143.00	0.0	7.4	7.2	0.87
19391221	2054	10.00	−85.00	0.0	7.3	7.1	0.62
19391226	2357	39.50	38.50	17.00	7.8	7.6	3.47
19400524	1633	−11.22	−77.79	30.00	7.9	7.7	2.00
19400801	1508	44.30	139.50	33.00	7.5	7.3	2.10
19410415	1909	18.85	−102.94	0.0	7.7	7.5	2.94
19410517	0224	−10.00	166.25	0.0	7.3	7.1	0.62
19410626	1152	12.16	92.57	60.00	7.7	7.5	4.23
19411108	2337	0.50	122.00	0.0	7.3	7.1	0.62
19411118	1646	32.00	132.00	0.0	7.8	7.6	3.47
19411125	1803	37.50	−18.50	0.0	8.2	8.0	15.70
19411205	2046	8.50	−83.00	0.0	7.5	7.3	1.23
19411216	1919	21.50	120.50	0.0	7.2	7.0	0.44
19420408	1540	13.50	121.00	0.0	7.5	7.3	1.23
19420514	0213	0.01	−80.12	19.70	7.9	7.7	4.90
19420806	2336	14.00	−91.00	50.00	7.9	7.7	4.10
19420824	2250	−14.52	−74.81	0.0	8.2	8.0	4.31
19421020	2321	8.50	122.50	0.0	7.3	7.1	0.62
19421110	1141	−49.50	30.60	0.0	7.9	7.7	13.00
19421220	1403	40.50	36.50	0.0	7.3	7.1	0.62
19430222	0920	17.62	−101.15	16.00	7.5	7.3	1.56
19430309	0948	−60.00	−27.00	0.0	7.2	7.0	0.44
19430406	1607	−30.98	−71.27	20.00	7.9	7.7	25.00
19430503	0159	12.50	125.50	0.0	7.3	7.1	0.62
19430525	2307	7.50	128.00	0.0	7.7	7.5	2.45
19430608	2042	−2.80	102.00	50.00	7.3	7.1	0.62
19430609	0306	−1.00	100.91	50.00	7.6	7.4	1.74
19430613	0511	42.80	143.30	20.00	7.2	7.0	0.44
19430729	0302	19.25	−67.50	0.0	7.7	7.5	2.45
19430906	0341	−53.90	159.20	0.0	7.7	7.5	2.45
19430910	0836	35.50	134.20	10.00	7.4	7.2	0.36
19430914	0201	−22.00	171.00	50.00	7.4	7.2	0.87
19431023	1723	26.00	93.00	0.0	7.2	7.0	0.44
19431102	1808	−57.00	−26.00	0.0	7.3	7.1	0.62
19431103	1432	61.90	−150.84	15.00	7.4	7.2	0.87
19431106	0831	−6.00	134.50	0.0	7.7	7.5	2.45
19431113	1843	−19.00	170.00	0.0	7.3	7.1	0.62
19431126	2220	41.00	34.00	15.00	7.6	7.4	1.74
19431223	1900	−5.50	153.50	50.00	7.3	7.1	0.62

Date (y-m-d)	Time	Lat.	Long.	Depth	M_s	M_{corr}	$\times 10^{20}$ Nm
19440115	2349	− 31.25	− 68.75	50.00	7.2	7.0	0.44
19440201	0322	41.50	32.50	15.00	7.4	7.2	0.87
19440427	1438	− 0.50	133.50	50.00	7.3	7.1	0.62
19440525	1258	− 2.50	152.75	0.0	7.5	7.3	1.23
19440923	1213	54.00	160.00	40.00	7.2	7.0	0.44
19441116	1210	− 12.50	167.00	0.0	7.3	7.1	0.62
19441207	0435	33.75	136.00	30.00	8.0	7.8	15.00
19450415	0235	57.00	164.00	0.0	7.2	7.0	0.44
19451127	2156	24.50	63.00	0.0	8.0	7.8	10.20
19451228	1748	− 6.00	150.00	0.0	7.7	7.5	2.45
19460105	1957	− 16.00	167.00	50.00	7.2	7.0	0.44
19460401	1228	53.32	− 163.19	0.0	7.3	7.1	11.00
19460411	0152	− 1.00	− 14.50	0.0	7.3	7.1	0.62
19460503	2223	− 6.00	154.00	0.0	7.4	7.2	0.87
19460623	1713	49.75	− 125.40	25.00	7.3	7.1	2.50
19460804	1751	19.25	− 69.00	0.0	8.0	7.8	6.92
19460808	1328	19.50	− 69.50	0.0	7.6	7.4	1.74
19460912	1517	23.50	96.00	0.0	7.5	7.3	1.23
19460912	1520	23.50	96.00	0.0	7.8	7.6	3.47
19460929	0301	− 4.50	153.50	0.0	7.7	7.5	2.45
19461102	1828	41.50	72.50	0.0	7.5	7.3	1.23
19461104	2147	39.75	54.50	0.0	7.2	7.0	0.44
19461110	1742	− 8.50	− 77.80	15.00	7.3	7.1	0.17
19461112	1728	− 20.00	− 173.50	0.0	7.2	7.0	0.44
19461220	1919	33.10	135.80	30.00	8.2	8.0	15.00
19461221	1018	44.00	149.00	0.0	7.3	7.1	0.79
19470317	0819	33.00	99.50	0.0	7.6	7.4	1.74
19470402	0537	− 1.50	136.00	0.0	7.3	7.1	0.62
19470506	2030	− 6.50	148.50	0.0	7.5	7.3	1.23
19470527	0558	− 1.50	135.25	0.0	7.3	7.1	0.62
19470729	1343	28.50	94.00	0.0	7.5	7.3	0.98
19470805	1424	25.50	63.00	0.0	7.3	7.1	0.23
19471016	0209	64.50	− 147.50	0.0	7.2	7.0	0.44
19471101	1458	− 10.70	− 75.00	30.00	7.3	7.1	4.00
19480124	1746	10.50	122.00	0.0	8.2	8.0	13.80
19480502	0909	18.50	119.00	0.0	7.2	7.0	0.44
19480417	1611	33.00	135.75	40.00	7.3	7.1	0.62
19480514	2231	54.71	− 160.88	0.0	7.5	7.3	1.23
19480525	0711	29.50	100.50	0.0	7.3	7.1	0.62
19480628	0713	36.10	136.20	20.00	7.3	7.1	0.33
19480908	1509	− 21.00	− 174.00	0.0	7.8	7.6	12.50
19481005	2012	37.50	58.00	0.0	7.3	7.1	0.62
19490223	1608	41.00	83.50	0.0	7.3	7.3	1.23
19490327	0634	3.50	127.50	0.0	7.0	7.0	0.44
19490710	0353	39.30	70.60	20.00	7.5	7.5	2.40
19490822	0401	53.62	− 133.27	0.0	8.1	8.1	13.00
19491019	2100	− 5.50	154.00	60.00	7.1	7.1	2.20
19491217	0653	− 53.40	− 69.22	0.0	7.7	7.7	4.90
19491217	1507	− 53.99	− 68.77	0.0	7.7	7.7	4.90
19491229	0303	18.00	121.00	0.0	7.2	7.2	0.87
19500202	2333	22.00	100.00	0.0	7.0	7.0	0.44

Date (y-m-d)	Time	Lat.	Long.	Depth	M_s	M_{corr}	$\times 10^{20}$ Nm
19500815	1409	28.70	96.60	30.00	8.6	8.6	95.00
19501005	1609	10.35	−85.00	0.0	7.7	7.7	5.30
19501008	0323	−3.75	128.25	0.0	7.4	7.4	1.74
19501023	1613	14.50	−91.50	0.0	7.2	7.2	2.20
19501108	0218	−10.00	159.50	0.0	7.0	7.0	0.44
19501202	0104	−20.00	169.50	60.00	7.2	7.2	0.87
19501214	1415	16.81	−98.92	16.00	7.1	7.1	0.89
19510213	2212	55.55	−156.35	0.0	7.1	7.1	0.62
19511021	2134	23.75	121.50	0.0	7.4	7.4	1.74
19511022	0329	23.75	121.25	0.0	7.2	7.2	0.87
19511022	0543	24.00	121.25	0.0	7.0	7.0	0.44
19511106	1640	47.75	154.25	0.0	7.2	7.2	0.87
19511118	0935	30.50	91.00	0.0	8.0	8.0	4.60
19511124	1850	23.00	122.50	0.0	7.3	7.3	1.23
19511208	0414	−34.00	57.00	0.0	7.4	7.4	1.74
19520214	0338	−7.50	126.50	66.00	7.1	7.1	0.62
19520304	0122	42.50	143.00	15.00	8.3	8.3	17.00
19520309	1703	42.50	143.00	10.00	7.1	7.1	0.62
19520319	1057	9.50	127.25	0.0	7.6	7.6	3.74
19520721	1152	35.00	−119.00	0.0	7.8	7.8	0.90
19520817	1602	30.50	91.50	0.0	7.6	7.6	3.47
19521104	1658	52.75	159.50	0.0	8.2	8.2	350.00
19521106	1947	−5.00	145.00	50.00	7.0	7.0	0.44
19521206	1041	−8.00	156.50	0.0	7.2	7.2	0.87
19521224	1839	−5.50	152.00	0.0	7.0	7.0	0.44
19530105	0748	54.00	170.50	0.0	7.1	7.1	0.62
19530105	1006	49.00	155.50	40.00	7.0	7.0	0.44
19530226	1142	−11.00	164.25	0.0	7.0	7.0	0.44
19530318	1906	40.00	27.25	0.0	7.2	7.2	0.87
19530423	1624	−4.00	154.00	0.0	7.5	7.5	2.45
19530506	1716	−36.63	−72.60	60.00	7.4	7.4	1.74
19530812	0923	38.25	20.25	0.0	7.1	7.1	0.62
19531104	0349	−13.00	166.50	0.0	7.4	7.4	1.74
19531125	1748	34.00	141.50	0.0	7.9	7.9	8.90
19531212	1731	−4.00	−81.00	0.0	7.4	7.4	1.74
19540211	0030	39.00	101.50	0.0	7.0	7.0	0.44
19540331	1825	12.50	58.00	0.0	7.0	7.0	0.44
19540429	1134	28.50	−113.00	0.0	7.0	7.0	0.44
19541216	1107	39.30	−118.10	16.00	7.1	7.1	0.53
19550105	0050	−50.00	164.00	0.0	7.0	7.0	0.44
19550227	2043	−28.00	−175.50	0.0	7.7	7.7	4.90
19550318	0006	54.00	161.00	0.0	7.3	7.3	1.23
19550331	1817	8.00	124.00	0.0	7.6	7.6	3.47
19550414	0129	29.50	102.00	0.0	7.4	7.4	1.74
19550415	0340	40.00	75.00	0.0	7.0	7.0	0.44
19550517	1449	7.00	94.00	0.0	7.2	7.2	0.87
19551010	0857	−5.00	152.50	0.0	7.3	7.3	1.23
19560609	2313	35.00	67.50	0.0	7.5	7.5	2.45
19560709	0709	36.70	25.80	0.0	7.7	7.7	4.90
19560716	1507	22.25	96.00	0.0	7.0	7.0	0.44
19561024	1442	11.50	−86.50	0.0	7.2	7.2	0.87

Date (y-m-d)	Time	Lat.	Long.	Depth	M_s	M_{corr}	$\times 10^{20}$ Nm
19570223	2026	24.25	121.00	0.0	7.1	7.1	0.62
19570309	1422	51.63	−175.41	0.0	8.1	8.1	100.00
19570309	2039	52.43	−169.58	0.0	7.1	7.1	0.62
19570311	0958	52.66	−169.02	0.0	7.0	7.0	0.44
19570312	1144	51.10	−176.73	0.0	7.0	7.0	0.44
19570314	1447	51.32	−176.70	0.0	7.1	7.1	0.62
19570316	0234	51.47	−178.78	0.0	7.0	7.0	0.44
19570322	1421	53.61	−165.76	36.00	7.0	7.0	0.44
19570414	1918	−15.00	−174.00	0.0	7.4	7.4	1.74
19570425	0225	36.50	28.75	0.0	7.0	7.0	0.44
19570526	0633	40.50	31.25	0.0	7.1	7.1	0.62
19570622	2350	−1.75	137.25	0.0	7.3	7.3	1.23
19570627	0009	56.50	116.60	20.00	7.6	7.6	1.40
19570702	0042	36.00	53.00	0.0	7.0	7.0	0.44
19570728	0840	16.76	−99.55	16.74	7.5	7.5	5.13
19570924	0821	5.50	127.00	0.0	7.6	7.6	3.47
19571204	0337	45.20	99.20	25.00	8.0	8.0	18.00
19580119	1407	1.22	−79.37	40.00	7.3	7.3	5.20
19580407	1530	65.99	−156.55	0.0	7.3	7.3	1.23
19580531	1932	−15.00	168.50	0.0	7.0	7.0	0.44
19580710	0615	58.34	−136.52	15.00	7.9	7.9	5.30
19581106	2258	44.38	148.58	32.00	8.1	8.1	44.00
19581112	2023	44.50	148.75	0.0	7.2	7.2	0.36
19590122	0510	37.60	142.10	43.00	7.1	7.1	0.62
19590504	0715	53.20	159.80	0.0	8.2	8.2	12.60
19590815	0857	22.10	120.00	0.0	7.1	7.1	0.62
19590817	2104	−7.80	156.40	0.0	7.0	7.0	0.44
19590818	0637	44.70	−110.80	10.00	7.5	7.5	0.95
19590914	1409	−28.50	−177.80	0.0	7.7	7.7	4.90
19600320	1707	39.90	143.20	20.00	7.7	7.7	4.90
19600521	1002	−37.17	72.96	0.0	7.9	7.9	20.00
19600522	1032	−37.52	−72.35	0.0	7.2	7.2	0.17
19600522	1855	−37.79	−72.49	0.0	7.8	7.8	6.92
19600522	1910	−38.05	−73.34	32.00	8.5	8.5	1900.00
19600522	1911	−38.20	−73.50	32.00	8.5	8.5	3200.00
19600606	0555	−45.71	−73.00	0.0	7.1	7.1	0.62
19600620	0201	−38.21	−72.75	0.0	7.1	7.1	0.38
19600620	1259	−39.10	−73.05	0.0	7.0	7.0	0.44
19601120	2201	−6.90	−80.80	0.0	7.0	7.0	5.30
19601124	0652	−24.90	−176.30	0.0	7.0	7.0	0.44
19601202	0910	−24.40	−70.00	0.0	7.1	7.1	0.62
19601213	0736	−50.80	160.30	0.0	7.1	7.1	0.62
19610226	1810	31.80	131.60	56.00	7.6	7.6	3.47
19610307	1010	−28.80	−175.60	0.0	7.0	7.0	0.44
19610723	2151	−18.30	168.20	0.0	7.3	7.3	1.23
19610811	1551	42.90	145.20	37.00	7.1	7.1	0.62
19620412	0052	38.10	142.50	33.00	7.1	7.1	0.62
19620511	1411	16.93	−99.99	37.00	7.0	7.0	0.93
19620726	0814	7.50	−82.80	0.0	7.1	7.1	0.62
19630213	0850	24.40	122.10	28.00	7.4	7.4	1.00
19630316	0844	46.80	154.80	26.00	7.2	7.2	0.87

Date (y-m-d)	Time	Lat.	Long.	Depth	M_s	M_{corr}	$\times 10^{20}$ Nm
19630326	0948	−30.00	−177.70	20.00	7.0	7.0	1.40
19630416	0129	−0.90	128.00	23.00	7.2	7.2	0.87
19630915	0046	−10.40	165.60	43.00	7.2	7.2	1.95
19630917	1920	−10.20	165.40	0.0	7.4	7.4	1.74
19631012	1126	44.70	149.20	40.00	7.0	7.0	0.43
19631013	0517	44.90	149.60	40.00	8.1	8.1	75.00
19631020	0053	44.90	150.30	26.00	7.2	7.2	7.00
19631218	0030	−24.80	−176.50	32.00	7.1	7.1	3.70
19640206	1307	55.75	−155.79	26.00	7.0	7.0	0.44
19640315	2230	36.19	−7.65	14.00	7.1	7.1	0.14
19640328	0336	61.10	−147.60	30.00	8.4	8.4	750.00
19640428	0332	−5.14	133.99	33.00	7.0	7.0	0.44
19640616	0401	38.40	139.30	20.00	7.5	7.5	3.20
19641117	0815	−5.80	150.70	60.00	7.0	7.0	0.44
19650124	0011	−2.40	126.00	23.00	7.5	7.5	24.00
19650204	0501	51.30	178.60	35.00	8.2	8.2	140.00
19650204	0840	51.40	179.60	40.00	7.0	7.0	5.12
19650330	0227	50.60	177.90	20.00	7.5	7.5	3.40
19650520	0040	−14.60	167.40	3.00	7.1	7.1	2.51
19650811	0340	−15.50	166.90	14.00	7.0	7.0	0.74
19650811	2231	−15.80	167.10	15.00	7.3	7.3	3.00
19650813	1240	−15.90	166.80	28.00	7.1	7.1	1.00
19650823	1946	16.28	−96.02	16.00	7.6	7.6	1.70
19660307	2129	37.40	115.00	34.00	7.0	7.0	0.10
19660312	1631	24.20	122.70	42.00	7.8	7.8	1.60
19660322	0819	37.50	115.10	28.00	7.1	7.1	0.15
19660615	0059	−10.40	160.90	38.00	7.7	7.7	0.54
19660615	0132	−10.20	161.00	20.00	7.2	7.2	1.01
19660704	1833	52.00	179.90	16.00	7.0	7.0	1.00
19661017	2141	−10.92	−78.79	21.00	7.8	7.8	20.00
19661228	0818	−25.50	−70.70	23.00	7.7	7.7	4.50
19661231	1823	−11.90	166.40	35.00	7.9	7.9	5.6
19661231	2215	−12.10	165.70	36.00	7.1	7.1	0.62
19670105	0014	48.20	102.90	10.00	7.5	7.5	0.32
19670209	1524	2.90	−74.80	36.00	7.1	7.1	0.62
19670722	1656	40.70	30.70	33.00	7.1	7.1	1.50
19671221	0225	−21.90	−70.10	47.00	7.3	7.3	1.43
19671225	0123	−5.30	153.70	55.00	7.2	7.2	0.87
19680129	1019	43.50	146.70	20.00	7.3	7.3	1.20
19680212	0544	−5.50	153.40	46.00	7.1	7.1	1.69
19680219	2245	39.40	24.90	7.00	7.5	7.5	0.67
19680226	1050	22.80	121.50	8.00	7.1	7.1	0.62
19680401	0042	32.50	132.30	37.00	7.6	7.6	1.80
19680516	0048	40.90	143.40	35.00	8.1	8.1	28.00
19680516	1039	41.00	143.60	26.00	7.7	7.7	4.90
19680520	2109	44.70	150.30	44.00	7.0	7.0	0.44
19680523	1724	−41.70	172.00	21.00	7.1	7.1	0.62
19680612	1341	39.40	143.10	33.00	7.3	7.3	0.51
19680725	0723	−30.70	−178.30	17.00	7.1	7.1	0.98
19680801	2019	16.30	122.10	31.00	7.2	7.2	3.70
19680802	1406	16.75	−98.08	16.00	7.2	7.2	1.00

Date (y-m-d)	Time	Lat.	Long.	Depth	M_s	M_{corr}	$\times 10^{20}$ Nm
19680803	0454	25.70	128.50	19.00	7.0	7.0	0.44
19680810	0207	1.40	126.20	30.00	7.5	7.5	2.45
19680814	2214	0.10	119.70	22.00	7.3	7.3	1.23
19680831	1047	34.20	59.00	13.00	7.1	7.1	0.86
19681023	2104	−3.40	143.30	21.00	7.0	7.0	0.44
19690228	0240	36.00	−10.60	15.00	7.8	7.8	6.00
19690718	0524	38.40	119.50	6.00	7.1	7.1	0.61
19690811	2127	43.60	147.20	30.00	8.2	8.2	22.00
19690811	2352	1.73	126.47	34.00	7.0	7.0	0.44
19691121	0205	1.90	94.60	20.00	7.5	7.5	2.45
19691122	2309	57.60	163.60	33.00	7.1	7.1	5.30
19691225	2132	15.80	−59.60	42.00	7.0	7.0	0.78
19700104	1700	24.10	102.50	15.00	7.3	7.3	0.87
19700407	0534	15.80	121.70	30.00	7.1	7.1	0.62
19700429	1401	14.70	−92.60	25.00	7.1	7.1	1.20
19700531	2023	−9.36	−78.87	64.00	7.6	7.6	10.00
19700611	1646	−59.00	157.30	5.00	7.1	7.1	1.00
19700624	1309	51.80	−131.00	22.00	7.0	7.0	0.16
19700725	2241	32.18	131.70	30.00	7.0	7.0	0.41
19701210	0434	−3.79	−80.66	42.00	7.4	7.4	0.57
19710110	0717	−3.20	139.70	40.00	7.9	7.9	4.06
19710709	0303	−32.50	−71.20	42.00	7.7	7.7	5.60
19710714	0611	−5.50	153.90	53.00	7.8	7.8	12.00
19710714	0741	−5.60	153.80	43.00	7.0	7.0	0.44
19710726	0123	−4.90	153.20	48.00	7.7	7.7	18.00
19710802	0724	41.40	143.40	45.00	7.1	7.1	0.62
19710905	1835	46.45	141.24	22.00	7.3	7.3	0.95
19711215	0829	56.00	163.20	39.00	7.5	7.5	6.70
19720125	0206	22.45	122.26	14.00	7.4	7.4	2.20
19720229	0922	33.40	141.00	50.00	7.4	7.4	1.74
19720425	1930	13.37	120.34	37.00	7.1	7.1	0.62
19720730	2145	56.80	−135.90	29.00	7.4	7.4	3.00
19721202	0019	6.47	126.60	33.00	7.2	7.2	12.00
19721204	1016	33.30	140.80	62.00	7.5	7.5	2.45
19730130	2101	18.39	−103.21	32.00	7.3	7.3	3.00
19730206	1037	31.40	100.58	20.00	7.2	7.2	1.70
19730228	0637	50.49	156.58	27.00	7.0	7.0	0.44
19730617	0355	43.10	145.70	30.00	7.7	7.7	6.70
19730624	0243	43.32	146.44	50.00	7.3	7.3	1.23
19731228	1341	−14.46	166.60	26.00	7.3	7.3	1.23
19731229	0019	−15.12	166.90	30.00	7.0	7.0	0.29
19740110	0851	−14.43	166.86	34.00	7.0	7.0	0.44
19740131	2330	−7.50	155.90	34.00	7.0	7.0	1.00
19740201	0312	−7.80	155.60	40.00	7.0	7.0	1.40
19740702	2326	−29.20	−175.90	33.00	7.0	7.0	1.60
19740713	0118	7.80	−77.60	12.00	7.1	7.1	0.61
19740811	0113	39.46	73.83	7.00	7.2	7.2	0.43
19740927	0547	43.20	146.70	43.00	7.0	7.0	0.26
19741003	1421	−12.39	−77.66	27.00	7.6	7.6	15.00
19741008	0950	17.37	−62.00	47.00	7.3	7.3	0.25
19741023	0614	−8.42	154.03	48.00	7.0	7.0	0.44

Date (y-m-d)	Time	Lat.	Long.	Depth	M_s	M_{corr}	$\times 10^{20}$ Nm
19741109	1259	−12.64	−77.56	20.00	7.0	7.0	0.44
19750202	0843	53.11	173.50	10.00	7.4	7.4	0.51
19750204	1136	40.70	122.60	12.00	7.2	7.2	0.31
19750510	1427	−38.18	−73.78	6.00	7.6	7.6	3.47
19750526	0911	36.00	−17.65	25.00	7.8	7.8	7.00
19750720	1437	−6.59	155.05	49.00	7.6	7.6	3.40
19750720	1954	−7.10	155.15	44.00	7.5	7.5	1.20
19751011	1435	−24.89	−175.12	30.00	7.7	7.7	1.40
19751031	0828	12.54	125.99	50.00	7.4	7.4	2.30
19751129	1447	19.33	−155.02	15.00	7.1	7.1	1.80
19751226	1556	−16.26	−172.47	33.00	7.5	7.5	3.90
19760114	1556	−29.50	−177.60	29.00	7.7	7.7	4.90
19760114	1647	−28.43	−177.66	33.00	7.9	7.9	9.77
19760121	1005	44.92	149.12	41.00	7.0	7.0	0.44
19760204	0901	15.32	−89.10	5.00	7.5	7.5	3.70
19760727	1942	39.57	117.98	23.00	7.8	7.8	1.80
19760728	1045	39.66	118.40	26.00	7.2	7.2	0.80
19760816	1611	6.26	124.02	33.00	7.8	7.8	19.00
19761124	1222	39.32	43.73	15.00	7.1	7.1	0.75
19770402	0715	−16.70	−172.10	25.00	7.4	7.4	1.00
19770420	2342	−9.89	160.35	19.00	7.3	7.3	0.90
19770420	2349	−9.84	160.82	16.00	7.2	7.2	0.50
19770421	0424	−9.97	160.73	45.00	7.6	7.6	2.32
19770729	1115	−8.03	155.54	24.00	7.0	7.0	0.63
19770819	0608	−11.09	118.46	23.00	8.1	8.1	24.00
19771010	1153	−25.86	−175.41	23.00	7.0	7.0	1.00
19771123	0926	−31.03	−67.76	17.00	7.2	7.2	1.90
19780209	2135	−30.68	−177.36	23.00	7.0	7.0	0.39
19780323	0031	44.20	148.90	41.00	7.1	7.1	0.44
19780323	0315	44.93	148.44	28.30	7.4	7.4	2.70
19780324	1947	44.24	148.86	31.00	7.5	7.5	2.30
19780324	2105	42.84	78.61	35.00	7.0	7.0	0.25
19780612	0814	38.15	142.23	43.00	7.5	7.5	3.10
19780723	1442	22.28	121.51	29.00	7.2	7.2	0.86
19780916	1535	33.39	57.43	11.00	7.2	7.2	1.50
19781129	1952	16.03	−96.67	18.00	7.6	7.6	3.20
19790228	2127	60.50	−141.39	18.80	7.0	7.0	1.30
19790314	1107	17.41	−101.45	20.00	7.4	7.4	2.34
19790912	0517	−1.68	136.04	16.30	7.7	7.7	2.58
19791012	1025	−46.54	165.20	20.30	7.2	7.2	1.00
19791212	0759	1.60	−79.36	24.00	7.6	7.6	29.00
19800708	2319	−12.41	166.38	43.00	7.3	7.3	2.00
19800717	1942	−12.52	165.92	33.00	7.7	7.7	5.60
19801010	1225	36.19	1.35	10.00	7.1	7.1	0.50
19801025	1100	−21.89	169.85	11.00	7.0	7.0	2.00
19801108	1027	41.12	−124.25	19.00	7.2	7.2	1.10
19810130	0852	51.74	176.27	20.00	7.0	7.0	0.40
19810525	0525	−48.79	164.36	20.00	7.6	7.6	5.00
19810706	0308	−22.29	171.74	58.30	7.0	7.0	2.59
19810715	0759	−17.26	167.60	30.00	7.0	7.0	0.58
19810728	1722	30.01	57.79	11.00	7.1	7.1	0.67

Date (y-m-d)	Time	Lat.	Long.	Depth	M_s	M_{corr}	$\times 10^{20}$ Nm
19810901	0929	−14.96	−173.08	22.00	7.7	7.7	1.90
19811016	0325	−33.13	−73.07	14.00	7.2	7.2	0.51
19811025	0322	18.04	−102.08	20.00	7.3	7.3	1.14
19811219	1410	39.24	25.23	10.00	7.2	7.2	0.23
19811226	1705	−29.93	−177.74	8.00	7.1	7.1	0.46
19820111	0610	13.75	124.36	38.00	7.1	7.1	0.50
19820607	1059	16.56	−98.36	15.00	7.0	7.0	0.24
19820707	1043	−51.22	160.51	10.00	7.0	7.0	0.46
19820805	2032	−12.59	165.93	28.00	7.1	7.1	0.32
19821219	1743	−24.13	−175.86	29.00	7.7	7.7	2.00
19830117	1241	38.03	20.23	10.10	7.0	7.0	0.23
19830403	0250	8.72	−83.12	28.00	7.3	7.3	1.80
19830526	0259	40.46	139.10	13.00	7.7	7.7	7.60
19830806	1543	40.14	24.77	2.00	7.0	7.0	0.12
19831004	1852	−26.53	−70.56	15.00	7.3	7.3	3.40
19831028	1406	44.06	−113.86	10.00	7.3	7.3	0.31
19831130	1746	−6.85	72.11	10.00	7.6	7.6	4.10
19840207	2133	−10.01	160.47	18.00	7.5	7.5	3.75
19840319	2028	40.32	63.35	14.00	7.0	7.0	0.35
19840324	0944	44.00	148.12	42.00	7.0	7.0	0.64
19841101	0448	8.19	−38.79	10.00	7.1	7.1	0.40
19841117	0649	0.20	98.03	18.00	7.2	7.2	0.58
19841228	1037	56.19	163.46	21.50	7.0	7.0	0.14
19850303	2247	−33.13	−71.87	44.00	7.8	7.8	11.50
19850409	0156	−34.13	−71.62	38.00	7.2	7.2	0.50
19850510	1535	−5.60	151.04	27.00	7.1	7.1	0.69
19850703	0436	−4.44	152.83	26.00	7.2	7.2	0.83
19850823	1241	39.43	75.22	15.40	7.3	7.3	0.33
19850919	1317	18.14	−102.71	17.00	8.1	8.1	10.70
19850921	0137	17.82	−101.67	22.00	7.6	7.6	2.60
19850926	0727	−34.69	−178.65	51.00	7.0	7.0	0.24
19851117	0940	−1.63	134.91	13.30	7.1	7.1	0.78
19851128	0225	−14.04	166.24	24.20	7.0	7.0	0.30
19851128	0349	−13.99	166.18	44.40	7.1	7.1	0.36
19851221	0113	−14.03	166.51	43.00	7.1	7.1	0.57
19860430	0707	18.40	−102.97	20.70	7.0	7.0	0.31
19860507	2247	51.33	−175.44	31.30	7.7	7.7	14.50
19860814	1939	1.79	126.52	20.20	7.2	7.2	2.30
19861020	0646	−27.93	−176.43	50.40	8.1	8.1	8.50
19861114	2120	23.96	121.82	33.20	7.8	7.8	1.30
19870130	2229	−60.06	−26.92	15.00	7.0	7.0	0.19
19870208	1833	−6.09	147.69	55.00	7.4	7.4	0.54
19870305	0917	−24.39	−70.16	41.90	7.3	7.3	2.50
19870903	0640	−58.89	158.51	15.00	7.3	7.3	4.00
19871006	0419	−17.94	−172.23	16.00	7.3	7.3	0.89
19871016	2048	−6.27	149.06	48.00	7.4	7.4	1.30
19871025	1654	−2.32	138.36	15.00	7.0	7.0	0.19
19871130	1923	58.68	−142.79	10.00	7.6	7.6	7.30
19880224	0352	13.48	124.62	25.00	7.0	7.0	0.86
19880306	2235	56.95	−143.03	10.00	7.6	7.6	4.90
19880412	2319	−17.19	−72.31	15.00	7.0	7.0	0.48

Date (y-m-d)	Time	Lat.	Long.	Depth	M_s	M_{corr}	$\times 10^{20}$ Nm
19880618	2249	26.86	−111.00	10.00	7.0	7.0	0.11
19880810	0438	−10.37	160.82	16.20	7.4	7.4	2.50
19881106	1313	22.79	99.61	15.00	7.3	7.3	0.37
19890523	1054	−52.34	160.57	50.00	8.2	8.2	24.00
19891018	0004	37.04	−121.88	19.00	7.1	7.1	0.27
19891027	2104	−11.02	162.35	25.20	7.0	7.0	0.29
19891101	1825	39.83	142.76	24.00	7.4	7.4	1.36
19891215	1843	8.34	126.73	36.90	7.3	7.3	2.37

References

Agnew, D.C., and L.M. Jones, 1991. Prediction probabilities from foreshocks, *J. Geophys. Res., 96,* 11959–11971.

Aitchison, J., and J.A.C. Brown, 1957. *The Lognormal Distribution* (Cambridge, Univ. Press, Cambridge, 176 pp.)

Aki, K., 1965. Theory of earthquake prediction with special references to monitoring the quality factor of lithosphere by coda method, *Earthq. Predict. Res., 3,* 219–230.

Aki, K., 1989. Ideal probabilistic earthquake prediction, *Tectonophysics, 169,* 197–198.

Aki, K., and B. Chouet, 1975. Origin of coda waves: Source, attenuation, and scattering effects, *J. Geophys. Res., 80,* 3322–3342.

Aki, K., and K.L. Larner, 1970. Surface motion of a layered medium having an irregular interface due to incident plane SH waves, *J. Geophys. Res., 75,* 1921–1941.

Aki, K., and P.G. Richards, 1980. *Quantitative Seismology* (W. H. Freeman, San Francisco).

Aki, K., and W.D. Stuart, 1987. Introduction, in *Proc. Workshop XXXVII: Physical and observational basis for intermediate-term earthquake prediction,* Vol. 1, v-viii, Open-file Rep. 87–591, USGS, Menlo Park, CA.

Allen, C.R., 1983. Procedures for evaluation of earthquake predictions: Experience in USA, in *Proc. Seminar on Earthq. Prediction Case Histories* (UNDRO, Geneva). See also *Bull. Seismol. Soc. Am., 72,* S334, 1982.

Anderson, P.W., 1991. Is complexity physics? Is it science? What is it? *Physics Today, 44,* 9–11.

Bak, P., C. Tang, and K. Wiesenfeld, 1988. Self-organized criticality, *Phys. Rev. A, 38,* 364–374.

Bakun, W.H., 1988. History of significant earthquakes in the Parkfield area, *Earthquakes & Volcanoes, 20*, 45–50.

Bakun, W.H., and A.G. Lindh, 1985. The Parkfield, California earthquake prediction experiment, *Science, 229*, 619–624.

Bakun, W.H., and T.V. McEvilly, 1984. Recurrence models and Parkfield, California, earthquakes, *J. Geophys. Res., 89*, 3051–3058.

Baldwin, R.B., 1972. The tsunami model of the origin of ring structures concentric with large lunar craters, *Phys. Earth Planet. Interiors, 6*, 327–339.

Barrientos, S., and E. Kausel, 1990. Pre- and postseismic time dependent signals associated with large subduction earthquakes, *EOS, 71*, 1451.

Barrientos, S., and S.N. Ward, 1990. The 1960 Chile earthquake: coseismic slip from surface deformation, *Geophys. J. Int., 103*, 589–598.

Benioff, H. 1951. Colloquium on plastic flow and deformation within the earth, *Trans. Am. Geophys. Union, 32*, 508–514.

Benioff, H. 1955. Symposium on the crust of the earth, *Geol. Soc. Am. Spec. Pap. 62*, 61–74.

Ben-Zion, Y., T.L. Henyey, P.C. Leary and S.P. Lund, 1990. Observations and implications of water well and creepmeter anomalies in the Mojave segment of the San Andreas fault zone, *Bull. Seismol. Soc. Am., 80*, 1661–1676.

Bernard, P., 1991. How far from the seismic source can electrotelluric precursors be observed? *Proc. Int. Conf. Earthq. Predict., Strasbourg, EMSC*, pp. 292–297.

Bertero, V.V., 1990. Lessons learned from the Loma Prieta earthquake, *4th Nat. Conf. Earthq. Eng., Special Lecture*, Earthquake Eng. Res. Inst., Berkeley, CA.

Boltzmann, L., 1992. A German professor's trip to El Dorado, *Phys. Today, 45*, 44–51.

Boullé, P.L., 1990. Will the 1990s be a decade of increasingly destructive natural disasters? *Earthq. & Volcanoes, 22*, 173–175.

Brady, B.T., and G.A. Rowell, 1986. Laboratory investigations of the electrodynamics of rock fracture, *Nature, 321*, 488–492.

Brown, George, Chairman, 1992. *Report of the Task Force on the Health of Research* (U.S. Congress, House Committee on Science, Space, and Technology, Washington, Sep. 15).

Brownlee, K.A., 1965. *Statistical Theory and Methodology in Science and Engineering*, 2nd ed. (John Wiley, New York).

Brune, J.N., 1968. Seismic moment, seismicity, and rate of slip along major fault zones, *J. Geophys. Res., 73*, 777–784.

Brune, J.N., 1979. Implications of earthquake triggering and rupture propagation for earthquake prediction based on premonitory phenomena, *J. Geophys. Res., 84*, 2195–2197.

Brune, J.N., 1991. Seismic hazard at Tehri Dam, India, *Proc. 1991 Strong-Motion Sympos., Santiago, Chile*.

Brune, J.N., W. Nicks, and A. Aburto, 1992. Microearthquakes at Yucca Mountain, Nevada, *Bull. Seismol. Soc. Am., 82*, 164–174.

Bush, Susan, 1992. California earthquake risk reassessed, *EOS, 73*, 362.

Bush, Vannevar, 1945. Science—the endless frontier, *Rept. to the President* (reprinted by National Science Foundation, Washington, DC, 1990).

Calderón, C., S.J. Sánchez-Sesma, and M.A. Bravo, 1992. Seismic response of soft soil deposits using a hybrid method, *Proc. Int. Symp. Effects Surf. Geol. Seismic Motion, Odawara, Japan,* vol. 1, 179–184.

Chin Byan-Heng and K. Aki, 1991. Simultaneous study of the source, path, and site effects of strong ground motion during the 1989 Loma Prieta earthquake: A preliminary result on pervasive nonlinear effects, *Bull. Seismol. Soc. Am., 81,* 1859–1884.

Cornell, C.A., and S.R. Winterstein, 1988. Temporal and magnitude dependence in earthquake recurrence models, *Bull. Seismol. Soc. Am., 78,* 1522–1537.

Cox, D.R., and H.D. Miller, 1965. *The Theory of Stochastic Processes* (John Wiley, New York).

Daley, D.J., and D. Vere-Jones, 1988. *An Introduction to the Theory of Point Processes* (Springer-Verlag, Heidelberg, 702 pp.)

Darwin, C., 1860. *The Voyage of the Beagle* (London, 768 p.; re-edited by Anchor/Doubleday, New York, 1962).

Davies, P., 1989. The new physics: a synthesis, in *The New Physics,* P. Davies, Ed. (Cambridge U. Press, Cambridge, pp. 1–6).

De Groot, S.R., 1952. *Thermodynamics of Irreversible Processes* (North-Holland Publishing Co., Amsterdam).

Deng Qidong, Jiang Pu, L.M. Jones and P. Molnar, 1981. A preliminary analysis of reported changes in ground water and anomalous animal behavior before the 4 February 1975 Haicheng earthquake, in *Earthquake Prediction,* D. Simpson and P. Richards, Eds., Maurice Ewing Series, vol 4., Am. Geophys. Union, Washington, DC, pp. 543–565.

Deshpande, B.G., 1987. *Earthquakes, Animals and Man* (Maharashtra Assoc. Cultiv. Science, Pune, 120 pp.).

Dombrowsky, W., 1987. Critical theory in sociological disaster research, in *Sociology of Disasters,* R.R. Dynes, B. de Marchi and C. Pelanda, Eds. (Franco Angeli, Milano, pp. 331–356).

Drakopoulos, J., and G.N. Stavrakakis, 1991. A false alarm based on the largest SES recorded at a VAN station in northern Greece, *Proc. Int. Conf. Earthq. Predict., Strasbourg, EMSC,* 309–313.

Einstein, A., 1918. Address delivered at the celebration of Max Planck's sixtieth birthday, in *Mein Weltbild* (Querido-Verlag, Amsterdam, 1934).

Epstein, B., and C. Lomnitz, 1966. A model for the occurrence of large earthquakes, *Nature, 211,* 954–956.

Feder, J., 1988. *Fractals* (Plenum Press, New York, NY, 283 pp.)

Fedotov, S.A., 1965. Regularities of the distribution of strong earthquakes in Kamchatka, the Kurile Islands, and northeast Japan. *Tr. Inst. Fiz. Zemli Akad. Nauk SSSR, 36,* 66–93.

Fedotov, S.A., 1968. O seismicheskom cycle, in *Seismicheskoye Rayonnirovaniye SSSR* (Nauka, Moscow, pp. 121–150).

Fedotov, S.A., and Y.V. Riznichenko, 1984. Long-term prediction of strong earthquakes, in *Earthquake Prediction* (Terra/UNESCO, Tokyo/ Paris, pp. 477–485).

Felix, J., and H.Lenk, 1890. *Beiträge zur Geologie und Paläontologie der Republik Mexiko* (Arthur Felix, Leipzig).

Filson, J.R., 1988. The role of the federal government in the Parkfield Earthquake Prediction Experiment, *Earthquakes & Volcanoes, 20,* 56–59.

Finn, W.D.L., 1991. Site conditions and seismic response, *Proc. Int. Symp. Effects Surf. Geol. Seismic Motion, Odawara, Japan,* vol. 1, 3–31.

Fraser-Smith, A.C., A. Bernardi, R. Helliwell, P.R. McGill, and O.G. Villard, Jr., 1993. Analysis of low-frequency electromagnetic field measurements near the epicenter of the Ms 7.1 Loma Prieta earthquake, *U.S.G.S., Loma Prieta earthquake, Professional Paper* (in press).

Friedman, H.W., 1966. The 'little variale favtor': a statistical discussion of the reading of seismograms, *Bull. Seismol. Soc. Am., 56,* 593–604.

Friedman, H.W., 1967. Estimating earthquake magnitude, *Bull. Seismol. Soc. Am., 57,* 747–760.

Fu Chengyi, 1976. *Ten Lectures on the Earth* (Scientific Press, Beijing, in Chinese).

Gao Xiang-lin, 1991. Preseismic crustal deformation associated with intraplate earthquakes: the character and mechanism, *Int. Conf. Earthq. Predict, Preprints,* (CSEM, Strasbourg, pp. 381–395).

García Cubas, Antonio (1904). *El libro de mis recuerdos* (Mexico).

Gauss, C.F. (1823). *Theoria Combinationis Observationum Erroribus Minimis Obnoxiae* (Henricus Dieterich, Göttingen). This work was read before the Royal Society of Göttingen in two parts: part one, on February 15, 1821, and part two, on February 2, 1823.

Geller, R.J., 1991. Shake-up for earthquake prediction, *Nature, 352,* 275–276. See also *Nature, 353,* 612.

Giesecke, A.A., 1983. Case history of the Peru prediction for 1980–81, in *Proc. Semin. Earthq. Predict. Case Histories* (UNDRO, Geneva, pp. 51–75).

Gilbert, F., 1967. Gravitationally perturbed Rayleigh waves, *Bull. Seismol. Soc. Am., 57,* 783–794.

Gilbert, G.K., 1909. Earthquake forecasts, *Science, 29,* 121–138.

Gouldner, .W., 1976. *The Dialectics of Ideology and Technology* (New York).

Gómez, José de, 1854. Diario Curioso de México, de 14 de agosto de 1776 a 26 de junio de 1798, en *Documentos para la Historia de México, III* (T.S. Gardida, México).

Green, N.B., 1987. *Earthquake-resistant Building Design and Construction* (Elsevier, Amsterdam).

Gumbel, E.J., 1958. *Statistics of Extremes* (Columbia Univ. Press, New York, NY, 375 pp.)

Gutenberg, B., and C.F. Richter, 1954. *Seismicity of the Earth and Associated Phenomena* (Princeton U. Press, Princeton, NJ, 310 pp.)

Habermann, R.E., 1988. Precursory seismic quiescence: past, present and future, *Pageoph, 126,* 277–318.

Habermas, J., 1985. *Theorie des kommunikativen Handelns* (Suhrkamp, Frankfurt).

Hadley, P.K., A. Askar, and A.S. Cakmak, 1991. Subsoil geology and soil amplification in Mexico Valley, *Soil Dyn. Earthq. Eng., 10,* 101–109.

Hardin, B.O., and V.P. Drnevich, 1972. Shear modulus and damping in soils: design equations and curves, *J. Soil Mech. Found. Div., Proc. m. Soc. Civil Eng., SM7, 98,* 667–692.

Hawkes, A.G., 1971. Point spectra of some mutually exciting point processes, *J. R. Stat. Soc. B, 33,* 438–443.

Hawking, S.W., 1988. *A Brief History of Time* (Bantam Books, New York, NY, 198 pp.)

Hewitt, K., 1983. Calamity in a technocratic age, in *Interpretations of Calamity,* K. Hewitt, ed. (Allen & Unwin, New York).

Homsy, G.M., 1987. Viscous fingering in porous media, *Annu. Rev. Fluid Mech., 19,* 271–311.

Hudnut, K.W., L. Seeber, and J. Pacheco, 1989. Cross-fault triggering in the November 1987 Superstition Hills earthquake sequence, southern California, *Geophys. Res. Lett., 16,* 199–202.

Idriss, I.M., 1990. Response of soft soil sites during earthquakes, *Proc. H.B. Seed Memorial Symp. (*U.C. Berkeley, CA.*),* II.

Imamura, A., 1937. *Theoretical and Applied Seismology* (Maruzen, Tokyo).

Infeld, E., and G. Rowlands, 1990. *Nonlinear Waves, Solitons and Chaos* (Cambridge Univ. Press, Cambridge).

Isacks, B.L., J. Oliver, and L.R. Sykes, 1967. Seismology and the new global tectonics, *J. Geophys. Res., 73,* 5855–5899.

Ito, T., Y. Uesugi, H. Yonezawa, K. Kano, M. Someno, T. Chiba, and T. Kimura, 1987. Analytical method for evaluating superficial fault displacements in volcanic air fall deposits: case of the Hirayama fault, south of Tanzawa Mountains, central Japan, since 21,500 years b.p., *J. Geophys. Res., 92,* 10683–10695.

Ito, T., K. Kano, Y. Uesugi, K. Kosaka, and T. Chiba, 1989. Tectonic evolution along the northernmost border of the Philippine Sea plate since about 1 Ma, *Tectonophysics, 160,* 305–326.

Jacob, K.H., 1991. Seismic zonation and site response, submitted to *4th Int. Conf. Seismic Zonation, Stanford, CA.*

Jin, A., and K. Aki, 1988. Spatial and temporal correlation between coda Q^{-1} and seismicity in China, *Bull. Seismol. Soc. Am., 78,* 741–769.

Johnston, R.L., 1955. Earthquake damage to oil fields and to the Paloma cycling plant in the San Joaquin Valley, *Bull. Calif. Div. Mines, 171,* 221–226.

Jongmans, D., and M. Campillo, 1989. Influence de la source et de la structure géologique sur la distribution des dégâts, *Bull. Soc. Géol. Fr., 8,* 849–857.

Joyner, W.B., and D.M. Boore, 1981. Peak horizontal accelerations and velocities from strong-motion records including records from the 1979 Imperial Valley, California, earthquake, *Bull. Seismol. Soc. Am., 71,* 2011–2038.

Kadanoff, L.P., 1992. Hard times, *Phys. Today, 45, (10),* 9–11.

Kagan, Y.Y., and D.D. Jackson, 1991. Seismic gap hypothesis: ten years after, *J. Geophys. Res., 96,* 21419–21431.

Kanamori, H., 1981. The nature of seismicity patterns before large earthquakes, in *Earthquake Prediction,* D. Simpson and P. Richards, Eds., Maurice Ewing Series, vol 4 *(*Am. Geophys. Union, Washington, DC, pp. 1–19*)*.

Kawase, H., and K. Aki, 1981. A study on the response of a soft basin for incident S, P, and Rayleigh waves with special reference to the long duration observed in Mexico City, *Bull. Seismol. Soc. Am.*, *79*, 1361–1382.

Keilis-Borok, V.I., L. Knopoff, I.M. Rotwain, and C.R. Allen, 1988. Intermediate-term prediction of occurrence times of strong earthquakes, *Nature*, *335*, 690–694.

Khintchine, A.J. 1960. *Mathematical Methods in the Theory of Queuing* (Griffin, London).

Kisslinger, C., 1986. Seismicity patterns in the Adak Seismic Zone and the short-term outlook for a major earthquakes, in *Minutes Nat. Earthq. Predict. Eval. Council, Sep. 8–9, 1985, Anchorage, AK*, C.R. Shearer, Ed., Open-File Rep. 86–92, USGS, 119–134.

Kisslinger, C., 1988. An experiment in earthquake prediction and the 7 May 1986 Andreanof Islands earthquake, *Bull. Seismol. Soc. Am.*, *78*, 218–229.

Klaus, A., B. Taylor, G.F. Moore, F. Murkami, and Y. Okamura, 1992. Back-arc rifting in the Izu-Bonin island arc: structural evolution of Hachijo and Aoga Shima Rifts, *Isl. Arc, 1*, 16–31.

Knopoff, L., 1971. A stochastic model for the occurrence of main-sequence earthquakes, *Rev. Geophys. Space Phys.*, *9*, 175–188.

Kokusho, T., Y. Yoshida, and Y. Esashi, 1982. Dynamic properties of soft clay for wide strain range, *Soils & Found.*, *22*, 1–18.

Kolmogorov, A.N., 1941. Über das logarithmisch normale Verteilungsgesetz der Dimensionen der Teilchen bei Zerstückelung, *Dokl. Akad. Nauk SSSR, 31*, 99–101.

Kolmogorov, A.N., 1956. The Theory of Probability, in *Mathematics* (S.H. Gould, trans., M.I.T. Press, Cambridge, MA, Vol. 2, 229–264).

Kraemer, Smith, and Levine, 1976. An animal behavior model, *Conf. Abnormal Animal Behavior Prior to Earthquakes, I*, U.S. G. S., Menlo Park, CA. (not open-filed).

Küppers, A., 1992. Japan und die IDNDR: Wird die japanische Erdbebenvorhersage zum Exportschlager für Katastrophenländer? *DGEB, Schriftenr.* (Weimar), *2*, 173–192.

Lawson, A.C. 1922. Earthquake prediction, *Christian Sci. Monit.*, Feb. 14.

Le Pichon, X., J. Francheteau, and J. Bonnin, 1973. *Plate Tectonics* (Elsevier, Amsterdam).

Liu Defu, 1990a. Unusual atmospheric phenomena before large earthquakes, in *Earthquake Prediction*, Ma Zongjin, Ed. (Seismological Press/Springer-Verlag, Springer, Beijing/Heidelberg, 172–188).

Lomnitz, C., 1956. Creep measurements in igneous rocks, *J. Geol.*, *64*, 473–479.

Lomnitz, C., 1957. Linear dissipation in solids, *J. Appl. Phys.*, *28*, 201–205.

Lomnitz, C., 1961. On thermodynamics of planets, *Geophys. J. Roy. Astr. Soc.*, *5*, 157–161.

Lomnitz, C., 1966. Magnitude stability in earthquake sequences, *Bull. Seismol. Soc. Am.*, *56*, 247–249.

Lomnitz, C., 1969. Sea-floor spreading as a factor of tectonic evolution in southern Chile, *Nature*, *222*, 366–369.

Lomnitz, C., 1970. Some observations of gravity waves in the 1960 Chile earthquake, *Bull. Seis. Soc. Am., 60,* 669–670.

Lomnitz, C., 1974. *Global Tectonics and Earthquake Risk* (Elsevier, Amsterdam, 320 pp.)

Lomnitz, C. 1985. Tectonic feedback and the earthquake cycle, *Pageoph, 123,* 667–682.

Lomnitz, C., 1988. The 1985 Mexico earthquake, in *Natural and Man-made Hazards,* M.I. El-Sabh and T.S. Murty, Eds. (D.Reidel, Dordrecht, pp. 63–79).

Lomnitz, C., 1993. Moment-ratio imaging of seismic regions for earthquake prediction, *Geophys. Res. Lett., 20,* 2171–2174.

Lomnitz-Adler, J., 1985. The statistical dynamics of the earthquake process, *Bull. Seismol. Soc. Am., 75,* 441–454.

Lomnitz-Adler, J., 1989. Statistical dynamics calculations of time-dependent seismicity, *Tectonophysics, 169,* 207–213.

Lomnitz-Adler, J., and X. Lemus-Díaz, 1989. A stochastic model for fracture growth on a heterogeneous seismic fault, *Geophys. J. Int., 99,* 183–194.

Lomnitz-Adler, J., and C. Lomnitz, 1978. New magnitude-frequency relation, *Tectonophysics, 49,* 237–245.

Lomnitz-Adler, J., and F. Lund, 1992. The generation of quasi-dynamical accelerograms from large and complex seismic fractures, *Bull. Seismol. Soc. Am., 82,* 61–80.

Lomnitz-Adler, J., G. Martinez-Mekler and L. Knopoff, 1991. Fracture propagation: from time to ensemble averages and back again, in *Nonlinear Phenomena in Fluids, Solids and other Complex Systems,* P. Cordero and B. Nachtergaele, Eds. (Elsevier, Amsterdam, p. 187–201).

Ma Zongjin, Fu Zhengxiang, Zhang Yingzhen, Wang Chengmin, Zhang Guomin, and Liu Defu, Eds., 1990. *Earthquake Prediction* (Seismological Press/Springer-Verlag, Beijing/Heidelberg, 332 pp.)

Mandelbrot, B.B., 1983. *The Fractal Geometry of Nature* (W.H. Freeman, San Francisco).

Mandelbrot, B.B., and J.R. Wallis, 1969a. Some long-run properties of geophysical records, *Water Resourc. Res., 5,* 321–340.

Mandelbrot, B.B., and J.R. Wallis, 1969b. Robustness of the rescaled range R/S in the measurement of nonclyclic long-run statistical dependence, *Water Resources Res., 5,* 967–988.

Mantovani, E., E. Boschi, D. Albarello, D. Barbucci and M. in *Earthquake Prediction, Proc. Int. School of Solid Earth Geophys., Erice, Italy* (Il Cigno, Galileo Galilei, Roma, 1992, p. 181–198)

Mao Zedong, 1937. *On Practice* (Foreign Languages Press, Peking).

Matuzawa, T., 1925. On the possibility of gravitational waves in soils and allied problems, *J. Inst. Astr. Geophys., Tokyo, 3,* 161–174.

Martiel, J.L., and A. Goldbeter, 1987. *Biophys. J., 52,* 807.

McCann, W.R., S.P. Nishenko, L.R. Sykes, and J. Krause, 1979. Seismic gaps and plate tectonics: seismic potential for major plate boundaries, *Pageoph, 117,* 1082–1147.

McKenzie, D., and R.L. Parker, 1967. The North Pacific: an example of tectonics on a sphere, *Nature, 216,* 1276–1280.

Melosh, H.J., 1989. *Impact Cratering—A Geologic Process* (Oxford Univ. Press, London-Oxford).

Meunier, J.M., 1991. Are some earthquakes triggered by the strong reversals of the atmospheric electric field? *Proc. Int. Conf. Earthq. Predict., Strasbourg, EMSC,* pp. 344–348.

Mjachkin, V.I., B.V. Kostrov, G.A. Sobolev and O.G. Shamina, 1984. The physics of rock failure and its links with earthquakes, in *Earthquake Prediction, Proc. Int. Symp., Paris, 1979* (Unesco/Terra, Paris/Tokyo, pp. 319–341).

Moehle, J.P., 1989. Experiments on the Cypress Street Viaduct and indications regarding performance during the 17 October earthquake. *Testimony, Governor's Board of Inquiry,* Oakland, CA., 14 Dec.

Mogi, K., 1984. Fundamental studies on earthquake prediction, in *On Continental Seismicity and Earthquake Prediction* (Seismological Press, Beijing, p. 619–652).

Mogi, K., 1985. *Earthquake Prediction* (Academic Press, Tokyo).

Mogi, K., 1992. Earthquake prediction research in Japan, in *Earthquake Prediction—Proc. Int. Sch. Solid Earth Geophys., Erice, Italy* (Il Cigno, Galileo Galilei, Rome).

Molnar, P., and Q. Deng, 1984. Faulting associated with large earthquakes and the average rate of deformation in central and east Asia, *J. Geophys. Res., 89,* 6203–6214.

Montessus de Ballore, F., 1907. *La Science Sismologique* (Armand Colin, Paris, 579 pp.)

Montessus de Ballore, F., 1915. Algunas palabras sobre las cuatro memorias del General D. Manuel Cortés y Agullo, *Bol. Serv. Sismol. Chile, XI, Mem.,* Santiago, 207–208.

Moore, S.E., 1962. Seismic considerations in nuclear power plants, *Nucl. Saf., 3,* 48–68.

Morgan, W.J., 1968. Rises, trenches, great faults and crustal blocks, *J. Geophys. Res., 75,* 285–309.

Mucciarelli, 1992. Medium term earthquake prediction in Italy, in *Earthquake Prediction—Proc. Int. Sch. Solid Earth Geophys., Erice, Italy* (Il Cigno, Galileo Galilei, Roma, pp. 181–198).

National Academy of Sciences, 1975. *Earthquake Prediction and Public Policy* (Washington, DC).

Nicolis, G., 1986. *Dynamics of Hierarchical Systems* (Springer, Berlin).

Nims, D.K., E.I. Miranda, I.D. Aiken, A.S. Whitaker, and V.V. Bertero, 1989. Collapse of the Cypress Street Viaduct as a result of the Loma Prieta earthquake, *Rept. UCB/EERC-89–16,* Univ. California, Berkeley, CA.

Nirei, H., T. Kusuda, K. Kamura, K. Furuno, Y. Hara, K. Satoh, and O. Kazaoka, 1990. The 1987 East Off Chiba Prefecture earthquake and its hazards, *Mem. Geol. Soc. J., 35,* 31–46.

Nishenko, S.P., 1985. Seismic potential for large and intermediate earthquakes along the Chilean and southern Peruvian margins of South America: quantitative reappraisal, *J. Geophys. Res., 90,* 3589–3615.

Nishenko, S.P., and R. Buland, 1987. A generic recurrence interval distribution for earthquake forecasting, *Bull. Seismol. Soc. Am., 77,* 1382–1399.

Nishenko, S.P., and S.K. Singh, 1987. The Acapulco-Ometepec, Mexico earthquakes of 1907–1982: evidence for a variable recurrence history, *Bull. Seis. Soc. Am., 77,* 1359–1367.

Nur, A., 1972. Dilatancy, pore fluids, and premonitory variations in t_S/t_P travel times, *Bull. Seismol. Soc. Am., 62,* 1217–1222.

Ogata, Y., 1991. Detection of precursory relative quiescence before great earthquakes through a statistical model (II), *preprint, Inst. Stat. Math., Tokyo.*

Ogata, Y., and K. Abe, 1991. Some statistical features of the long-term variation of the global and regional seismic activity, *Int. Stat. Review, 59,* 139–161.

Ohtake, M., T. Matumoto, and G. V. Latham, 1977. Seismicity gap near Oaxaca, southern Mexico, as a probable precursor to a large earthquake, *Pageoph, 115,* 375–385.

Ohtake, M., T. Matumoto, and G.V. Latham, 1981. Evaluation of the forecast of the 1978 Oaxaca, southern Mexico earthquake based on a precursory seismic quiescence, in *Earthquake Prediction, Maurice Ewing Series 4, D.W. Simpson and P.G. Richards, Eds.,* 53–66 (American Geophysical Union, Washington, D.C.)

Olson, R.S., 1989. *The Politics of Earthquake Prediction* (Princeton University Press, Princeton, NJ, 187 pp).

Palm, C., 1943. Intensitätsschwankungen im Fernsprechverkehr, *Ericsson Techniks, 44,* 1–189.

Parkinson, C.N., 1960. *The Law and the Profits* (John Murray, London, 192 pp.)

Press, F. (Chairman), 1965. Earthquake Prediction: A Proposal for a Ten-year Program of Research (*Office of Science and Technology, Ad-hoc Panel on Earthquake Prediction,* Washington, DC, 39 pp.)

Press, F., 1975. Earthquake prediction, *Sci. Am., 232,* 14–23.

Prigogine, I., 1947. *Etude Thermodynamique des Processus Irréversibles* (Dunod, Paris, 259 pp.)

Ralchovsky, T., and L. Komarov, 1991. On electric precursors of earthquakes, *Tech. Contributions (Preprints), International Conf. Earthq. Predict., Strasbourg* (EMSC, pp. 351–356).

Rampino, M.R., and K. Caldeira, 1993. Major episodes of geologic change: correlations, time structure and possible causes, *Earth Planet. Sci. Lett., 114,* 215–227.

Reasenberg and Jones, 1989. *Science, 243,* 1173.

Reid, H.F., 1910. *The California Earthquake of April 18, 1906.* Rept. State Earthq. Invest. Comm., vol. 2, 1–192 (Carnegie Inst., Washington, DC).

Reid, H.F. 1911. The elastic-rebound theory of earthquakes, *Univ. Calif. Dep. Geol. Bull. 6 (19),* 413–444.

Rhoades, D.A., and F.F. Evison, 1989. On the reliability of precursors, *Phys. Earth Planet. Int., 58,* 137–140.

Richter, C.F., 1955. Aftershocks of the earthquake, in *Earthquakes in Kern County, California, during 1952* (Calif. Dept. Nat. Resources, Div. Mines, Bulletin 171, Sacramento, CA.)

Richter, C.F., 1958. *Elementary Seismology* (W.H. Freeman, San Francisco).

Rikitake, T., 1976. *Earthquake Prediction* (Elsevier, Amsterdam).

Rikitake, T., 1982. *Earthquake Forecasting and Warning* (Center for Academic Publications/Reidel, Tokyo).

Roeloffs, E., 1988. Hydrological precursors to earthquakes, *Pageoph, 126,* 177–209.

Rogers, J.D., 1991. Brief engineering history and observations of damage to the San Francisco-Oakland Bay Bridge and I-880 Cypress Structure, *Assoc. Eng. Geol. Spec. Public. 1, Loma Prieta Earthq.,* J. E. Baldwin and N. Sitar, Eds., pp. 151–170.

Russell, J.S., 1844. Report on waves, *14th Meeting, Brit. Assoc., Rept., York,* 311–390.

Sacks, I.S., A.T. Linde, J.A. Snoke, and S. Suyehiro, 1981. A slow earthquake sequence following the Izu-Oshima earthquake of 1978, in *Earthquake Prediction,* D. Simpson and P. Richards, Eds., Maurice Ewing Series vol. 4 (Am. Geophys. Union, Washington, DC, pp. 617–628.

Savage, J.C., 1976. Technical Report, Liaoning Earthquake Study Team. USGS Internal Report (unpublished). 20 pp. + figs.

Savage, J.C., 1991. Criticism of some forecasts of the National Earthquake Prediction Evaluation Council, *Bull. Seismol. Soc. Am., 81,* 862–881.

Savage, J.C., 1993. The Parkfield prediction fallacy, *Bull. Seismol. Soc. Am., 83,* 1–6.

Savage, J.C., and R.S. Cockerham, 1987, Quasi-periodic occurrence of earthquakes in the 1978–1986 Bishop-Mammoth Lakes sequence, eastern California, *Bull. Seismol. Soc. Am., 77,* 1347–1358.

Savage, J.C., W.H. Prescott, M. Lisowski, and N.E. King, 1981. Strain on the San Andreas fault near Palmdale, California: rapid, aseismic change, *Science, 211,* 56–58.

Schaefer, E., and D. Swinbanks, 1990. Betting on an inexact science, *Nature, 348,* 273.

Scholem, G., 1977. Zur Kabbala und ihrer Symbolik (Suhrkamp, Zurich).

Scholz, C.H., 1990. *The Mechanics of Earthquakes and Faulting* (Cambridge U. Press, Cambridge, 439 pp.)

Scholz, C.H., L.R. Sykes, and Y.P. Aggarwal, 1973. Earthquake prediction: a physical basis, *Science, 181,* 803–809.

Schwartz, D.P., and K.J. Coppersmith, 1984. Fault behavior and characteristic earthquakes: examples from the Wasatch and San Andreas faults, *J. Geophys. Res., 89,* 5681–5698.

Seed, H.B., and I.M. Idriss, 1983. Ground Motions and Soil Liquefaction during Earthquakes (Earthquake Engineering Research Institute, El Cerrito, CA).

Shapiro, M.H., J.D. Melvin, T.A. Tombrello, M.J. Mendenhall, P.B. Larson, and J.H. Whitcomb, 1981. Relationship of the 1979 southern California radon anomaly to a possible regional strain event, *J. Geophys. Res., 86,* 1725–1730.

Shimazaki, K. and T. Nakata, 1980. Time predictable recurrence for large earthquakes, *Geophys. Res. Lett., 7,* 279–282.

Shimazaki, K., 1987. Reported intermediate-term earthquake precursors in the Izu Peninsula, Japan, *Proc. Workshop XXXVII, Physical and Observational Basis for*

Intermediate-Term Earthq. Prediction, vol. *1*, Open-File Rept. 87–591 (U.S.G.S., Menlo Park, CA., pp. 26–53).

Sibson, R.H., 1981. Fluid flow accompanying faulting: field evidence and models, in *Earthquake Prediction*, D. Simpson and P. Richards, Eds., Maurice Ewing Series vol. 4, Am. Geophys. Union, Washington, DC, p. 593).

Sieh, K., 1984. Lateral offsets and revised dates of large prehistoric earthquakes at Pallett Creek, southern California, *J. Geophys. Res.*, *89*, 7641–7670.

Singh, S.K., E. Mena, and R. Castro, 1988. Some aspects of the source characteristics and the ground amplification in and near Mexico City from the acceleration data of the September 1985 Michoacan, Mexico earthquakes, *Bull. Seismol. Soc. Am.*, *78*, 451–477.

Sornette, A., and D. Sornette, 1989, *Europhys. Lett.*, *9*, 197.

Sosa Ordoño, M., 1984. Pinotepa Nacional: A case of a seismic pseudo-prediction: causes and effects, in *Earthquake Prediction* (Terra/UNESCO, Tokyo/Paris, pp. 673–682).

Stillwell, H.D., 1992. Natural hazards and disasters in Latin America, *Nat. Hazards*, *6*, 131–159.

Sugiyama, Y., 1990. Seismotectonics of the Suruga Bay and Enshunada region, *Zisin*, *43*, 439–442.

Sugiyama, Y., 1992. The Cenozoic tectonic history of the forearc region of southwest Japan, based mainly on the data obtained from the Shizuoka distict, *Bull. Geol. Surv. J.*, *43*, 91–112.

Suh, N.P., 1985. Statement before the Senate Subcommittee on Science, *Congressional Record*, October 3, 1985, Washington, DC.

Sun Tzu, about 500 B.C. *The Art of War*. Trans. Samuel B. Griffith (Oxford Univ. Press, London, 1963).

Swinbanks, 1992. Trying to shake Japan's faith in forecasts, *Nature 356*, April 9.

Sykes, L.R., 1971. Aftershock zones of great earthquakes, seismicity gaps, and earthquake prediction for Alaska and the Aleutians, *J. Geophys. Res.*, *76*, 8021–8041.

Sykes, L.R., and J.F. Pacheco, 1992. Seismic moment catalog of large, shallow earthquakes, 1900–1989, *Bull. Seismol. Soc. Am.*, *82*, 1306–1349.

Tang Xiren, 1988. *A General History of Earthquake Studies in China* (Science Press, Beijing).

Thatcher, W., 1984. The earthquake deformation cycle, recurrence, and the time-predictable model, *J. Geophys. Res.*, *89*, 5674–5680.

Thoreau, H.D., *Walden* (Signet, New York, 1949).

Trifunac, M.D., 1982. A note on rotational components of earthquake motions on ground surface for incident body waves, *Soil Dynamics & Earthq. Eng.*, *1*, 111–119.

Turcotte, D.L., 1991. Earthquake Prediction, *Ann. Review Earth Planet. Sciences*, *19*, 268.

Updike, R.G., 1989. Proceedings of the National Earthquake Prediction Evaluation Council, June 6–7, 1988. Open-File Rep. 89–144, USGS, Reston, VA., 25 pp + attachments.

Utsu, T., 1969–1970. Aftershocks and earthquake statistics (two papers), *J. Fac. Sci. Hokkaido U., Ser. VII, 3*, 129–195 and 379–441.

Utsu, T., 1979. Calculation of the probability of success of an earthquake prediction (in the case of Izu-Oshima-Kinkai earthquake of 1978), *Rep. Coord. Comm. Earthq. Predict.*, 164–166.

Uyeda, S., M. Kinoshita, M. Uyeshima, H. Iino, and T. Kawase, 1992. Progress report on an earthquake prediction study by means of geoelectric potential monitoring in Japan, in *Earthquake Prediction, Proc. Int. Sch. Solid Earth Geophys., Erice, Italy* (Il Cigno, Galileo Galilei, Rome, pp. 467–497).

Van Dorn, W.G., 1968. Tsunamis on the moon? *Nature, 220,* 1102–1107.

Varotsos, P., and M. Lazaridou, 1991. Latest aspects of earthquake prediction in Greece based on seismic electric signals, *Tectonophysics, 188,* 321–347.

Vere-Jones, D. 1988. On the variance properties of stress release models, *Austral. J. Stat., 30A,* 123–135.

Vere-Jones, D., and Y.L. Deng, 1988. A point process analysis of historical earthquakes from North China, *preprint.*

Vere-Jones, D., and Y. Ogata, 1984. On the moments of a self-correcting point process, *J. Appl. Probab., 21,* 315, 342.

Vere-Jones, D. and T. Ozaki 1982. Some examples of statistical inference applied to earthquake data, I. Cyclic Poisson and self-exciting models, *Ann. Inst. Stat. Math.,* B34, 189–207.

Vucetic, M., and V. Thilakaratne, 1989. Liquefaction of the Wildlife site: Effect of soil stiffness and seismic response, in *Soil Dynamics and Liquefaction*

Wadati, M., and K. Sawada, 1980. New representations of the soliton solution for the Korteweg-de Vries equation, *J. Phys. Soc. J., 48,* 312–318.

Wakita, H., 1981. Precursory changes in groundwater prior to the 1978 Izu-Oshima-Kinka earthquake, in *Earthquake Prediction,* D.W. Simpson and P.G. Richards, eds., Maurice Ewing Series vol. 4 (Am. Geophys. Union, Washington, DC, pp. 527–532).

Wang Chengmin, 1990. Abnormal changes of ground water (gas). In *Earthquake Prediction,* Ma Zongjin, Ed., *(Seismological Press/Springer-Verlag, Beijing/Heidelberg, pp. 143–171).*

Wang Chengmin, Wang Yaling, and Guo Yixin, 1984. Some results of groundwater level observations in earthquake areas in China during the past 15 years, in *Internat. Symp. Continental Seismicity Earthq. Predict.* (Seismological Press, Beijing, pp. 501–513).

Watts, M., 1983. On the poverty of theory: Natural hazards research in context, in *Interpretations of Calamity,* K. Hewitt, ed. (Allen & Unwin, New York).

White, G.F., and J.E. Haas, 1975. *Assessment of Research on Natural Hazards* (MIT Press, Cambridge, Mass.)

Wiener, N. 1956. Nonlinear prediction and dynamics, *Proc. 3rd. Berkeley Symp. Stat. Probl., Univ. Calif. Berkeley, 3,* 247–252.

Winchester, P., 1992. *Power, Choice and Vulnerability* (James & James, London).

Wittgenstein, L., 1918. *Logisch-philosophische Abhandlung* (Routledge & Kegan Paul, London, 1981).

Working Group on California Earthquake Probabilities, 1988. Probabilities of large earthquakes occurring in California on the San Andreas Fault, *U.S.G.S. Open-File Rep.* pp. 88–398.

Wyss, M., Ed., 1991a. *Evaluation of Proposed Earthquake Precursors* (Am. Geophys. Union, Washington, DC,94 pp.)

Wyss, M., 1991b. An artificial and a precursory seismic quiescence, *Proc. Int. Conf. Earthq. Predict., Strasbourg* (EMSC, pp. 157–166).

Wyss, M., and R.E.Habermann, 1987. Precursory seismic quiecence, *Proc. Workshop XXXVII,* vol. 2, Open-File Rept. 87–591, U.S.G.S. Menlo Park, CA., pp. 526–536.

Yamazaki, Y., K. Seo, and T. Samano, 1988. Interpretation of strong ground motions in Mexico City during the Mexico earthquake of Sept. 19, 1985, *Proc. 9th World Conf. Earthq. Eng., J.,* vol. II, pp. 609–614.

Zhang Guomin, 1990. Anomalous variations of the geophysical field, in *Earthquake Prediction,* Ma Zongjin, Ed. (Seismological Press/ Springer-Verlag, Beijing/Heidelberg, pp. 86–111).

Zhang Guomin and Fu Zhengxiang, 1981. Some features of medium- and short-term anomalies before great earthquakes, in *Earthquake Prediction,* D.W. Simpson and P.G. Richards, eds., Maurice Ewing Series vol. 4 (Am. Geophys. Union, Washington, DC).

Zhang Guomin, Ma Zongjin, Liu Defu and Fu Zhengxiang, 1984. On the procedure of earthquake prediction, in *On Continental Seismicity and Earthquake Prediction* (Seismological Press, Beijing, p. 844).

Zhang Yingzhen, 1990. Earthquake field, in *Earthquake Prediction,* Ma Zongjin, Ed. (Seismological Press/Springer-Verlag, Beijing/ Heidelberg, pp. 261–287).

Zhu Fengmi, Quan Yingdao, Gu Haoding, and Guan Xingguo, 1984. Re-examination of the anomalous phenomena taken as precursors before the Haicheng earthquake of 1975, in *On Continental Seismicity and Earthquake Prediction* (Seismological Press, Beijing, p. 571).

Index